Debating Judicial Appointments in an Age of Diversity

What should be the primary goals of a judicial appointments system, and how much weight should be placed on diversity in particular? Why is achieving a diverse judiciary across the UK taking so long? Is it time for positive action? What role should the current judiciary play in the appointment of our future judges?

There is broad agreement within the UK and other common law countries that diversity raises important questions for a legal system and its officials. However, there is much less agreement about the full implications of recognizing diversity as an important goal of the judicial appointments regime. Opinions differ on the methods, forms, timing and motivations for judicial diversity. To mark the tenth anniversary of the creation of the Judicial Appointments Commission (JAC) in England and Wales, this collection includes contributions from current and retired judges, civil servants, practitioners, current and former commissioners on the JAC and leading academics from Australia, Canada, South Africa and across the UK. Together they provide timely and authoritative insights into past, current and future debates on the search for diversity in judicial appointments.

Topics discussed include the role and responsibility of independent appointment bodies; assessments of the JAC's first ten years; appointments to the UK Supreme Court; the pace of change; definitions of 'merit' and 'diversity'; mandatory retirement ages; the use of ceiling quotas; and the appropriate role of judges and politicians in the appointments process.

Graham Gee is Professor of Public Law at the University of Sheffield, UK.

Erika Rackley is Professor of Law at the University of Birmingham, UK.

Debating Judicial Appointments in an Age of Diversity

Edited by
Graham Gee and Erika Rackley

Routledge
Taylor & Francis Group
LONDON AND NEW YORK

First published 2018
by Routledge

2 Park Square, Milton Park, Abingdon, Oxfordshire OX14 4RN
52 Vanderbilt Avenue, New York, NY 10017

Routledge is an imprint of the Taylor & Francis Group, an informa business

First issued in paperback 2019

British Library Cataloguing-in-Publication Data
A catalogue record for this book is available from the British Library

Library of Congress Cataloging-in-Publication Data
Names: Gee, Graham, editor. | Rackley, Erika, editor.
Title: Debating judicial appointments in an age of diversity / edited by Graham Gee and Erika Rackley.
Description: New York, NY : Routledge, 2017. | Includes bibliographical references and index.
Identifiers: LCCN 2017012480 | ISBN 9781138225350 (hardback) | ISBN 9781315400051 (adobe reader) | ISBN 9781315400044 (epub) | ISBN 9781315400037 (mobipocket)
Subjects: LCSH: Judges–Selection and appointment.
Classification: LCC K2146 .D43 2017 | DDC 347/.014–dc23
LC record available at https://lccn.loc.gov/2017012480

ISBN: 978-1-138-22535-0 (hbk)
ISBN: 978-0-367-33682-0 (pbk)

Typeset in Galliard
by Taylor & Francis Books

Contents

Preface

This book grew out of an international conference held at the University of Birmingham in November 2015 to mark the tenth anniversary of the Judicial Appointments Commission (JAC). The conference brought together members of the JAC, the judiciary, civil servants from the Ministry of Justice and the UK Supreme Court, practitioners and academics from Australia, Canada, South Africa as well as from across the UK. The keynote address was given by Lady Hale, and is included in this collection. We are very grateful to all of those who participated at the conference. The conference was generously funded by the Centre for the Study of Law in Society at the University of Sheffield, the College of Arts and Law at the University of Birmingham and the Socio-Legal Studies Association. We thank these sponsors for their support.

We are grateful to the JAC for their assistance in organizing the conference and also in collating some of the contributions to this collection from members of the JAC. A special debt of gratitude is owed to Martin Wimpole, who is currently a civil servant in the Attorney General's Office, but was previously Private Secretary to the JAC's Chairman. The JAC came in for fairly sharp criticism at the conference, and does so again in some of the contributions to this collection. It is to the JAC's considerable credit that it is an outward-looking and engaged public body which – even in the face of often heated criticism – remains very keen to participate in the vital debates about judicial appointments and diversity. The final proofs were submitted to the publisher before the announcement in July 2017 of Lady Hale's promotion to President of the UK Supreme Court, Lady Black's appointment to the same Court, and Singh LJ's appointment to the Court of Appeal.

We would like to thank the editorial team at Routledge, and in particular Olivia Manley. The sketch on the front cover of this book is by Isobel Williams, to whom we are also very grateful.

Graham Gee
Erika Rackley
February 2017

Contributors

Cordella Bart-Stewart is a solicitor and the Executive Director of the Black Solicitors Network. She is also a Fee paid Judge of the First Tier Tribunal (Immigration and Asylum).

Samreen Beg is a lawyer practising in the area of securities regulation in Canada, and has regulatory and policy experience at the federal and provincial level.

Alysia Blackham is a Senior Lecturer at Melbourne Law School at the University of Melbourne.

Graham Gee is Professor of Public Law at the University of Sheffield.

Lady Hale is President of the UK Supreme Court.

Cora Hoexter is a Professor in the School of Law at the University of the Witwatersrand, Johannesburg.

Rosemary Hunter is Professor of Law and Socio-Legal Studies at Queen Mary, University of London.

Frances Kirkham served as a judicial member of the Judicial Appointments Commission between 2006 and 2011. A former solicitor, she was appointed a Senior Circuit Judge in 2000, serving in the Technology and Construction Court.

Sir Thomas Legg worked in the Lord Chancellor's Department from 1962, serving as Permanent Secretary between 1989 and 1998.

Noel Lloyd is an Emeritus Professor of Mathematics and was Vice Chancellor of Aberystwyth University from 2004 until his retirement in 2011. He has been a lay member of the Judicial Appointments Commission since 2012.

Andrew Lynch is a Professor and Co-Director of the Judiciary Project at the Gilbert + Tobin Centre of Public Law, Faculty of Law, University of New South Wales.

Kate Malleson is Professor of Law at Queen Mary, University of London.

Karon Monaghan is a barrister at Matrix Chambers. She also sits as a Deputy High Court Judge (Administrative Court) and as a Recorder in the Crown Court.

John Morison is Professor in the School of Law at Queens University Belfast and was formerly a lay commissioner on the Northern Ireland Judicial Appointments Commission.

Alan Paterson is Professor of Law at Strathclyde University, and Director of the Centre for Professional Legal Studies, a think tank on the legal system. He served as a lay member on the Judicial Appointments Board for Scotland from 2002 to 2008.

Erika Rackley is a Professor in the Law School at the University of Birmingham.

Jenny Rowe was the first Chief Executive of the UK Supreme Court.

Hilary Sommerlad is Professor of Law and Social Justice at the University of Leeds.

Lorne Sossin is Dean and Professor at Osgoode Law School, York University, Canada.

Christopher Stephens was Chairman of the Judicial Appointments Commission (JAC) between 2011 and 2016. He had previously served on the Civil Service Commission and the Senior Salary Review Board.

Jan van Zyl Smit is an Associate Senior Research Fellow at the British Institute of International and Comparative Law, where he is a member of the Bingham Centre for the Rule of Law.

Charlie Webb is an Associate Professor at the London School of Economics and Political Science.

1 Introduction

Diversity and the JAC's first ten years

Graham Gee and Erika Rackley

This is an age of diversity. In a pluralistic polity such as the UK, diversity often serves as shorthand for a series of related questions about how best to respond to our mutual differences of, amongst other things, gender, race, sexuality and social background. Over the last twenty-five years or so there has been growing recognition that these questions are as relevant to the courts and tribunals as for other areas of public life. Today, across the UK, there is widespread agreement that the judiciary should reflect the society it serves. Especially welcome is the evidence in recent years that this agreement traverses the judicial and political spheres, with the need for faster and more visible progress on judicial diversity increasingly acknowledged across the ideological spectrum. There is, in other words, a political salience to debates about judicial diversity largely absent just a few years ago. This has significant spill-over effects for the design, working and assessment of judicial appointments: previously relatively discrete debates about the independence, legitimacy and accountability of the appointments regime are frequently now framed in terms of, and by reference to, widely shared concerns about the need for judges who are more visibly reflective of society. Diversity is not the only goal of a selection regime of course, but it has begun to shape how those other goals are viewed. In brief, there is now such widespread agreement about its importance that judicial diversity 'has in recent years become a truth almost universally acknowledged'.[1]

Although most now accept the pressing need for a more diverse judiciary, there is considerably less agreement about the implications of recognizing diversity as an important goal of the judicial appointments regime. In fact, beneath the veneer of agreement that a diverse judiciary is – all else being equal – normatively desirable, there is substantial disagreement about almost everything else including the methods, forms, timescales and justifications for bringing it about. Differently put: the risk is that the consensus amongst politicians, judges, lawyers, officials and lay people about the need for a diverse judiciary conceals tricky and largely unaddressed questions about not only how to achieve diversity, but also the very meaning of diversity in this context. Some questions have a conceptual

1 E. Rackley, 'Rethinking Judicial Diversity' in U. Schultz and G. Shaw (eds), *Gender and Judging*, Oxford: Hart Publishing, 2013, pp. 501, 503.

orientation. For instance, precisely how diverse is a diverse judiciary? Do understandings of diversity change if we think in terms of the over-representation of traditionally privileged groups rather than the under-representation of historically marginalized groups? How is judicial diversity best secured when the wider social environment is informed by entrenched patterns of power, privilege and perhaps even prejudice? Do changes to the judicial role – a greater emphasis on leadership, case management and communicating with litigants and the public at large – suggest that traditional understandings of 'merit' need to evolve? Other questions are more practical. For example, how does the need to diversify the judiciary align with policies on retirement? What degree and sort of involvement in appointment processes for judges, ministers, lawyers and lay people helps or hinders the pursuit of diversity? What lessons – if any – can be drawn from the approach to promoting diversity in other legal systems?

This collection brings together current and retired judges, officials, lawyers and academics from Australia, Canada, South Africa and the UK to debate these and other questions. It is the first collection investigating diversity debates in light of the changed institutional terrain of judicial appointments in England and Wales. The collection's premise is that debates about diversity are complex and interrelated, with transformation of the judiciary's composition likely only via a *systematic* and *collaborative* approach. Systematic insofar as diversity must be addressed not only within the appointments process itself, but when thinking about a myriad of other matters as well: retention as well as recruitment; the terms and conditions of judicial service; the provision of training; arrangements for judicial welfare; promotion and professional development across a career; policies on retirement and post-retirement and so forth.[2] A systematic approach also extends more broadly to include thinking about how judicial recruitment is influenced by multiple political and social changes, including changes to the public sector, legal regulatory regimes, legal labour markets and the career choices and working arrangements of lawyers. Insofar as debates about diversity should be informed by the perspectives, experiences and insights of the many different actors with a stake in the judicial system, the approach must also be collaborative.[3] This requires, at a bare minimum, that all of those with a stake in the judicial system engage in good faith, reasoned and constructive debate. Of course no single collection could address all of the interrelated issues implicated in these debates nor include all of the perspectives on them. All that having been said, this collection strives to discuss a number of conceptual and practical questions relating to judicial diversity, and to do so via several lenses: judicial and non-judicial, legal and lay; practitioner and academic; domestic and international; analytical and experiential; and insider and outsider.

2 *The Report of the Advisory Panel on Judicial Diversity 2010* at para 4.

3 For discussion of the new judicial appointment regime as collaborative, see G. Gee, 'Judicial Policy in England and Wales: A New Regulatory Space' in R. Devlin and A. Dodek (eds), *Regulating Judges: Beyond Independence and Accountability*, Cheltenham: Edward Elgar, 2016, p. 145.

Debates about diversity must be attentive to the real world institutional settings in which individual selection decisions are made. The institutional focus for this collection is the Judicial Appointments Commissions ('JAC'). Created under the Constitutional Reform Act 2005, beginning its work in 2006 and marking its tenth anniversary last year, the JAC is the body responsible for recommending candidates for appointment to courts and tribunals in England and Wales (as well as certain tribunals whose jurisdictions extend to Scotland or Northern Ireland). The JAC is of course only one part – albeit a very significant part – of the new architecture of appointments that plays host to debates about diversity. The statutory context, the structure of the legal professions and the behaviour of other stakeholders in the judicial system remain key determinants of the rate of progress on recruiting candidates from a wider pool of talent that is more reflective of society at large. Inevitably, however, the JAC is today the primary focus of many of the most pressing debates about diversity – and, as illustrated throughout this collection, views differ on the extent to which its processes and policies have helped or hindered the transformation of the judiciary. Perhaps unsurprisingly, one site of disagreement is between those on the inside of the JAC-managed regime (i.e. the JAC, senior judges and officials at the Ministry of Justice) and those on the outside (i.e. academics and lawyers, particularly those from groups under-represented in the judiciary). Insiders and outsiders often have markedly differing assessments of the scale of the diversity deficit, the pace of progress so far and the tools needed to address it, and in particular whether the JAC has utilized the levers available to it as fully as it might. They also often have rival views on whether the levels of judicial and ministerial involvement in JAC-run selections help or hinder the push for a more diverse bench. In short, insiders and outsiders appear to have different experiences of and expectations for the JAC's selection regime. Across the last ten years, constructive debate has proved very challenging because views diverge so markedly, with insiders and outsiders often seeming to speak past each other.

This collection encompasses both insider and outsider perspectives on the JAC, with many of the contributors using their essays not only to reflect on the many challenges that the JAC has confronted during its first decade, but also to chart how it can tackle the challenges that are likely to define the next ten years. In addition to a dozen chapters written by academics, this collection includes six 'reflection essays' by people with practical, first-hand experience of the judicial appointment processes in England and Wales. The authors of these experiential essays have all been involved in judicial appointments in one guise or another. They include former and current commissioners on the JAC (Frances Kirkham and Noel Lloyd respectively), two former senior civil servants (Sir Thomas Legg and Jenny Rowe), and two prominent practitioners who have been vocal critics of the rate of progress on diversifying the judiciary (Karon Monaghan QC and Cordella Bart-Stewart). Between them, these authors' involvement with judicial appointments dates from the early 1980s to today. The collection also contains an opening essay reflecting on the JAC's first ten years by its recently retired chair, Christopher Stephens. It closes with a longer essay by Lady Hale on the process for selecting the Justices of the UK Supreme Court. Lady Hale is, of course, not only the Court's Deputy President, but also one of the most powerful voices in the common law world on the importance of judicial diversity.

The collection's objectives are threefold. First, it aims to illustrate the range of views on and experiences of the JAC-run regime, which is after all more inclusive than the pre-2005 regime, involving as it does ministers, judges, civil servants, lawyers and lay people. Second, it attempts to identify possible reasons for, and suggestions on how to respond to, the contrasting assessments of those on the inside and outside of the regime, especially as those assessments relate to the rate of progress on diversity. Third, the collection attempts to reframe in novel and fruitful ways some of the familiar debates that have led to an impasse between insiders and outsiders: debates relating to, among other things, 'merit', quotas and the respective roles of judges and politicians in the selection process. In doing all of this, the collection furnishes a number of competing assessments of the JAC's first decade as well as mapping out alternative paths that the JAC could pursue in its second. In this Introduction, we offer an outsider's account of the JAC's first decade, albeit one that draws on interviews and conversations with insiders. Our goal is to give readers a flavour of the highs and lows and ups and downs of the JAC's first ten years and to sketch some of the main challenges that will confront it in its second decade.

The new institutional terrain of judicial appointments

The terrains on which diversity debates play out have changed. In line with the international trend, there are now central roles across the UK for independent commissions in the appointment of judges to courts and tribunals.[4] Just as there are multiple domestic judiciaries in the UK, so there are also a number of selection processes, each anchored around its own commission.[5] The Judicial Appointments Board for Scotland ('JABS') was created in 2002; the Northern Ireland Judicial Appointments Commission ('NIJAC') in 2005, whilst the JAC was established in 2006.[6] (This collection includes contributions from former lay commissioners at

4 In 81 per cent of Commonwealth jurisdictions there is now a judicial appointments body that plays some role in the selection or short-listing of candidates for appointment to the judiciary: generally J. van Zyl Smit, *The Appointment, Tenure and Removal of Judges under Commonwealth Principles: A Compendium and Analysis of Best Practice*, London: Bingham Centre for the Rule of Law, 2015 at para 1.6. See also K. Malleson, 'Introduction' in K. Malleson and P. H. Russell (eds), *Appointing Judges in an Age of Judicial Power: Critical Perspectives from Around the World*, Toronto: University of Toronto Press, 2006, pp. 3, 6–7.

5 We do not discuss the process for selecting UK judges that sit on the Court of Justice of the European Union or the European Court of Human Rights or any other international courts. For useful recent treatments, see M. Bobek, *Selecting Europe's Judges: A Critical Review of the Appointment Procedures to the European Courts*, Oxford: Oxford University Press, 2015; and R. Mackenzie, K. Malleson, P. Martin and P. Sands, *Selecting International Judges: Principles, Process and Politics*, Oxford: Oxford University Press, 2010.

6 See A. Paterson, 'The Scottish Judicial Appointments Board: New Wine in Old Bottles?' in K. Malleson and P. H. Russell (eds), *Appointing Judges in an Age of Judicial Power: Critical Perspectives from Around the World*, Toronto: University of Toronto

JABS and NIJAC: Alan Paterson and John Morison respectively). The Supreme Court, itself a recent creation which only began its work in 2009, has its own recruitment process involving ad hoc commissions that are specifically constituted whenever vacancies arise.[7] But the changing institutional landscape extends much further than this. In England and Wales, for example, there has been continuing change over the last decade to the roles and responsibilities of several crucial actors in the selection regime such as the Lord Chancellor and the Lord Chief Justice. Transferring staff and functions from the Ministry of Justice to the JAC and the Judicial Office (which was created in 2005 to support senior judicial leaders in England and Wales) has also moulded relations between crucial stakeholders in the selection regime. Other new bodies are charged with important coordinating functions, including the Judicial Diversity Forum, the Judicial Diversity Taskforce and the Judicial Diversity Committee of the Judges' Council. The UK Parliament also takes a greater interest in the appointments regime.[8] This changed terrain inevitably influences the tenor and direction of debates about diversity, although as shall become evident across this collection the new selection regime in England and Wales is marked by continuity as well as change (for example, the continued dominance of a traditional understanding of 'merit').

The JAC has a heavy workload, overseeing the recruitment of between 300 and 800 judges each year. The exact number of vacancies varies from year to year, depending on the number and type of competitions that the JAC is requested to run. (See Appendix I for a breakdown of the number of recommendations that the JAC has made over its first decade.) Partly because of this large and variable workload, it has a relatively large membership by international standards, with 15 members: seven holding judicial office, one of whom is a magistrate, two lawyers, and six lay people, one of whom serves as the JAC's chair. More information on the identity of the commissioners is set out in Appendix II. In contrast to the informality and secrecy that for a long time characterized the selection regime run by the Lord Chancellor, the JAC runs a much more formal and relatively inclusive regime. Its recommendations for judicial office are made following open competition, with the process of evaluating a person's suitability for judicial office requiring the input of multiple actors at several different stages. The JAC is under a statutory duty to select candidates 'solely on merit',[9] but where two or more are assessed to be of equal merit then it can recommend a candidate on the basis of increasing diversity on the bench.[10] We explain the selection processes overseen by the

Press, 2006, p. 13; and G. Gee, R. Hazell, K. Malleson and P. O'Brien, *The Politics of Judicial Independence in the UK's Changing Constitution*, Cambridge: Cambridge University Press, 2015, pp. 159–193 and 239–249.

7 S. Shetreet and S. Turenne, *Judges on Trial: The Independence and Accountability of the English Judiciary*, Cambridge: Cambridge University Press, 2nd edn, 2013, pp. 140–150.

8 See Gee et al, *The Politics of Judicial Independence*, pp. 188–189.

9 Constitutional Reform Act 2005, s. 63.

10 Crime and Courts Act 2013, Schedule 13.

JAC in more detail in Appendix III, including the slightly different process for senior appointments, but for now it suffices to offer a brief summary of a typical selection exercise run by the JAC.

At the outset of a selection exercise the Lord Chancellor is required to consult with the Lord Chief Justice. Supported by their officials, the Lord Chancellor and Lord Chief Justice discuss the details of the job description. This discussion is informed by advice and data from H.M. Courts & Tribunals Service about the judicial vacancy in question. Upon receiving a vacancy request from the Lord Chancellor, the JAC runs the process (advertising the post; compiling a short-list; running a selection day at which the short-listed candidates will be interviewed and may also be required to participate in role-play activities; and then recommending a single candidate for each vacancy). Despite its name, the JAC was created as a recommending body, not an appointing body. It makes initial recommendations for judicial office, with the final say whether or not to appoint lying with, depending on the exact vacancy in question, the Lord Chancellor (for the High Court and above), the Lord Chief Justice (for all lower level courts) or the Senior President of Tribunals (for most tribunal vacancies). Before 2014, the JAC made all of its recommendations to the Lord Chancellor. However, the Lord Chancellor's role was diluted by the Crime and Courts Act 2013, which transferred the final say over appointments to the lower courts to the Lord Chief Justice and over most tribunal appointments to the Senior President of Tribunals.[11] As a result, the Lord Chancellor has the final say over only five per cent of all selections. Between 2006 and 2016, there were only six occasions out of nearly 5,000 appointments where the final appointing authority did not accept the JAC's recommended candidate. In other words, the JAC's recommendations were accepted 99.9 per cent of the time. What this means is that although created as a recommending body, the JAC effectively functions as an appointing body.

Even though the terrain of judicial appointments has been reshaped since 2005, there has been significantly less change in the composition of the judiciary itself, especially at the highest echelons of the courts in England and Wales. It is true that there has been progress in the lower courts and the tribunals. For example, more than half of both court judges (51 per cent) and tribunal judges (64 per cent) under the age of 40 are female,[12] with 1,800 women appointed to judicial office between 2006 and 2016.[13] Particular progress has been made in the two crucial entry-level positions to the judiciary; namely, Recorder and Deputy District Judges. For example, there has been an increase over the last decade in the proportion of female Deputy District Judges from 25 per cent to 37 per cent. It is also true that some progress has been seen in higher courts. From 2005, the number of women judges in the High Court and the Court of Appeal rose from

11 Crime and Courts Act 2013, Schedule 13.

12 *Judicial Diversity Statistics 2016: Judicial Office Statistics Bulletin* (Published 28 July 2016. Revised 2 December 2016), p. 5.

13 Letter dated 7 April 2016 from Christopher Stephens (Chair of the JAC) to the Lord Chancellor.

10 to 22 and from two to eight respectively.[14] This is indeed progress – but the numbers are still exceptionally small, representing only 21 per cent and 19 per cent of the total number of judges sitting on those courts, with no women at the time of writing occupying any of the five most senior leadership roles in the English and Welsh judiciary.

The statistics for Black, Asian and Minority Ethnic ('BAME') judges tell an even more dispiriting story. The numbers of BAME candidates applying for and being selected for judicial office is greater than when the JAC was created, with 400 BAME judges appointed since 2006. But BAME judges still represent a very small minority in the judiciary. Of the approximately 3,200 professional judges in England and Wales, ethnicity information is known for 84 per cent, with 174 (six per cent) declaring their background as BAME.[15] The numbers are slightly higher in the tribunals where 10 per cent of judges declared their background as BAME, with this rising to 16 per cent for under-40s. At the time of writing, however, there are still no BAME judges in the Court of Appeal, and only two on the High Court. For many selection rounds, the proportion of applicants from BAME is equal to or greater than the eligible pool, yet the proportion of applicants recommended for appointment is often substantially lower. A similar story is seen in terms of professional background: around a third of court judges (34 per cent) and two-thirds of tribunal judges (65 per cent) have been appointed from non-barrister backgrounds, but there is only one solicitor out of 105 judges sitting on the High Court, and none on the Court of Appeal.[16] The unrepresentative Bar, in other words, still retains a disproportionate presence at all levels of the court judiciary, especially the top courts. In practice, this consolidates the stranglehold that white, middle and upper class men enjoy on judicial office. Other more diverse pools of talent – such as solicitors, government lawyers, legal executives and academics – are still not successfully progressing through the new selection processes in sufficient numbers.

Although the JAC (through its Chair or his or her nominee) plays only a limited role as one of five members of the UK Supreme Court ad hoc appointment commissions, it is important to note that progress over the last decade in changing the composition of the UK's apex court has been positively glacial, if indeed it is even apt to talk of any progress at all. Every one of the thirteen appointments over the last decade has been a white man, and all but one has spent the majority of his career at the Bar, prior to appointment as a judge. Even the somewhat contentious expansion of the pool of potential appointees beyond the Court of Appeal, which enabled direct appointments to the Court, could do nothing to stem the tide. At the time of writing, it has been used once: to appoint another white, male barrister. A number of appointments will be made to the Supreme Court in the next couple of years, and it might be that the UK's top court looks more diverse than it

14 *Judicial Diversity Statistics 2016: Judicial Office Statistics Bulletin* (Published 28 July 2016. Revised 2 December 2016), pp. 6–7.

15 Ibid., pp. 8–9.

16 Ibid., p. 5.

does at the time of writing. This would of course be welcome, but diversity will remain a real and enduring challenge at all levels of the judiciary even if there is a sudden influx of more diverse appointments to a Supreme Court that is currently staffed by only one women. Indeed, there is also the real risk that very visible progress in the UK's top court will conceal the continued dispiriting lack of progress in other parts of the senior judiciary.

Ten years on, then, some limited progress on diversity has been made, but this greater diversity has not been evenly distributed across the judiciary as a whole. The rate of progress has also been much slower than many had expected, with England and Wales still lagging very far behind comparable countries in terms of judicial composition.[17] No doubt a complex mix of related reasons accounts for this. A major impediment to faster progress is the continued stratification of the legal profession, with the upper echelons of legal practice not reflecting the growing diversity found at the early stages of a legal career or in the branches of legal practice traditionally regarded as less prestigious than the Bar. Another impediment is the fact that judicial careers have traditionally lacked flexibility, especially in terms of part-time posts[18] and the traditional expectation that High Court judges who are generally based in London will go 'on circuit' (i.e. to sit on courts outside of London, often for many weeks at a time).[19]

But what of the JAC itself? Whilst recognizing the importance of these impediments, and whilst acknowledging that the statutory framework confers only limited tools to promote diversity on it, some commentators argue that the JAC's timidity is part of the explanation for why there has not been faster progress over the last ten years. The JAC's 'passivity',[20] it is often argued, is seen in inter alia: its failure to displace traditional understandings of 'merit'; its reluctance to downgrade the importance attached within the selection process to judicial references and statutorily required consultations with senior judges; and its failure to resist selection criteria that can disadvantage candidates from non-traditional backgrounds (for example, the requirement to have 'fee-paid' experience in a part-time judicial position whilst continuing in a day job, which might not be practicable for

17 See e.g. Council of Europe, *European Judicial Systems. Efficiency and Quality of Justice: CEPEJ Studies No 23* (2016) 101, where the UK ranks alongside Armenia and Azerbaijan at the very bottom of Council of Europe Contracting Parties in terms of the percentage of women in professional judicial roles.

18 This is changing. The Crime and Courts Act 2013 amended the Senior Courts Act 1981 to allow the maximum number of judges in the High Court and the Court of Appeal to be comprised of a specified number of full-term equivalents (i.e. a mix of full-time and part-time positions) rather than a maximum number of individual judges. There are also similar provisions applicable in respect of the Supreme Court.

19 The requirement to go on Circuit is also changing. The formal policy is that no High Court judge is required to go on Circuit unless they wish to do so. It remains to be seen, however, if the decision not to go on Circuit will be held against an individual who later applies for promotion. See Lord Thomas, *Speech for the City of London Solicitors' Company* (13 March 2017).

20 See L. Barmes and K. Malleson, 'The Legal Profession as Gatekeeper to the Judiciary: Design Faults in Measures to Enhance Diversity' *Modern Law Review* 74, 2011, pp. 245, 258–261.

some types of legal practice such as solicitors in city firms or high-street practices). There can be little doubt that the JAC's timidity is related to and partly a consequence of its difficult and sometimes tumultuous relations with other stakeholders in the judicial system, and the senior judiciary and the Ministry of Justice in particular. Or to put this more bluntly: the JAC's willingness to agitate for faster progress on diversity (or for that matter to make full and effective use of the tools available to it under the statutory scheme) has been limited by the need at various points during its first ten years to placate its stakeholders in order to safeguard its position on the constitutional map.

The JAC's first decade: securing an institutional foothold

Over ten years on from its creation, the JAC today occupies what most regard as a secure place on the constitutional map.[21] The new model of appointments overseen by the JAC attracts 'broad consensus', with few proposing significant departures from it.[22] However, this belies the number and scale of challenges that the JAC confronted during what at times was a tumultuous first decade. Much of this tumult resulted from rocky relationships between the JAC and its stakeholders (the judiciary, the legal professions and the Ministry of Justice), with the JAC's future seeming to be uncertain at various points during the ten years as a result. In brief: although the JAC now enjoys a secure position on the institutional landscape, the history of its first decade illustrates that it occupies an extremely narrow constitutional space, with its ability to drive policy change limited by, amongst other things, the need to nurture the confidence of multiple stakeholders whose interests do not always coincide. This is a useful reminder that, in the real world, debates about diversity do not occur in the abstract, but can be buffeted by the competing interests, priorities and personalities of the various stakeholders in the judicial system. For these purposes, it is possible to divide the JAC's first decade into three phases: an initial period between 2006 and 2010 defined by tensions and even hostility between the JAC and its main stakeholders; a period of stabilization and further change from 2011 to 2014; and finally, some evidence of renewed tensions with the judiciary between 2014 and 2016. A golden thread that runs throughout the decade is the way in which opposition from stakeholders crimps the JAC's willingness to innovate in bold and novel ways.

Tensions and hostility (2006–2010)

From the very beginning of its work in 2006, the JAC faced a number of serious financial, staffing and workload challenges.[23] The financial challenge took the form

21 It is overstating matters, however, to suggest, as the Ministry of Justice did in 2015, that the JAC is 'a universally respected part of the constitutional landscape': Ministry of Justice, *Triennial Review: Judicial Appointments Commission* London: Ministry of Justice, 2015, p. 3.

22 House of Lords, Select Committee on the Constitution, *Judicial Appointments*, 25th Report of Session 2010–12, (HL 272), para 5.

23 See Gee et al, *The Politics of Judicial Independence*, pp. 166–167.

of a five per cent budget cut in its first year. That most of its staff was seconded from the Department of Constitutional Affairs (i.e. the predecessor ministerial department to the Ministry of Justice) led not only to some officials struggling to adapt to the new way of selecting judges, but also to a perception among some outsiders that the JAC was not independent from, but rather an adjunct of, the government.[24] The workload challenges included a lack of reliable forecasting data from the Courts Service about the number of likely vacancies to arise in any one year. All of this occurred at the same time as the JAC was devising its own processes for identifying well-qualified candidates as well as managing a number of selection rounds underway under the pre-2006 processes which were inherited from the Department of Constitutional Affairs.

This translated into the JAC's early years being marked by criticism, suspicion and hostility, as powerfully recounted in the essay in this collection by Frances Kirkham (who served as a judicial commissioner on the JAC from 2006 to 2011). Many in the legal profession criticized the JAC for the length of time it took for judicial vacancies to be filled under the new selection regime. However, most of this criticism was misplaced insofar as delays mainly resulted from the time that it took the Ministry to finalize its vacancy request at the outset of the process (a step that was required before the JAC could initiate a selection exercise) and then to accept the JAC's recommendation at the process's end. Many judges and barristers also criticized the JAC's reliance on application forms, qualifying tests, interviews and evidence-based evaluations that relate to explicitly stated criteria for appointment. Typical were complaints that several barristers widely viewed as high-flyers had not been successful in securing an appointment under the new processes even though they would almost certainly have done so under the pre-2006 processes. This period was also characterized by tensions between the JAC and the Ministry of Justice, with ministers and officials left frustrated that the government was formally responsible for the new appointments regime yet lacked effective levers to influence its day-to-day workings.[25] Jack Straw, the Lord Chancellor from 2007 to 2010, was frustrated by both the slow progress on diversity as well as his limited input into senior appointments.[26] In brief: whilst the JAC stressed its role as an independent body performing an important constitutional task in identifying candidates for judicial office, the Ministry regarded the JAC as insufficiently responsive to the concerns of judges and lawyers.

One measure of the level of unease is that the Ministry initiated two reviews of the JAC within the first two years of its birth, with a total of seven reviews of one sort or another between 2006 and 2012. Relations deteriorated to such an extent around 2009–2010 that the Ministry mulled the possibility of abolishing the JAC and either bringing judicial appointments back in-house or delegating the responsibility for

24 Baroness Prashar, 'Translating Aspirations into Reality: Establishing the Judicial Appointments Commission' in Judicial Appointments Commission, *Judicial Appointments: Balancing Independence, Accountability and Legitimacy*, London: Judicial Appointments Commission, 2010, p. 47.

25 This section draws on the account of the JAC's early years in Gee et al, *The Politics of Judicial Independence*, pp. 164–170.

26 See J. Straw, *Aspects of Law Reform: An Insider's Perspective*, Cambridge: Cambridge University Press, 2013, pp. 58–59.

appointments to the senior judges, although neither option was pursued with seriousness. This was the JAC's first 'near death experience' (as it came to be known inside the JAC), with a second to follow in 2010 when the JAC was included in Schedule 7 of the Public Bodies Bill, which sought to empower ministers to abolish or restructure a wide range of non-departmental public bodies. The bodies listed in Schedule 7 would not inevitably be scrapped or restructured but would have remained subject to the risk that ministers could use their delegated powers to purge them at some point in the future. This was the Cabinet Office's Bill, and the JAC was included in it against the Ministry's advice that this would lead to substantial resistance from the judiciary and the legal professions. The Ministry's prediction was accurate, with judges and lawyers setting aside their misgivings about the new appointment processes to defend the JAC, with their efforts successful in securing the JAC's removal from the Bill. According to some insiders, these near death experiences helped to cement much more constructive relationships between the JAC, senior judges and the legal professions.

Stability and change (2011–2014)

In one sense, the JAC survived these near death experiences. In another sense, what emerged from these series of bruising encounters with the Ministry was in effect a 'new' JAC. There were significant staff changes throughout the JAC. By 2011, Christopher Stephens and Nigel Reeder had been appointed as the new Chair and Chief Executive, replacing Baroness Prashar and Claire Pelham respectively. By 2012, the JAC was staffed by a new cohort of commissioners. This was no accident; it was a state of affairs that the Ministry engineered by extending some of the inaugural commissioners' terms by just a single year to ensure that most of their terms in office would conclude by early 2012. Budget cuts of 18 per cent introduced in the new age of austerity led to reductions between 2006 and 2013 in the JAC's personnel from 109 to 79. Accompanying all of this was the JAC's renewed effort to be more responsive to the business needs of the judicial system. It is only a slight exaggeration to say that by 2011 the JAC – with its new leadership, a new cohort of commissioners and a streamlined internal organization – was willing to embrace a new vision of its own role.

Some of the tensions in the earlier period had derived from competing visions of the JAC's role. In the face of suspicion and hostility from judges and lawyers, the JAC's initial leadership sought to secure its place on the institutional map by stressing both its independence and the importance of its role in identifying suitably qualified candidates for judicial office. In its early years, the JAC's first leadership team was particularly concerned to protect the boundaries of its role from interference by judges, ministers or civil servants. On this 'constitutional' vision, the JAC was a proactive actor playing a central role in directing policy on appointments and diversity. One concrete example of this can be seen in the willingness of the JAC's initial commissioners to challenge the use of fee paid experience as an additional criterion for appointment. The JAC objected to this criterion on the grounds that it would tend to disadvantage candidates from non-traditional backgrounds. It took this stand even though both the judiciary and the Ministry felt that those appointed to the bench should have some prior experience of fee-paid judicial office in order that newly appointed judges could 'hit the ground running'. This was one of a number of issues in respect of which there were intense clashes between the JAC on the one hand and the Ministry and the judges on the other.

In contrast to a 'constitutional' vision of the JAC's role, the Ministry embraced a 'recruitment' vision. This envisaged the JAC serving as a recruitment agency whose chief responsibility was to respond to the business needs and workforce requirements of the judiciary, as determined by senior judges and the Ministry. By 2011, with new leadership at its helm, the JAC was more sympathetic to the Ministry's recruitment vision. The new leadership team reshaped the JAC into a leaner, cheaper and more responsive outfit. As Christopher Stephens explains in this collection, the JAC's leadership oversaw a change agenda that included: cutting the JAC's costs; reducing the length of the end-to-end selection process from up to 40 weeks to an average of less than 20 weeks; improving satisfaction levels with the JAC's processes amongst those who applied for judicial office; and better supporting the business needs of the justice system. Emblematic was the fact that, in its more responsive mode, the JAC largely abandoned its policy of resisting fee paid experience as an additional eligibility criterion, accepting instead the argument that business needs required those appointed to 'hit the ground running'. The JAC did so even though a practical effect of this was to narrow – and in all likelihood also render less diverse – the pool of potential candidates who would meet this additional criterion. On one reading, then, the JAC prioritized the need to stabilize relations with the senior judiciary and the Ministry over the need to aggressively promote judicial diversity.

By subscribing to the Ministry's 'recruitment' vision of its own role, the JAC repaired relations with its primary stakeholders and stabilized its foothold on the institutional map. More generally, this period was one of both stability and change. Important changes were made to the statutory framework. The Crime and Courts Act 2013 further diluted the involvement of the Lord Chancellor in individual selections by passing the final decision whether or not to appoint the candidates recommended by the JAC to the Lord Chief Justice (for all court vacancies below the High Court) or the Senior President of Tribunals (for most tribunal vacancies). What bears emphasis is how during this period stability and change were interrelated. Stability flowed in large part from change: as the JAC adopted a more conciliatory approach to its stakeholders by becoming much more responsive to the business needs of the justice system, so its institutional position stabilized. Change in turn flowed from this new found stability: with the confidence of its main stakeholders on the rise, and its institutional position secured, the JAC's new leadership team won notable victories that had eluded its inaugural leadership. These included the introduction of advertisements, application forms, short-listing and interviews for appointments to the Court of Appeal and leadership positions such as Heads of Division.[27] Another example was the extension of

27 Gee et al, *The Politics of Judicial Independence*, p. 184.

the JAC's remit to include the role of Deputy High Court Judges, a fee-paid position that is widely seen as a stepping-stone to a full-time appointment to the High Court.[28] These fee-paid positions had originally been excluded from the JAC's regime. That filling these positions had been regarded instead as deployment decisions within the Lord Chief Justice's discretion – with an accompanying lack of transparency and formality, and with no publicly available data by which to measure diversity – had been a 'running sore' during the JAC's early years.[29] But it was only when its own place on the institutional map had been stabilized that the JAC was able to persuade the Ministry and judiciary that its remit should embrace appointing Deputy High Court judges.

Renewed tensions with the senior judiciary (2014–2016)

By 2014, critics were already characterizing the JAC as an excessively cautious body that so far as possible would avoid innovating in ways that would unsettle its critical stakeholders. The publication in 2014 of its policy on the 'equal merit provision' confirmed this characterization.[30] The Crime and Courts Act clarified that the requirement for the JAC to recommend candidates 'solely on merit' (as provided under s. 63 of the Constitutional Reform Act 2005) did not prevent it preferring a candidate on diversity grounds where two or more candidates were of 'equal merit'.[31] Views differed on whether this new provision would translate into more diverse appointments. Some doubted whether there are really many occasions where two or more candidates can be deemed to be equal; the JAC's then chair Christopher Stephens had suggested in 2011 that there had been no two indistinguishable candidates out of the nearly 500 recommendations made by the JAC since he had assumed office earlier that year.[32] Others involved in the appointments process – notably, the JAC's former Vice Chair, Lady Justice Hallett – had opposing views, suggesting that it was 'not as rare as people think that you have candidates who are equally qualified'.[33] Either way, the statutory change created space for the JAC to devise its own policy on how to implement the 'equal merit' provision.

In designing the policy the JAC had two questions to address. First, should the equal merit provision apply at multiple stages of the selection process (including short-listing) or only at the final stage when the JAC makes a recommendation? Second, to which groups of people should the provision apply? That the JAC answered both questions in a very narrow, minimalist fashion is in keeping with its

28 See Judicial Appointments Commission Regulations 2013.
29 See House of Lords, Select Committee on the Constitution, *Judicial Appointments*, para 166.
30 Judicial Appointments Commission, *Equal Merit Provision Policy* (April 2014).
31 Crime and Courts Act 2013, Schedule 13. This provision derives from s. 159 of the Equality Act 2010.
32 House of Lords, Select Committee on the Constitution, *Judicial Appointments: Oral and Written Evidence* 25th Report of Session 2010–12, (HL 272) Q.364.
33 Ibid., Q.240.

cautious approach to policy innovation. The JAC initially decided that the provision would only apply at the final stage of recommendation, and not at short-listing. This minimalist approach was short-sighted, to say the least. The premise that there can be candidates exhibiting different combinations of strengths and weaknesses who are determined to be of equal merit is as relevant to short-listing as final recommendation. Applying the provision at short-listing could conceivably help counteract deep-seated barriers that prevent candidates from being invited to an interview.

In answering the second question, the JAC further resolved that the provision would only apply to race and gender on the grounds that the provision should only be used where under-representation can be substantiated by reference to published data. Gathering reliable data for groups other than race and gender can indeed be problematic, but some suggest that the JAC needs to devote more of its time and resources to become a pioneer on such matters.[34] That in 2015–2016 the provision was only invoked in a mere 14 out of 308 recommendations is scarcely surprising given the narrowness of the JAC's policy.[35] There was thus a very real risk that the JAC's policy would be dismissed as 'merely another positive headline backed by very little positive impact in terms of addressing the glaring diversity deficit'.[36] The cautiousness of the JAC's policy was a response to the judiciary's concerns. Over half of the responses to the JAC's consultation on how to implement the equal merit provision were from judges and their representative bodies. There were also detailed negotiations in private between the JAC, the Ministry and the judges. Suggestions of the strength of judicial concerns were apparent when Christopher Stephens commented that 'there is serious caution among many', with the JAC's 'stakeholders ... cautious about the equal merit provision'.[37] He noted that the reaction from the judges and lawyers was 'mixed'. Augmenting this picture of a body that is hemmed in by its main stakeholders is the fact that the JAC sought to revisit its policy shortly after its introduction. An internal report prepared in 2016 had recommended that the JAC should extend the provision to short-listing.[38] This proposal triggered considerable controversy with senior judges. On this occasion, the opposition of some judicial members on the JAC delayed the widening of the equal merit policy. This seems to confirm both the degree to which the JAC has to placate its stakeholders and the degree of the judicial influence on its internal decision-making. Nevertheless, in January 2017 the JAC published a slightly tweaked version of their equal merit policy which explains that whilst the provision would not formally be applied at

34 G. Gee and K. Malleson, 'Judicial Appointments, Diversity and the Equal Merit Provision' *UK Constitutional Law Blog*, 6 May 2014.

35 *Judicial Selection and Recommendations for Appointment Statistics, April 2015 to March 2016.*

36 A. Paterson and C. Paterson, *Guarding the Guardians: Towards an Independent, Accountable and Diverse Senior Judiciary*, London: CentreForum, 2012, p. 48.

37 House of Commons Justice Committee, *The Work of the Judicial Appointments Commission* (HC 1132) (5 March 2014) Q.31.

38 Judicial Appointments Commission,*Minutes* (July 2016) para 4.1.

short-listing, the JAC will increase the number of candidates who are shortlisted where there are two or more applicants assessed as being of equal merit, including some women or BAME applicants.[39] Perhaps inevitably, this too seems like a fudge, representing neither a full-throated application of the rationale for, nor the spirit of, the equal merit provision. And as such it seems unlikely to make much, if any, difference to the appointments ultimately made.

This episode coincided with another change in the JAC's leadership. In 2016, Christopher Stephens's term as chair ended. Repairing the JAC's relations with the judiciary had been one of his priorities when first appointed chair five years earlier. After initial success on this front, Stephens's relationship with the senior judiciary proved more challenging towards the end of his term. The JAC's leadership found it difficult at times to cultivate a constructive working relationship with Lord Thomas, the Lord Chief Justice between 2013 and 2017. Inside the JAC it was felt that the Lord Chief Justice was second-guessing many of its decisions (although the Crime & Courts Act 2013 envisages the Lord Chief Justice having a limited quality assurance role vis-à-vis the JAC's recommendations, and the difference between second-guessing and quality assurance might be in the eye of the beholder). There was also concern that some in the senior judiciary were keen to reverse some of the major elements of the JAC's selection processes (for example, the requirement that all applicants complete a standardized and competence-based application form, and the use of interviews for senior competitions). For their part, some senior judges felt that the JAC lacked an effective strategy for encouraging judicial diversity while others complained that its selection processes made too many onerous demands of the senior judiciary (for example, in terms of writing references, providing feedback as consultees and sitting on interview panels). These tensions occurred during a period of low judicial morale, caused in part by changes to judicial pensions as well as more general concerns about the increasing workload pressures placed on individual judges.[40] Many judges believe that the stature of the judiciary has been seriously diminished by substantial cuts in real terms to pay and pensions, with this commonly cited as the reason why two recent recruitment exercises for the High Court have not filled all of the vacancies. Indeed, working out how to promote a positive relationship with the senior judiciary – one that takes account of judicial concerns but does not submit unthinkingly to them – is a central challenge for Lord Kakkar, who was appointed the JAC's third chair in October 2016.

The JAC's next decade: continuity and change

Without doubt the JAC's first decade has been tumultuous at times. Some of this tumult has been of its own making. Some of it has not. Either way, it is important

39 Judicial Appointments Commission, *Equal Merit Provision Policy.* First published in 2014 and revised in 2017.

40 See generally C. Thomas, *2016 UK Judicial Attitudes Survey: Report of Findings Covering Salaried Judges in England & Wales Courts and UK Tribunals*, London: UCL Judicial Institute, 2017.

not to lose sight of the fact that the idea of a selection process that is organized around an independent recommending body is now accepted as an integral part of the judicial system. Despite all of the criticism it receives – much of it justified – the JAC is today widely viewed as performing a critical role in nurturing the rule of law by overseeing the appointment of qualified candidates who are recruited following a fair and open competition. Over the decade, the JAC has succeeded in introducing quicker, more efficient and more candidate-focused selection processes, and has done so on a smaller budget and with fewer staff. In terms of corporate governance, the JAC is a small and inexpensive public body that secures value for money. And with the publication of its annual report and accounts, board minutes and policy papers, the JAC is in many respects an exemplar of an open and accountable public body. It is certainly the case that the JAC ends its first decade on a stronger institutional and reputational footing than when it began its work in 2006, and certainly stronger than at many points during its first ten years.

But what of the next ten years? What are the issues, opportunities and challenges facing the JAC as it enters its difficult teenage years? For all of its success in establishing itself on the institutional landscape, the JAC has had much less success in transforming the judiciary. It has rightly been criticized for publishing press releases that cherry-pick statistics that could lead casual readers to conclude that greater progress has been made on addressing the diversity deficit than is in fact the case.[41] Of course, the JAC's (limited) effectiveness at securing greater judicial diversity should be assessed in a wider context that acknowledges the systemic issues that impact on diversity. Much has been made of the fact that the JAC's ability to drive change is limited by the lack of diversity within the legal profession. However, the JAC is also limited by a statutory framework that is not designed to be a full-throated endorsement of diversity, but instead serves multiple other goals as well (for example, enhancing the independence, legitimacy and transparency of the appointment processes). The diversification of the judiciary is, at best, a secondary goal of the statutory framework. Even the statutory duty imposed on the JAC is relatively weak, only requiring it to have regard to the need to encourage diversity among those who are available for selection.[42] The impact of the equal merit provision – one of the few diversity-oriented tools conferred by statute on the JAC – has been largely stymied by judicial opposition. In all of this lies evidence of the 'regulatory bind'[43] that has ensnared the JAC for the last ten years: it has a specific albeit weak statutory duty relating to judicial diversity, but very limited scope to influence several of the key determinants of success. At the same time, notwithstanding these wider systemic factors, the JAC has been too timid. It could – and, over the next decade, should – do more. Many of the contributions to this collection offer thoughts on how the JAC should approach the next ten years. For our part, we would suggest that there are five main tasks that should animate the JAC's second decade.

41 K. Malleson and R. Hunter, 'Women judges: inconvenient truth' *Law Society Gazette*, 20 January 2014.
42 Constitutional Reform Act 2005, s. 64.
43 Barmes and Malleson, 'The Legal Profession as Gatekeeper to the Judiciary', p. 259.

First, the JAC should do more to challenge the judiciary to not merely pay lip-service to diversity, but to pursue policies that will lead to faster change in the composition of the bench. While there are some judges who have a long-standing commitment to judicial diversity, for many more – including, often, those in leadership positions – this commitment is qualified by a deeply-seated reluctance to unsettle traditional understandings of what (or who) makes a 'good' judge. For sure, the judiciary has introduced a number of welcome initiatives such as a Judicial Working Shadowing Scheme (which enables lawyers considering a career in judicial office to spend time observing the work of sitting judges) and a Judicial Role Models Scheme (where judges from a range of diverse backgrounds assist outreach events and serve as mentors).[44] What is undeniable, however, is that the judiciary needs to be encouraged – and even harried – into doing more. The JAC has an important role to play here. It should, for example, challenge many judges' continued attachment to traditional understandings of merit. It should resist the judiciary's insistence on fee-paid experience since this not only favours long-serving barristers, but also reinforces that same traditional understanding of merit. And it should insist on a bolder equal merit policy that applies at short-listing in the same way as well as at the final recommendation, and it should look out for opportunities to use it more often.

Second, the JAC should work to weaken the Bar's grip on access to a judicial career in the courts. It should, for example, work with professional associations to ensure that candidates from unconventional backgrounds who have the potential to make excellent judges have the information and opportunities to develop skills and undergo activities that prepare them for judicial office (such as fee-paid experience, training and mentoring). The JAC should build and strengthen relationships with key interest groups such as the Women Judge's Association, the Black Solicitors Network and the Lawyers with Disabilities Division of the Law Society. These groups not only have enormous expertise which should help to inform the JAC's future policies and direction, but are also excellently placed to operate as a conduit between the JAC and highly-qualified non-traditional candidates. It is also vital that the JAC focus on the implementation and outcomes (and not simply the inauguration) of measures designed to put pressure on key gatekeepers in the legal profession; for example, by asking questions about the action taken to give effect to commitments made by leading Magic Circle and other law firms in initiatives to encourage senior staff to apply for judicial appointment.[45] The JAC should also do more to puncture continuing myths – identified in its own research as well as elsewhere – surrounding the appointments process and the judicial role; an example is the persistent misconception that a reference from a High Court judge is needed to apply successfully for lower level judicial vacancies. Many myths are still widely held by under-represented groups.[46] Here actions

44 See e.g. Judicial Diversity Committee of the Judges' Council, *Report on Progress 2013–2016*, London: Judges' Council, 2016.

45 J. Rayner, 'Leading firms sign up to judicial recruitment campaign', *Law Society Gazette*, 27 July 2012.

46 Judicial Appointments Commission, *Barriers to Application to Judicial Appointment: Report* (July, 2013).

speak louder than words. The quickest and most effective way to demonstrate the JAC's commitment to widening the appointment pool would be a significant and sustained step-change in the number of appointments made from across all branches of the legal profession, including solicitors, academics, lawyers in the public sector, lawyers from the employed Bar and legal executives.

Third, the JAC should review – and, where necessary, improve – its own internal practices and operations. To be fair, the JAC has not been short of internal and external reviews during its first decade. It is important, however, that the JAC continues to scrutinize and improve its processes and procedures – for example, in relation to the collation of diversity data and the operation of its online tests – as well as innovating new ones.[47] In particular, there should be greater transparency of the short-listing and selection day processes, particularly the role of the (non-JAC) lay and judicial panellists in these processes. Reviewing its internal processes should not be used, however, as an excuse for senior judges to reverse important progress that the JAC has made in the formalization of the selection process, especially in respect of senior vacancies. Attention should also be paid to ensuring the effective engagement of all of the JAC's commissioners. At times, some commissioners seem somewhat disengaged from some aspects of the JAC's work, especially its ongoing tensions with key stakeholders. For sure, the commissioners all have busy and demanding day-jobs, and their remuneration for the JAC's work is limited to around 28 days per year. It is especially important, however, that the JAC's leadership team ensures that the newly appointed commissioners – especially but not only the lay commissioners – are able to contribute to the JAC's work as soon as possible following appointment. According to one official at the JAC, it can take up to a year for a lay commissioner to find his or her feet in their new role. The JAC must ensure that the risk of being 'captured' by key stakeholders is highlighted as part of the training of new commissioners.

Fourth, the JAC should take more 'ownership' of the process for making senior appointments. At present, statute specifies the membership of the ad hoc panels that select candidates for appointment to the Court of Appeal and senior leadership positions such as Heads of Division and the Lord Chief Justice. Strictly speaking, these panels operate as 'committees' of the JAC, with their membership comprising senior judges as well as commissioners from the JAC. These appointments do not fall under the full auspices of the regular JAC-run regime. The precise composition of these panels depends on the senior vacancy in question, but each includes senior judges who do not sit on the JAC. There is no clear rationale for having these appointments lie outside the usual JAC processes other than to give senior judges greater say in the selection of their colleagues. However, as academic critics have argued, senior judges have too much influence over the

47 See e.g. criticism of the disproportionate failure rate of BAME candidates in the online tests and recommendation that the JAC monitor the social and educational background of applicants, shortlisted candidates, those recommended for appointment and current post-holders in Geoffrey Bindman and Karon Monaghan's report on judicial diversity (G. Bindman and K. Monaghan, *Judicial Diversity: Accelerating Change*, London: Labour Party, 2014, pp. 33, 49–50).

selection of other senior judges.[48] Several (but admittedly not all) of the lay commissioners who have sat on selection panels for senior posts have expressed concern about their ability to challenge the judicial panellists. According to one study, the lay commissioners on these panels tend to perform a limited, secondary role of corroborating the senior judicial panelists' assessment of the candidates.[49] If indeed acting in this way, the JAC's lay commissioners can perform an important role in helping senior judges to understand the importance of leadership skills and people management. They can also help to ensure that decisions are evidence-based and made in terms of and by reference to the selection criteria. What it also means, however, is that there is likely to be limited change in the type of candidates who succeed in the competitions for senior posts. It is also likely to mean that traditional understandings of merit will continue to prevail. Addressing this would ideally involve statutory change to bring top appointments fully within the normal JAC regime, with selection panels that are drawn wholly from the JAC's cohort of commissioners. The JAC should push for this statutory change. However, short of statutory change, the JAC should take greater responsibility for these selections. At present, it is commonplace to hear commissioners and staff at the JAC talk about selections above the High Court as not 'one of ours'. This reveals a mindset in which the JAC self-identifies as a secondary actor in top appointments, with the senior judges who participate on the ad hoc panels having the decisive say. This is concerning since some who are closely involved in the JAC concede that there are still 'who is next in line?' and 'whose turn is it?' attitudes amongst senior judges when it comes to deciding appointments to the Courts of Appeal and leadership roles.

Finally, and implicit in the four preceding points, the JAC must provide much stronger and more forceful leadership on diversity. It should provide active and strategic leadership on the need for, and design of, the fundamental and far-reaching changes to the selection process. But its leadership should extend more broadly to include judicial working conditions, training, mentoring and appraisal. The JAC should be forward-thinking in its interpretation of policies and changes already introduced (for example, around the availability and publication of part-time and flexible working arrangements). And it should be provocative in its support and lobbying for new ones (including further changes to historical relics, such as the requirement to go out on circuit, and – where these unnecessarily limit the applicant pool – statutory and non-statutory minimum qualifications for judicial appointments). Indeed, in relation to the latter, the JAC is uniquely placed to offer evidence-based arguments for change. The JAC should also encourage the judiciary and the Ministry to provide more resources to the cash-strapped Judicial College so that more extensive training and mentoring can be made available for newly appointed judges. To do this requires the JAC to demonstrate clear and deliberate leadership. At various points during the last decade the JAC has seemed to lack the nerve for proactive leadership.

48 See generally A. Paterson and C. Paterson, *Guarding the Guardians: Towards an Independent, Accountable and Diverse Senior Judiciary*, London: CentreForum, 2012.

49 Gee et al, *The Politics of Judicial Independence*, p. 185.

The recent Ministry of Justice consultation on *Modernising Judicial Terms and Conditions* in late 2016 is arguably a case in point.[50] As part of a package of measures aimed at improving diversity, the Government proposed single non-renewable terms for fee-paid judicial posts. The Government argued that this would allow for a larger and more diverse cohort of candidates to obtain fee-paid experience prior to applying for a salaried judicial role. This is not a trivial concern: as noted earlier, rightly or wrongly, considerable weight is placed on fee-paid judicial experience as an eligibility criterion for appointment to a salaried judicial position, and often this requirement can disadvantage non-traditional candidates. Driving the Government's proposal was the hope that a wider cohort of candidates with fee-paid experience might in turn lead to a more diverse salaried judiciary. Admittedly, views differed on the proposal. Those in favour welcomed the opportunity to widen the pool of candidates for judicial office who had fee-paid experience, with the hope that over time this would disturb settled expectations about the type of lawyers who are appointed to fee-paid positions.

However, many fee-paid judges and lawyers' associations were opposed, citing training and workload concerns relating to the time that fee-paid judges need to acquire experience. Their worry was that many fee-paid judges would not have sufficient opportunity before their non-renewable term lapsed to develop relevant experience in certain types of case (for example, serious sex offences). Some also contended that the Government's proposal might actually make the fee-paid role less attractive to particular groups, for example those with child caring responsibilities who preferred the flexibility of a part-time role and who might not have any desire to progress to a salaried role. Their worry was that the introduction of single non-renewable appointments might offset the benefits to diversity brought by a quicker turnover of fee-paid judges, and could disproportionately disadvantage particular groups. The Law Society also cited concerns that those employed in law firms would need to negotiate arrangements with their employer to undertake a part-time fee-paid judicial role. Although law firms might become more amenable to letting their employees pursue a fee-paid role if their tenure as a fee-paid judge were time-limited, this willingness might be undermined if there is greater uncertainty as to whether their employee would be leaving the firm for a salaried judicial role at the end of the term. Plainly, this was a difficult policy question with a range of competing arguments, including opposing arguments grounded on diversity concerns. But what was the JAC's view? Although it submitted a response to the consultation, the JAC's view was unclear.[51] It failed to take a strong stance, choosing instead to simply offer a risks/benefits analysis of the proposal, including of the implications of the proposal for its own workload and resources. It may be that this ambivalence reflected split

50 Ministry of Justice, *Modernising Judicial Terms and Conditions: Consultation on proposals to introduce a new tenure for fee paid office holders, provide for fixed term leadership positions, and modernise judicial terms and conditions*, London: Ministry of Justice, 2016.

51 Judicial Appointments Commission, *Ministry of Justice Consultation on Modernising Terms and Conditions: JAC Response*, London: Judicial Appointments Commission, 2016.

views on the JAC itself. However, this represents a missed opportunity to draw on its expertise and experience. For whatever reason, the JAC opted not to offer clear and deliberate leadership on a difficult question of diversity.

Reflecting on the JAC's first decade, what seems clear is that change will only come once the scale of the current diversity deficit is recognized and greater weight is attached (by the JAC, the judiciary, ministers and the legal profession) to the importance of remedying it. What is also clear is that clear, positive and strategic leadership is essential to making this happen. If the JAC is serious about providing such leadership (and it should be) then it is important that every opportunity is taken to make and demonstrate this point. No doubt JAC insiders would say that they have been endeavouring to do all of these things, to varying degrees. The same insiders might also add that it can be difficult for the JAC to exhibit leadership on judicial diversity given the narrow constitutional space that it occupies, with the constant need to navigate the concerns and interests of the senior judiciary, the Ministry and the different branches of the legal professions. Perhaps so, but the JAC needs to be bolder. It should have greater confidence in its ability to weather external pressures. Similarly, it should feel more confident in its ability to withstand and challenge the preoccupations of ministers, a self-interested legal profession and an embattled judiciary. After the various ups and downs of its first decade, the JAC has acquired some political 'capital'. It should begin to spend it.

2 The JAC's first ten years

Christopher Stephens CBE

I am pleased to have been asked to contribute to this collection and to have the opportunity to reflect on some of the important constitutional changes introduced by the Constitutional Reform Act 2005 (CRA).

Prior to my appointment as Chairman of the Judicial Appointments Commission (JAC) in 2011, I had read much about the arrangements that existed before the CRA and in particular before the creation of the JAC: judges were appointed by a politician, the Lord Chancellor. There was a network of 'secret soundings' that took place within the legal and judicial community. Openness and transparency did not feature largely in the arrangements. And there was little in the way of advertising and objective assessment of candidates.

But that is not an entirely fair description. In the lead up to the CRA and the creation of the JAC, the then Lord Chancellor, Lord Mackay of Clashfern, had introduced a good deal of modernization: posts were advertised, job descriptions and statements of eligibility were introduced as were selection criteria for each judicial office. Candidates were required to complete application forms designed to elicit information to enable them to be assessed against the published selection criteria. However, private consultation with judges and members of the legal profession did still take place prior to final interviews. These arrangements were largely maintained by Lord Mackay's successors.

The CRA provided a greater and clearer separation of powers and the JAC was the instrument though which the CRA would ensure future judicial appointments would be made more independently, with greater openness and transparency. It provided a clear statutory focus on increasing diversity while ensuring that selections were to be made solely on merit. The creation of the JAC also introduced a lay element to bring broader perspectives to the process. But early on some members of the judiciary, the executive and the legal profession had misgivings about the new arrangements. The loss of patronage and influence; the inevitable changes to established practices and the impact that a drive towards greater diversity might have on the quality of appointments reinforced a view that the old system had worked perfectly well. Public confidence in the judiciary was high, and the concern was that this could be damaged by a new appointments system.

The new statutory arrangements introduced by the CRA also prescribed roles with new responsibilities for some and a loss of duties for others. Tensions in the new relationships inevitably arose and the newly formed JAC faced a substantial challenge. It had to introduce a much more open and transparent process with new selection processes which encouraged applications from a wider and diverse pool. At the same time, it had to change the culture of judicial appointments and win the hearts and minds of all of those involved in the process. Moreover, during the first five years of operation the JAC faced six external reviews about various aspects of its operation.

Despite the inevitable tensions, the first Commissioners, led by my predecessor Baroness Usha Prashar, carefully protected the boundaries of the JAC's role. They put in place a selection process characterized by openness, fairness, and transparency. Importantly, the Commission and its selections were palpably independent. They focused on making selections, as required by the CRA, 'solely on merit'; they developed and applied good character considerations to their selection, and they encouraged diversity in their selections.

Just prior to my appointment as Chairman, the JAC had been included in a list of bodies under the Public Bodies Bill that was published in late 2010, which ministers were to be able to alter or abolish without fresh primary legislation. The then Lord Chief Justice, Lord Judge, was unflinching in his support for the continuation of an independent Judicial Appointments Commission and shortly after my appointment, the JAC was removed from the Bill.

When I took up post in February 2011, the then Lord Chancellor, Rt Hon Kenneth Clarke MP, was clear that the appointments process took too long and cost too much. During my five years in office, while I wanted to focus on improving relations with our partners I also wanted to address the areas of concern expressed by the Lord Chancellor and those of the JAC's other stakeholders. The JAC's programme for change therefore focused on: reducing the cost of the JAC, better supporting the business need of the courts, improving the experience of our candidates, reducing the time to make an appointment, improving diversity outcomes, and ensuring the quality of JAC selections.

Speed was my first area of focus. Together with colleagues in the senior judiciary, Judicial Office, Ministry of Justice (MoJ), and Her Majesty's Courts and Tribunals Service, the JAC put in place a series of measures to reduce the length of the end-to-end appointments process. Where previously this could take up to 40 weeks, there is now an average of less than 18 weeks between the launch of an exercise and the JAC making its recommendations.

Secondly, I launched a comprehensive review of the JAC's selection processes and tools. This was informed by a review by external experts. They identified a number of strengths including the high quality work of our selection panels, and the consistency and transparency of its processes. They also made a number of recommendations for improvement, most of which have now been implemented.

To make brief mention of the key changes, we introduced a new competency framework tailored to each role, and aligned with the Judicial Skills and Abilities Framework (which is used by the Judicial College and Judicial Office and identifies the skills and abilities required by judicial office-holders). Existing selection tools were also refined to assess these competencies, particularly at shortlisting stages. This was particularly important because in large exercises the JAC can receive more than a thousand applications; distinguishing between large numbers of highly able candidates is a considerable challenge. These changes were made in parallel with the launch in 2015 of a new digital recruitment system.

Separately, the JAC also worked closely with the senior judiciary to support the ad hoc selection panels – 'committees' of the JAC – which make recommendations for appointments above the High Court, to the Court of Appeal and Heads of Division. Through joint effort, these selections were made more open, transparent and evidence-based.

Due to the expertise the JAC has developed, it has received an increasing number of requests to advise on, assist with or run selection exercises beyond its core statutory responsibilities. The Government's Triennial Review of the JAC recommended the exploration of options to clarify and expand the JAC's functions in a wide range of appointments, as well as in promoting the international rule of law. The Review also concluded that the MoJ and JAC should consider the potential to enable the JAC to charge for the provision of assistance with appointments beyond its statutory responsibilities. Modest but important steps have been taken in response to these recommendations (such as running exercises for the Government of Wales on a cost recovery basis, and providing technical advice on judicial appointments to the new government of Myanmar), and the work is ongoing.

Thirdly, the JAC continued to develop its original three-pronged strategy to increase diversity. This was supported by measures in the Crime and Courts Act 2013, including the introduction of the 'equal merit' provision which has been applied by the JAC since July 2014. I am also encouraged by the recent strengthening of the Judicial Diversity Forum, both in terms of its remit and the commitment of the high-level representatives who now attend. I hope that this momentum can be maintained.

Women have continued to make good progress, comprising between 44 and 52 per cent of all candidates recommended to legally qualified roles in each year between 2012 and 2016. Over the past ten years, 1,800 women have been recommended; the number of women has more than doubled in both the High Court (to 22) and the Court of Appeal (to eight), albeit from a very low base. BAME candidates have applied, and been recommended, in greater numbers since the JAC was created; the level of recommendations remains broadly in line with their level in the eligible pool at 10 per cent (over 400 recommended BAME candidates in total). However, there is little progress at more senior levels, and there is more to do in encouraging and supporting BAME candidates throughout the selection process.

Overall the proportion of recommended candidates who declare a disability is in line with the proportion of applicants, but there is no robust eligible pool data maintained by the professions or the judiciary against which the JAC can benchmark its performance. Finally, the picture on solicitors is fairly static, despite efforts by senior judges, the Law Society, the JAC, and some major firms to encourage and support applications. More work is clearly needed here.

Finally, for 2015/2016 both the JAC's budget allocation and staffing complement were around half their level in 2008/2009.

Despite the JAC's achievements over the last ten years, it was never complacent during my tenure, and I know that continues to be the case. A continuing programme of work is needed to ensure that JAC selections are fair, made solely on merit, and open – to non-traditional candidates in particular. The support of the JAC's partners in the judiciary and the profession is key to this work. There are some key areas – such as flexible working patterns, appraisal and development – where I believe continued or increased momentum could accelerate the rate of progress.

I would like to have seen greater numbers of diverse, non-traditional candidates joining the judiciary, particularly at more senior levels – not only from its four key target groups but also from other pools of talent such as academia, the employed Bar, chartered legal executives and government lawyers. There are barriers for some of these groups which I believe should be kept under regular review. The pressure to provide judges who can 'hit the ground running' – demonstrating previous judicial experience and/or specific jurisdictional knowledge – inevitably reduces the opportunities for unconventional candidates who have gained good experience and skills in different ways. If such candidates are to apply and succeed in greater numbers, this needs to be enabled and supported by all parts of the system – from the detail of the vacancy request, through the selection process, to the training and development provided and beyond.

Inflexible working patterns are another barrier for many potential candidates, and I welcome the recent steps taken toward increasing the availability of salaried part-time working. While recognizing the challenges involved, I hope this will start to become the default position. Together with further modernization of employment conditions and practices more generally, this would assist in attracting and retaining the best candidates from the broadest range of backgrounds.

A crucial element of this modernization, in my view, is the implementation of effective appraisals throughout the judiciary. As well as supporting development, appraisal evidence usefully informs judicial references on existing office-holders as part of the selection process. It could also potentially be used to inform an assessment of the quality and effectiveness of JAC recommendations. While on an anecdotal basis I have consistently been told that the high calibre of appointments has been maintained if not raised under the JAC, and public confidence in the judiciary remains high, there are no external measures available to confirm the quality of recommendations that the JAC is making. In my view the development of such 'performance metrics', recognized as a significant gap by the Triennial Review, should be a high priority for the future.

It is important that I should also recognize the support and contribution of those colleagues – both currently and formerly on the Commission. The work of a Commissioner is fascinating and rewarding but also demanding, including in terms of the time needed to learn about and fulfil the responsibilities. It is essential to attract and retain Commissioners of the calibre and diversity that have been appointed to date. I should also pay tribute to the staff of the JAC who, during the term of my appointment, have worked hard to achieve considerable efficiencies in the operation of the JAC while introducing many new and improved systems and processes against a backdrop of financial austerity and uncertainty.

I welcome Parliamentary scrutiny of the JAC, including in relation to the appointment of the Chairman, the requirement to lay an Annual Report before Parliament, and the occasional public hearings at which the work of the Commission is called to account. I consider all of this to be an appropriate Parliamentary engagement in the process of appointing judges, which stops short of Parliamentary review of individual appointments. I hope that Parliament continues to be engaged with the work of the JAC, as this oversight is a very important aspect of the JAC's legitimacy.

Reflection

Sir Thomas Legg KCB QC

Sir Thomas Legg KCB QC was Permanent Secretary to the Lord Chancellor and Clerk of the Crown in Chancery from 1989 to 1998. His 36-year career in the old LCD (now subsumed in the Ministry of Justice) included working on law reform, European and International Law, courts administration and, especially in this context, extensive experience of appointing judges, magistrates and Queen's Counsel. During the years after he retired from the Civil Service, he did a wide variety of other public service appointments.

I contribute to this debate as a voice from the past. I was responsible for the appointment of judges and magistrates, and Queen's Counsel, in the old Lord Chancellor's Department from 1982 to 1989, and then as Permanent Secretary from 1989 to 1998. Much has changed since then, but in many ways the landscape still looks familiar. At any rate, I hope that a longer-range view from the past may help in looking to the future.

The 'old' system of the 80s and 90s was in fact at the time a new system, mainly devised by my predecessor Sir Derek Oulton. With the Civil Service as our model, we tried to make the process more regular, recorded and objective. We based our advice to the Lord Chancellor on widespread and systematic confidential consultations about individuals, combined with continuous liaison with the Judiciary. The Lord Chancellors of the day, who of course were themselves senior barristers or judges, usually but by no means always made their appointments in agreement with the senior judges.

The group working this system was about a dozen strong of all ranks, and it was rare for vacancies not to be filled at once or reasonably promptly.

This system worked a lot better than its predecessor, and I would be content for it to be judged by the quality of its product. However, it fell short in respect of diversity. We were increasingly aware of this at the time, and accepted the need for further development. In particular, I became concerned over time about our evident failure to appoint enough women. At the time, I supposed that this problem would solve itself in due course, mainly because of the growing number of women coming into the legal profession. It turned out that I was wrong about that, and I have retained an interest ever since in the issue of diversity in judicial appointments.

In due course, the 'old' system was replaced by the Judicial Appointments Commission (JAC), the first 10 years of whose work we celebrated at a conference at the University of Birmingham in 2015, which formed the impetus for this collection. The JAC has clearly made good progress in many respects, and they can be justly proud of their work so far. The fact that problems persist is not their fault, but because those problems run deeper.

I don't myself believe that we need to spend too much time debating exactly how many women, BMEs etc. we need to achieve an acceptably diverse judiciary. We plainly need a better balance to achieve even a broad 'reflection'. But to achieve this looks likely to require re-structuring the whole appointments system, and to some extent of the judicial system and culture.

In approaching this task, some limits must be borne in mind. The work of our judges is responsible and demanding. First-instance judges at every level must have the personal and professional qualities and experience to handle trials in our adversarial system, and to make decisions directly determining the rights and lives of their fellow-citizens. And, at the appellate level, they must also have the intellect and wisdom to settle the law for us all, subject only to the legislative power of Parliament. Moreover, the fortified security of tenure that our judges necessarily enjoy means that there is little room for taking risks with judicial appointments.

On the other hand, the future credibility and quality of our judiciary do depend on recruiting judges from a wider stream of lawyers than before. To achieve this, I wouldn't rule out quotas, but they would bring problems of their own, and I would hope to try other means first and see if they work sufficiently by themselves.

Against this background, I think we need to look at getting rid of, or cutting down on, part-time sitting and substituting more intensive training; and also at further changing the working patterns and career prospects of the judiciary. Such changes would be aimed at widening the recruiting field, and making appointment and judicial life more friendly to a more diverse pool of candidates, especially for the lower ranks of the judiciary.

However, I will concentrate here on the merit test. What *is* 'merit'? The Shorter Oxford defines it as 'that which is deserved; due reward or punishment ... Excellence, worth'. In the context of judicial appointments, that doesn't get us very far. Here it surely means a measure of both absolute and comparative *qualification* for the judicial post in question, in terms both of personal ability and character, and also of professional experience and skills, all of which combine to enable an estimate of the candidate's likely capacity for, and competence in, that post. In short, a combination of moral, intellectual and professional qualities. This is a complex cocktail.

We appear to owe the concept of merit for public appointments originally to the Chinese Civil Service in the Qin and Han dynasties (221 BCE to 220 CE). However, it is worth recalling how relatively recent has been its arrival in our own field. Many centuries passed before it was taken up by the British Raj in appointing the Indian Civil Service, after which it came to Britain, and especially to the home Civil Service through the Northcote-Trevelyan Report in 1854. And even then, it was controversial to begin with.

Moreover, it did not immediately apply to judicial appointments, where spoils rather than merit long ruled the roost. Indeed, Lord Salisbury, one of our most intelligent Prime Ministers, stated explicitly around the turn of the twentieth century that it was an

> unwritten law of our party system that party claims should always weigh very heavily in the disposal of the highest legal appointments … Perhaps it is not an ideal system … but it is our system for the present.

This did not trouble Lord Salisbury too much, since he added that 'within certain limits of intelligence, honesty and knowledge of the law, one man would make as good a judge as another, and a Tory mentality was *ipso facto* more trustworthy than a Liberal one'.

But times changed, and later in the twentieth century we were determined to eradicate the remaining vestiges of that mentality. So in devising the 'old' appointments system, we took our primary aim to make all appointments on merit. We took this to mean, as in the Civil Service (being Civil Servants ourselves), that all available candidates must be ranked in order of merit, and that only the single most meritorious candidate could be recommended.

However, with experience I came to realize how subjective the concept of merit was, and how vague and inexact a measure it was and is. Of course, it is not without content: some candidates are plainly not up to the job, and some are equally clearly very well qualified. But within those broad limits, there can be little precision, especially in comparing candidates. The more so because, beneath the visible tip of conscious and rational decision-making there inevitably lies a subconscious mass of assumptions, impressions and even prejudices. This is so for everybody and is therefore not blameworthy. But the system must do everything possible to counter them. The first defence is, of course, to involve not one, but a group in the process. But that alone is not enough.

The present ground-rules are rational enough. The combined effect of the Constitutional Reform Act 2005 and the Crime and Courts Act 2013 requires that candidates for judicial office must be selected 'solely on merit', but that where there are two candidates of equal merit, that candidate can be selected who will most improve diversity.

This would appear to give important scope for increasing judicial diversity, but of course it depends on the width of the approach to the decision that there are two or more candidates of equal merit. Graham Gee and Kate Malleson have raised concerns about this.[1] They feared that, in spite of its potential, 'as narrowly interpreted by the JAC, the equal provision is likely to have very little impact' in improving judicial diversity. They attribute this minimalist approach of the JAC to 'excessive judicial influence on judicial appointments'.

1 G. Gee and K. Malleson 'Judicial Appointments, Diversity and the Equal Merit Provision' *UK Constitutional Law Association Blog*, 6 May 2014.

I tend to share Gee and Malleson's concern. My own experience of assessing hundreds of candidates for various judicial posts makes me agree with the view of Lady Justice Hallett, whom they also cite, that it is not 'as rare as people think that you have candidates who are equally qualified'. When you bear in mind how subjective *any* merit criterion is, that is hardly surprising. The fact that, under the 'single best candidate' rule, you *must* choose one candidate as more meritorious than the others can easily become a self-fulfilling device to obscure a broad equality of 'merit'.

More broadly, the 'single best candidate' approach embodies what I have elsewhere called a *maximalist* approach to merit.[2] I would prefer the selecting authority to employ a *minimalist* approach. This would mean determining always which of the available candidates are 'appointable'. If only one is appointable, or more than one is but one of them is clearly head and shoulders above the others, then that one should be selected. But if more than one is appointable, and none stands out above the others, then the authority should be free to select the most 'diverse' candidate. I do not pretend that such an approach is much easier to apply. I claim only that it corresponds better in most cases to reality, and tends therefore to be fairer both to the candidates and the system.

I believe that the application of this approach across the board would go far to increase diversity. It would be especially helpful in appointing the judges of appellate courts. There one is not selecting a soloist but composing a chamber orchestra, and a balance of different experience, skills and attitudes – such as women can often bring – is desirable. In this connection, I have long believed that there is also scope for appointing a few 'outside' experts, especially distinguished academics, direct to our appellate courts.

As an envoi, I must add that I also share Gee and Malleson's concern about judicial influence. Of course, the judiciary *should* have an important involvement in all judicial appointments: they are an essential ingredient. However, the removal of the old-style Lord Chancellor, who acted as a well-informed and powerful counter-weight to the judges, may have tilted the balance too far in the latter's favour. For many reasons, lay members are often likely to defer to their judicial colleagues in these decisions. And no group of professionals, however distinguished, should be effectively self-perpetuating. From here, I cannot judge if that line has been crossed; but it must, I think, be counted as a risk.

For this reason, I would myself like to see the re-introduction of a 'political' element in the appointments process, especially at the most senior levels. The Lord Chancellor's involvement has now been diluted almost to vanishing point. That is understandable now that the Lord Chancellor is a mere 'politician', often without legal qualifications or knowledge. It is defended on the ground that 'politics' must be taken out of the appointment of judges. But at senior levels, the appointment of judges is in fact a political act, with political implications for the future governance of the country. To exclude politicians altogether, and treat senior

2 T. Legg 'Brave New World – the Supreme Court and Judicial Appointments', *Legal Studies* 24, 2004, pp. 45–54.

appointments as if they were an entirely professional matter, not only ignores some realities, but runs long-term risks of its own for the judiciary. At any rate at the highest judicial levels, both the other branches of government, the Executive and the Legislature, should have some involvement and therefore some responsibility – as they do, in one way or another, in other major Western democracies, both in the Common Law and Civil Law jurisdictions.

That is why, for the protection of our judiciary and its independence, I would personally like to see Ministers and Parliament play a suitable, and not merely formal, role in the appointment of our most senior judges. Indeed, I foresee that at some stage this may well be demanded by Parliament, maybe in the context of a serious dispute with the Judiciary. Surely it would be better to introduce it now, in advance.

3 Power and judicial appointment

Squaring the impossible circle

Alan Paterson OBE

Introduction

The very title of the volume in which this chapter appears – *Debating Judicial Appointments in an Age of Diversity* – alerts us to the fact that judicial appointments and senior judicial appointments in particular remain contested territory as they have been on and off for more than a century in the UK. Why should this be so? Essentially the debate is about 'power' and who should wield it in relation to the appointment of the senior members of a branch of the state. To ask how the different branches of the state exercise power over judicial appointment is, of course, to beg the question of what is meant by power.

For the purposes of this chapter – power will be used in the sense so evocatively expounded by Steven Lukes.[1] Lukes' argument is that power is best seen as a three-dimensional concept. The first dimension focuses on observable behaviour and the ability to compel a particular outcome to be achieved. The second dimension famously includes the 'mobilization of bias',[2] whereby a group or elite sustains a predominant set of values or beliefs which work to their benefit through influencing what is included, and especially what is excluded, from the belief set. This dimension extends the notion of power to include not just decision-making but also non-decision-making – ensuring that certain decisions are not even considered. The third dimension takes this last notion further by focusing on the ability to ensure that some issues never get on the agenda, by controlling the decision-making arena such that certain decisions are not even contemplatable.[3] In the policymaking arena Lukes' argument means that we should look beyond the ability to impose one's policy preferences on others, or even the ability to confine the scope of the debate over policymaking in certain ways, to the ability to

1 S. Lukes, *Power: A Radical View*, London: Palgrave Macmillan, 2nd edn, 2005. Unlike Lukes I will use 'power', 'influence' and 'control' interchangeably – each will be used in a three-dimensional way.

2 See E. E. Schattshneider, *The Semi-Sovereign People*, New York: Harper & Row, 1960. See also P. Bachrach and M. S. Baratz, *Power and Poverty: Theory and Practice*, New York: Oxford University Press, 1970.

3 For reasons of brevity this is necessarily a gross over-simplification of the richness of Lukes' thesis.

have one's perception of the policy universe accepted as the obvious and only one available.[4] Applied to judicial appointments the first dimension involves getting one candidate appointed rather than another. The second dimension would include the elite controlling the attributes deemed essential for a judge and thus preventing candidates from even being considered for appointment, and an exercise of the third dimension of power would be where the elite controls the paradigm within which judicial appointments are made such that no one considers that any other paradigm is possible. Gee, in this volume, makes a similar argument to Lukes when he suggests that we need to move beyond a focus on the influence exercised by some on others' choices as to who should become a senior judge (conduct shaping), to the behaviour of those who by their actions shape the context in which these decisions are made (context shaping).[5] In this chapter it will be argued that the senior judiciary in the UK – particularly in England and Wales – have over the last one hundred and fifty years gradually acquired the lion's share of power in all three of Lukes' senses over the appointment of senior judges. It will further be argued that this evolution, although it is genuinely and understandably believed by the senior judges to be in the public interest, is in fact unhealthy for democracy and for the judiciary itself.

Historical evolution

Historically, the courts were the monarch's courts – a key part of the apparatus by which the kingdom was governed. In England the three main branches of the state – the Courts, Parliament and the Cabinet all emanated from the monarch's Council.[6] Each had specialized functions but it was very far from a pure separation of powers – a concept that was some centuries off. The Lord Chancellor was the monarch's senior law officer and subsequently, most senior judge, yet for several centuries he sat in the Cabinet and for a while so too did the Lord Chief Justice. Hardly surprising then that such significant wielders of state power in the monarch's name, should be appointed by the monarch. After the Glorious Revolution in 1688 had ushered in the foundation of the constitutional monarchy, judicial appointments, especially senior ones, continued to be done in the name of the monarch. In truth, the real power in such appointments had shifted to the executive (and ultimately, to Parliament) as it had done in the country as a whole – in recognition of the fact that wielders of state power must derive their legitimacy from the constitutional accountability measures of the time. However, in practice, although Prime Ministers took a keen interest in appointments to the highest judicial positions (including Law Lords) up until the end of the Second World War,[7] for other senior judicial positions (including the High Court and the

4 For Lukes, the third dimension has close parallels with Antonio Gramsci's notion of hegemony.

5 See G. Gee, 'Judging the JAC: How Much Judicial Influence Over Judicial Appointments Is Too Much?' in this collection.

6 See A. V. Dicey, *The Privy Council*, London: Macmillan & Co, 1887.

7 See A. Paterson, 'Scottish Lords of Appeal, 1876–1988', *Juridical Review*, 1988, p. 235.

Court of Appeal) it was not really the Prime Minster who chose the candidates for the monarch's approval, it was the Lord Chancellor.[8] Similarly, in Scotland it was not the Secretary of State for Scotland who played the major part in the selection of judges in practice, but the chief law officer, the Lord Advocate, another political appointee.[9] In one sense this was simply a delegation of authority by the Prime Minister/Secretary of State since throughout the nineteenth and for much of the twentieth centuries Lord Chancellors and Lord Advocates were political appointments of the Prime Minster and his party, and when the Government fell the officeholders lost their post.

To the executive, ministerial appointment of the judiciary made perfect sense – what external critics might, and often did, dismiss as 'political' appointments – the executive saw as either (1) a 'reward' to lawyer MPs for loyal party service and sacrifice (of which elevating a Law Officer to a senior judicial position was a particular form), or (2) as a way of ensuring that 'right thinking' individuals of the same political persuasion as the party in power were making the decisions in all three branches of the state, or (3) latterly, a way of recognizing that political experience from any party was an asset for senior judges given the policy content of some of their decisions. The senior appointments for much of the nineteenth century certainly seemed to bear this out – Harold Laski's research[10] indicated that of the 139 judicial appointments in England from 1832 to 1906, 80 were sitting MPs at the time of the their appointment (63 being appointed when their party was in office) and a further 11 had been candidates. This does look like Lukes' notions of the second and third dimensions of power – the ability to confine the scope of the debate over who should be judges or further to have one's perception of the judicial role and who might best fill it accepted as the obvious and only viewpoint available – since the legitimacy of appointing judges from a political background was widely accepted. Lord Salisbury was the Tory Prime Minster on several occasions at the end of that century and his approach to judicial appointments was described by his biographer (his daughter) as follows:

> With regard to many non-political posts, he would be frankly partisan in his selections. Legal promotions did not come under his direct appointment, but he would never apologize for the practice of making them a reward for political 'right thinking'. Within certain limits of intelligence, honesty, and

8 Almost invariably Prime Ministers would seek the advice of their Lord Chancellor even for appointments to the most senior judicial positions including Lord of Appeal and very rarely was it not followed. See R. F. V. Heuston, *Lives of the Lord Chancellors 1885–1940*, Oxford: Oxford University Press, 1964, p. 24; R. F. V. Heuston, *Lives of the Lord Chancellors, 1940–1970*, Oxford: Clarendon Press, 1987, pp. 146, 155 and 173. On p. 199 Heuston records that Gerald Gardiner as LC stated that in terms of promotions to the Law Lords he was always consulted by PM and his advice was always taken.

9 Paterson, 'Scottish Lords of Appeal', p. 241.

10 H. J. Laski, 'The Technique of Judicial Appointment', in H. J. Laski (ed.) *Studies in Law and Politics*, London: Allen and Unwin, 1932, p. 168.

> knowledge of the law, one man would make as good a judge as another, and a Tory mentality was, ipso facto, more trustworthy than a Liberal one.[11]

In the 1897 Lord Salisbury wrote to his Lord Chancellor, Lord Halsbury to say that it was:

> the unwritten law of our party system; and there is no clearer statute in that unwritten law than the rule that party claims should always weigh very heavily in the disposal of the highest legal appointments. In dealing with them you cannot ignore the party system as you do in the choice of a general or an archbishop. It would be a breach of the tacit convention on which politicians and lawyers have worked the British Constitution together for the last 200 years.[12]

Salisbury practised what he preached. Four of the six Lords of Appeal that he and Balfour appointed to sit in the House of Lords were Conservative MPs and five of the six retired judges that they promoted to the peerage (thus becoming Law Lords) had a history of conservative if not Conservative decision-making. By comparison, Halsbury appears quite circumspect – of his 30 appointments to the High Court, only ten were clearly rewards for party service or promotion for a 'right-thinking' candidate,[13] although another four were Liberals. In fact Halsbury would have appointed more judges with a political background but at several stages in his period as Lord Chancellor there was an edict from the party whips and the Prime Minister that the party's majority in the House was too slender to brook the risk of a by-election. However, already the tide was beginning to turn. Ironically, after a much criticized political appointment, when Halsbury proposed to appoint another Tory MP to the High Court in 1897, Lord Salisbury wrote to suggest that it would be sensible in the light of the current 'public taste' if Halsbury was to desist, since 'the judicial salad requires both legal oil and political vinegar; but disastrous effects will follow if due proportion is not observed' and that a lawyer of good practice (not in the House) be appointed and the 'promising political lawyer' asked to wait.[14] This letter, and the very fact that not a few of Halsbury's appointments were severely criticized by the Bar and the Media (and the senior judiciary, in private),[15] either for political cronyism or for a lack of obvious legal merit, strongly suggest that the ministerial power of judicial appointment was no longer being taken on trust in the wider world. The executive's untrammeled ability to decide which politically minded lawyer should be appointed to the senior judiciary had been taken too far – this was

11 G. Cecil, *Life of Lord Salisbury*, 1931, Vol. iii, pp. 192–193.
12 See Heuston, *Lives of the Lord Chancellors 1885–1940*, p. 53.
13 See A. Paterson, 'Judges: A Political Elite?', *British Journal of Law and Society* 1, 1974, p. 118.
14 See Heuston, *Lives of the Lord Chancellors 1885–1940*, p. 57.
15 See Heuston, *Lives of the Lord Chancellors 1885–1940*, p. 35ff.

undisguised or first dimensional power in Lukes' terms and the media had had enough.[16]

The 'Liberal Landslide' in the 1905 election ushered in a new era in judicial appointments. Lord Loreburn, Halsbury's successor was opposed to appointing judges on anything other than professional merit as was Lord Haldane who succeeded Loreburn. Lord Haldane persuaded Asquith, the Liberal Prime Minister to agree to this change of policy and after that political 'reward' and 'right-thinking' appointments in England and Wales greatly declined (with the exception of the promotion of Law Officers). However, Haldane considered that political experience (of whatever party) was an advantage for senior judicial appointments – especially the House of Lords. Thus Loreburn, Haldane and Asquith between them appointed seven Lords of Appeal and all but one had political experience as had two of their four judicial elevations to the Lords during the years 1905–1915.[17] The Liberals tried to keep a balance of party political experience in these appointments but this did not solve the problem that the Courts were manned by many more former Tory MPs than Liberal ones. Thus in 1910 the Liberal Attorney General (Robson) wrote to Loreburn asking him to appoint more Liberal Lords of Appeal:

> The Lord Chancellor is no doubt anxious to exclude from his Court any appointment he believes to be political, but the political complexion of the Court cannot be altogether ignored especially in view of future developments. The tribunal would have to play a great part in disputes that are legal in form but political in fact, and it would be idle to deny the resolute bias of many of the Judges.[18]

Haldane did not accede to this request. Lloyd-George when Prime Minister from 1916 to 1923 tried to restore political 'reward' or 'right-thinking' judicial appointments but he was partly thwarted by Lord Birkenhead his Lord Chancellor and after Lord Hailsham became Lord Chancellor in 1928 appointments to the higher courts in England and Wales were based overwhelmingly on professional merit alone. Perhaps because Lord Chancellors were beginning to place more emphasis on their judicial duties rather than their ministerial duties they were growing uncomfortable with any suggestion that the Prime Minster might be consulted over High Court appointments. As Hailsham wrote to Lord Sankey his predecessor, in 1933, 'I don't think it is any business of the Prime Minister to have a voice in the selection of a judge … I think you and I both agree that that would be very undesirable'. Clearly ministerial appointment was on the wane. This approach was further underlined by Lord Jowitt the Lord Chancellor for the new

16 Indeed *The Economist* was to be found criticising political 'reward' appointments to the judiciary as early as 1859. See 'Mr Justice Blackburn', *The Economist*, 9 July 1859, p. 758.
17 See Paterson, 'Judges: A Political Elite?'.
18 Heuston, *Lives of the Lord Chancellors 1885–1940*, p. 151.

Labour Government after the Second World War. He went out of his way not to appoint any of the Labour sympathizers put up to him by the Labour Whips[19] and during his six-year tenure as Lord Chancellor he was proud that he had only appointed two members of his own party to the bench.

With respect to some of the most senior judicial appointments however, political experience was still seen as an advantage. Thus, promotion to the Heads of Division or the Lord Chief Justiceship were often from the ranks of the Law Officers[20] or other politically experienced lawyers, up until the later 1940s and as late as the 1970s half of the Lords of Appeal had had party political experience.[21] J. L. Edwards argues that any claim of the law officers to high judicial office in England and Wales died in 1873 with the Judicature Act of that year.[22] In this he was supported by Gladstone's letter to Queen Victoria in the same year which states that the Cabinet were of the opinion that with the passing of the Judicature Act all claims of the law officers to a succession as of right to any particular judicial office have naturally dropped. However the facts of history do not bear out the assertion that the law officers were no longer seen to have any claims to senior judicial posts after 1873. Of the 20 Attorney-Generals between 1874 and 1964 only three failed to be appointed to the post of Lord Justice or above (and two of these had consistently refused such offers), of the 19 Lord Chancellors between 1874 and 1964 only five had not been a law officer and of the eight Lord Chief Justices between 1873 and 1946 seven had been Attorney General.[23]

Similarly, in Scotland in the 100 years prior to 1972 whenever the top two most senior judicial posts became vacant they were filled by the chief law officer (the Lord Advocate) or one of his predecessors. Indeed the top position – the Lord President – had been filled by the current or former Lord Advocates on every occasion in the 250 years before 1972. Unsurprisingly, a very high percentage of Lords Advocates during these centuries were promoted to the senior judicial bench. As for Scottish Lords of Appeal they – until the 1960s – were chosen by the Prime Minister on the advice of the Lord Chancellor rather than the Lord Advocate (who might be a candidate) and as such had a very similar profile in terms of political experience as their English counterparts.[24] In the last fifty years, however, as lawyer participation in the House of Commons has tended to decline political experience has played very little part in the appointment of Lords of Appeal in England or Scotland. At the High Court level in Scotland the claims of the law officers to judicial preferment took longer to shake off. They may have given up their claims to the top two judicial posts in the early 1970s, but their claims to High Court appointment strengthened – not least since they could appoint themselves. Thus in 2000 12 of the last 15 Lord Advocates to hold the position had been appointed to the High Court in Scotland and 22 of the 71

19 Heuston, *Lives of the Lord Chancellors 1940–1970*, p. 118.

20 The Attorney General and the Solicitor General.

21 See Paterson, 'Judges: A Political Elite?', p. 125.

22 J. Edwards, *The Law Officers of the Crown*, London: Sweet and Maxwell, 1964.

23 See *inter alia* Paterson, 'Judges: A Political Elite?', pp. 126–127.

24 See Paterson, 'Scottish Lords of Appeal', p. 235.

appointments to that court from 1955 to 1999 had been active in politics.[25] With Devolution the First Minister replaced the Prime Minister for appointments to the High Court and (in practice) even for the top two judicial appointments in Scotland, but in the modern era fewer and fewer Scottish judges have had political experience and in the last ten years we have seen the emergence of the non-political Lord Advocate.[26]

This account, including the survival of some political 'reward' appointments until the 1970s, might tend to suggest that for much of the nineteenth and twentieth centuries the selection of the senior judiciary in Great Britain was entirely in the hands of the Executive. That may have been the legal position but it was far from the whole story. A scrutiny of Campbell's *Lives of the Lord Chancellors* (1851) reveals that Lord Chancellors as far back as the seventeenth century, when faced with vacancies in the common law courts (as opposed the equity courts in which they presided) were not averse to consulting the Chief Justices as to the possible candidates from the common law Bar. Indeed, in a fascinating letter from Lord Chief Justice Coleridge to Lord Halsbury LC in 1892, Coleridge reveals that from at least 1800 onwards all Lord Chancellors had consulted the Chiefs of the courts in which a vacancy had arisen about possible candidates and given them the opportunity to comment on the candidates before making an appointment to that vacancy. Coleridge is quick to assert that the Chiefs did not have a veto of any proposed appointment – 'not should they' – since the responsibility was the Lord Chancellor's. Coleridge notes that his advice was not always accepted by certain of the Halsbury's predecessors but it was always requested. However, Halsbury did not consider this universal practice for nigh on a century to be a convention which was binding on him and his practice was generally to inform the Chief after an appointment had been made.[27] Coleridge was clearly hurt at this departure from past practice and adds that it is part of a general trend to give more statutory power to the Lord Chancellor and less to the Lord Chief Justice, whose office may even be abolished.[28] An earlier letter from Coleridge to Halsbury in 1886 indicates that when the Chief knew of a vacancy he would mention candidates to the Lord Chancellor but the latter might not only ignore the suggestion but make the appointment without even telling the Chief what he had done. This he felt deprived him of the opportunity to remonstrate if the Lord Chancellor was planning to make an appointment

25 See A. Paterson, T. St J. N. Bates and M. R. Poustie, *The Legal System of Scotland*, Edinburgh: W Green, 4th edn., 1999, p. 226.

26 Elish Angiolini broke the mould in numerous ways. The first female Lord Advocate, she was also the first non-barrister Lord Advocate and so successful was she that when the Labour Government that had appointed her fell, the incoming Nationalist government asked her to stay on.

27 Halsbury was possibly influenced by the fact that Coleridge was from the Liberal Party and Halsbury was not.

28 This is an ironic comment in the light of the current position of the Lord Chief Justice as head of the judiciary.

which was manifestly suspect. In 1890 Coleridge writes again on behalf of himself and a judicial colleague to press the merits of a barrister for a particular vacancy in his Division, this time with success.

With the return of Liberal Lord Chancellors at the start of the twentieth century so the practice of consultation with the senior judges about suitable candidates for vacancies in their Divisions once again became more commonplace, and under Jowitt LC in the first Labour government after the Second World War not only were there no 'reward' or 'experience' appointments to politically active lawyers, but a formal consultation system was established involving all the Heads of Division (MR, V-C Chancery Division and President Family Division) depending on which Court the vacancy arose.[29] Lord Hailsham LC (the son) described the practice of senior judicial appointments in England and Wales during the 1980s as 'a delicate mechanism, composed in part of the judiciary themselves, the Lord Chancellor, and the Prime Minister (who must never act out of political considerations), with the officials of the Lord Chancellor's office acting as the secretariat and liaison between the working parts'.[30] In fact, when a senior appointment was being considered Hailsham would convene a meeting with the Heads of Division and discuss the candidates. It is clear that if his candidate was rejected by the Heads then he would not push the candidate further.[31] Confirmation for this comes from the Justice Report[32] on judicial appointment which had had the benefit of extensive discussions with the then Lord Chancellor's Permanent Secretary. The Report indicates that the system for appointment to the High Court in the late 1980s gave special weight to the four Heads of Division. 'If any of these persons opposed a senior appointment, it was most unlikely to go through',[33] later describing the four senior judges as having a 'virtual power of veto' on such appointments.[34] Ten years later little had changed. The research of Gee *et al*[35] revealed that in the 1990s the Lord Chancellors of that era had monthly meetings with the Heads of Division at which only rarely would Lord Chancellors depart from a collective judicial view, if there was one – which there usually was. As one former official observed – most appointments reflected 'the dominant school of thought among the senior judges'. Similarly, by that stage when Lord of Appeal appointments were mooted to the House of Lords all of the Law Lords would be consulted about the leading candidates at a joint meeting with the Lord Chancellor. Very, very rarely was the collective view of the Law Lords overridden by the Lord Chancellor.

29 See Heuston, *Lives of the Lord Chancellors* 1940–1970, p. 119

30 See Lord Hailsham, *A Sparrow's Flight: The Memoirs of Lord Hailsham of St Marylebone*, London: Collins, 1990, p. 424.

31 Ibid., pp. 426–427.

32 The Justice Committee Report on *The Judiciary in England and Wales* 1992.

33 Ibid., p. 7.

34 Ibid., p. 12.

35 G. Gee *et al, The Politics of Judicial Independence in the UK's Changing Constitution*, Cambridge: Cambridge University Press, 2015, p. 161.

In short, it would be fair to say that in England and Wales in the decade prior to the introduction of the Judicial Appointments Commission in 2005 the senior judiciary had acquired a decisive role in appointments to the senior judiciary, even though the legal responsibility for these appointments remained with ministers and the executive. Moreover the sophistication of the appointment machinery introduced by Derek Oulton and other Permanent Secretaries in the twentieth century was such that the input of the Heads of Division extended not only to current appointments but to succession planning for future appointments.

At first blush it would seem that the same could not be said of Scotland. Thus it is clear from Gordon Stott's diary as Lord Advocate in the 1960s that the senior judiciary had no significant power over his nominations to the High Court or the House of Lords. Lord Stott and the Lord President (the chief judge) did not get on and although the Lord President when intimating a vacancy in the High Court to the Lord Advocate might suggest a candidate, the Lord Advocate did not have to accept that suggestion. Equally, it is clear that Lord Stott felt no compunction in appointing a candidate to the High Court (including himself)[36] without any consultation with the Lord President or the Secretary of State. Later Lord Advocates were probably more circumspect in their handling of the Lord President, and in terms of the Scotland Act 1998[37] appointments to the Court of Session must be the subject of consultation with the Lord President and appointments to the office of Lord President or the Lord Justice-Clerk require to be consulted on with both the Lord President and the Lord Justice-Clerk unless the office is vacant.[38] Indeed by the new millennium the practice had also grown up that the Dean of the Faculty of Advocates (the Head of the Scots Bar) would also be consulted about possible candidates for appointments to the Outer House of the Court of Session (High Court), the top two judicial posts in Scotland as well as to Scottish Lords of Appeal vacancies in the House of Lords. Generally speaking the Lord Presidents are thought to have confined themselves to observations when something significantly negative is thought to arise in relation to one or more of the candidates – rather than providing a general assessment of the strengths and weaknesses of all the candidates. As a result the Lord President's observations were probably not as influential as those of the Lord Chief Justice were in England and Wales. However, successive Lord Presidents found other ways of circumventing the preferences of the Lord Advocate or the First Minster. If a High Court judge retired it was the Lord President who decided whether he/she needed to be replaced. If the Lord President didn't want a nomination from a particular Lord Advocate he didn't need to declare a vacancy. Again, under the traditional reading

36 In his autobiography he records (probably tongue in cheek) 'I appointed myself and a jolly good appointment I turned out to be!'. See G. Stott, *Lord Advocate's Diary 1961–1966*, Aberdeen: Aberdeen University Press, 1991.

37 s. 95.

38 This seems to imply that an outgoing very senior judge must be consulted about his or her replacement. This enhances the power of the senior judges but such a practice has now been rejected in England and Wales and is not thought to be an acceptable practice in modern human resources terms.

of the 1825 Court of Session Act promotion from the High Court to the 'Court of Appeal'[39] in Scotland was done by seniority – from their original appointment date to the High Court. Lord Clyde in his dealings with Gordon Stott (as Lord Advocate) implied that he didn't necessarily accept this reading of the 1825 Act and the 1988 Act left the position unclear. In 1990s Lord Hope changed the rule on seniority so that Lord President (with the help of the second senior judge – the Lord Justice Clerk) could chose who to promote from Outer House to the Inner House.[40] Although portrayed as a sensible way of ensuring that there was an appropriate mix of specialisms on the Inner House, it clearly represented a substantial enhancement of the power of the leaders of the judiciary to make senior judicial appointments and to succession plan, not least because there was and is no statutory requirement to make such promotions on merit or with an eye to equal opportunities. When exercised the power had a tendency to embitter those who were very publicly 'passed over' in a small community, whilst leaving the successful appointee with the potential taint of cronyism. Perhaps for these reasons the power has been used pretty sparingly by some Lord Presidents and not at all by others, although one was thought to exercise the power with a degree of ruthlessness.

The advent of the judicial appointment commissions

The forces that led to the introduction of the Judicial Appointments Board in Scotland in 2002 and the Judicial Appointment Commissions in England and Wales and Northern Ireland in 2005 have been described at length in other publications[41] however, the election of Blair's New Labour Government in 1997 brought with it a real impetus to discussions around the replacement of much of the executive's role in judicial appointment – especially at levels below the High Court – by an independent judicial appointments commission. Such commissions had been introduced by the UK in a range of Commonwealth countries – leading to voices suggesting that similar commissions might be introduced in the UK. The discussions focused on the perceived flaws with the millennial system of judicial appointment. The critics of the status quo identified:

a A lack of transparency and formality in the process – at the senior level there were no applications forms, no job descriptions, no selection criteria and no interviews. The 'tap on the shoulder' was usually the first the candidate knew that he was in the frame. In practice, who was in the frame was partly the

39 Otherwise known as the Inner House of the Court of Session.

40 Law Reform (Miscellaneous Provisions) (Scotland) Act 1990 (c. 40, SIF 36:1), s. 35 (2), 'where a vacancy arises in a Division of the Inner House the Lord President and the Lord Justice Clerk, with the consent of the Secretary of State and after such consultation with judges as appears to them to be appropriate in the particular circumstances, shall appoint a Lord Ordinary to fill that vacancy'.

41 See e.g. K. Malleson and P. H. Russell (eds), *Appointing Judges in an Age of Judicial Power*, Toronto: University of Toronto Press, 2006.

result of the extensive system of 'secret soundings' of senior and mid-level judges about potential candidates;

b The prevailing system therefore contained no demonstrable commitment to 'equal opportunities' merit based appointments – quite the reverse. The work of the Commission for Judicial Appointments revealed that the old-boys network of 'secret soundings', and the 'blackballing' that accompanied it, were occasionally a vehicle for misogyny or even something closely akin to racism;[42]

c Others pointed to the breadth of ministerial discretion set out in the relevant legislation and unaware of the decisive role played in practice by senior judiciary called for a dramatic reduction in ministerial involvement based on the doctrine of the separation of powers and the risk of political appointments (even although all three forms of such appointments had been a thing of the past for twenty years);

d A rather different group of critics (academics) who were aware of the senior judiciary's power in relation to senior appointments considered that it was too great since it had a tendency to lead to judicial self-replication or white male cloning. This in turn lead to the final criticism;

e The appointment system, particularly at the most senior level, was marked by a widescale lack of diversity.

Where one stood on these arguments strongly influenced whether you favoured the introduction of judicial appointments commissions in the UK, whether they should be appointing commissions (i.e. replacing ministerial appointment) or only recommending commissions (i.e. leaving the final choice with the executive from the recommendations of the commissions) and what the composition and membership of such commission should be.

When the Government's initial enthusiasm for a JAC in England and Wales seemed to falter the coalition Lib/Lab government in Scotland took up the baton. With the active encouragement of the then Lord Advocate (Andrew Hardie), the Justice Minister (Jim Wallace) and the relevant civil servant (David Stewart) a consultation paper was produced proposing the introduction of a Judicial Appointments Board for Scotland (JABS). Interestingly, all four judicial bodies which responded to the consultation paper, including the senior judiciary, favoured this development presumably seeing it as a way to drastically reduce the power of the executive in the shape of the Lord Advocate whilst at the same time hopefully boosting their own influence, since they would have had little doubt that, as in the Commonwealth the judicial members would dominate the decision-making of the commission.[43] Jim Wallace had proposed that JABS be a recommending commission with a lay chair and a 50:50 split of ten members – five lay, three judicial and two lawyers, but the senior judiciary would have been hopeful that from the consultation process they would get more judges on the Board. To

42 Commission for Judicial Appointments *Annual Reports* 2001–2004.

43 For a similar view voiced by a former Permanent Secretary to the Lord Chancellor's Department see T. Legg, 'Judges for the New Century', *Public Law*, 2001, p. 62.

Jim Wallace's great credit he held firm and JABS opened its doors with the 50:50 composition contained in the consultation paper.

Equally challenging for the senior judiciary were some of the initial decisions of JABS. Early on it was suggested that JABS should, 'of course', continue to take secret soundings from the senior judges and the head of the Bar, and that the judicial and legal members of JABS should share their personal knowledge of the candidates with the lay members. Acceptance of these suggestions would have considerably enhanced the power of the senior judiciary (in all three of Lukes' dimensions – being both conduct shaping and context shaping) over senior judicial appointments, and thus enhanced the potential for cloning and judicial self-replication. The suggestions were gently rebuffed by the majority of JABS but the rejections caused resentment in certain quarters which led to a push back from some in the judicial and legal establishment in the years that followed. However, there was a potential weakness in JABS which was clear to all from the outset. JABS was not a statutory Board. The Government was as good as its word and accepted every recommendation of JABS bar one[44] in the first six years (during which JABS appointed over a third of the whole Scots Judiciary). Yet the success of JABS in the coalition Government's eyes was to work against it, because the coalition did not feel the need to make legislative time to make JABS statutory until it was too late. By the time that this was considered there was a new Government and the senior judiciary took the opportunity of the change of justice minister and a new civil service team to engage in a fresh dialogue with the Government. The Lord President selected four High Court judges to negotiate confidentially[45] with the civil servants over the package of reforms including (1) the judiciary taking charge of the running of the courts and their staff, (2) complaints and discipline for judges and (3) JABS and its operation. While the senior judges appeared to get almost all they asked for in respect of (1) and (2), it was JABS that proved the stumbling block. Try as they might they were unable to persuade the Government to alter the composition of JABS to include more judicial members and thus give the judiciary a greater say in its decision-making. However, they extracted a 'quid pro quo' instead. They persuaded the Government to give the legal and the judicial members of JABS a veto on who might be considered sufficiently legally qualified to be considered for judicial appointment. The key provision is s. 13 of the Judiciary and Courts (Scotland) Act 2008, which reads:

> *s. 13. Assessment of legal knowledge, skills and competence*
>
> Only the judicial and legal members of the Board may take part in any assessment by the Board of an individual's –
>
> (a) knowledge of the law, or
>
> (b) skills and competence in the interpretation and application of the law.

44 Even that one was merely held up whilst a policy determination was made by JABS.

45 Unlike the English Concordat negotiations – the existence of the Scottish negotiations was not widely known.

In one sense this was simply the enactment of an understanding on which JABS had worked for its first six years, namely that if all the legal and judicial members considered that a candidate was unappointable due to a lack of sufficient legal knowledge and skill, then they would not be appointed. In practice this power was almost never invoked but it was there as protection in case the lay members were won over by a slick competency based application and interview. However, once the provision was enshrined in the legislation making JABS a statutory Board, one of the four judge negotiating team was appointed to JABS by the Lord President[46] and it was indicated to the Board that the meaning to be given to s. 13 was that in future there would effectively be a two-tier Board with the legal and judicial members meeting to sift all the applicants in a competition as to their legal knowledge, skills and potential (thus increasing the risk of cloning and judicial self-replication). Only once this sift had been completed would the lay members be permitted to comment on the candidates who had survived the legal/judicial veto. This suggestion had the potential to destabilize the operation of the Board by splitting it along tribal lines.[47] It also would potentially give the senior judiciary a level of control over judicial appointments in Scotland that they had not had before JABS and which they had not been able to obtain from the coalition Government or through the private negotiations with the next Government. There was a further advantage for those who had pushed for s. 13 – JABS would look evenly balanced in its membership and committed to equal opportunities merit selection whilst in its necessarily hidden decision-making involving sifts, legal/judicial vetoes would be in operation. Fortunately for the harmonious operation of the Board, the creation of a de facto two-tier Board was defeated through the lay members insisting on transparency and making it clear that there would be no private meetings of the legal/judicial members in their absence and that they would sit in on any such meeting to check that any vetoes were based on merit justifiable grounds.

England and Wales were slower off the mark to consult about a judicial appointments commission and it was only startled into action by Tony Blair's shock announcement in June 2003 that the second stage of constitutional reform was at hand, and that in the name of a more rigorous separation of powers the Lord Chancellor would be abolished, a Judicial Appointments Commission (JAC) established and a new Supreme Court introduced. This took the world – including

46 This is another area for the exercise of power by the senior judiciary – the two most senior judicial members of JABS were (and still are) nominated to sit on JABS by the Lord President and by the other Sheriffs Principal respectively, not by the normal public appointments procedure used for all other members of JABS, including the Chair. This left open the question as to whom these judicial members owed their allegiance whilst on JABS. Was it to the Board and its members or to the person(s) who had appointed them?

47 It is to the credit of the legal and judicial members of the JACs in Northern Ireland, and England and Wales that they were considerably taken aback at this interpretation of s. 13 when it was presented to them, seeing very clearly its potential to undermine the effective working of a judicial appointments commission.

the senior judiciary and the Lord Chief Justice aback since they had had no inkling that such far-reaching proposals were in the offing. The senior judges' initial reaction was concern. The loss of their representative in the Cabinet, putting the judicial viewpoint and protecting the judges from unfair political attacks was a major blow. Indeed, immediately after the Blair announcement there was a concern that the new announcement would mask an attempt by the executive to seize greater control of judicial appointment.[48] The consultation paper in July 2003 very quickly dispelled such notions – ministerial input to judicial appointments was to be drastically scaled back. The Government favoured a recommending commission rather than an appointing one, but the discretion of the Secretary of State/Lord Chancellor would be confined to accepting or rejecting the single name put forward by the JAC. However, the paper suggested that for Court of Appeal or Heads of Division appointments the Secretary of State might wish to have a 'more direct input' (unspecified in the paper) whilst still consulting the senior judiciary. As Malleson notes the lack of guidelines as to when a minister would be justified in rejecting a commission nomination was symptomatic of the executive's lack of clear thinking in relation to the retention of ministerial appointment.[49] As for membership the Government favoured 15 commissioners (five lay, five judges and five lawyers) appointed in the main by a public appointments procedure applying Nolan principles. To maintain a balance between the executive and the senior judiciary the paper suggested that a senior judge should serve on the three-person appointing panel along with the Permanent Secretary of the Department of Constitutional Affairs and an independent assessor. However, the paper also suggested that the judicial members of the commission should be appointed by the Judges' Council rather than an independent public appointments procedure, making it unclear to whom these members would owe their allegiance in the event of a disagreement arising between the JAC and the senior judiciary.[50]

Although the senior judiciary lamented the loss of their champion in the Cabinet – a loss still felt by many[51] – they quickly saw the threats and opportunities that the consultation paper offered. If the executive was going to step back from

48 K. Malleson, 'Creating a Judicial Appointments Commission: Which Model Works Best?', *Public Law*, 2004, p. 102.

49 Ibid., pp. 112–113.

50 It is understood that the Judges' Council, a large and unwieldy body, invites applications from interested judges to be considered for appointment to the JAC. It seems likely that the Lord Chief Justice effectively makes the decision as to who he favours and gets that name through the Council. In practice it appears to come down to the respective personalities of the Lord Chief Justice and the successful candidate the extent to which latter confides in the former and if tensions arise between the JAC and the senior judiciary, where the judicial appointees consider their loyalties to lie.

51 See Gee *et al*, *The Politics of Judicial Independence*, p. 35, and the comments of Lord Judge when the *Daily Mail* attacked the Divisional Court judges as 'Enemies of the people' when deciding the Brexit case and the Lord Chancellor failed to defend the judges for 48 hours (See, H. Agerholm, 'Liz Truss may have broken law in failing to defend Brexit judges, warns former Lord Chief Justice', *The Independent*, 19 November 2016).

active involvement with the judicial appointment process and possibly also the appointment of senior judges then the senior judiciary were going to fill that power vacuum – rather than any of the other stakeholders. This was and remains very understandable. The senior judiciary has an unshakeable belief that since they know better than anyone what the job entails (which they undoubtedly do), they are necessarily the group best placed to choose who should be appointed to these posts, and that it is in the public interest that they should play the major part in that process. Who better to appoint a brain surgeon than experienced brain surgeons? If we do not object to any cloning effect for brain surgeons, why should we do so for senior judges? This opt-repeated argument overlooks a key distinction. Brain surgeons do not wield state power – senior judges do. If a commentator was to assert that MPs know best what is required of an MP and what are the most desirable qualities in an MP there would not be many supporters for the corollary that therefore MPs are the best people to appoint their successors. One sign that the senior judiciary understand Lukes' third dimension of power (context shaping) is that they have succeeded in portraying themselves as nearer to brain surgeons than MPs in the eyes of the commentariat.[52] Yet this is surely fallacious – in today's constitutional democracy, the senior judiciary are an arm of government and as Lord Sumption has argued[53] they have been given unprecedented powers to challenge the executive and Parliament.[54] This inevitably creates an accountability problem and the only place where this can be made to bite is at the appointment of senior judges.

The response of the senior judiciary to the consultation paper came in two forms. First, from the Judges' Council. Like the judicial bodies in Scotland, they welcomed the establishment of a judicial appointments commission but could not see the point of having so many lay members. They favoured a JAC composition of five judges, two lay magistrates, two lawyers and two lay members, although the chair would be a lay person.[55] This they claimed would allow the judges to be outvoted by the others – ignoring the likelihood that lay magistrates were much more likely to see themselves as judges rather than lay persons. In relation to senior judicial appointments above High Court level they favoured a panel chaired by the lay Chair of the JAC, with the four Heads of Division and two lay members from the JAC (i.e. a clear judicial majority).

The second response came in the shape of the Concordat negotiations between the Lord Woolf LCJ and Lord Falconer LC which culminated with the publication of the Concordat agreement in January 2004, whose provisions were enacted

52 The re-emergence of the declaratory theory of lawmaking – that the judges only find rather than create the law – dovetails neatly with this portrayal – some critics would say that this too, is an exercise of Lukes' third dimension of power.

53 Lord Sumption, *Judicial and Political Decision-Making: The Uncertain Boundary*, F. A. Mann Lecture 2011.

54 This was amply demonstrated in the histrionic approach of some of the media to the Brexit case when it was before the Supreme Court towards the end of 2016.

55 *Constitutional Reform: A new way of appointing judges – Summary of responses to consultation*, DCA, CP (R) 10/03 January 2004, p. 51

in the Constitutional Reform Act 2005. It was meant to establish a partnership between the executive and senior judiciary on a number of fronts[56] but its effect was to put the senior judiciary firmly in charge of the judicial appointments process in England and Wales. The Lord Chief Justice became the head of the judiciary. Membership of the JAC was slightly altered. Now there were to be six lay members (including the Chair), five judicial members (the senior of whom would be the vice chair of the JAC), two lawyers, one lay justice and one tribunal member. Members of the senior judiciary have tended to claim that this makes the lay input the largest single bloc on the JAC. However, that assumes that the lay justice and the tribunal member will not see themselves as part of the judiciary. The real successes, however, were elsewhere. First, the selection panel for the JAC would not have a balance between the executive and the judiciary. Instead it would be chaired by the Commissioner for Public Appointments, there would be no civil servant or member of the government on it, the Lord Chief Justice would sit on it and a third independent member selected by the Commissioner. This panel would choose the lay Chair of the JAC (and all future lay chairs) who would then sit on the appointing panel. Second, the ad hoc panels to appoint to the Court of Appeal would consist of the Lord Chief Justice (in the chair and with a casting vote), another Head of Division or senior judge, the chair of the JAC and another lay member of the JAC. Similarly, appointments to the Heads of Division would have the President of the Supreme Court in the chair (with the casting vote), a Head of Division, the chair of the JAC and another lay member of the JAC. The third success was the retention of the elaborate system of statutory consultations, very largely with senior judges, whenever a senior judicial vacancy arose. Thus in the case of appointments to the new Supreme Court the panel, on paper, consisted of the President (in the chair), the Deputy President and a representative of each of the three judicial appointments commissions. Only one of these was required to be a lay member and in practice, for most contests there has been a judicial majority. However, the effect of the statutory consultations meant that the assessment of the merits of the candidates was done essentially by 20 senior judges (including all the existing Justices on the Court), one junior judge and two laypersons. The description of this as a 'self-perpetuating oligarchy' seems apt – the senior judiciary had left nothing to chance, power to appoint to the Supreme Court in all three of Lukes' dimensions had been ceded to them – but as Legg had predicted, democracy was the loser.[57] There was also a further loss – to diversity. All but one of these 20 senior judges was a white male – hardly the most promising mechanism for tackling the diversity deficit on the Supreme Court – and so it has proved. Thirteen years and more than ten straight contests have come and gone since Lady Hale was appointed and still no other candidate than a white male has made it onto the Court in that period, although strenuous efforts are now being made to rectify this.

56 Gee *et al*, *The Politics of Judicial Independence*, p. 38
57 See A. Paterson and C. Paterson, *Guarding the Guardians: Towards an Independent, Accountable and Diverse Senior Judiciary*, London: CentreForum, 2012, p. 29.

In theory a strong lay chair of the JAC might have wrested some 'context shaping' power back from the senior judiciary, but the odds were always stacked against them. To do so would have required a stable and well-grounded relationship with the executive. Ironically, the JAC's relationship with the executive quickly soured as the departmental civil servants gradually appreciated that Lord Woolf LCJ had outmanoeuvered Lord Falconer LC at every turn – leaving the executive with 'responsibility without influence'.[58] This was hardly the fault of the JAC, far less its chairs, but it was they who bore the brunt of the executive's backlash. In its first six years the JAC experienced seven reviews and although peace was finally established thereafter, the JAC's appetite to challenge the executive's perception of its role as recruitment agency to meet the workforce requirements assessed by the Ministry, the Courts Service and the senior judiciary had considerably waned.[59] The then chair Christopher Stephens had a measure of success in introducing a degree of procedural formality on the ad hoc panels for senior appointments but it was unpopular with some in the senior judiciary and only bought at a price. In any event in senior appointments, as we have seen, the statutory consultation process was key, reinforced by the lack of a judicial appraisal programme. The very limited discretion left to the Lord Chancellor to reject the recommendations of the JAC and the ad hoc panels, was narrowed still further by Lord Chancellors even after the Constitutional Reform Act 2005, giving the senior judges effectively the same power of veto on the appointment of candidates recommended to the Lord Chancellor as their predecessors had had before the Act.[60] By 2012 Kenneth Clarke LC had concluded that his power to reject recommendations from the JAC or the ad hoc panels for senior appointments was so constrained that he was never likely to use it and that he would be better off giving it up[61] in return for joining the membership of the ad hoc appointment panels. This attempt to take back a minor amount of power to the executive was not well received by the senior judiciary and when Chris Grayling, the first non-lawyer Lord Chancellor was appointed in 2012 the leaders of the judiciary (backed up by vigorous campaign in the Lords) swiftly persuaded him that this part of the Crime and Courts Bill should just be dropped.[62] The Bill, which came after a major review of judicial appointment and diversity by the Constitution Committee of the House of Lords and a parallel review of judicial appointment by the Ministry of Justice, could have been an opportunity for those favouring reform of the appointment process and greater diversity on the senior bench to challenge the judiciary's hegemonic

58 Gee *et al*, *The Politics of Judicial Independence*, p. 167.

59 Ibid., p. 169.

60 Ibid., p. 174.

61 Only one Lord Chancellor since 2005 (Jack Straw) actually rejected a nomination of a senior appointment and even he did not follow through with it. See J. Straw, *Judicial Appointments*, Hamlyn Lecture, 4 December 2012, reproduced in J. Straw, *Aspects of Law Reform: An Insider's Perspective*, Cambridge: Cambridge University Press, 2013.

62 It was replaced with a requirement for the panel to consult the Lord Chancellor about the leadership qualities which the Ministry is looking for in such appointments. See Gee *et al*, *The Politics of Judicial Independence*, p. 186.

control of the definition of 'merit' in judicial appointments. However, the leaders of the judiciary, once again, appeared to emerge as the winners. Henceforth all lower court appointments would be by the LCJ on the recommendation of the JAC and the senior appointments although still nominally by the Lord Chancellor would come from the JAC or ad hoc panels both of which were significantly open to the influence of the senior judiciary either now or in the future. True, the Act when passed did contain two potentially unsettling areas: first, it established that the Equality Act provisions about a 'tipping point' did apply to judicial appointments[63] and secondly that the size of the ad hoc panels for appointing senior judicial posts was expanded to five with the potential for a lay majority[64] and the Deputy President was removed from the panel to appoint Supreme Court Justices, however these developments might be managed by the judiciary as the ones before had been. Here the critics and the senior judiciary were as one. The latter might hope (with the justification of past history) to find ways to make the reforms work in line with their perception of the public interest, the former equally were in little doubt that (as some commentators had presaged) the senior judiciary would succeed in co-opting the appointment commissions and the ad hoc senior appointment panels in particular. For those seeking a more constitutionally balanced appointment system for senior judges the Act was an opportunity wasted.

Summary and analysis

In this chapter it has been argued that the last 150 years of senior judicial appointments in England and Wales has witnessed an ever greater transfer of power over the process (de jure and de facto) from the executive to the senior judiciary, with a few minor hiccups on the way. This transfer has related to all of Lukes' dimensions of power (and both conduct and context shaping in Gee's language). In terms of conduct shaping the senior judiciary now appoint all English judges below the High Court (albeit on the recommendation of the JAC – which the senior judiciary significantly influences), and have an effective veto of all senior judicial appointments and a major influence on them which increases the higher up the hierarchy the appointment. As for context shaping we have seen that the leaders of the judiciary in the twentieth century changed the way senior judges were appointed first by helping to take reward appointments off the agenda (except for law officers), then political experience appointments off the agenda and finally law officer appointments off the agenda. Faced with the threat to their influence on senior appointments in 2003 the English judicial leaders responded vigorously to fill the vacuum created by the executive as they stepped back from their pre-eminent (de jure) role in the appointment of senior judges. In contrast, in Scotland the transfer of power by the executive took longer and

63 Schedule 13 para 10 (aka s. 63(4) CRA 2005); see Gee *et al*, *The Politics of Judicial Independence*, p. 176.

64 Gee *et al*, *The Politics of Judicial Independence*, p. 183 record that the JAC saw the loss of the Lord Chief Justice's casting vote as an 'important dilution of judicial control'.

judicial leaders of Scotland have had more of a struggle to achieve a major or controlling influence over senior judicial appointments.

How have the leaders of the judiciary been so successful in garnering power (in all senses) over senior judicial appointments and what accounts for some of the more recent differences between Scotland, and England and Wales? The first point to make is that since the new millennium judicial leaders have had a major advantage over other stakeholders – continuity. The judiciary as an arm of government has been strengthened immeasurably by the move to a more defined form of separation of powers. Further, despite the handicap of the mandatory retirement age of 70, the senior judiciary have greater continuity and more of an institutional memory and a greater ability to play for the long game than either the executive or the legislature. Before the millennium this could be counterbalanced by the esprit de corps of the civil servants of the Lord Chancellor's Department which was a small, self-contained department with little turnover of the staff and a strong institutional memory. The creation of the Ministry of Justice has changed all that – now a huge ministry with a much greater remit, the turnover of civil servants has increased dramatically and with the transfer of the bulk of the original staff to the Judicial Office in 2011[65] much of ministry's ability to monitor and challenge the growing hegemony of the senior judiciary has been lost.

Playing for the long game – gaining and keeping the major influence over senior judicial appointments – dovetails neatly with the senior judiciary's second advantage. They know what they are trying to achieve in this area. Interestingly, it is not necessarily to gain more and more control over senior judicial appointments, although that may be a by-product of their actions. Often the leaders of the judiciary seem to have engaged in pre-emptive strikes to prevent other, less palatable forms of stakeholder influence gaining or retaining traction in this area. This they genuinely believe to be in the public interest since they know best what the role of the senior judge entails and their vigilance safeguards the independence of these appointments from what they consider to be inappropriate external influence. Such clarity of vision has made it easier for the leaders of the judiciary to employ their skills of persuasion to achieve their goal. This soft power of the senior judiciary should not be underestimated. History suggests that lay members of judicial appointment boards or parliamentarians on the justice or constitution committees can be susceptible to the charm or advocacy of high status judicial leaders.[66] It is also easier to win round other stakeholders to your line of thinking if time and patience are on your side. It can plausibly be argued that during the nineteenth and twentieth centuries the senior judiciary gradually co-opted the post of Lord Chancellor from being a political adviser to the executive who dabbled in judicial work into a bridge between the executive and the judiciary, whose primary role

65 Gee *et al*, *The Politics of Judicial Independence*, p. 169.

66 Lacking the hard power to resist Lord Halsbury LC, Lord Coleridge LCJ resorted to flattery to try to win him round on the matter of judicial appointments (see Heuston, *Lives of the Lord Chancellors 1885–1940*, Lord Halsbury ch. V). Leaders of the judiciary wield their soft power on a very regular basis today.

was to appoint judges[67] and to protect the independence of the judiciary in the cabinet.[68] By the 1960s Lord Hailsham had ceded the virtual veto on senior judicial appointments to the other judicial leaders and established formal consultations with them. This too looks like co-option. As for judicial appointments commissions, early critics asserted that it would be inevitable that the judiciary would be tempted to co-opt these and so it has proved. We have seen the efforts made by the judicial leaders during the Concordat negotiations in England and Scotland to influence the composition and operation of the appointment commissions. The efforts to influence the commissions did not stop there. The ambiguity as to whether the judicial members of these commissions (nominated in effect by head of the judiciary) are perceived as owing their allegiance to the commission or to the senior judiciary, remains a weakness in the commissions which could be exploited by future judicial leaders should a tension between the JAC and the judicial leaders arise as it might on a range of issues, for example job descriptions, the content of the assessment tests, the use of personal knowledge, or the use of the tipping point test. Moreover, should the chair of the JAC be vacant for any reason, as it was in 2016 for several months, the vice chair, a senior judge nominated effectively by the head of the judiciary, takes over.[69] Here again any ambiguities in the role of the judicial members of the JAC are not helpful for the perceived independence of the JAC. Finally, the head of the judiciary plays a key role in the selection of the JAC's lay chair[70] and given that the latter chairs the selection panel for the appointment of the Lord Chief Justice and the President of the Supreme Court and is a member of the selection panels for the other senior judicial posts it would be strange if the judicial leaders did not seek to appoint candidates who they hoped would be amenable to their line of thinking on key issues to do with judicial appointment or seek to win any appointee round to their way of thinking. Given also that the chair's job description requires him or her to make strong and constructive working relationships with the judiciary it is entirely predictable that the two should converse very regularly with and without the support of civil servants. Perhaps for these reasons Gee *et al* refer to the 'high level of judicial influence on the JAC'.[71]

67 Certainly Lord Gardiner in 1968 considered this to be his most important role as Lord Chancellor. See Heuston, *Lives of the Lord Chancellors 1940–1970*, p. 222.

68 Lord Hailsham (the son) attests to the significance of this aspect of the Lord Chancellor's role in his two autobiographies See Lord Hailsham, *The Door Wherein I Went*, London: Collins, 1975, chs 36–37 and Lord Hailsham, *A Sparrow's Flight*.

69 The appointment of a new chair has not entirely resolved this issue since he has indicated that he can only devote two thirds of the time to the post that his predecessor did. This may mean that work that in the past was done by the chair will now be done by his judicial deputy.

70 The head of the judiciary in Scotland has no such role.

71 Gee *et al*, *The Politics of Judicial Independence*, p. 180. The contrast between the JAC and the Irish Judicial Appointments Commission proposed in their JAC Bill 2017 could not be more striking. There the Commission will be chaired by a lay person selected by the Public Appointments Commission and have a majority of lay persons for every judicial appointment. The JAC will give the executive a choice of 3 names for each senior appointment.

It would be surprising if the senior judiciary's use of soft power were to stop there. Faced with the perceived threats from the CRA 2005 it is only to be expected that the leaders of the judiciary would seek to bring others to share their viewpoint. This might be through engagement with key voices in the media[72] or through the cultivation of sympathy or support from potential allies amongst the intelligentsia or parliamentarians. Thus in the responses of the senior judiciary to Government consultation papers or in appearances before parliamentary committees since 2003 the message has been clear and consistent: that they had lost (without being consulted) the voice of the staunch protector of judicial independence in the cabinet and accordingly that judicial independence was now more at threat from the executive. It followed, they said, that the input of politicians into the appointment process for senior judges should be reduced or eliminated. It may be that the genuine discomfort felt by the judicial leaders at the Lord Chancellor's departure as the head of the judiciary is a testament to the success of the judiciary's long-term project to shape the office of Lord Chancellor along lines they considered to be defensible in the public interest.[73] More importantly the stress on the perceived threat to the independence of judicial appointment commissions was a message repeated by many commentators. The message from the judiciary internationally in a series of declarations[74] has been subtly different. Appointment commissions must be independent *of the executive*, a message taken up by liberal commentators and academic respondents to the consultation papers or parliamentary reviews on judicial appointment in the last 15 years. The interesting aspect of this, at least in the UK, is that it is 30 years since the executive have tried to interfere with senior judicial appointment in a political way. This had no inhibiting effect on the judiciary's message. It was clearly an exercise of context shaping power or Lukes' second dimension of power – keeping issues off the agenda. By concentrating the focus of attention on the potential threat of the executive to the independence of the JAC and the ad hoc senior appointment panels the judiciary's leaders kept attention away from the elephant in the room, namely how independent the commissions and senior appointment panels should be from the senior judiciary itself. The Bingham Report which reviewed the use of appointment commissions throughout the Commonwealth asserts the importance of judicial appointments being made by a 'manifestly independent body',[75] an argument repeated in the Latimer House Guidelines and the Venice Commission, but all of their

72 Gordon Stott, when Lord Advocate, recommended his Solicitor General for appointment to the Scots High Court. The Lord President opposed the move, according to Stott, by briefing the national newspapers repeatedly against the appointment. See G. Stott, *Lord Advocate's Diary 1961–1966*, p. 172.

73 This did not include sitting or presiding any longer in the Appellate Committee of the House of Lords.

74 E.g. the Latimer House Guidelines for the Commonwealth (1998), the Venice Commission, *Judicial Appointments*, CDL-AD (2007)028 and the Dublin Declaration on *Standards for the Recruitment and Appointment of Members of the Judiciary*. It is probably not unfair to note that each of these bodies was composed mainly of judges and lawyers.

75 J. van Zyl Smit, *The Appointment, Tenure and Removal of Judges under Commonwealth Principles*, London: Bingham Centre for the Rule of Law, 2015, p. 31 (The Bingham Report).

texts concentrate overwhelmingly on the threat from the executive.[76] This is clearly context shaping behaviour on the part of the judiciary.

Why has Scotland been different? Historical differences are part of the explanation as we saw earlier. Curiously a more resolute executive also plays a part. This influenced the composition of JABS, the composition of the panels for the top two judicial posts in Scotland,[77] the provision that the First Minster is not required to accept the nomination provided by these panels,[78] and the provision that the Scottish Ministers can give guidance to JABS as to the procedures it should follow.[79] However, the Scots judiciary did less well in their Concordat negotiations than the English, at least as regards composition of the appointments board. Perhaps as a result, JABS under an exceptionally strong lay chair was able to protect the independence of the lay members from the personal knowledge of the legal and judicial members and to safeguard the independence of JABS from the influence of the senior judiciary by greatly constraining the operation of statutory consultations for senior Scottish posts below the UK Supreme Court. There was a pushback from some of the senior judiciary in the subsequent years through the threat of a two-tier Board by the operation of s. 13 of the Judiciary and Courts (Scotland) Act 2008, but that too has been contained. However, there have been occasions when one or two senior judges in Scotland have sought to use both soft and not so soft power in relation to senior appointments.[80] While no Lord President has exercised his power to issue guidance to JABS as to the procedures it should follow, they have retained effectively the power to promote judges to the Scottish 'Court of Appeal' with no requirement to use a transparent, competency based, equal opportunities procedure. Further, Lord Presidents retain the power to appoint temporary high court judges also without a merit-based contest.

However, these differences should not be exaggerated. The leaders of both the Scots and English judiciaries necessarily have a pretty significant influence over senior judicial appointments. In England and Wales statutory consultation for senior appointments plays a major role particularly in relation to appointments to the UK Supreme Court, as we have seen. So too does the setting of the job

76 The UN Special Reporter Annual Report 2009 para 28 similarly concentrates on the threat from the politicians. (The Bingham Report, p. 34). That said, the Venice Commission, judicial appointments, cdl-ad(2007)028 paras 27–30 and the Dublin Declaration on Standards for the Recruitment and Appointment of members of the judiciary para 11.2 point to the dangers of judicial corporatism or the judicial members of commissions furthering the interests of the judiciary, including the adoption of narrow and traditional definitions of 'merit'.

77 s.19(2) and Schedule 2 of the *Judiciary and Courts (Scotland) Act 2008* provides for ad hoc panels of four – the lay chair of JABS and another lay commissioner together with two senior judges selected by the First Minister. Nothing is said about the chairing of the panel or a casting vote. The criteria for selecting the judicial members are opaque, leaving scope for the exercise of soft judicial power.

78 s.19(5).

79 s.16.

80 E.g. there have been occasional communications from senior judges to the lay chair about appointment rounds and the failure of certain candidates.

description by the judicial leaders which can predispose towards one candidate or another. Lord Dyson MR on his retirement publicly indicated that he had applied for the job because the Lord Chief Justice of the time (who chaired the appointment panel) had suggested that he applied. Again when Jonathan Sumption was first offered a position on the Supreme Court it was on the basis that the Master of the Rolls post was about to become vacant and that Lord Neuberger would get it. Given that the vacancy had not yet been declared and the contest for it had yet to take place, this left little doubt that the judiciary's leaders were very confident of persuading not only the candidate to apply but that they could persuade the lay commissioners that 'their' candidate would get the post. Since then there have been other instances where the lay members of senior appointment panels have been left in little doubt as to who the senior judiciary expected should get the job.[81]

Conclusions

It is important to stress that it is not being argued that significant judicial involvement in senior judicial appointments should not exist. Quite the reverse, it is both inevitable and highly desirable – they really do know better than anyone what the job entails and who might be some of the best candidates. Further, they also genuinely believe that this is in the best interest of the country. This is a powerful combination. Yet allowing the leaders of the judiciary the lion's share of the power over senior judicial appointments is a real matter for concern for democracy for several reasons. The first is that their hegemony has a cloning effect on appointments. As Tom Legg observed in 2001 when predicting that the judiciary would come to dominate the appointment commissions, 'It is no reflection on our judges to say that this would be undesirable. No branch of government should be effectively self-perpetuating'.[82] Michael Kirby of the Australian High Court was equally hostile to appointment commissions, asserting that they would reinforce the senior judiciary's preference for traditionalist appointments and inhibit the cause of diversity including the appointment of gay judges. It is hard not to conclude that the appointment of thirteen white male Justices since Baroness Hale's appointment in 2004 reflects the continuing power of traditionalist thinking amongst senior judges. A tendency to clone is not confined to the UK's judiciary – in civilian countries as disparate as the Netherlands, Germany[83] and China whilst the majority of lower court judges are female, when it gets to the higher courts the routes to advancement are controlled by male judges and partly as a result, at the level of the higher courts, males continue

81 See Gee *et al*, *The Politics of Judicial Independence*, pp. 182–5.

82 T. Legg, 'Judges for the New Century', p. 62.

83 See e.g. U. Schultz, '"I was noticed and I was asked …" Women's Careers in the Judiciary: Results of an Empirical Study for the Ministry of Justice in Northrhine-Westfalia, Germany', in U. Schultz and G. Shaw (eds), *Gender and Judging*, Oxford: Hart Publishing, 2013, ch. 2.2.

to predominate. The cloning tendency is another reason why the use of soft power by England's judicial leaders (who are overwhelmingly male) to engage in succession planning through the wording of job descriptions or through appointments to the office of Senior Presiding Judge (now a known stepping stone to the post of Lord Chief Justice) is suspect. It either runs the risk of appearing to open the door to cronyism (as with the appointment of Scots judges to the Inner House of the Court of Session) or of seeming to work against the advancement of diverse judges through subconscious bias.[84]

Secondly, the principal rationale of affording the senior judiciary such a dominant influence in the appointment of the senior judiciary appears to be an extension of the attempt to protect judicial independence in the context of the new separation of powers enshrined in the CRA 2005. However, this is a fundamental misconception:

> Of course the separation of powers is an important underlying factor in the appointment and operation of the judges, but that principle cannot be an absolute one in relation to the appointment of judges because the judges cannot be purely a self-appointing body.[85]

It is in no way disrespectful to the judges themselves to recognize that it is deeply problematic in a democracy for one branch of state to have anything like a decisive voice in choosing their own colleagues and successors. This begins to look like oligarchy not democracy. Lord Justice Etherton described the current situation as 'quite unacceptable ... for constitutional legitimacy'.[86] To quote from *Guarding the Guardians:*

> [T]he legitimate exercise of power in the political sphere in a democratic society requires some degree of connection between the office holder in question and the public from whom that power is derived. As Lady Hale notes, the process of Supreme Court appointments 'currently lacks any democratic accountability'[87] – it involves no input whatsoever from the legislature, minimal input from the executive and actually requires no participant with a substantive role to be an elected office-holder. While undoubtedly crucial, judicial independence cannot be an absolute ... Particularly in light of the new constitutional settlement, it is important to recognise that the appointment of senior judges is, in the broad sense, a political act. As such, it is 'for the long-term health, quality and therefore standing and independence of the senior judiciary [that] there should also

84 See Gee *et al*, *The Politics of Judicial Independence*, ch. 7.

85 Lord Justice Etherton, Oral Evidence to the House of Lords Select Committee on the Constitution Inquiry into the Judicial Appointments Process, 13 July 2011, Q.41.

86 Ibid., Q.48.

87 Baroness Hale, Written Evidence to the House of Lords Select Committee on the Constitution Inquiry into the Judicial Appointments Process, para 7.

> be an equal involvement of [the] other branches of government'.[88] In the context of the expanded role and political significance of the judiciary, it is more important than ever to protect the legitimacy of this branch of government by ensuring that it is buttressed by a constitutionally appropriate appointments process. The current method of appointing our senior judiciary – and our Supreme Court Justices in particular – is, in short, not fit for purpose.[89]

The response of many of the senior judiciary to such arguments is that there is no accountability or democratic deficit in their exercise of judicial power at the higher appellate levels. To those schooled in the seminal lecture by Lord Reid of Drem where he dismissed mechanical jurisprudence with a robust 'we don't believe in fairy tales anymore'[90] the reappearance of the declaratory theory in recent pronouncements of the senior judiciary has been striking:

> the introduction of the European dimension to our law and the increasing use of judicial review of government action in particular has not altered the basic principle, which is that we try to discover the law, and … having discovered it, we say what it is.[91]

This denial of the increased power of the senior judiciary in the last 20 years may be seen as an exercise in context shaping or Lukes' third dimension of power to downplay the accountability problems that greater recognition of this increased power would create. In contrast, Lord Sumption's open recognition that in relation to the Human Rights Act and the expansion of Judicial Review the judiciary are engaged in the 'resolution of inherently political issues'[92] has resonances of Lord Robson's dictum quoted earlier. Whilst few of Lord Sumption's colleagues on the Supreme Court have overtly agreed with him, several are troubled by a perception that the HRA has put them in the world of politics with a small 'p' or required them to make decisions with political ramifications.[93] For them, and others, this has created an accountability problem.[94] Given that sacrificial accountability for judges is incompatible with judicial independence,[95] and

88 T. Legg, Written Evidence to the House of Lords Select Committee on the Constitution Inquiry into the Judicial Appointments Process.
89 Paterson and Paterson, *Guarding the Guardians*, p. 32.
90 Lord Reid, 'The Judge as Law Maker', *Journal of the Society of Public Teachers of Law* 12, 1972, p. 22.
91 Lord Judge LCJ, Oral Evidence to the House of Lords Select Committee on the Constitution Inquiry into the Judicial Appointments Process, 19 October 2011, Q.162. See also A. Paterson, *Final Judgment*, Oxford, Hart Publishing, 2013, pp. 267–268, 273 fn. 85.
92 Lord Sumption, *Judicial and Political Decision-Making*.
93 Paterson, *Final Judgment*, p. 307 fn. 255.
94 Ibid., p. 308.
95 See V. Bogdanor, *The New British Constitution*, Oxford: Hart Publishing, 2009, p. 85 and A. Le Sueur, 'Developing Mechanisms for Judicial Accountability in the UK', *Legal Studies*, 2004, p. 73.

occasional appearances before the parliamentary committees do not cut the mustard, the focus of attention has to be on the appointment of the senior judiciary. Here we have seen the bulk of the power move from the executive to the senior judiciary which for the reasons already outlined is incompatible with constitutional democracy.

Two correctives are needed. First, to reject the cloning tendency by expressly accepting, as Lord Bingham did,[96] that 'merit' in senior judicial appointments includes the institutional requirements of the Court into which the appointment is being made and further, that this includes issues of diversity and gender.[97] It has been announced that the UK Supreme Court appointment contests for the six vacancies which are coming up in the next two years will be grouped together in joint selection exercises to encourage the broadest and most diverse range of applications.[98] Hopefully this is an indication that the Bingham thesis is gaining support amongst today's Justices.[99] Second, a better balance of power is needed between the three arms of the state in relation to judicial appointment – a genuine partnership at the level of appointment of the senior judiciary.[100] This is entirely consistent with the separation of powers because that concept is about checks and balances, and in relation to the appointment of the senior judiciary there are now insufficient checks to the power of the leaders of the judiciary.

How is such a balance to be achieved? As in many other countries[101] a greater residual role is required for the executive or for Parliament. Three options have gained a measure of support from the commentators:

96 See Lord Bingham, 'The Law Lords: Who Has Served' in L. Blom-Cooper, B. Dickson and G. Drewry (eds), *The Judicial House of Lords 1876–2009*, Oxford: Oxford University Press, 2009, p. 126.

97 Recognizing the importance of diversity in this way would be a significant advance on the most recent diversity initiative – the application of the 'tipping point' provision of the Equalities Act to judicial appointments. The latter provides that where two or more candidates for judicial office are of equal merit then a preference may be given to the candidate(s) who belong to the less represented category. This is a potentially useful provision but its utility depends in part on how broadly it is interpreted and whether it is applied only at the final stage in the selection process or also at the sift stage(s).

98 Statement released by the Supreme Court 11 July 2016.

99 Lord Mance, in an interview in 2015 commented: 'My feeling is that one possible problem over the years has been that it's easy to take quite a narrow view about what is meant by merit and I think account should be taken of the overall composition and balance of the court, especially of the highest court. I think it would be entirely appropriate to look at diversity as one aspect of merit.' (C. Hopkins and R. Dolby-Stevens, 'UKSC Blog Interviews Lord Mance', *UK Supreme Court Blog*, 5 October 2015).

100 Gee *et al*, *The Politics of Judicial Independence*, p. 61.

101 See The Bingham Report. While Truss LC undoubtedly wrong footed the senior judiciary in 2017 by indicating that any candidate for the position of Lord Chief Justice had to be able to stay for 4 years - inadvertently knocking out the top two candidates in the senior judiciary's eyes - this was not a real change to the balance of power between senior judiciary and the executive.

1 That the relevant selection panel should offer the Minister responsible for the appointment a choice of two or three names rather than the single name that is currently put forward by the panel.[102]
2 Widening the selection panel for appointments to the Supreme Court and the Heads of Division to include parliamentarians.[103]
3 Holding a post-appointment parliamentary confirmation hearing. This could involve not only the successful candidate but the chair of the selection panel.[104]

What is proposed is unlikely to appeal to some, since even a relatively modest realignment of the distribution of power between the different arms of the state in this way would mean the senior judiciary losing some of their power in the broadest sense of the word. However, as this chapter has shown – when it comes to judicial appointments it is necessary to look at power in all three of Lukes' dimensions, that is in its 'conduct shaping' and its 'context shaping' forms. The very fact that the senior judiciary can play a long game in this area and have a far greater institutional memory than the executive or legislature, has given them the edge in the balance of power between the three arms of the state in relation to senior judicial appointments. We can no longer ignore the 'soft power' that senior judges can exercise over the appointment of senior judges – some redressing of the balance is now needed. The movement away from senior judicial appointments that were largely controlled by the executive was a desirable one. Unfortunately the pendulum in relation to these appointments has swung too far towards control by the senior judiciary and ironically this has begun to erode the legitimacy of judicial power at the highest levels[105] because balance has been lost between the three arms of government in this area. It may be too late to turn the clock back but it is only

102 This proposal is supported by Baroness Hale (in her evidence to the to the House of Lords Select Committee on the Constitution Inquiry into the Judicial Appointments Process), and Kate Malleson ('Taking the Politics out of Judicial Appointments?' *UK Constitutional Law Association Blog*, 21 February 2012) and discussed in the Bingham Report, p. 55. In the past decade appointments to Canadian Federal Courts have used this system. Lord Hailsham (the son) records in his autobiography that when recommending senior judicial appointments to the Prime Minister he would always give him three names (albeit in ranked order) See Lord Hailsham, *A Sparrow's Flight*, p. 427.

103 Baroness Hale and several other witnesses to the House of Lords Select Committee on the Constitution supported this proposal which is discussed in the Bingham Report, p. 39, and is used to appoint the South African Constitutional Court (South African Constitution, ss.105, 174–178). One possible variation would be to have a lay majority on these selection panels.

104 This is not the same as the Senate confirmation hearings in the USA for Supreme Court Justices which have received little support in UK discussions. In August 2016 the Canadian Government announced that post-appointment parliamentary confirmation hearings would be held for appointments to the Canadian Supreme Court, S. Chase, 'Ottawa overhauls how it picks justices' *The Globe and Mail*, 2 August 2016, p. 1, A11, A12.

105 First, because no arm of government in a democracy can be self-replicating. Second, because of the 'cloning effect' which works against diversity of judicial appointment. Thus, it is difficult not to conclude that the legitimacy and standing of the UK Supreme Court internationally has been damaged by the longstanding failure to improve the diversity of its membership.

now becoming apparent that the pre-2005 Constitutional Reform Act role of the Lord Chancellor enshrined a wisdom built on many years of political evolution involving as it did a balance between elements of the judiciary, the executive and the legislature. It was moreover – at least in the latter part of the twentieth century[106] – more democratic and less oligarchic than what we now have.

106 In that era most Lord Chancellors were eminent lawyers as well as politicians. As such they were accountable in Parliament for judicial appointments in a way that is very difficult for today's non-lawyer Lord Chancellors. Both Lords Hailsham of St Marylebone and Lord Mackay of Clashfern expressly recognized that part of their role included being accountable to the legislature for individual judicial appointments. See in particular Lord Hailsham, *A Sparrow's Flight*, pp. 426–428.

4 'Opening up' Commonwealth judicial appointments to diversity?

The growing role of commissions in judicial selection

Jan van Zyl Smit

Introduction

Entrusting the selection of judges to a commission or council 'looks likely to become the most popular selection system of the twenty-first century'.[1] It is estimated that over the past 30 years the global incidence of councils and commissions has increased from 10 per cent to 60 per cent of jurisdictions.[2] An important part of this phenomenon is the still-unfolding story of the spread of such bodies across much of the Commonwealth. By 2015, no fewer than 81 per cent of Commonwealth jurisdictions had commissions with at least some responsibility for selecting judges of the superior courts (high courts and appellate courts).[3] The aim of this chapter is to tease out how prospects for greater judicial diversity – the overarching theme of this volume – have been affected by the design of these bodies, especially their composition and the nature of their judicial selection processes.

The chapter takes a broadly historical approach. It examines the establishment and reform of commissions through periods of decolonization and autochthonous constitutional change, as well as considering the emergence during the last 20 years of Commonwealth norms such as those contained in the *Latimer House Principles* and *Guidelines*. The chapter draws on the author's study of Commonwealth judicial appointment systems as they stood in 2015.[4] It is not possible to describe historical developments in all 52 member states, so the discussion mostly concentrates on larger jurisdictions and those which pioneered particular design features. Specific attention is paid to the Judicial Appointments Commission (JAC) for England and Wales, which is the main subject of other chapters in this volume. The legal framework of the JAC was only established in 2005 and is

1 K. Malleson, 'Introduction', in K. Malleson and P. H. Russell (eds), *Appointing Judges in an Age of Judicial Power: Critical Perspectives from around the World*, Toronto: University of Toronto Press, 2006, p. 6.
2 N. Garoupa and T. Ginsburg, *Judicial Reputation: A Comparative Theory*, Chicago: University of Chicago Press, 2015, p. 101.
3 J. van Zyl Smit, *The Appointment, Tenure and Removal of Judges under Commonwealth Principles*, London: Bingham Centre for the Rule of Law, 2015, para 1.6.1.
4 Ibid.

comparatively elaborate by Commonwealth standards, which makes it well suited to illustrate contemporary debates on the design of such bodies.

Preliminary doubts and observations

Any attempt to assess how judicial diversity is affected by the legal frameworks for judicial selection in a large number of jurisdictions must address doubts about the feasibility of such an inquiry. There are at least three reasons to doubt how much can be said in a comparative essay on this subject. First and foremost, the diversity challenges facing Commonwealth jurisdictions are a function of the patterns of privilege, prejudice, group socialization and power dynamics that exist within particular legal communities and their societies. It is by no means clear that the same strategies would be effective in addressing, for example, race in South Africa, religion and caste in India, or regional and ethnic divisions in Kenya or Nigeria. The underrepresentation of women in the judiciary is a pervasive problem, but differences in social and professional practices and attitudes relating to gender are also likely to be relevant in addressing it. Furthermore, the challenge of ensuring an appropriate diversity of jurisprudential outlook among members of the judiciary is highly contingent on the legal and political culture of a jurisdiction. In view of these complexities, any comparative analysis must proceed with caution and remain sensitive to local dynamics which may cast doubt on otherwise workable diversity strategies.

Secondly, it is beginning to be understood, at least in the UK, that targeting the appointment process alone will never be an adequate way of promoting judicial diversity.[5] After all, it is not only appointment bodies that make choices, but also the would-be members of a diverse judiciary, whose initial interest in judging must survive their experiences of whatever branch of the legal profession they enter and their estimation of what it would be like to be a judge. In England and Wales, diversity efforts in the past few years have been widened to encompass developing a 'legal and judicial career'[6] that would appeal to a more diverse pool of applicants, starting well before the moment of actual appointment to the bench. One striking result has been the introduction of fractional judicial posts all the way up to the highest courts, partly in response to the fact that women still have a disproportionate share of child-rearing and caring responsibilities.[7] In similar vein, Commonwealth associations of judges and lawyers have called for working conditions

5 See Advisory Panel on Judicial Diversity, *The Report of the Advisory Panel on Judicial Diversity 2010*, London: Ministry of Justice, 2010; L. Barmes and K. Malleson, 'The Legal Profession as Gatekeeper to the Judiciary: Design Faults in Measures to Enhance Diversity', *Modern Law Review* 74, 2011, p. 245.

6 *Report of the Advisory Panel on Judicial Diversity*, para 4. The recommendations of the Advisory Panel are addressed to the government, the judiciary, the JAC and the organized legal profession. These bodies have met under the auspices of the Judicial Diversity Taskforce (2011–2014) and Judicial Diversity Forum (since 2015) to co-ordinate their implementation of the Panel's recommendations.

7 Senior Courts Act 1981, ss. 2 and 4 (as amended by the Crime and Courts Act 2013).

of judges to be adapted to 'encourage women and those from diverse backgrounds to apply for judicial appointments'.[8] It is beyond the scope of this chapter, however, to assess the progress that individual Commonwealth countries have made with any initiatives falling outside the scope of the processes of judicial selection and appointment.

A third reason to doubt the utility of a comparative discussion is that the legal frameworks under which judges are appointed rarely seem to give much prominence to considerations of diversity, even if those frameworks are relatively new. In England and Wales, the Constitutional Reform Act 2005 provides that the JAC is to select candidates 'solely on merit'.[9] The opening provisions of the Act refer to the rule of law and the independence of the judiciary, which suggests that the Act is principally aimed at securing these values. The Act does require the JAC to 'have regard to the need to encourage diversity in the range of persons available for selection', but it would be easy to infer that this duty relates mainly to outreach activities.[10] In 2013, the Act was amended to allow the JAC to take judicial diversity into account when choosing between candidates of 'equal merit',[11] but this further reference to diversity only seems to underscore that it is not normally central to the selection process.

It would be a mistake, however, to confine one's examination of legal frameworks to a search for explicit references to judicial diversity. Such an approach overlooks the reality that a constitutional or legislative scheme can be designed to serve multiple objectives which are not all made equally explicit. It also forecloses the discussion of unintended effects that may benefit judicial diversity. In the case of the Constitutional Reform Act, government statements suggest that improving judicial diversity was one of its principal objectives, albeit that its pursuit was intertwined with others. A 2003 consultation paper argued that a judicial appointment commission would not only provide a 'guarantee of judicial independence', but also 'work to make our judiciary more reflective of the society it serves'.[12] Judicial independence would be more visibly protected if appointments were no longer in the gift of the Lord Chancellor, a cabinet member serving at the pleasure of the Prime Minister.[13] As far as diversity was concerned, the consultation paper recognized that there was a long history of Lords Chancellor selecting mainly white men from a narrow social and educational background. It noted that 'Whether or not the system really is biased, the perception has an impact which is

8 Commonwealth Lawyers' Association, Commonwealth Legal Education Association, Commonwealth Magistrates' and Judges' Association and Commonwealth Parliamentary Association, *Edinburgh Plan of Action for the implementation of the Commonwealth Latimer House Principles,* 2008, para 1.4.1.

9 Constitutional Reform Act 2005 (CRA), s. 63.

10 CRA, s. 64.

11 CRA, s. 63(4).

12 Department for Constitutional Affairs, *Constitutional Reform: A New Way of Appointing Judges*, Consultation Paper CP 10/03, 2003, para 21.

13 Ibid., paras 22–23.

real enough.'[14] An independent commission, operating transparently, might encourage a wider range of potential candidates to consider applying for judicial office. The consultation paper described the changes it was proposing as 'opening up the system of appointments ... to attract suitably qualified candidates from a wider range of social backgrounds'.[15]

This chapter borrows the phrase 'opening up' to describe how a larger number of Commonwealth jurisdictions have reformed their judicial appointment systems by shifting responsibility from the Executive to independent commissions and making the process of judicial selection more transparent. These shifts are often a matter of degree, and in many Commonwealth jurisdictions their potential to affect judicial diversity may not have received as much attention as other objectives (in the case of some of the early commissions, there is little evidence that judicial diversity was considered at all).

Three concerns other than judicial diversity are worth highlighting for the influence they have had on the design of judicial appointment frameworks in the Commonwealth, including those built around commissions. The first is the independence of the judiciary, which has been a constant thread in the discourse since the first commissions were established. Secondly, professional standards of judging have also been invoked. For example, prior to the Constitutional Reform Act 2005, the UK government sought to address concerns about a possible decline in the quality of judges.[16] Kate Malleson has noted that this stance was surprisingly timid, since if the government was confident that the commission would attract a more diverse pool of potential candidates it should also have expected standards to rise through competition.[17] Other Commonwealth states have been more enthusiastic about the potential for commissions to raise, rather than merely maintain, professional standards.

Last but not least, concerns about the legitimacy of the judiciary, and in particular the role of the superior courts in reviewing legislation and government action, have also played a substantial part in shaping judicial appointment frameworks. In some Commonwealth jurisdictions this has led to a continued insistence that members of the Executive or the legislature should play a central part in the selection of judges, whereas in the UK the Constitutional Reform Act heralded a very substantial withdrawal of elected politicians from this process.[18] Although it is not possible to explore these issues in full, this chapter remains cognizant that underlying debates about such matters have shaped the composition and selection processes of commissions established by Commonwealth jurisdictions.

14 Ibid., para 24.
15 Ibid., para 27.
16 Ibid., para 28.
17 K. Malleson, 'The New Judicial Appointments Commission in England and Wales: New Wine in New Bottles?' in K. Malleson and P. H. Russell (eds), *Appointing Judges in an Age of Judicial Power*, Toronto: University of Toronto Press, 2006, pp. 44–45.
18 Ibid., pp. 39–42.

The first wave of commissions

The use of commissions to select superior court judges in the Commonwealth began when decolonization reached British colonies and territories in Sub-Saharan Africa in the mid-1950s.[19] When Ghana led the way to independence in 1957, its constitution made provision for a Judicial Service Commission, which had in fact already been established in 1954 when the country secured self-government.[20] Commissions quickly became a standard feature of other independence constitutions across much of Africa and the Caribbean from the 1960s onwards.[21]

The introduction of commissions represented a departure from the approach of Commonwealth states which had gained their independence earlier, all of which chose in one form or another to continue with the Executive selection of superior court judges.[22] However, there was already some experience with the use of commissions as a mechanism to appoint magistrates or other judicial staff, starting with the Judicial and Legal Services Commission of Ceylon (now Sri Lanka) established at the time of independence in 1948.[23] More broadly, the final years of colonial rule had seen experiments with entrusting the recruitment and selection of civil servants to a Public Service Commission in an effort to replicate the British tradition of a politically neutral civil service.[24] The advent of these bodies meant that it was a smaller leap to take the selection of judges out of Executive hands.

The commissions established by the African independence constitutions were small, and based on a common model. Chaired by the Chief Justice, the membership usually consisted of one or two other judges, the chairman of the Public

19 The following brief sketch of these developments is based on contemporary accounts by British jurists who advised on some of the independence constitutions: S. A. De Smith, *The New Commonwealth and Its Constitutions*, Dallas: Stevens, 1964; K. Roberts-Wray, *Commonwealth and Colonial Law*, Dallas: Stevens, 1966. It also draws on studies of post-independence judicial systems, including B. O. Nwabueze, *Judicialism in Commonwealth Africa*, London: Hurst Publishing, 1977; T. O. Elias, *Judicial Process in the Newer Commonwealth*, Lagos: University of Lagos Press, 1990; A. N. E. Amissah, *The Contribution of the Courts to Government: A West African View*, Oxford: Oxford University Press, 1981; J. Hatchard, M. Ndulo and P. Slinn, *Comparative Constitutionalism and Good Governance in the Commonwealth: An Eastern and Southern African Perspective*, Cambridge: Cambridge University Press, 2004; and D. O'Brien, *The Constitutional Systems of the Commonwealth Caribbean*, Oxford: Hart Publishing, 2014.

20 Amissah, *The Contribution of the Courts*, pp. 146–147.

21 Nwabueze, *Judicialism in Commonwealth Africa*, pp. 267–268; O'Brien, *The Constitutional Systems*, p. 198.

22 Roberts-Wray, *Commonwealth*, pp. 479–480; De Smith, *The New Commonwealth*, p. 137. The exact form of Executive selection system varied between jurisdictions. The formal appointment power was typically vested in the head of state and exercised upon advice of the Attorney-General or a senior minister, in some countries after consultation with the Chief Justice.

23 Roberts-Wray, *Commonwealth*, p. 482; De Smith, *The New Commonwealth*, p. 142; Amissah, *The Contribution of the Courts*, p. 101.

24 Amissah, *The Contribution of the Courts*, p. 101. See also De Smith, *The New Commonwealth*, pp. 73–74, 77, 146–150.

Service Commission and in some cases also the Attorney-General.[25] The Commission was charged with selecting judges for appointment to the superior courts (except for the position of Chief Justice, which remained in the gift of the government).[26] The Commission's selection decisions were binding on the head of state, who was responsible for the formal act of appointment. Contemporary accounts describe the purpose of these arrangements as being to 'insulate' judicial appointments from political control in order to enhance the independence of the judiciary.[27] This was seen as necessary because the courts of the newly independent states would be called upon enforce bills of rights, federal divisions of power and other restraints on government.[28]

However laudable the objective of securing an independent judiciary, a closer look at the early commissions in their historical context suggests that they were in some respects a rather conservative measure. Under British rule, the Colonial Office had played an active role in the selection of superior court judges, whose appointment required approval from London.[29] Transferring this task to commissions in newly independent states was also a decision to continue excluding local politicians from involvement in the selection of judges. Some observers suggest that there was also a specific intention to secure the position of the white expatriate or colonist judges, who still held many of the senior judicial positions and so would be well represented on most commissions.[30] After independence, some African jurisdictions continued to make use of expatriate judges for decades, although not all of these judges may have been perceived as representatives of the former colonial power as some came from other Commonwealth countries in Africa and the Caribbean.[31] Demands for indigenization of the judiciary were accommodated by appointing expatriates on fixed-term contracts rather than permanently, and there were jurisdictions in which any expatriate judge could be compulsorily retired in the event that a suitable local replacement was identified.[32] Such compromises may have provided a temporary source of judges with skills and experience. However, they were clearly problematic. Expatriate judges without security of tenure were more vulnerable to pressure from authoritarian governments to rule in their favour.[33] The same governments were also

25 De Smith, *The New Commonwealth*, p. 142; Roberts-Wray, *Commonwealth*, p. 481; Amissah, *The Contribution of the Courts*, pp. 102–103.

26 De Smith, *The New Commonwealth*, p. 138; Roberts-Wray, *Commonwealth*, p. 482.

27 De Smith, *The New Commonwealth*, pp. 136, 136–138; Roberts-Wray, *Commonwealth*, p. 481; Elias, *Judicial Process*, p. 157; Amissah, *The Contribution of the Courts*, p. 99.

28 De Smith, *The New Commonwealth*, pp. 106–109, 136–143; Nwabueze, *Judicialism in Commonwealth Africa*, pp. 266–267.

29 Nwabueze, *Judicialism in Commonwealth Africa*, pp. 265–266; Amissah, *The Contribution of the Courts*, pp. 60–68; Hatchard, Ndulo and Slinn, *Comparative Constitutionalism*, pp. 151–152.

30 Elias, *Judicial Process*, pp. 172, 174.

31 Ibid., 174; Paul Mwangi, *The Black Bar: Corruption and Political Intrigue within Kenya's Legal Fraternity*, Nairobi: Oakland Media, 2001.

32 Nwabueze, *Judicialism in Commonwealth Africa*, pp. 273–274, 277.

33 On Kenya, see M. Mutua, 'Justice Under Siege: The Rule of Law and Judicial Subservience in Kenya', *Human Rights Quarterly* 23, 2001, pp. 96, 107–111.

enabled to neglect the important work of developing a pool of local judges by investing in legal education and judicial training.

The prospects for judicial diversity were also affected by the fact that most commissions inherited the Westminster 'tap on the shoulder' selection system, which did not allow interested persons to apply for judicial office.[34] Commissions enjoyed a broad discretion to select candidates who met basic requirements of eligibility, as the applicable legal frameworks did not commonly specify a full set of criteria against which candidates could be evaluated. Perhaps the independence-era drafters, more concerned with judicial independence than diversity, considered structured processes of application and evaluation unnecessary. In the view of the eminent Nigerian jurist T. O. Elias, who served as Chief Justice of Nigeria and later President of the International Court of Justice, the best safeguard for judicial independence was the natural wish of accomplished lawyers to retain the respect of their professional peers once appointed to the Bench.[35] But there was a clear danger that a commission could abuse its discretion to favour smaller cliques of lawyers or an 'old boys' network', rather than building a rapport with the entire local legal community as it became more diverse.[36] Even with the best of intentions, a small and homogenous commission might be prone to elitism or other forms of unconscious bias.[37]

Another shortcoming of first wave commissions was that some failed to insulate the judiciary from political influence as they were intended to. Their crucial vulnerability was that the Chief Justice was chosen by the Executive, and between them the Chief Justice and the Executive usually had the power to choose most of the other members of the commission.[38] Authoritarian governments in Kenya and Uganda are said to have obtained control over judicial selection by installing compliant Chief Justices, and over time the Kenyan judiciary in particular developed a reputation for political bias and corruption.[39] The opacity of tap on the shoulder selection processes facilitated this subversion of the judiciary as it was not possible for critics to identify procedures that had not been followed or point to applicants for judicial office who had been unfairly overlooked.

34 Elias,*Judicial Process*, p. 172. T. Robinson, A. Bulkan and A. Saunders, *Fundamentals of Caribbean Constitutional Law*, Yorkshire: Sweet & Maxwell, 2005, pp. 382–383.

35 Elias, *Judicial Process*, p. 175.

36 Hatchard, Ndulo and Slinn, *Comparative Constitutionalism*, p. 153; Robinson, Bulkan and Saunders, *Fundamentals of Caribbean Constitutional Law*, pp. 376, 383.

37 Hatchard, Ndulo and Slinn, *Comparative Constitutionalism*, pp. 152–153.

38 Nwabueze, *Judicialism in Commonwealth Africa*, p. 272; Hatchard, Ndulo and Slinn, *Comparative Constitutionalism*, p. 152. This problem was anticipated by De Smith, *The New Commonwealth*, p. 138.

39 Mutua, 'Justice Under Siege', pp. 104–105. Hatchard, Ndulo and Slinn, *Comparative Constitutionalism*, p. 154 discuss the experience of Uganda, which in 1995 adopted a new Constitution which banned the Chief Justice from being a member of the Judicial Service Commission.

The second wave of commissions

It did not take long for some political leaders to challenge the selection of judges by commissions as an unjustified restraint imposed by the departing colonizers, while observing that selecting judges was still a function of the Executive in Britain and the older Commonwealth countries.[40] This was essentially an argument about legitimacy. Judicial service commissions were abolished in Ghana and Nigeria, while in several other states the commission was retained but lost its role in the selection of superior court judges.[41]

However, the pendulum soon began to swing back. Before the end of the 1960s, 'local demand' led both Ghana and Nigeria to establish new selection bodies with judges among their members.[42] The membership of the new bodies and role in judicial selection decisions remained in flux during this period of frequent coups and constitutional upheaval; yet, remarkably, even military governments tended to follow their advice.[43] Local Bar Associations were among their strongest supporters and called for their selections to be made binding on the Executive.[44] Entrusting judicial selection to an independent body may also have had a broader appeal to minority politicians and their supporters in societies marked by deep ethnic and regional divisions. According to the leading Nigerian constitutional scholar B. O. Nwabueze, this would have been preferable to a situation in which the government, possibly controlled by a rival ethnic group, could select its own judges to enforce its laws and policies.[45]

This second wave of commissions reached its peak in the 1990s. That decade saw both Ghana and Nigeria make transitions from military rule to civilian political systems under constitutions which remain in place today, and which have provided a relatively stable framework specifying the composition and functions of the relevant judicial selection bodies.[46] A Judicial Service Commission was established in South Africa in 1994, which merits separate discussion in view of the apartheid history from which it emerged.[47] The second wave certainly includes the

40 Nwabueze, *Judicialism in Commonwealth Africa*, pp. 268, 272; Elias, *Judicial Process*, p. 173.

41 Nwabueze, *Judicialism in Commonwealth Africa*, p. 268; Amissah, *The Contribution of the Courts*, p. 159. The judicial service commissions in Sierra Leone and Tanzania were confined to selecting magistrates (professional judges of the lower courts) and other legal officers (Nwabueze, *Judicialism in Commonwealth Africa*, p. 268). Similar changes occurred in Malaya prior to the formation of federal Malaysia (De Smith, *The New Commonwealth*, p. 137), and in Barbados (Robinson, Bulkan and Saunders, *Fundamentals of Caribbean Constitutional Law*, p. 367).

42 Elias, *Judicial Process*, p. 174. See also Nwabueze, *Judicialism in Commonwealth Africa*, pp. 268–269; Amissah, *The Contribution of the Courts*, pp. 104–105, 205–206.

43 Elias, *Judicial Process*, p. 174; Amissah, *The Contribution of the Courts*, p. 205.

44 Elias, *Judicial Process*, p. 174.

45 B. O. Nwabueze, *A Constitutional History of Nigeria*, London: Hurst Publishing, 1982, pp. 113–114.

46 Constitution of the Republic of Ghana 1992, art 153; Constitution of the Federal Republic of Nigeria, s. 153.

47 See text to nn 60–69 and the chapter by C. Hoexter, 'The Judicial Service Commission: Lessons from South Africa', in this collection.

substantially revamped commissions which were established in other African jurisdictions such as Malawi, Uganda and Zambia, in each case as part of constitutional reforms which heralded a return to multi-party politics.[48] The establishment of new commissions with responsibility for judicial selection was part of the design for securing an independent judiciary that could enforce the new constitutional settlements. At the same time, many of these jurisdictions made senior judicial appointments subject to parliamentary confirmation, which could be understood either at face value as conferring added legitimacy on the judiciary for the exercise of their constitutional review powers or, more cynically, as an attempt by politicians to retain influence over judicial appointments.[49]

Whereas first wave commissions were small and dominated by senior judges, the second wave commissions have tended to be significantly larger and with a more varied membership. Judges, practising lawyers and lay persons all found a place on the new commissions. The numbers of seats allocated to each these groups varied, and some of the arguments that may have weighed for or against granting influence to each group can be gathered from the literature.[50] It was recognized that judicial members possessed valuable experience with which to assess the qualities of potential judges. Their participation thus appeared to be conducive to raising the professional standard of judging, although there were concerns that if the judges dominated the membership of a commission as before that might lead to an elitist approach in which judicial members would insist on choosing new judges in their own image.[51] Like judges, practising lawyers were also thought to be well placed to assess the legal skills of candidates who were their professional peers.[52] To reduce the possibility of political influence, it was desirable that commission seats allocated to practising lawyers should be filled by the Bar Association as an independent body representing the legal profession.[53] However, this brought with it the danger that such representatives might work together as a professional lobby to sway the commission's decisions.[54] Lobbying could have the effect of strengthening the prospects of the most senior or influential lawyers at the Bar, and not necessarily advancing judicial diversity.

Perhaps the most innovative feature of the second wave commissions was the inclusion of lay members.[55] Two reasons sometimes given for doing so were that

48 On the empowerment of the judiciary under these reforms see K. Prempeh, '*Marbury* in Africa: Judicial Review and the Challenge of Constitutionalism in Contemporary Africa', *Tulane Law Review* 80, 2006, p. 1.

49 Hatchard, Ndulo and Slinn, *Comparative Constitutionalism*, p. 156; van Zyl Smit, *The Appointment, Tenure and Removal of Judges under Commonwealth Principles*, paras 1.5.1–1.5.11.

50 Amissah, *The Contribution of the Courts*, pp. 120–126; Hatchard, Ndulo and Slinn, *Comparative Constitutionalism*, pp. 152–153.

51 Nwabueze, *Judicialism in Commonwealth Africa*, pp. 271–272; Amissah, *The Contribution of the Courts*, pp. 120–121.

52 Hatchard, Ndulo and Slinn, *Comparative Constitutionalism*, p. 153.

53 Ibid.

54 Amissah, *The Contribution of the Courts*, p. 126.

55 Ibid., pp. 125–126.

lay members would enhance the ability of commissions to assess the general suitability of candidates rather than concentrating only on their technical legal skills (an influence which could be expected to improve judicial diversity), and that lay participation would improve the legitimacy of the judiciary by giving members of the wider public a say in how they were selected.[56] A desire to foster greater legitimacy could perhaps account for the common provision that lay members would be chosen by the elected branches of government. However, such arrangements are more plausibly explained as attempts by the Executive to gain informal influence over judicial appointments. For example, in the case of Uganda's second wave Judicial Service Commission established in 1995, the President appoints the two lay members of the Commission with the approval of Parliament.[57] The President's influence in fact extends to appointing a majority of members of the Commission, including the chair, and there have been allegations of judicial selection decisions being influenced by government patronage.[58] The potential for such abuses in Uganda has been exacerbated by the commission's continued use of secretive 'tap on the shoulder' methods of selection. As already noted in relation to first wave commissions, this approach was also not calculated to bring the commission into contact with the most diverse range of candidates. Other second wave jurisdictions also initially retained this method of selection, although some have now adopted application procedures.

Post-apartheid South Africa made an unequivocal commitment to inclusive and transparent methods of judicial selection when establishing its Judicial Service Commission.[59] Previously, the secrecy of the tap on the shoulder method had helped the apartheid government, even during the years of constitutional negotiations, to maintain a judiciary which was almost entirely white and male.[60] Constitutional negotiators and drafters had access to a wide range of legal models, including an extensive comparative study of how judges were selected elsewhere in the Commonwealth.[61] Canada's 'advisory committees', in particular, had demonstrated that a system in which the committees would advertise judicial posts, receive applications and then shortlist and interview appointable candidates was a

56 Ibid., pp. 120–121.
57 Constitution of the Republic of Uganda 1995, art 146.
58 See the views of a distinguished member of the Supreme Court of Uganda, G. Kanyeihamba, *Commentaries on Law, Politics and Governance*, Kampala: Renaissance Media, 2006, pp. 170–171; M. Twesiime-Kirya, 'The Independence and Accountability of the Judiciary in Uganda: Opportunities and Challenges', in F. Jjuuko (ed.), *The Independence of the Judiciary and the Rule of Law: Strengthening Constitutional Activism in East Africa*, Kampala: Kituo Cha Katiba, 2005.
59 See Hoexter, 'Lessons from South Africa'; M. Olivier, 'The Selection and Appointment of Judges', and C. Hoexter and M. Olivier, 'The Judicial Service Commission', both in C. Hoexter and M. Olivier (eds), *The Judiciary in South Africa*, Cape Town: Juta, 2014.
60 Olivier, 'The Selection and Appointment of Judges', pp. 117–119.
61 Hoexter and Olivier, 'The Judicial Service Commission', pp. 155–157. The leading comparative article from this period is H. Corder, 'The Appointment of Judges: Some Comparative Ideas', *Stellenbosch Law Review*, 1992, p. 207.

viable alternative to the tap on the shoulder method.[62] The South African selection process builds on this approach. All judicial vacancies are advertised and the application process is supplemented by a nomination procedure, which allows Commissioners and others to approach promising candidates to make themselves available.[63] This process attempts to cast the net as wide as possible, which is understandable in the view of the magnitude of the diversity challenge posed by an almost all-white and all-male judiciary at the outset.

It may seem odd to emphasize applications and nominations when the features of the South African judicial selection process that most often attract comment are the politician-heavy membership of the Judicial Service Commission and its practice of interviewing shortlisted candidates in public. As Cora Hoexter discusses in this collection, these features have led to some troubling episodes in recent years, in which the Commission reportedly subjected candidates with distinguished human rights records to abrasive questions with a pro-executive slant, before going on to reject their applications.[64] The loss of these accomplished candidates appears to be a setback to the diversity of legal philosophies on the South African bench, in contrast to the strides made on race and gender diversity,[65] and the public nature of questioning may well have deterred other strong candidates from applying for judicial office.[66] Nonetheless, it is hard to say whether the structure and processes of the Commission have made South African judicial appointments more politicized than they might otherwise have been. Given the need to rebuild the legitimacy of the judiciary after apartheid, the way the Commission was designed arguably has the benefit of containing the inevitable political debates within its own proceedings.[67] Unlike many other second wave jurisdictions, South Africa did not adopt a parliamentary confirmation requirement for judicial appointments, which could have led to equally public attacks on individual candidates from politicians who do not have the familiarity with the judicial system that membership of the Commission and long-term involvement in judicial selections have the potential to foster. Moreover, the publication of the names of shortlisted candidates prior to interview has enabled civil society to engage constructively with the Commission by providing information relevant to their suitability for judicial office.[68]

62 Corder, 'The Appointment of Judges', pp. 210–215.
63 Olivier, 'The Selection and Appointment of Judges', pp. 124–126.
64 See also C. Oxtoby, 'Managing a Fraught Transition: The Practice of the South African JSC', in H. Corder and J. van Zyl Smit (eds), *Securing Judicial Independence: The Role of Commissions in Selecting Judges in the Commonwealth*, Cape Town: Siber Ink, forthcoming.
65 According to statistics cited by Hoexter in Lessons from South Africa, by 2016 the judiciary was 44% black African and 36% white, with the balance from other minority groups. Women made up 35% of the judiciary.
66 Oxtoby, 'Managing a Fraught Transition'.
67 cf. Hoexter and Olivier, 'The Judicial Service Commission', pp. 164–172.
68 The work of the Democratic Governance and Rights Unit of the University of Cape Town, described in Oxtoby, 'Managing a Fraught Transition', has been particularly notable in this regard.

The development of Commonwealth norms

The Latimer House Principles *and* Guidelines

The second wave of judicial selection commissions in the 1990s coincided with a period of increased activity in the formulation of norms of good government at the Commonwealth level, possibly due in part to the end of the Cold War and the dismantling of apartheid in South Africa making it easier to find common ground.[69] As far as the judiciary is concerned, the most important instruments are the *Commonwealth Principles on the Three Branches of Government* and an accompanying set of *Guidelines*, which together are informally known as the *Latimer House Principles* and *Guidelines.*[70] The name reflects their origin and rather unusual history of development. Although more detailed than the *Principles*, the *Guidelines* came first, being drawn up at a conference of Commonwealth parliamentary, judicial and legal associations held at Latimer House, Buckinghamshire in 1998.[71] Over the ensuing several years, the *Guidelines* became a focus of inter-governmental discussions and were revised in consultation with the Commonwealth associations for possible adoption by the Commonwealth Heads of Government.[72] Ultimately, however, the member-state governments preferred a briefer set of norms, which were distilled from the *Guidelines* and adopted at the Heads of Government Meeting in Abuja in 2003. These *Principles* are stated to be 'in the spirit' of the *Latimer House Guidelines*, and both texts are usually issued together by the Commonwealth Secretariat.

The *Latimer House Principles* deal with judicial appointments under the heading of 'The Independence of the Judiciary'.[73] Judicial diversity is also identified as an objective, although there is little guidance as to what actions should be taken to pursue it: while appointments are to be made 'on merit', the *Principles* also state that the selection process should ensure 'equality of opportunity for all who are eligible for judicial office' and 'that appropriate consideration is given to the need

69 The 1991 Harare Commonwealth Declaration was the first engagement by Commonwealth Heads of Government with fundamental principles of good government since the 1971 Singapore Declaration of Commonwealth Principles, which did not mention courts or the independence of the judiciary.

70 The full titles of the two instruments are *Commonwealth Principles on the Accountability of and the Relationship Between the Three Branches of Government* and *Guidelines on good practice governing relations between the Executive, Parliament and the Judiciary in the promotion of good governance, the rule of law and human rights to ensure the effective implementation of the Harare Principles.* An official text is at <http://thecommonwealth.org/sites/default/files/history-items/documents/LatimerHousePrinciples.pdf> (accessed 13 January 2017).

71 The original 1998 version of the *Guidelines* is reproduced in the proceedings of the Latimer House conference, published as J. Hatchard and P. Slinn (eds), *Parliamentary Supremacy and Judicial Independence: A Commonwealth Approach*, London: Cavendish, 1999.

72 *Latimer House Principles*, pp. 5–7 [Preface].

73 *Latimer House Principles*, Principle IV.

for the progressive attainment of gender equity and the removal of other historic factors of discrimination'.[74]

As far as the methods of selection are concerned, the *Principles* state that judicial appointments 'should be made on the basis of clearly defined criteria and by a publicly declared process'.[75] Taken together with the reference to equality of opportunity, this strongly suggests that judicial positions should be open to applications from any qualified candidate.[76] The *Guidelines* recommend that 'Judicial vacancies should be advertised', which implies that applications or at the very least nominations would have to be invited.[77] The tap on the shoulder system is thus decisively rejected.

While the *Principles* are silent on the role of different institutions and branches of government in the selection of judges, the *Guidelines* recommend the use of commissions to ensure an 'independent process', unless another satisfactory appointment mechanism is already in place:

> Jurisdictions should have an appropriate independent process in place for judicial appointments. Where no independent system already exists, appointments should be made by a judicial services commission (established by the Constitution or by statute) or by an appropriate officer of state acting on the recommendation of such a commission.[78]

Contemporary accounts indicate that this was a compromise to avoid blanket criticism of all jurisdictions where the Executive was still responsible for selecting judges.[79]

Judicial selection in the Commonwealth after Latimer House

In 2015, more than a decade after the publication of the *Latimer House Principles* and *Guidelines*, 19 per cent of Commonwealth member-state jurisdictions still adhered to the Executive model of judicial selection.[80] It is beyond the scope of this chapter to consider whether all these jurisdictions – which include highly developed legal systems such as Australia, Canada, New Zealand and Singapore – are able to conduct an 'independent process' of judicial selection in the sense contemplated in the *Latimer House Guidelines.* Among this group, perhaps the most elaborate process is provided by Canada under the system of advisory committees which has already been mentioned.[81] However, the advisory committees

74 *Latimer House Principles*, Principle IV(a).
75 Ibid.
76 Ibid.
77 *Latimer House Principles*, Guideline II.1.
78 Ibid.
79 Hatchard and Slinn, *Parliamentary Supremacy*, p. 15.
80 van Zyl Smit, *The Appointment, Tenure and Removal of Judges under Commonwealth Principles*, paras 1.4.6–1.4.17.
81 Text to Corder, 'The Appointment of Judges'. See further R. Devlin, 'Dirty Laundry: Judicial Appointments in Canada', in H. Corder and J. van Zyl Smit (eds), *Securing*

merely serve to provide a pool of approved judicial candidates from which the Executive then makes its own selections, and they have no role in appointments to appellate courts.[82] In the last years prior to the establishment of the JAC in England and Wales, the Lord Chancellor's department began to advertise and receive applications for judicial posts and an independent Commission on Judicial Appointments was established to monitor the process and adjudicate complaints.[83] The government nonetheless came to the conclusion that it was necessary to establish a new appointments commission with direct responsibility for selecting judicial candidates, arguing that 'If the judiciary is to be seen and trusted as independent of the government of the day, it must be appointed by a process which must be seen to be open and independent.'[84]

An overwhelming majority of 81 per cent of Commonwealth jurisdictions had by 2015 established a commission with a constitutional or statutory mandate to play some part in the selection of superior court judges.[85] However, the extent of a commission's responsibilities can vary significantly. In almost all jurisdictions there is still a minor role for the Executive, as the head of state is responsible for the formal act of appointment.[86] There are also various ways in which some jurisdictions give the Executive a more substantial say. Notably, in 8 per cent of jurisdictions with a commission the Executive is solely responsible for selecting all the members of the highest court,[87] while in no fewer than 38 per cent of these jurisdictions it is solely responsible for choosing the Chief Justice (these are mostly jurisdictions with unreconstructed first wave commissions).[88] There are also jurisdictions which require the commission to present a shortlist of candidates to the Executive, enabling the latter to make the final choice for certain judicial positions.[89]

It would be wrong to attribute the contemporary prevalence of commissions to the *Latimer House Principles* and *Guidelines*. The first two waves of commissions meant that by the 1990s these bodies were well established in numerous Commonwealth jurisdictions across Africa and the Caribbean. Since the formal adoption of the *Principles* and *Guidelines* in 2003, most of the activity in establishing new commissions to select judges has occurred in England and Wales, and in Commonwealth jurisdictions in Asia. However, in some several Asian jurisdictions the attempts to establish new commissions encountered serious resistance,[90] and

Judicial Independence: The Role of Commissions in Selecting Judges in the Commonwealth, Cape Town: Siber Ink, forthcoming.

82 Devlin, 'Dirty Laundry'.

83 S. Shetreet and S. Turenne, *Judges on Trial: The Independence and Accountability of the English Judiciary*, Cambridge: Cambridge University Press, 2013, 2nd edn, pp. 106–108.

84 Department for Constitutional Affairs, *Constitutional Reform*, para 22.

85 van Zyl Smit, *The Appointment, Tenure and Removal of Judges under Commonwealth Principles*, para 1.6.1.

86 Ibid., para 1.4.27.

87 Ibid., paras 1.4.18–1.4.20.

88 Ibid., paras 1.4.21–1.4.24.

89 Ibid., paras 1.7.24–1.7.25.

90 In Bangladesh, a 2008 Ordinance of the interim government establishing a Supreme Judicial Commission expired while in Sri Lanka the 17th Amendment to the

currently Malaysia and Pakistan are the only states in the region where such bodies have managed to survive.[91]

The most dramatic reversal occurred in India, where in 2015 the Supreme Court struck down a newly established National Judicial Appointments Commission.[92] This was not a decision in favour of the Executive selection of judges. On the contrary, the Supreme Court held that selection decisions should remain in the hands of the *collegium*, a small committee of five senior judges headed by the Chief Justice. In substance, the *collegium* resembles the first wave commissions that exist in other Commonwealth jurisdictions, although it is not explicitly created by the Constitution of India in 1952, but rather extrapolated from the text by the Supreme Court in the 1990s as a necessary mechanism to safeguard judicial independence.[93] The *collegium*'s opaque selection methods, which effectively amount to the tap on the shoulder system, remain controversial.[94] However, as long as the *collegium* endures, India can be regarded as fitting within the overall Commonwealth trend of judicial selection responsibility shifting from the Executive to independent commissions.

Emerging norms and innovative features

The *Latimer House Principles* and *Guidelines* leave open many questions about the selection and appointment of judges, and there have been no further declarations or statements of the Commonwealth Heads of Government dealing with these issues.[95] However, there is a growing body of evidence from which less official norms may be ascertained.[96] The Commonwealth associations have developed

Constitution provided for a Constitutional Council with responsibility for selecting appellate judges, but was repealed by the 18th Amendment.

91 On Malaysia, see M. Ershadul Bari, M. Ehteshamul Bari and S. Naz, 'The Establishment of the Judicial Appointments Commission in Malaysia to Improve the Constitutional Method of Appointing the Judges of the Superior Courts: A Critical Study', *Commonwealth Law Bulletin* 41, 2015, p. 231. The Judicial Commission of Pakistan has been the subject of extensive constitutional litigation, as discussed in I. Bin Haris, 'Judicial Review of Constitutional Amendments – Pakistan's Uneasy Subscription to the Basic Structure Doctrine', *UK Constitutional Law Association Blog*, 24 September 2015.

92 *Advocates-on-Record Association v Union of India*, Writ Petition (Civil) No 13 of 2015, discussed in J. van Zyl Smit, 'Judicial Appointments in the Commonwealth: Is India Bucking the Trend?', *UK Constitutional Law Association Blog*, 7 March 2016.

93 *Supreme Court Advocates-on-Record Association v Union of India* (1993) 4 SCC 441; AIR 1994 SC 268 and *In re Special Reference No 1 of 1998* (1998) 7 SCC 739; AIR 1999 SC 1.

94 van Zyl Smit, 'Judicial Appointments in the Commonwealth'.

95 The *Latimer House Principles* are affirmed by the *Charter of the Commonwealth* adopted by the Commonwealth Heads of Government in 2012.

96 One recent attempt to formulate norms by a group of academics from Commonwealth jurisdictions is the *Cape Town Principles on the Role of Independent Commissions in the Selection and Appointment of Judges*, published online in February 2016 by the Bingham Centre for the Rule of Law and forthcoming in H. Corder and J. van

various guides on the implementation of the Latimer House norms, including a *Model Constitutional Clause on Judicial Appointment Commissions.*[97] It is also relevant to consider the features of the newest commissions, not only in jurisdictions which previously had Executive selection systems such as England and Wales, but also in first wave jurisdictions such as Kenya, where the 2010 Constitution introduced a new Judicial Service Commission with an expanded and rebalanced membership and a mandate which explicitly includes the advancement of judicial diversity.[98] Interesting guidance can also be extracted from the declarations, reports and other statements of regional and global bodies whose membership extends beyond the Commonwealth.[99] However, space precludes discussion of such materials in this chapter.

A balanced membership

The first version of the *Latimer House Guidelines* stated that commissions should have 'a majority of members drawn from the senior judiciary', but this recommendation proved controversial and was omitted from the final version of the *Guidelines.*[100] The omission meant that the debate about which composition of a commission would be most conducive to an 'independent process' of judicial selection was left open at the Commonwealth level.

Among the commissions established since the *Latimer House Principles*, only one (the Judicial Service Commission of Swaziland) contains neither a judicial majority nor a joint majority of judges and lawyers.[101] Overall, a gap has opened up between the group of Commonwealth jurisdictions where the commission has

Zyl Smit (eds), *Securing Judicial Independence: The Role of Commissions in Selecting Judges in the Commonwealth*, Cape Town: Siber Ink, 2017.

97 K. Brewer, J. Dingemans and P. Slinn, *Judicial Appointments Commissions: A Model Clause for Constitutions*, Report on behalf of the Commonwealth Magistrates' and Judges' Association, the Commonwealth Lawyers' Association and the Commonwealth Legal Education Association, 2013. See also the *Edinburgh Plan of Action for the implementation of the Commonwealth Latimer House Principles* (2008), adopted by the same three associations in conjunction with the Commonwealth Parliamentary Association. The *Edinburgh Plan of Action* was based on the earlier *Nairobi Plan of Action for Africa* (2005) drafted by Commonwealth associations and the Commonwealth Secretariat.

98 Constitution of Kenya 2010, arts 27, 171–173; Judicial Service Act 2011.

99 See van Zyl Smit, *The Appointment, Tenure and Removal of Judges under Commonwealth Principles*, and in particular the Introduction and Chapter 1 for a discussion of Commonwealth judicial appointments with reference to the output of bodies such as the UN Special Rapporteur on the Independence of Judges and Lawyers, the Venice Commission, the European Network of Councils for the Judiciary and the African Commission on Human and Peoples' Rights.

100 Hatchard, Ndulo and Slinn, *Comparative Constitutionalism*, p. 154. For the original recommendation see Hatchard and Slinn, *Parliamentary Supremacy*, p. 20.

101 van Zyl Smit, *The Appointment, Tenure and Removal of Judges under Commonwealth Principles*, para 1.6.13. The Judicial Service Commission established in the Maldives also falls short of a joint majority of judges and lawyers, but in 2016 the Maldives left the Commonwealth.

a judicial majority (44 per cent of jurisdictions), and the larger group where there is either a judicial majority or a joint majority of judges and lawyers chosen by the practising or academic branches of the legal profession (62 per cent of jurisdictions).[102] Whereas the former group is dominated by small commissions established during decolonization, the latter has been boosted by the second wave of commissions and by newer bodies established in the period since the *Latimer House Principles* were issued. To cite two recent examples, Kenya as well as England and Wales both have commissions which are balanced between judges and lawyers, in the sense that neither group holds a majority of seats on its own but they do so jointly.

The Commonwealth associations have lent their support to this approach in their *Model Constitutional Clause on Judicial Appointment Commissions*, which proposes a 13-member commission with five judicial members, two representatives of the legal profession, one legal academic and five lay members.[103] This suggests that opinion is turning towards the balanced model, which has the advantage of preventing a judicial majority from importing conscious or unconscious selection bias detrimental to diversity. However, it would be wrong to rule out the possibility that in circumstances where the judiciary and senior members of the legal profession have strong vested interests in common it may be necessary to search for ways of achieving an 'independent process' that do not require a judicial-legal majority.[104]

Questions of gender balance and ethnic diversity in the membership of commissions have belatedly begun to receive attention in recent years. The *Model Clause* indicates that the lay members of the commission 'should broadly reflect the composition of the community in terms of gender, ethnicity, social and religious groups and regional balance'.[105] The Kenyan constitution stipulates that 'one woman and one man' shall occupy the pair of Judicial Service Commission seats allocated to members of the public, and likewise the pair of seats allocated to the legal profession, and two of the judicial seats.[106] India's ill-fated National Judicial Appointments Commission included two seats for 'eminent persons', at

102 Ibid., para 1.6.13.

103 Brewer, Dingemans and Slinn,*Model Clause*, para 2.

104 As Graham Gee argues in his essay ('Judging the JAC: How Much Judicial Influence Over Judicial Appointments Is Too Much?') in this collection on the JAC in England and Wales, there is reason to think that a commission which is strongly influenced by a judicial-legal majority (or even an extremely influential minority) may sometimes be insufficiently independent from the institutional interests of the judiciary as perceived by the most senior judges and practising lawyers. This may be specifically detrimental to the advancement of judicial diversity if the judicial-legal contingent is reluctant to permit reconsideration of existing concepts of judicial merit and their application in the selection process. In such situations, it becomes crucial to find mechanisms by which a substantial contingent of lay members can be selected without bringing the commission under political control. The present chapter touches on that challenge in text to nn 112–116.

105 Brewer, Dingemans and Slinn, *Model Clause*, para 5.

106 Constitution of Kenya 2010, art. 171(2)(d),(f),(h).

least one of whom had to be a woman or a member of certain designated minority groups.[107] Since 2013, it has been recognized as 'desirable' to have gender and racial diversity in selection panels for senior judicial posts in England and Wales.[108] It is probably too early to evaluate the effect of such requirements on the recruitment of a diverse judiciary. Beneficial effects may include counteracting conscious or unconscious bias among members of the commission or other selection body, and making it easier for candidates from a wide range of backgrounds to feel comfortable in interview situations.[109] The symbolism of a commitment to diversity may also help to attract a more diverse group of applicants.

Who appoints (and guards) the appointers?

The independence of a commission can arguably be instrumental to promoting both judicial independence and judicial diversity by giving a wider range of potential candidates the confidence that their application for judicial office will be impartially assessed and considered. That was one of the arguments considered at the outset of this chapter.[110] To ensure the manifest and effective independence of a commission, it is necessary to go beyond the question of a balanced membership and ask how the various judicial, legal and lay members are chosen. Senior judges such as the Chief Justice often hold their seats *ex officio*, and there is now some support for the view that other judicial members should be elected by their peers,[111] in much the same way as lawyer members are often chosen by their professional bodies.

The *Model Clause* endorses these developments,[112] and provides further that lay members should be selected by the commission itself after receiving applications from members of the public.[113] The closest parallel to this provision is the

107 Constitution of India, art. 124A(1)(d) as it would have read following the 99th Constitution Amendment Act 2014 but for the decision of the Supreme Court in *Advocates-on-Record Association v Union of India*.
108 Judicial Appointment Regulations 2013.
109 In the UK, the *Report of the Advisory Panel on Judicial Diversity*, p. 104 received submissions that 'people can feel intimidated by being utterly different from those on the selection panel'. The panel recommended (at 38) that '[t]here should always be a gender and, wherever possible, an ethnic mix' on selection panels.
110 See text to nn 15–16.
111 Council of Europe's Commission for Democracy Through Law (the Venice Commission), *Report on the Independence of the Judicial System – Part One: The Independence of Judges*, CDL-AD (2010)004, para 32. Hatchard, Ndulo and Slinn, *Comparative Constitutionalism*, note that 'presidential influence as to the choice of the commission's judicial members is a cause of concern' and argue for a combination of *ex officio* positions and peer selection (at p. 152).
112 In Brewer, Dingemans and Slinn, *Model Clause*, para 2 proposes that the five judicial members should consist of three *ex officio* members (the Chief Justice, the President of the Court of Appeal and the Chief Magistrate) and two judges elected by a representative body such as a Judges' Council. It also proposes that the two legal practitioner members should 'shall be selected by the relevant professional bodies in accordance with a transparent and published procedure' (para 3).
113 Ibid., para 4.

elaborate procedure for indirect selection of lay members in England and Wales, which is carried out by a selection panel including the chairman of the JAC and senior members of the judiciary.[114] The proposal in the *Model Clause* is presented as a safeguard against '[t]he temptations on the Executive to influence the appointment of Judges'.[115] The selection procedure for the two 'eminent persons' who were to serve on India's six-member National Judicial Appointments Commission became one of the grounds on which the Indian Supreme Court held that the establishment of the Commission undermined judicial independence. These two seats were to be filled by a committee consisting of the Prime Minister, the Leader of the Opposition and the Chief Justice, but the Court considered that the likelihood of political bargaining among these actors risked politicizing in turn the work of the Commission in selecting judges.[116]

Other features that have been introduced to strengthen the independence of commissions include guaranteeing the security of tenure to members for the duration of their period of service,[117] and providing for the financial and administrative autonomy of the commission.[118]

Selection criteria and process

The *Latimer House Principles* and *Guidelines* provide a very clear indication that commissions should advertise judicial posts, invite applications, and assess them 'on the basis of clearly defined criteria and by a publicly declared process'.[119] The *Model Clause* adds an important gloss to this by arguing that the published criteria should not merely define eligibility for judicial office (matters such as age and legal qualifications), but should also deal with the full range of judicial qualities which a commission needs to consider. The authors of the *Model Clause* argue that there is 'remarkable uniformity of view about what criteria make a person fit for judicial office' and suggest that these include 'intellectual capacity; integrity and independence; judgement; objectivity; an ability to understand and deal fairly with all persons and communities served by the Courts; authority and communication skills; and efficiency'.[120] The act of publishing a full list of criteria undoubtedly makes the judicial selection process more transparent. Potential applicants are placed in a better position to anticipate how they will be assessed, and to include appropriate evidence in their applications or nominate referees who have observed them in situations where they have displayed the requisite qualities. This may

114 Judicial Appointment Commission Regulations 2013, regs 9 and 13.
115 Brewer, Dingemans and Slinn, *Model Clause*, p. 10 [commentary on para 4].
116 *Advocates-on-Record Association v Union of India*.
117 van Zyl Smit, *The Appointment, Tenure and Removal of Judges under Commonwealth Principles*, para 1.6.23.
118 Brewer, Dingemans and Slinn, *Model Clause*, para 11–12; and van Zyl Smit, *The Appointment, Tenure and Removal of Judges under Commonwealth Principles*, para 1.6.24–1.6.25.
119 *Latimer House Principles*, Principle IV(a).
120 Brewer, Dingemans and Slinn, *Model Clause*, para 13 and commentary.

make the application process more appealing to candidates who might otherwise fear that a broad selection discretion is likely to be exercised against them due to conscious or unconscious bias.

There is considerable variation in the extent to which the newer Commonwealth selection commissions are subject to binding criteria, or left to develop their own. In Kenya, the Judicial Service Commission operates within a statutory framework of eight evaluation criteria, with 19 specified elements and further sub-elements.[121] In England and Wales, by contrast, the JAC is simply required to select judges 'solely on merit', with added permission to advance judicial diversity in 'equal merit' situations.[122] The JAC has produced, published and revised several sets of criteria and receives input from the Lord Chief Justice well as the Lord Chancellor, who may by agreement impose criteria for a particular selection exercise.[123] The two approaches offer contrasting advantages. The Kenyan model may appear too rigid, while the position of the JAC offers room for adaptation in the light of changing circumstances, including improved understandings of barriers to diversity. However, in some jurisdictions the flexible model might tempt authoritarian governments to demand a return to minimal criteria and a broad discretion, which would facilitate patronage appointments.

The strongest way in which selection criteria can be used to advance diversity is by imposing quotas, followed by targets. To date, both have been rare in the Commonwealth. The South African constitution requires that consideration be given to 'the need for the judiciary to reflect broadly the racial and gender composition of South Africa'.[124] Despite the extreme racial and gender disparities of the South African judiciary in the 1990s, the Judicial Service Commission has never adopted a rigid policy to limit the number of white male candidates it selects. However, it is widely understood to have accorded preference at times to candidates from other groups and some have criticized the Commission's somewhat unclear selection criteria for obscuring its approach to diversity.[125] In Kenya, the 2010 Constitution states with apparent precision that 'the State shall take legislative and other measures to ensure that no more than two-thirds of elective or appointive bodies shall be of the same gender'.[126] When only two female Justices were appointed to the seven-member Supreme Court, a court held that this constitutional requirement was not immediately enforceable.[127] This meant that what appeared to be a quota became a target. An informal norm has since

121 Judicial Service Act 2011, sch 1, s. 13.
122 CRA, s. 63.
123 CRA, ss. 65–66.
124 Constitution of the Republic of South Africa 1996, s. 174(2).
125 Oxtoby, 'Managing a Fraught Transition'.
126 Constitution of Kenya 2010, art 27(8).
127 *Federation of Women Lawyers Kenya and others v Attorney-General and another*, High Court Petition No 102 of 2011 [2011] eKLR, discussed in Y. Ghai *et al*, 'Constitutional Reforms and Judicial Appointments in Kenya', in H. Corder and J. van Zyl Smit (eds), *Securing Judicial Independence: The Role of Commissions in Selecting Judges in the Commonwealth*, Cape Town: Siber Ink, forthcoming.

developed that the number of women should not fall below two, and male candidates have generally refrained from applying to fill vacancies left by the departure of the first two female Justices. The Kenyan Judicial Service Commission has been more successful in appointing an ethnically diverse Supreme Court, which is another dimension of diversity which it is required by statute to consider.[128]

Just as transparency about selection criteria has the potential to encourage a wider range of applications, transparency about the nature of the selection process may also have that effect of allaying the concerns of potential applicants (especially if the information indicates that the process is manifestly fair). The *Latimer House Principles* call for a 'publicly declared process' of selection, which in many Commonwealth jurisdictions is set out in a combination of primary and delegated legislation (and increasingly also publicized by commissions on their websites). However, there is less appetite for the identity of individual applicants to be made public or for shortlisted candidates to undergo a public interview. According to the Commonwealth associations responsible for the *Model Clause*, 'reports have shown that although candidates are prepared to put themselves through an open and fair process, they are less willing to share their candidature, and any lack of success, with the public at large'.[129] There is thus a concern that transparency of this kind may deter potential candidates, and in a divided society it is possible that candidates of disadvantaged groups may be deterred to a greater extent if they consider themselves more likely to be rejected by the commission. Kenya is the only Commonwealth jurisdiction that has followed the South African example by requiring its commission to interview shortlisted candidates in public. This is one of several respects in which Kenya has emulated the South African constitutional project of rebuilding the legitimacy of the judiciary so that the courts could become credible guardians of a socially progressive constitution.[130] Public interviews certainly have the potential to widen the focus of media scrutiny and popular debate, as the commission may question candidates about issues such as the separation of powers and judicial activism. The South African experience shows that the attitudes of commission members are often exposed in these exchanges.[131] There is a clear public interest in such differences being aired as part of the process of nurturing debate about constitutional democracy, which is to be weighed against the costs, including potential candidates who are deterred from applying.

The interests of individual applicants may be better served by making provision for targeted and confidential scrutiny of commission proceedings in the event that a candidate wishes to raise a complaint. The authors of the *Model Clause* recommend that commissions should keep a full and confidential record of its proceedings so that complaints may be 'dealt with by the Appointments Ombudsman or

128 Judicial Service Act 2011, First Schedule, s. 14(1), discussed in Ghai *et al*, 'Constitutional Reforms'.

129 Brewer, Dingemans and Slinn,*Model Clause*, p. 13 [commentary on para 14].

130 Ghai *et al*, 'Constitutional Reforms'; J. Thuo Gathii, *The Contested Empowerment of Kenya's Judiciary, 2010–2015*, Nairobi: Sheria Publishing, 2016.

131 Oxtoby, 'Managing a Fraught Transition'.

through an appeal system'.[132] Whereas internal appeals would be heard by the commission, an external mechanism may be more appropriate in many cases, particularly if complaints concern matters such as alleged discrimination by the commission (which would be relevant to judicial diversity). Ombudsman offices with a specific remit to investigate judicial appointment processes exist in England and Wales, and in Northern Ireland, but it is difficult to find other examples in the Commonwealth.[133] The publication of anonymized reports by an ombudsman may improve the confidence of potential applicants more widely, and so contribute to advancing judicial diversity. There is a similar case to be made for commissions to produce annual reports which include statistical information on diversity, and to be held accountable for their performance by way of public and parliamentary debate.[134]

Conclusion

The historical and contemporary developments examined in this chapter suggest that the advancement of judicial diversity depends on much more than simple act of establishing a commission with a mandate to select superior court judges. The primary purpose of the small, judge-dominated commissions of the decolonization era was said to be to 'insulate' judicial selection from political influence.[135] Unfortunately, these commissions also risked becoming insular – selecting judges from their own narrow circles or, if the commission came under government influence, dispensing patronage. The second wave of commissions brought in wider perspectives by adding members from the legal profession and also lay persons, although in some jurisdictions these members were also liable to become politicized.

By the time the *Latimer House Principles* and *Guidelines* were finalized in 2003, a model of judicial selection had emerged that offered greater potential to improve judicial diversity. The Latimer House norms not only affirmed the need for an 'independent process' of selection – best conducted by an independent commission – but also clarified that such a process should involve a commission advertising judicial posts, receiving applications, and assessing candidates in accordance with published criteria and selection procedures. This finally spelled the end of the 'tap on the shoulder' methods used by the Lord Chancellor and the early commissions alike.

Questions remain about how a commission can most effectively attract, and perhaps actively recruit, applicants who will enhance the diversity of the judiciary. Contemporary developments discussed in the final part of this chapter have focused on improving the independence of commissions, the diversity of their

132 Brewer, Dingemans and Slinn, *Model Clause*, p. 13 [commentary on para 14].

133 CRA, ss. 100–101 and sch 13, para 1.

134 Brewer, Dingemans and Slinn, *Model Clause*, para 15.

135 See De Smith, *The New Commonwealth*, pp. 136, 136–138; Roberts-Wray, *Commonwealth*, p. 481; Elias, *Judicial Process*, p. 157; Amissah, *The Contribution of the Courts*, p. 99.

membership, the relevance of selection criteria and the transparency and accountability of selection processes. There are very few examples so far of Commonwealth jurisdictions taking more radical steps to address their diversity challenges at the judicial selection stage, for instance by the introduction of quotas or targets. Most of the recent reforms discussed in this chapter are not attributable solely to efforts to advance judicial diversity but have also been influenced by other concerns such as judicial independence, professional standards of judging and the legitimacy of the courts. It makes little sense to attempt to disentangle these strands of reform completely, particularly in a time when diversity has become integral to modern legal and political values and increasingly shapes our understandings of the independence, professionalism and legitimacy of the courts.

5 The Judicial Service Commission

Lessons from South Africa

Cora Hoexter

Introduction

South Africa's transition from white minority rule to constitutional democracy demanded the transformation of all her public institutions, including the judiciary. Before the watershed year of 1994 there was a Supreme Court of South Africa consisting of a number of provincial and local divisions, with the Appellate Division at its apex. About 170 judges, almost uniformly white and male, served in these divisions. They were drawn mainly from the ranks of practising advocates, with occasional 'political' appointments from the public service. Appointments were made by the head of state on the advice of the Cabinet (in practice, the Minister of Justice), and were very much of the tap-on-the-shoulder type. In 1992, Hugh Corder described the appointments process as 'informal, secret and unaccountable', and pointed out that the process was susceptible to political pressure because it was substantially unregulated by law.[1]

The judiciary of the old era was hopelessly unrepresentative in terms of both race and gender. Its institutional legitimacy was also eroded by its close association with apartheid: for while not all the judges were executive-minded, even 'liberal' judges who were opposed to the political system could not avoid participating in it unless they resigned. Very few did.[2] It is not surprising, then, that by the end of this era the administration of justice and the legal system were both said to be suffering from a crisis of legitimacy.[3] The crisis was not as acute as one might imagine, for South African judges had never been corrupt and had not taken orders from politicians.[4] They still enjoyed a measure of professionalism and

1 H. Corder, 'The Appointment of Judges: Some Comparative Ideas', *Stellenbosch Law Review* 3, 1992, pp. 207, 226.

2 Only four judges are known to have resigned for political reasons in the apartheid era: see H. Corder, 'Judicial Accountability', in C. Hoexter and M. Olivier (contributing eds), *The Judiciary in South Africa*, Claremont: Juta & Co Ltd, 2014, pp. 200, 205.

3 See H. Corder, 'Establishing Legitimacy for the Administration of Justice in South Africa', *Stellenbosch Law Review* 6, 1995, p. 202; and S. Ellmann, 'Law and Legitimacy in South Africa', *Law and Social Enquiry*, 1995, pp. 407–408 and the works referred to there.

4 C. Forsyth, 'The Judiciary under Apartheid', in C. Hoexter and M. Olivier (contributing eds), *The Judiciary in South Africa*, Claremont: Juta & Co Ltd, 2014, pp. 26, 66.

relative autonomy.[5] Indeed, as Stephen Ellmann has observed, liberal lawyers still had considerable faith in the capacity of the courts to deliver justice: 'South African lawyers continued to challenge apartheid through the courts' and 'sometimes won'.[6] Nevertheless, in the eyes of the people the judiciary had lost much of the trust and credibility that confer legitimacy on state institutions.[7]

During the negotiations for a new democratic dispensation it was evident that South Africa would require judges committed to the values of what promised to be a remarkably progressive constitution. These judges would have to reflect an unusually diverse population, and they would have to be appointed in a suitably democratic and transparent manner. However, for reasons of practicality and in the prevailing spirit of reconciliation, the negotiating parties agreed that the existing divisions of the Supreme Court would remain in place and that the existing judges would be able to stay on subject to their taking a new oath.[8]

Efforts to restore the legitimacy of the courts were ultimately seen in two reforms in particular.[9] First, the Constitutional Court was established to act as the guardian of the democratic Constitution and its justiciable Bill of Rights. This was mainly a response to the feeling that the existing apex court, tainted by its association with apartheid, could not be trusted with the crucial task of interpreting and applying this instrument of transformation. Secondly, a new mechanism was created for the selection and appointment of judges (as opposed to magistrates),[10] with a judicial appointments commission taking a pivotal part in it. South Africa thus became one of the many Commonwealth jurisdictions to have opted for such a commission, and part of the 'second wave' of law reform in this regard.[11]

The Constitutional Court has been one of the great successes of the new South Africa, and in just over two decades it has achieved international acclaim as well as

5 E. Cameron, 'Nude Monarchy: The Case of South Africa's Judges', *South African Journal on Human Rights* 3, 1987, pp. 338, 339.
6 Ellmann, 'Law and Legitimacy in South Africa', p. 408.
7 See further D. Carter, *Sources of State Legitimacy in Contemporary South Africa: A Theory of Political Goods*, Afrobarometer Working Paper No. 134, September 2011.
8 See further M. Olivier, 'The Selection and Appointment of Judges', in C. Hoexter and M. Olivier (contributing eds), *The Judiciary in South Africa*, Claremont: Juta & Co Ltd, 2014, pp. 116, 120.
9 See Corder, 'The Appointment of Judges', p. 102.
10 Magistrates are appointed by the Minister of Justice after consulting the Magistrates' Commission, a body established under the Magistrates' Act 90 of 1993, and in some respects they are less independent than judges. For a full account of their selection and appointment, see M. Olivier, 'The Magistracy', in C. Hoexter and M. Olivier (contributing eds), *The Judiciary in South Africa*, Claremont: Juta & Co Ltd, 2014, pp. 319, 323ff.
11 In a recent study of practices in the Commonwealth by the Bingham Centre, Jan van Zyl Smit indicates that 39 of 48 (81%) of independent jurisdictions now have a judicial appointments commission. See J. van Zyl Smit, *The Appointment, Tenure and Removal of Judges under Commonwealth Principles*, London: Bingham Centre for the Rule of Law, 2015, paras 1.6.1–1.6.2.

domestic legitimacy.[12] The Judicial Service Commission (JSC), on the other hand, started off well but has already lost a good deal of its prestige and credibility as the body responsible for selecting judges for appointment. This chapter discusses the JSC's performance of that function in the expectation that other jurisdictions may learn from South Africa's sometimes painful experience. While the legitimacy of judicial appointments commissions around the world is increasingly being associated with or measured by their achievement of judicial diversity, the performance of South Africa's JSC is a salutary reminder that rapid progress in that area is not everything. Other qualities, such as rationality, fairness, impartiality and accountability, remain crucial to the process of judicial selection and cannot simply be taken for granted.

The next section briefly describes the composition and role of the JSC under the two democratic Constitutions that have governed South Africa since 1994. The chapter then goes on to acknowledge that the JSC and its selection process achieved a large measure of legitimacy in its first few years of operation, pointing out a number of areas where that legitimacy has been eroded more recently before offering a brief conclusion.

The Judicial Service Commission: then and now

Under the interim Constitution

The transitional or interim Constitution of 1993[13] made a break with the old system of untrammelled executive appointment by creating a JSC to select judges of the Supreme Court and participate in the selection of judges of the first Constitutional Court. Section 105 of the interim Constitution also gave the JSC two further and very broadly stated functions: making recommendations about the removal of judges from office and advising the government on 'all matters relating to the judiciary and the administration of justice'.

Three features set the JSC apart from judicial appointments commissions elsewhere in the world. First, it was unusually large. Section 105 of the interim Constitution identified 17 members, a number that expanded to 19 in matters affecting a particular provincial division. Secondly, just over half of the JSC's members were either politicians or political appointees, which is to say that they were drawn from the legislature and executive or designated by the President. Thirdly, there were no lay members apart from the politicians and political appointees.

12 H. Corder and J. Brickhill, 'The Constitutional Court', in C. Hoexter and M. Olivier (contributing eds), *The Judiciary in South Africa*, Claremont: Juta & Co Ltd, 2014, pp. 355, 400. See further H. Klug, *The Constitution of South Africa: A Contextual Analysis*, Oxford: Hart Publishing, 2010; K. O'Regan, 'A Pillar of Democracy: Reflections on the Role and Work of the Constitutional Court of South Africa', *Fordham Law Review* 81, 2012, p. 1169; and T. Roux, *The Politics of Principle: The First South African Constitutional Court, 1995–2005*, Cambridge: Cambridge University Press, 2013.

13 Constitution of the Republic of South Africa, Act 200 of 1993.

The interim Constitution did not say much else about the JSC and did not attempt to address its day-to-day functioning, for it was expected that such detail would be supplied by legislation. Unfortunately, the Judicial Service Commission Act 9 of 1994 proved to be of minimal assistance in this regard. It dealt briefly with commissioners' terms of office (five years in most cases), remuneration and expenses and touched on matters such as the JSC's annual report to Parliament, but was unhelpfully silent on the most crucial functions of the body: how to deal with complaints against judges[14] and how to go about selecting judges. Section 5 of the Act simply envisaged that the JSC would determine its own selection procedure, which it did in 1996[15] and again in 2003.[16]

A final point worth noting is that the interim Constitution contained 34 agreed constitutional principles (CPs) with which the 'final' Constitution would have to comply. Principles of particular relevance to this chapter were CP VI, calling for a separation of powers, and CP VII, which required the judiciary to be 'appropriately qualified, independent and impartial'.

Under the 1996 Constitution

Under the 1996 Constitution[17] the JSC retains its three main functions (selection and appointment, removal of judges and giving advice) but has an even more inflated membership, summarized below.

As regards selection and appointment, the influence of the JSC varies considerably under of section 174 of the Constitution. In relation to the Chief Justice (head of the Constitutional Court) and Deputy Chief Justice, the JSC is merely one of the parties to be consulted before the President of South Africa makes these appointments. The JSC has a greater role in relation to other judges of the Constitutional Court, for here it recommends candidates for the President to choose from. For this purpose the JSC must prepare a list of nominees 'with three names more than the number of appointments to be made' (section 174(4)). Finally, the JSC effectively has sole responsibility for deciding who will be judges of the High Court and the Supreme Court of Appeal,[18] for these judges are

14 This gap was eventually filled by the Judicial Service Commission Amendment Act 20 of 2008. See further M. Olivier and C. Hoexter, 'The Judicial Service Commission', in C. Hoexter and M. Olivier (contributing eds), *The Judiciary in South Africa*, Claremont: Juta & Co Ltd, 2014.

15 *Procedure of Commission* GN R114 *Government Gazette* 16952 of 2 February 1996, as amended by GN R795 of 13 June 1997 and GN R402 of 5 April 2002.

16 *Procedure of Commission* GN R423 *Government Gazette* 24596 of 27 March 2003.

17 Constitution of the Republic of South Africa, 1996 (hereafter simply 'the Constitution' unless the context demands specificity).

18 After 1994 the Appellate Division remained in existence as one of the two highest courts. Under the 1996 Constitution it was renamed the Supreme Court of Appeal, and since 2013 it has functioned as an intermediate court of appeal between the High Court and the Constitutional Court (the apex court). For further detail see C. Hoexter, 'The Structure of the Courts', in C. Hoexter and M. Olivier (contributing eds), *The Judiciary in South Africa*, Claremont: Juta & Co Ltd, 2014, p. 1.

appointed by the President on the advice of the JSC. Other statutes deal with the role of the JSC in relation to the judges of specialist courts, where again its influence varies. For example, the head of the Land Claims Court is appointed by the President on the advice of the JSC, whereas additional judges of that court are appointed after consultation with the JSC and the head of the court.[19]

The composition of the JSC is specified in section 178(1) of the Constitution. The total membership of the JSC is 23 and occasionally 25 members (that is, when a matter concerns a particular province). However, in terms of section 178 (5), the JSC sits without the members of the legislature when it is considering any matter other than the appointment of a judge. Other subsections make provision for alternates and deputies for some, though not all, members of the JSC, and section 178(3) provides that the nominated and designated members of the JSC serve 'until they are replaced by those who designated or nominated them'. The membership of the JSC may be summarized as follows.

The 'core' JSC consists of the following members who sit in all matters:

The Chief Justice, who presides at meetings (or Deputy)
The President of the Supreme Court of Appeal (or Deputy)
A Judge President designated by the Judges President (or alternate)
Two practising advocates (or alternates) nominated by their profession and appointed by the President
Two practising attorneys (or alternates) nominated by their profession and appointed by the President
A teacher of law (or alternate) designated by teachers of law at South African universities
The Minister of Justice (or alternate)
Four persons designated by the President after consulting the leaders of parties represented in the National Assembly[20]

In matters concerning judicial selection, the following also sit as commissioners:

Six members of the National Assembly, including at least three members of opposition parties
Four permanent delegates to the National Council of Provinces[21]

In matters (including selection matters) concerning a particular province, there are two additional commissioners:

19 Restitution of Land Rights Act 22 of 1994, s. 22.
20 The first house of Parliament; see further 1996 Constitution, ss. 46–59.
21 The second house of Parliament, which represents the provinces and ensures that their interests are taken into account in the national sphere of government. See further 1996 Constitution, ss. 60–72.

The Judge President of that province (or alternate)
The Premier of that province (or alternate)

I now turn to the question of the JSC's institutional legitimacy, something that was acquired quite rapidly in its first decade of existence but has more recently suffered some erosion.

The rise and fall of the JSC's legitimacy

> *How judges are selected is a matter of constitutional significance. Selection is not just about sterile processes. It is about balancing independence, accountability and legitimacy, and ensuring that the process for selection is not captured by any vested interest.*[22]

By the time the Constitutional Court was called upon to decide whether the 1996 Constitution was compliant with the constitutional principles,[23] the JSC was already gaining a reputation for independence, transparency, fairness and rational decision-making. This may help to explain the ease with which the court dismissed objections[24] concerning the composition and thus the independence of the JSC – issues that have become much more problematic in recent years.

More than one factor contributed to the growing legitimacy of the JSC in the early years. One of these was the openness of its process,[25] which includes wide advertising of vacancies and the publication of the names of short-listed candidates. Most significant of all was the JSC's decision to hold public interviews not only with candidates aspiring to the Constitutional Court, but for all other courts as well. This was a controversial move at the time, but it made an impressive contrast with the secrecy of the pre-1994 appointments process and soon began to pay off handsomely. Apart from the interviews themselves, which are not generally well attended by the public, the fact that they are advertised and reported on has done much for the public profile of the JSC as well as enhancing its accountability. Transcripts of interviews are usually available, and video recordings increasingly so.

Another major contribution to the legitimacy of the JSC and its process in the early years was its transformation of the demography of the judiciary in a remarkably short time. In early 1994, out of 166 superior court judges only three were black and two were (white) women. By September 2003, as recorded by François du Bois, 34 per cent of the judges were black (African, 'coloured' or mixed race,

22 Baroness Prashar CBE, 'Translating Aspirations into Reality: Establishing the Judicial Appointments Commission', in Judicial Appointments Commission, *Judicial Appointments: Balancing Independence, Accountability and Legitimacy*, 2010, pp. 43, 53.

23 *Ex parte Chairperson of the Constitutional Assembly: In re Certification of the Constitution of the Republic of South Africa, 1996*, 1996 (4) SA 744 (CC) (*First Certification* case).

24 Objections to the composition of the JSC were received inter alia from the Association of Law Societies and the Human Rights Committee of South Africa. As to objectors more generally, see *First Certification* case, paras 22–24.

25 See K. Malleson, 'Assessing the Performance of the Judicial Service Commission', *South African Law Journal* 116, 1999, pp. 36, 40ff.

and Indian) and 12 per cent were women.[26] While some were impatient with this rate of progress, it was undeniably significant in relation to the limited number of vacancies available and the limited size of the pool from which prospective candidates were being drawn.[27] Importantly, too, it did not entail a dramatic sacrifice of technical competence and experience. In most instances a reasonable balance was achieved and, with a few notable exceptions,[28] the selection record of the JSC in its first decade was a good one.

Further factors contributing to the legitimacy of the JSC were its generally fair and consistent treatment of interviewees and something less overt and tangible but nevertheless crucial: cohesiveness amongst its members. The body appeared to achieve what Kate Malleson describes as 'a coherence and common outlook which transcends the interests of each grouping or individual members'.[29] That, she explains, is a characteristic of notably independent commissions, and by 1998 it seemed to exist to some degree in the JSC. This is borne out by the recollections of a highly respected member regarding the first five years of the JSC: '[T]he culture was that you voted with your conscience, not your constituency, for the truly best candidates.'[30]

What has changed since then? From the point of view of racial demographics, the JSC's achievements are looking really impressive. At the end of March 2017 there were 246 judges, of whom 46 per cent were African, 34 per cent white, 11 per cent coloured and 9 per cent Indian.[31] Of the 20-odd heads of court, only one was white. Gender transformation of the judiciary was lagging behind as it has always done,[32] but was still showing a distinct improvement from 12 per cent women judges in 2004 to 35 per cent in 2017.

These are remarkable achievements – but in spite of them, the JSC has undeniably lost a good deal of its credibility and prestige in recent years. Its success at demographic transformation has been offset by some perverse decision-making, by erratic and unpredictable application of the selection criteria and uneven treatment of candidates in interviews. The independence of the JSC has often been questioned in recent years, and today few doubt the existence of a party-political

26 F. du Bois, 'Judicial Selection in Post-Apartheid South Africa' in K. Malleson and P.H. Russell (eds), *Appointing Judges in an Age of Judicial Power: Critical Perspectives from Around the World*, Toronto: University of Toronto Press, 2006, pp. 280, 287.

27 See Malleson, 'Assessing the JSC', p. 46ff, and on the JSC's efforts to expand the pool, see Du Bois, 'Judicial Selection', pp. 288–290.

28 For instance, the rejection of Geoff Budlender for a High Court position on three occasions. Budlender was an experienced practitioner with a fine human rights record, and he remains one of those 'who have brought only honour to the South African legal system': see R. Kadalie, 'ANC Turning "Justice" into a Game Only it Can Win', *Business Day* (Johannesburg, 20 May 2010).

29 Malleson, 'Assessing the JSC', p. 39.

30 Wim Trengove SC as quoted by N. Tolsi, 'Is the JSC Courting Favourites?' *Mail & Guardian Online* (Johannesburg, 26 April 2012).

31 Statistics as at 31 March 2017 supplied by the JSC and reflecting its terminology.

32 See C. Albertyn, 'Judicial Diversity', in C. Hoexter and M. Olivier (contributing eds), *The Judiciary in South Africa*, Claremont: Juta & Co Ltd, 2014, pp. 245, 283ff.

agenda in its selection decisions: a problem generally attributed to the large number of politicians on the body. The accountability of the JSC, too, was diminished by its refusal to give reasons for its decisions until ordered by a court to do so. Many are convinced that the JSC's composition is the source of all its woes, and that its unwieldy size also detracts from its effectiveness and efficiency. In what follows I deal in more detail with each of these issues, starting with the JSC's size and shape.

The JSC is too big to function effectively

As shown in the summary above, the 13 'core' commissioners who sit on all matters become 15 whenever one of the nine provinces has an interest in the question, i.e. in any matter relating to a division of the High Court. When judicial appointments are being considered, however, the JSC inflates to 23 members, and 25 when the appointment relates to a division of the High Court. This makes South Africa's JSC one of the three biggest judicial appointments commissions in Africa, the others belonging to Nigeria and Rwanda. The JSC is enormous in comparison with other commissions in southern Africa[33] and indeed by Commonwealth standards generally.[34] The most likely explanation for its size is the political horse-trading that went on during the constitutional negotiations.

As is increasingly recognized, these large numbers tend to make the JSC unwieldy. They render almost all its selection tasks more awkward or difficult, from interviewing candidates to distilling reasons for selection decisions. But even when performing its other functions with a reduced membership, the JSC remains clumsily large. This problem may have contributed to the JSC's slowness in resolving certain disciplinary matters[35] and may help to explain why its third function, that of advising the government, has been largely neglected up to now.

Most obviously, perhaps, the large numbers complicate the scheduling of the JSC's meetings and increase the chances of a legal challenge based on improper constitution. One such case confirmed that the Premier of the relevant province is entitled to be present not only when the JSC considers the appointment of a High Court judge, but also when it considers the removal of such a judge.[36] In another a selection meeting was declared invalid partly on account of the absence, without justification, of the President of the Supreme Court of Appeal or his deputy.[37]

33 Lesotho's JSC has four members, Namibia's has five, and those of Botswana and Swaziland have six respectively.

34 See van Zyl Smit, *The Appointment, Tenure and Removal of Judges under Commonwealth Principles*, p. 35.

35 For a full account see Olivier and Hoexter, 'The Judicial Service Commission', pp. 188–198.

36 *Acting Chairperson, Judicial Service Commission v Premier of the Western Cape Province* 2011 (3) SA 538 (SCA) paras 12–18, upholding the decision of the Western Cape High Court in *Premier, Western Cape v Acting Chairperson, Judicial Services Commission* 2010 (5) SA 634 (WCC).

37 *Judicial Service Commission v Cape Bar Council* 2013 (1) SA 170 (SCA) para 36, upholding the decision of the Western Cape High Court in *Cape Bar Council v Judicial Service Commission* 2012 (4) BCLR 406 (WCC).

Such challenges have made the JSC much more careful about ensuring that it is properly constituted at meetings, but problems persist and the unexpected absence of a member inevitably causes delay, inconvenience and expense. For example, when the Premier of the Free State province or his alternate failed to appear at a selection meeting in September 2015, the interviews relating to the High Court in that province had to be rescheduled at considerable cost.[38] Having fewer members might not eliminate such problems altogether, but it would almost certainly reduce their incidence.

A veteran observer of the JSC commented more than a decade ago that 'there are just far too many people involved'.[39] In recent years this has been acknowledged more widely.[40] Even the *National Development Plan 2030*, a major policy document commissioned by the government and adopted by the Cabinet in 2013, admits that the JSC may be 'too large to function effectively'.[41] A private member's Bill was introduced in that same year to reduce the size of the JSC as well as the number of politicians on the body. While the Bill seems to have fizzled out, it is hoped that the authorities have come to appreciate the problem that inspired it. Amazingly enough, only a few years ago the government had plans to enlarge the 'core' JSC still further: clause 10 the Seventeenth Constitution Amendment Bill (B6–2011) would have added the chairperson and deputy chairperson of a new committee proposed to oversee the appointment and promotion of magistrates. In the result, however, the provision was deleted before the Bill became law.[42]

The main justification for having such a large body is the need to reflect the diversity of South Africa's population – about 55 million people speaking 11 different official languages – and to facilitate the expression of diverse views. These are worthy aims, but they are not necessarily achieved by means of sheer numbers, particularly given the preponderance of politicians and the absence of lay members on the JSC. That is the next problem area to be discussed.

The JSC has no (truly) lay members and is overloaded with politicians

There are no lay members on the JSC, or at least none who are not also holders of executive office, parliamentarians or special appointees of the President. This contrasts with judicial appointments commissions in the rest of the Commonwealth, where judges and lawyers tend to be in the majority and politicians in the minority – and for good reason. Obvious and well-documented dangers are associated

38 See e.g. F. Rabkin, 'Judge Selectors Berate Magashule for Delays', *Business Day* (Johannesburg, 8 October 2015).

39 C. Rickard, 'The South African Judicial Service Commission', a response to Department of Constitutional Affairs, *Consultation Paper on Constitutional Reform: A New Way of Appointing Judges*, Pretoria, July 2003, p. 6.

40 See e.g. International Institute for Democracy and Electoral Assistance, *Assessing the Performance of the South African Constitution*, 2016, p. 95.

41 National Planning Commission, *National Development Plan 2030*, 2013, p. 453.

42 The Constitution Seventeenth Amendment Act of 2012.

with overly politicized judicial appointments commissions.[43] Lay membership, on the other hand, is generally credited with a range of benefits that include contributing specific expertise from other types of selection systems, reducing the likelihood of self-replication of the judiciary, and generally bringing 'new approaches and fresh ideas':[44] advantages that may be illustrated by the early experience of UK jurisdictions after the introduction of lay members. While lay membership also creates a risk of politicization, the risk can be substantially reduced by means of appropriately designed processes for choosing those members. A prime example is the process used by the Judicial Appointments Commission (JAC) in England and Wales, which includes open advertising and an independent selection panel.[45]

In South Africa the earliest expectations were that lay members would constitute a majority of the JSC, partly because this was a worldwide trend at the time and partly because this might help compensate to some extent for the untransformed nature of the legal profession and the judiciary. For Corder, writing in 1992, popular legitimacy demanded that 'fair representation of regions, gender and class be attained' on such a body, and it seemed likely that a lay majority on the JSC would be regarded as 'non-negotiable'.[46] This was not to be. As indicated above, the JSC is in fact composed of judges and other legal professionals; politicians drawn mainly from the legislature; and what are generally known as 'political appointees' – that is, members designated by the President. The main justification for this make-up is a link to democratic politics or electoral accountability.[47]

The four presidential appointees are sometimes referred to as lay members, but in practice the President has confined his choices almost entirely to legal professionals – and precisely because they are his choices, the independence of mind of these members may be questioned. There is a similar problem with the parliamentarians on the JSC, most of whom are aligned with the majority party. They are lay in the sense that many of them have not been lawyers, but their political allegiance obviously detracts from their independence and thus from the benefits to be gained by lay membership in the fullest sense. The ideal is, of course, 'to ensure that the selection of lay commissioners does not fall under political control'.[48]

South Africa's JSC is dominated by its political commissioners, who number 15 out of 23 and 16 out of 25. This domination was challenged when the 1996 Constitution was being certified by the Constitutional Court, as was the extent of the influence of the President – who also has indirect influence on the composition

43 See e.g. van Zyl Smit, *The Appointment, Tenure and Removal of Judges under Commonwealth Principles*, paras 1.6.6–1.6.8, referring to the *Latimer House Guidelines* and the recommendations of the Venice Commission on judicial appointments.

44 K. Malleson, 'Appointment, Discipline and Removal of Judges: Fundamental Reforms in the United Kingdom', in H. P. Lee (ed.), *Judiciaries in Comparative Perspective*, Cambridge: Cambridge University Press, 2011, pp. 117, 123.

45 See van Zyl Smit, *The Appointment, Tenure and Removal of Judges under Commonwealth Principles*, paras 1.6.16–1.6.17.

46 Corder, 'The Appointment of Judges', p. 227.

47 See Malleson, 'Assessing the JSC', pp. 39–40.

48 van Zyl Smit, *The Appointment, Tenure and Removal of Judges under Commonwealth Principles*, para 1.6.16.

of the JSC by virtue of his appointing the Chief Justice, the Minister of Justice and so on. Both challenges failed. The court reasoned that the constitutional principles did not even require the creation of a JSC, let alone stipulate how it ought to be constituted, and that the composition of the body was a political choice with which the court could not interfere.[49]

This deferential attitude seemed to be justified by the JSC's performance over the next few years. But the JSC's composition has again become controversial in more recent years, particularly since July 2009, when four new presidential appointments were named and the sole opposition delegate from the National Council of Provinces was also replaced. At the time there was speculation about packing the JSC with supporters of the governing party (the African National Congress or ANC),[50] and since then there have been many allegations of a party-political agenda in the selection of judges.[51]

Sad to relate, hardly any observer of the JSC has doubted the existence of such an agenda at some stage or another, for 'cadre deployment' is an official policy of the ANC, and its main thrust is to ensure that party members occupy important public positions.[52] In 2013 even the National Planning Commission seemed to accept the argument that the JSC is 'hamstrung by political interests';[53] and in 2016, an International IDEA report on the South African Constitution recommended that section 178 (regulating the JSC's composition) should be amended to reduce the number of political appointees.[54]

The JSC's application of the selection criteria has been erratic

The interim Constitution merely required the JSC to have regard to the need for a Constitutional Court that was 'independent and competent and representative in respect of race and gender'.[55] By contrast, the 1996 Constitution addresses judges in general. Section 174(1) states that judges must be 'appropriately qualified' and 'fit and proper'.[56] Section 174(2) contains an express demography or diversity

49 *First Certification* case, para 124.
50 P. de Vos, 'ANC Trying to "Load" the JSC?', *Constitutionally Speaking,* 10 July 2009.
51 Amongst many possible examples, see Kadalie, 'ANC turning "Justice" into a Game'; Editorial, 'Stuck with the ANC's JSC', *Business Day* (Johannesburg, 4 October 2011); D. Gleason 'From My Window', *Without Prejudice* (Johannesburg, May 2012); Tolsi, 'Is the JSC Courting Favourites?'; M. Ramphele and Z. Dawood, 'Crisis in Choosing Judges Needs Active Citizenship', *Business Day* (Johannesburg, 17 May 2012).
52 See e.g. C. Twala, 'The African National Congress (ANC) and the Cadre Deployment Policy in Post-Apartheid South Africa: A Product of Democratic Centralisation or a Recipe for a Constitutional Crisis', *Journal of Social Science* 41, 2014, p. 159 and other writing cited there; and in relation to the JSC in particular, see e.g. Kadalie, 'ANC turning "Justice" into a Game'.
53 National Planning Commission, *National Development Plan*, p. 453.
54 International IDEA, *Assessing the Performance of the South African Constitution,* p. 95.
55 Interim Constitution, s. 99(5)*(d)*.
56 In the *First Certification* case, para 122, the Constitutional Court held that these were 'objective criteria subject to constitutional control by the courts, and meet the requirements of CP VII in that regard'.

requirement that instructs the JSC to take into account '[t]he need for the judiciary to reflect broadly the racial and gender composition of South Africa' when appointments are being considered.

It need hardly be said that the legitimacy of South Africa's judicial selection process depends critically on the transparent, rational and consistent interpretation and application of these constitutional requirements. As others have pointed out, they are not simple or straightforward provisions: there is plenty of room for debate about the meaning and constituents of the merit requirements and about whether section 174 (2) speaks to demographic representation or to diversity in a deeper and more substantive sense.[57] The JSC, it seems, has generally favoured demographic representation and has prioritized race over other criteria.[58] That is a pity, for as Catherine Albertyn argues, a judiciary has far greater transformative potential when it is diverse in terms of culture, religion, politics, values and judicial philosophy. Focusing exclusively on race tends to reduce section 174(2) to a requirement of 'mere representivity'.[59]

But there are also problems of incoherence, inconsistency and irrationality in the application of the selection criteria, and this notwithstanding the JSC's publication of more detailed criteria and guidelines for questioning of candidates in 1994,[60] 1998[61] and most recently in 2010.[62] In practice these guiding documents have not prevented the JSC from applying the criteria with notable inconsistency, sometimes seeming to elevate technical competence and experience above all else, and at other times giving the impression of disregarding these qualities almost entirely in favour of demographic considerations. Even poor past performance as a judge has been disregarded in this way.[63] And it is not only technical competence that has been sacrificed: there has also been a very worrying tendency to pass over top performers who are also known for their commitment to the Constitution and its values.[64] The JSC has often seemed strangely suspicious of candidates with a

57 See Olivier, 'The Selection and Appointment of Judges', p. 131ff and Albertyn, 'Judicial Diversity', p. 275ff. On the interpretation and application of the criteria in earlier years, see Malleson, 'Assessing the JSC', p. 46ff and Du Bois, 'Judicial Selection', p. 290ff.

58 Albertyn, 'Judicial Diversity', pp. 279–283, 286.

59 Ibid., p. 281. International IDEA, *Assessing the Performance of the South African Constitution*, p. 96 concludes that 'a possibility for debate' is whether s. 178 ought to be amended to reflect the need for aspects of diversity apart from gender and race.

60 Judicial Service Commission, 'Guidelines for Questioning Candidates for Nomination to the Constitutional Court' (26 September 1994), in *JSC Handbook*, Pretoria, 2010, p. 67.

61 Judicial Service Commission, *Annual Report 1999.*

62 Judicial Service Commission, 'Summary of the Criteria Used by the Judicial Service Commission When Considering Candidates for Judicial Appointments', in *JSC Handbook*, Pretoria, 2010, p. 73.

63 For examples of promotion to a higher court notwithstanding negative reports, see Olivier and Hoexter, 'The Judicial Service Commission', p. 178.

64 Egregious examples from recent years include the passing over of Jeremy Gauntlett SC in respect of the Western Cape High Court (October 2012), on which there were five vacancies at the time; and Judge Clive Plasket (twice) in respect of the Supreme Court of Appeal.

strong background in human rights,[65] and this is one reason why the National Planning Commission has suggested that the criteria ought expressly to include a 'progressive philosophy'.[66]

This erratic performance has led to bitter accusations against the JSC from time to time, and even to a court challenge by the Helen Suzman Foundation on grounds of irrationality.[67] It has also shocked observers around the world. As Sir Jeffrey Jowell QC lamented in a keynote address in 2012, some of the candidates rejected

> would simply grace the bench of any top court in any country in the world, and if their rejection was due to their political affiliation or lack of affiliation, or to their habit of independence (and I venture no opinion on that) then the loss is South Africa's alone, and that loss is beyond calculation.[68]

Unfortunately, there is continuing uncertainty about how the merit and diversity requirements are interpreted and balanced by the JSC in practice. This has been widely acknowledged. In 2010, for instance, the Democratic Governance & Rights Unit (DGRU) at the University of Cape Town remarked on the JSC's apparent 'lack of a clear, unified vision of what criteria to apply',[69] and in 2013 the National Planning Commission suggested that there is 'little or no consensus' in the JSC about 'the qualities and attributes needed for the bench'.[70]

The JSC's interviewing of candidates has not always been even-handed

Writing in 1998, Malleson described the JSC's public interviews as generally being conducted 'politely and even-handedly' and 'with dignity and restraint'.[71] Indeed, in its first few years one commissioner, a professor of law, felt that the interviews were too bland and that the JSC was erring on the side of restraint.[72] By 2009, the JSC's interviewing style had changed along with its membership, and that year stands out as one in which the texture and tone of its interviews varied greatly. Corder records a trend towards 'intrusive and occasionally aggressive' questioning,

65 See e.g. Democratic Governance & Rights Unit, *Report of October 2010*, para 25.
66 National Planning Commission, *National Development Plan*, p. 453.
67 The main application, concerning the non-appointment of Jeremy Gauntlett SC, awaits the resolution of an interlocutory dispute about access to the full record of the JSC's deliberations. At the time of going to press such access had been refused both at first instance and on appeal, and the matter had been set down for hearing by the Constitutional Court. See further the text to notes 90–92 below.
68 Sir Jeffrey Jowell QC, 'The Appointment and Accountability of Judges', a lecture delivered on 16 May 2012 and published in Helen Suzman Foundation, *Delivering Justice: The Appointment and Accountability of Judges* (undated), pp. 10, 13.
69 Democratic Governance & Rights Unit, *Report of April 2010*, p. 2.
70 National Planning Commission, *National Development Plan*, p. 453.
71 Malleson, 'Assessing the JSC', p. 49.
72 E. Mureinik, *Report to Deans of Law by the Academic Representative on the Judicial Service Commission*, 1996.

particularly of white candidates, and particularly on the subject of transformation of the judiciary and the legal system.[73] Such interviews made a contrast with the far more deferential interviews of the JSC's 'sweethearts', including that of the current Chief Justice when he was being considered for a place on the Constitutional Court.[74]

This trend remained evident in subsequent years and reached its apogee in 2012 and 2013. Unfortunately it could not simply be attributed to an understandable wish to question white candidates more closely than others about their commitment to transformation; for some strong black candidates were also given a hard time,[75] while a few white candidates also appeared to be darlings of the JSC and had far cosier interviews than others. For example, there was a striking contrast between the 'intensity of scrutiny' as well as the length of the interviews of two white men for the same post on the Supreme Court of Appeal, a difference dubbed 'patently unfair' by observers from the DGRU.[76] These were amongst the troubling signs that the JSC and especially its ANC-aligned commissioners favoured politically compliant candidates, or candidates whom they imagined to be compliant, over more independent-minded or outspoken ones.

However, there are now hopeful signs that the JSC is regaining some of its earlier balance, for in October 2015 it was praised for sensitive and nuanced interviewing. The chair for that round, Deputy Chief Justice Dikgang Moseneke (who has since retired), evidently set an excellent example of rigorous but fair questioning, and showed how to handle difficult topics such as the long-term effects of racial discrimination. While the chair did not shy away from exposing white privilege and its structural legacy, he kept a tight rein on the proceedings and managed to give the interviews 'an air of sensitivity and grace'.[77]

Further good news is that the sexism and gender insensitivity sometimes evident in JSC interviews in previous years[78] seem largely to have been addressed. That said, in 2014 the JSC displayed an extraordinary lack of sympathy to a woman judge who was requesting a transfer to a different division in order to be closer to

73 H. Corder, 'Appointment, Discipline and Removal of Judges in South Africa', in H. P. Lee (ed.), *Judiciaries in Comparative Perspective*, Cambridge: Cambridge University Press, 2011, pp. 96, 104.

74 The transcript of his interview is available online at *Constitutionally Speaking* (www.constitutionallyspeaking.co.za) (accessed 12 October 2015).

75 An example is the interview of Judge Phineas Mojapelo for a Judge Presidency in 2012. Mojapelo drew fire from the JSC for an opinion piece in which he had called for more transparency and public participation in the appointment of Chief Justice.

76 Democratic Governance & Rights Unit, *Report of October 2013*, paras 17–18; and see also e.g. N. Tolsi, 'JSC conflict Laid Bare by Inconsistency', *Mail & Guardian*, 12 April 2013. The DGRU had commented previously that discrepancies in questioning tend to create the perception that 'interviews are not the main tool' used to establish the suitability of candidates: see Democratic Governance & Rights Unit,*Report of April 2010*, p. 2.

77 N. Tolsi, 'Light Grilling for Wannabe Judges', *Mail & Guardian* (Johannesburg, 9–15 October 2015), p. 9.

78 For examples see Olivier and Hoexter, 'The Judicial Service Commission', pp. 180–1.

her three children, one mentally disabled and the other two evidently traumatized by their father's arrest on a charge of rape.[79]

Consistency and fairness in the treatment of candidates who appear before the JSC are essential to the legitimacy of the commission and its selection process. Guidelines or protocols for conducting interviews are necessary and useful, but South Africa's experience suggests that they are not enough on their own: they have to be firmly enforced. The tone set by the chairperson is also critical, so it seems that the need for careful and tactful as well as confident chairing cannot be overstated.

The JSC fought against giving reasons

In terms of its governing statute the JSC is required to report to Parliament annually,[80] and the JSC's own Procedure of 2003 requires it to 'distil and record' its reasons for recommending any candidates for appointment to the Constitutional Court.[81] Apart from this, there is little explicit provision for the accountability of the JSC. In relation to the selection of judges of other courts, the 2003 Procedure is silent on the subject of reasons, as are the Constitution and the JSC Act. Furthermore, selection decisions of the JSC are expressly excluded from the definition of 'administrative action' in the Promotion of Administrative Justice Act 3 of 2000 (PAJA),[82] and thus cannot attract the general duty to give reasons under section 5 of that statute.

Perhaps the JSC cannot be blamed, then, for believing that it was not required to explain any of its selection decisions other than recommendations for appointment to the Constitutional Court. But for some time this belief was a source of further frustration to those bemused by apparently perverse selection decisions of the JSC.

This frustration boiled over in April 2011, when the JSC interviewed seven shortlisted candidates for three vacancies on the Western Cape High Court and decided to recommend only one of them, who happened to be the only candidate of colour amongst the seven. The decision to leave two positions vacant in a busy division struck many observers as irrational, particularly since the six other candidates included three silks, one of whom had been endorsed by the Cape Bar Council as especially suitable for the bench. By shortlisting all these candidates, the JSC had indicated that it regarded them all as appropriately qualified and fit and proper, as required by section 174(1) of the Constitution. Nor, when the case went to court, did the JSC seek to rely on diversity or race representivity to

79 See M. van Eeden, 'JSC Rejects Plea of Tearful Judge', *Litigator*, 10 October 2014; K. Hindle, 'The New JSC in a Man's World', *The Con*, 10 November 2014.

80 Judicial Service Commission Act, s. 6.

81 *Procedure of Commission,* GN R423. The Procedure gives effect to s. 174(4) of the Constitution, which allows the President to make his choice from a list of Constitutional Court nominees prepared by the JSC.

82 Section 1(*b*)(*gg*) excludes from the definition decisions 'regarding the nomination, selection or appointment of a judicial officer ... by the Judicial Service Commission'.

explain its decision. Its bland (and infuriating) answer was simply that none of the six had in the end received a majority vote. The JSC protested that it did not know the reasons why individual members had voted in a particular way, and that any demand to know would jeopardize the integrity of its voting procedure, which was by secret ballot.

The JSC's arguments failed to persuade the High Court.[83] On appeal by the JSC in *Judicial Service Commission* v *Cape Bar Council*,[84] the Supreme Court of Appeal rightly wondered why, if the JSC were able to distil reasons for one type of decision, it could not do so for others. The court confirmed that, like all who wield public power under South Africa's democratic Constitution, the JSC is bound to act rationally in accordance with the rule of law and a particular aspect of it, the principle of legality,[85] and bound to *demonstrate* that rationality if required. Ultimately, this meant that the JSC had to give reasons for its decisions if properly called upon to do so, for 'exemption from giving reasons will … almost invariably result in immunity from an irrationality challenge'.[86] Reasons, disparate or not, could be distilled from the deliberations preceding the vote, the court suggested, or they could be given anonymously.[87] In any event the JSC could not hide behind its voting procedure, but had to change that procedure if necessary in order to comply with its constitutional duty to act rationally.[88]

One cannot but feel that a great deal of trouble as well as litigation could have been avoided if this issue had been anticipated and expressly dealt with in the legislative framework or the JSC's Procedure. Given the emphasis placed on accountability, transparency and rationality by the Constitution, it seems obvious that the JSC should have to account for its decisions in this way.

The JSC has in fact been asked for, and has provided, written reasons for decisions since then, most famously for the non-selection of Jeremy Gauntlett SC for a vacancy on the Western Cape High Court.[89] The reasons given prompted a challenge based on irrationality as well as interlocutory litigation concerning access to the record of the JSC's decision-making. At first instance the High Court refused an application for access to the full record (including the audio recording and any transcript) of the JSC's deliberations in the Gauntlett matter.[90] After making a thorough survey of practices and attitudes in other jurisdictions, Le Grange J observed that South Africa's JSC is already far more transparent than many comparable judicial selection bodies – including the JAC

83 *Cape Bar Council v Judicial Service Commission*.
84 *Judicial Service Commission v Cape Bar Council*, para 50.
85 Ibid., paras 20–22.
86 Ibid., para 44.
87 Ibid., 50.
88 Ibid., 47.
89 See Hoexter and Olivier, 'The Judicial Service Commission', p. 183. In this instance the requester was the person who had nominated Gauntlett for appointment.
90 *Helen Suzman Foundation v Judicial Service Commission* 2015 (2) SA 498 (WCC).

in England and Wales.[91] He also noted several reasons for keeping the deliberations of such bodies confidential, such as the chilling and deterrent effects of too much transparency.[92] His judgment was upheld by the Supreme Court of Appeal, which agreed that the relief sought would 'hamper effective judicial selection'.[93] At the time of going to press the matter had been set down for hearing by the Constitutional Court.

Conclusion

South Africa's JSC was established as part of the answer to a crisis of legitimacy in the pre-1994 judiciary, and soon acquired credibility and respect for the transparency of its process, its fairness towards candidates and the rationality of most of its selection decisions. This chapter has argued, however, that the legitimacy won by South Africa's JSC in its first decade as an appointments commission has been eroded over the last few years, and particularly since 2009, by factors including its erratic and even irrational application of selection criteria, its uneven treatment of candidates and its unwillingness to give reasons for its decisions until ordered to do so. The JSC seems to have lost the sense of cohesiveness and common purpose that it achieved early on, and may be suffering from a legitimacy crisis of its own – notwithstanding the tremendous race and (to a lesser extent) gender transformation of the judiciary that it has accomplished over the last two decades. Indeed, the price paid for that transformation has been very high, for the dispiriting conclusion reached by a 2016 International IDEA report is that the South African Constitution 'has failed to ensure the creation of a process for the appointment of judges that is fully independent and credible in the eyes of the public'.[94]

This erosion of legitimacy no doubt has chilling effects on potential candidates for judicial office, as inconsistency, irrationality and unfairness are not likely to encourage good applicants to make themselves available for vacancies. It is not unusual after a round of JSC interviews for some of the positions advertised to be left unfilled; and it is especially worrying that in recent years the JSC has had to extend the deadline for applications for the highest court on three occasions (in 2012, 2015 and 2016) owing to an insufficient number of candidates to meet the constitutional threshold.[95]

91 Ibid., para 48; see the extract quoted from the JAC's publication policy at para 42 and decisions of the Information Tribunal and Information Commissioner referred to at para 43.

92 *Helen Suzman Foundation v Judicial Service Commission*, para 48.

93 *Helen Suzman Foundation v Judicial Service Commission* 2017 (1) SA 367 (SCA) para 39.

94 International IDEA, *Assessing the Performance of the South African Constitution*, p. 95.

95 As noted above, for a vacancy on the Constitutional Court the JSC is required by s. 174(4) of the Constitution to prepare a list of three more names than the number of appointments to be made. See e.g. F. Rabkin, 'Judges Fail to Apply for Vacancy at Top Court', *BDlive*, 1 March 2016.

The JSC is seemingly hampered by its size and general unwieldiness and has also been handicapped in some respects by the absence of a detailed legislative framework for its work. On the other hand, detailed guidelines for questioning and selecting candidates have not prevented the tendencies identified above, and there is little doubt that the root of the problem is the large contingent of politicians on the commission. South Africa opted for a JSC in the form of a broadly-based selection panel[96] in order to avoid a politically partisan system of appointing judges, but may have succeeded merely in replacing 'one form of undue influence with another'.[97]

96 *First Certification* case, para 124.
97 Malleson, 'Assessing the JSC', p. 37.

6 Diversity without a judicial appointments commission

The Australian experience

Andrew Lynch[1]

Introduction

Australia, at the Commonwealth, state and territory levels, remains faithful to the practice of appointing judicial officers by essentially unconstrained executive discretion. However, in the mid-2000s, Australian judges and legal academics did give substantial attention to the issue of reforming the means of judicial selection and appointment.[2] This development was undoubtedly prompted in part by some political frankness from government about seeking to make ideological appointments to the High Court of Australia ('the High Court') and also concerns about that body's all-male membership.[3] However, the more positive catalyst appeared to be the changes to the selection of judges for the courts of England and Wales that were introduced by the Constitutional Reform Act 2005, specifically the establishment of the Judicial Appointments Commission (JAC).[4] Various adaptations of the JAC were proposed by contributors to the Australian debate as a model for the reform of Australian appointment practices

1 Some parts of this chapter revisit arguments made in earlier work co-authored with Professor Elizabeth Handsley. I thank Gabrielle Appleby for comments on a draft of this chapter.

2 See notably, G. Brennan, 'The Selection of Judges for Commonwealth Courts', in Department of the Senate, *The Senate and Accountability*, Papers on Parliament No 48, January 2008, p. 1; R. Davis and G. Williams, 'Reform of the Judicial Appointments Process: Gender and the Bench of the High Court of Australia', *Melbourne University Law Review* 27, 2003, p. 819; S. Evans and J. Williams, 'Appointing Australian Judges: A New Model', *Sydney Law Review* 30, 2008, p. 295; R. Sackville, 'The Judicial Appointments Process in Australia: Towards Independence and Accountability', *Journal of Judicial Administration* 16, 2007, p. 125; and G. Williams, 'High Court Appointments: The Need for Reform' *Sydney Law Review* 30, 2008, p. 163.

3 See E. Handsley and A. Lynch, 'Facing up to Diversity? Transparency and the Reform of Commonwealth Judicial Appointments 2008–13', *Sydney Law Review* 37, 2015, pp. 187, 194.

4 Australian advocacy for an appointments commission pre-dates the establishment of the JAC in the United Kingdom by almost 30 years: G. Barwick 'The State of the Australian Judicature', *Australian Law Journal* 51, 1977, pp. 480, 494.

which were, particularly at the Commonwealth level, opaque and exclusively at the discretion of the executive.[5]

Enthusiasm for the JAC was not shared by Australia's elected representatives, although they were not immune to the significance of the English reforms. Shortly after the Labor government won office in late 2007, the new Commonwealth Attorney-General Robert McClelland implemented a number of modest, non-statutory changes to the method of selecting judges for the federal courts. McClelland's remarks when outlining the case for reform clearly illustrate that the importance of the creation of the JAC stretches beyond England and Wales. McClelland's agenda had much in common with the justifications that had supported establishment of the JAC, but although he pointedly did not rule out the prospect of establishing an Australian version of that body at some future time, he said that to do so 'would not be a step to be taken lightly'.[6] He explained that a commission did not feature in his immediate plans because there 'may well be as much controversy associated with selecting the selectors as with the judicial appointments themselves'.[7] McClelland noted criticisms that the JAC was 'overly bureaucratic and the whole appointments process is unreasonably intrusive as well as taking too long'.[8] McClelland's reluctance received endorsement from the Senate Legal and Constitutional Affairs References Committee which held an inquiry into the Australian judiciary in 2009.[9] Its members questioned the cost of establishing a commission and were 'not convinced that a JAC is the only way to implement effective and appropriate selection processes'.[10]

No Australian government has taken the path of establishing a judicial appointments commission. Undoubtedly, one consequence of the political preference for more limited reform has been to make those efforts inherently vulnerable. There are several illustrations of this phenomenon, but none as notable as the complete abandonment of McClelland's reforms after the federal Labor

5 For a contemporaneous description, see E. Handsley, '"The judicial whisper goes around": Appointment of Judicial Officers in Australia', in K. Malleson and P.H. Russell (eds) *Appointing Judges in an Age of Judicial Power: Critical Perspectives from Around the World*, Toronto: University of Toronto Press, 2006, p. 122. A recent report of practices in all nine Australian jurisdictions reveals that little has changed, although some states and territories have more sophisticated processes, at least for lower level courts, than others: Judicial Conference of Australia, *Judicial Appointments: A Comparative Study*, April 2015.

6 R. McClelland, 'Judicial Appointments Forum', Speech delivered at Bar Association of Queensland Annual Conference, Gold Coast, 17 February 2008, para 68.

7 Ibid.

8 Ibid., para 66. Early procedural inefficiencies have since been resolved: K. Malleson, 'Appointment, Discipline and Removal of Judges: Fundamental Reforms in the United Kingdom', in H. P. Lee (ed.), *Judiciaries in Comparative Perspective*, Cambridge: Cambridge University Press, 2011, pp. 117, 125. However, Australian perceptions of the process as overly elaborate endure: Justice Philip McMurdo, 'Hot Topics', Supreme Court and Federal Judges' Conference, Darwin, 9 July 2014.

9 Senate Legal and Constitutional Affairs References Committee, Parliament of Australia, *Australia's Judicial System and the Role of Judges*, 2009, p. 30, para 3.90.

10 Ibid., p. 29, para 3.89.

government lost office in 2013.[11] There were essentially three components to McClelland's enhancements to the process of selecting judges for appointment to the federal courts (excluding the High Court): (1) detailed, publicly available criteria; (2) the advertisement of vacancies and a call for expressions of interest and nominations; and (3) the use of narrowly constituted Advisory Panels to make recommendations to the Attorney-General.[12] The cessation of these processes by the Coalition government that took office in 2013 under Prime Minister Tony Abbott was not formally announced and the Commonwealth's only public information on the subject, beyond the bare statutory eligibility requirements, remains that: '[a]s the nation's first law officer, the Attorney-General is responsible for recommending judicial appointments to the Australian Government'.[13] If McClelland's reforms had involved transferring responsibility for some stage of the selection process to an appointments commission, they would presumably have taken a statutory form and enjoyed greater security against such reversal.

This chapter explores another consequence of the Australian reluctance to create a judicial appointments commission by asking what effect this has had on judicial diversity. The first part of that inquiry considers the extent to which the executive-based reforms implemented by McClelland possessed structural features that left space for diversity to be considered in selection. The simple answer to this is that the reforms imposed no constraint upon the executive's traditional discretion. But of course, without more, that discretion need hardly result in a more diverse judiciary, so the second issue to be considered is how diversity was expressly prioritized as an objective. Although Australian rhetoric on judicial appointments has been generally consistent with the United Kingdom's statutory

11 Another is provided by changes in the State of Victoria. In the first decade of the century, the Victorian Labor government advertised all judicial positions, but after 2010, the Coalition government abandoned that practice. Labor returned to power in 2014 and instituted a standing call for expressions of interest on its Courts website: Judicial Conference of Australia, *Judicial Appointments*, pp. 43–44. See further, C. Merritt, 'Mark Dreyfus: Liberals "have dropped ball" on reform', *The Australian*, 3 June 2016, p. 27.

12 See Attorney-General's Department, Australian Government, *Judicial Appointments: Ensuring a Strong, Independent and Diverse Judiciary through a Transparent Process*, April 2010. For commentary, see Handsley and Lynch, 'Facing up to Diversity?', pp. 196–198; and H. P. Lee, 'Appointment, Discipline and Removal of Judges in Australia', in H. P. Lee (ed.), *Judiciaries in Comparative Perspective*, Cambridge: Cambridge University Press, 2011, pp. 27, 29–30. The Advisory Panels were typically comprised of the head of jurisdiction of the relevant court (or their nominee), a retired judge or senior member of the federal or state judiciary and a senior officer in the Commonwealth Attorney-General's Department: Senate Legal and Constitutional Affairs References Committee, *Australia's Judicial System*, p. 14, para 3.17. Greater representation of former judicial officers seems to have occurred on occasion: see M. Kirby, 'A Darwinian Reflection on Judicial Values and Appointments to Final National Courts', in J. Lee (ed.), *From House of Lords to Supreme Court: Judges, Jurists and the Process of Judging*, Oxford: Hart Publishing, 2011, pp. 9, 29.

13 Attorney General's Department, 'Court appointments', Online, Available <www.ag.gov.au/LegalSystem/Courts/Pages/Courtappointments.aspx> (accessed 9 February 2017).

requirement that 'merit' alone determines selection while diversity is merely to be 'encouraged',[14] it is possible to see less reticence, at least amongst the judiciary, about the value of preserving executive discretion so that diversity may be deliberately addressed in the selection of judges.

The chapter then moves to consider actual progress towards greater gender diversity in the courts of Australia compared with those of England and Wales.[15] The disappointed expectations of those who hoped to see greater diversity on the bench follow the enactment of the Constitutional Reform Act in 2005 has been attributed to the 'disproportionate influence'[16] that the judiciary has in selection processes, especially, but not limited to, their presence and roles as commissioners of the JAC and the special selection commissions convened for senior appointments.[17] These concerns remain despite amendments made to the original arrangements in 2013.[18] By contrast, Australia's adherence to an exclusively executive model of judicial appointment highlights the ease with which judicial diversity may be advanced by political will – where it exists.[19]

On first impression, a comparison between the two jurisdictions may appear to confirm that the establishment of an independent commission limited to addressing diversity at the preliminary stage of identifying candidates will have only a muted impact on the profile of the judiciary. In particular, the stark disparity between female appointments to the final court in each jurisdiction in the last decade suggests that the elaborate English model has achieved independence from government in appointments at the expense of diversification. That observation may indeed be true, but the Australian experience needs to be more extensively considered before it can be said to provide compelling confirmation, let alone one

14 Constitutional Reform Act 2005 (CRA) (UK), ss. 63 and 64.

15 Judicial diversity obviously extends beyond gender to include many other attributes and experiences (see e.g. the factors discussed at E. Campbell and H. P. Lee, *The Australian Judiciary*, Cambridge: Cambridge University Press, 2nd edition, 2013, pp. 35–40), but reliable statistics on these in Australian courts are difficult to obtain: B. Opeskin, 'The State of the Judicature: A Statistical Profile of Australian Courts and Judges', *Sydney Law Review*, 2013, pp. 489, 512–513.

16 G. Gee, R. Hazell, K. Malleson and P. O'Brien, *The Politics of Judicial Independence in the UK's Changing Constitution*, Cambridge: Cambridge University Press, 2015, p. 191.

17 Ibid., pp. 170–193, 217–220; A. Paterson and C. Paterson, *Guarding the Guardians? Towards an Independent, Accountable and Diverse Senior Judiciary*, London: CentreForum, 2012, pp. 40–51.

18 Crime and Courts Act 2013 (UK), Sch 13; The Supreme Court (Judicial Appointments) Regulations 2013 (UK); The Judicial Appointments Regulations 2013 (UK), and The Judicial Appointments Commission Regulations 2013 (UK). See A. Blackham, 'Court Appointment Processes and Judicial Diversity', *Public Law Review* 24, 2013, p. 233; Gee *et al*, *The Politics of Judicial Independence*, pp. 177–179, 219; and P. O'Brien, 'Changes to Judicial Appointments in the Crime and Courts Act 2013', *Public Law*, 2014, p. 179.

19 J. van Zyl Smit, *The Appointment, Tenure and Removal of Judges under Commonwealth Principles*, London: Bingham Centre for the Rule of Law, 2015, pp. 16, 130.

that sustains that jurisdiction's own reluctance to embrace substantial judicial appointments reform.

Judicial diversity – an encouraging objective

The statutory obligation of the JAC to 'have regard to the need to encourage diversity in the range of persons available for selection for appointments'[20] is expressly subject to the requirement that selection is on merit alone.[21] Kate Malleson has lamented this as the result of judicial diversity having been 'downgraded' from an initial focus on who is actually appointed to simply an exercise in widening the pool from which individuals are selected.[22] That more modest emphasis is pointed to by some to explain the slow pace of change in the profile of the senior English judiciary that has been achieved under the new system.[23]

The traditional rhetoric of 'merit alone' has long been dominant in Australia,[24] but it was fortified by the statutory articulation of merit as the exclusive criterion for appointment in the Constitutional Reform Act. In 2006, the academic proponents of a new model of appointing Australian judges that drew directly on the design of the JAC, as representing 'best practices within the common law constitutional tradition', similarly insisted that 'selection must be solely on merit'.[25] That work was cited by the Senate Legal and Constitutional Affairs References Committee before it endorsed 'an approach consistent with the United Kingdom Constitution Reform Act 2005, which emphasises merit and promotes diversity'.[26]

20 CRA, s. 64(1).

21 CRA, ss. 63(2) and 64(2). A so-called 'tie-breaker' clause was added in s. 63(4) by the *Crime and Courts Act 2013* (UK) (see also, CRA, s. 27(5A)) which operates only where the 'two persons are of equal merit'. That scenario was initially perceived as one that would occur only rarely in practice (see Ministry of Justice, *Improving Judicial Diversity: Progress Towards Delivery of the 'Report of the Advisory Panel on Judicial Diversity 2010*, May 2011, p. 330), but between April 2016 and March 2017, just 12 out of 282 recommendations made by the JAC applied the provision: Judicial Appointments Commission, *Judicial Selection and Recommendations for Appointment Statistics 1 April 2016 to 31 March 2017*, 1 June 2017, p. 12.

22 Malleson, 'Appointment, Discipline and Removal of Judges: Fundamental Reforms in the United Kingdom', pp. 119–120; and K. Malleson, 'Diversity in the Judiciary: The Case for Positive Action', *Journal of Law and Society* 36, 2009, pp. 376, 378–380.

23 E. Rackley, *Women, Judging and the Judiciary: From Difference to Diversity*, London: Routledge, 2013, p. 93. See also J. Straw, *The Hamlyn Lectures – Aspects of Law Reform: An Insider's Perspective*, Cambridge: Cambridge University Press, 2013 pp. 51–59, Cf. Lord Sumption, 'Home Truths about Judicial Diversity', speech delivered at the Bar Council Law Reform Lecture, London, 15 November 2012, pp. 8–9.

24 See B. Debelle, 'Judicial Appointments: the Case for Reform', in *Upholding the Australian Constitution – Volume 21*, Sir Samuel Griffith Society, 2009, p. 82; and H. Gibbs, 'The Appointment of Judges', *Australian Law Journal* 61, 1987, pp. 7, 10.

25 Evans and Williams, 'Appointing Australian Judges', p. 313. See also Sackville, 'The Judicial Appointments Process in Australia', p. 143.

26 Senate Legal and Constitutional Affairs References Committee, *Australia's Judicial System*, p. 23, para 3.60.

The Committee saw no awkwardness in so expressly adopting the English lead on the basis for appointment while nevertheless declining to follow its example as to process through the creation of an independent appointments commission similar to the JAC.

In revealing his modest plans for reform to a wary profession, Attorney-General McClelland was careful not to deviate from the accepted formula, saying, 'I am firmly wedded to the principles of greater transparency, selection of candidates on merit only and ensuring greater diversity in appointments where possible'.[27] He certainly did not follow the example of his Labor predecessor, Commonwealth Attorney-General Michael Lavarch, who in 1993 had initiated a discussion on judicial appointments by including in a suggested list of possible selection criteria both 'fair reflection of society by the judiciary' and 'temper, gender and cultural sensitivity'.[28] Fifteen years later, McClelland candidly acknowledged that his reforms had the objective of 'pursuing the evolution of the federal judiciary into one that better reflects the rich diversity of the Australian community'.[29] In that respect, the government specified gender, geography, professional background and experience, and cultural background as the relevant focus of moves to improve diversity.[30] But crucially, unlike Lavarch, McClelland did not include diversity among the stated criteria for appointment. Formally at least, diversity played no part at the point of selection under these reforms.

There have been a few Australian challengers to the view that diversity is something merely to be 'encouraged'. In 2008, George Williams, an academic at the University of New South Wales, said he would include 'diversity in the judiciary' as one of four broad categories to 'give meaning and substance to the inherently subjective notion of merit'.[31] In the same year, the barrister Stephen Gageler SC, since appointed to the High Court of Australia, advocated a classic 'minimal merit' approach:[32]

> I would have one method for identifying the pool of potential judicial candidates and another for choosing amongst them. Both stages would be transparent. The first stage would be solely concerned with identifying persons having what I have described as the essential judicial attributes. At the second stage, I would be happy to see the broader considerations to which I have referred openly brought to the fore and debated.[33]

27 McClelland, 'Judicial Appointments Forum', para 70.
28 Commonwealth of Australia, *Discussion Paper: Judicial Appointments – Procedure and Criteria*, 1993, pp. 5–10. Handsley has said 'the radical nature of this list cannot be overestimated': Handsley, '"The judicial whisper goes around"', p. 132.
29 Attorney-General's Department, *Judicial Appointments*, p. 1.
30 Ibid.
31 Williams, 'High Court Appointments', p. 163.
32 D. Oliver, *Constitutional Reform in the United Kingdom*, Oxford: Oxford University Press, 2003, p. 340.
33 S. Gageler, 'Judicial Appointment', *Sydney Law Review* 30, 2008, pp. 159, 161.

Of those 'broader considerations', Gageler said 'geography, gender and ethnicity all can, and should, legitimately weigh in the balance'.[34]

This approach is often criticized because the danger of being 'solely concerned' with identifying merit at the primary stage is that a homogenous ideal of 'merit' will exclude from consideration those persons whose attributes and experiences differ from those already found on the bench.[35] Looking for diversity at the secondary stage will, in effect, be too late. But this may be remedied by tackling any such distortions in the meaning of merit; despite Erika Rackley's concerns about this approach, it seems an overstatement to say that we are required 'to abandon appointment on merit'.[36] Gageler himself evidently took an expansive rather than constricted view of the question, with the result that the first stage of 'identifying the pool of potential judicial candidates' still left a meaningful role for diversity to play at the second stage. Indeed, he said the essential attributes 'can be shared by a fairly wide pool of potential judicial candidates' and thus 'at any time there would be fifty people in Australia quite capable of performing the role of a High Court justice'.[37] Such an assessment accords with Malleson's argument that 'the use of a threshold merit system is both inevitable and necessary' given the inability of merit alone to determine selection of individuals from the field.[38] Ultimately, then, what Gageler called the 'broader considerations' must influence the choice to be made between those individuals.

Despite McClelland's cautious adherence to the rhetoric of 'merit alone' in his initial broaching of the topic of judicial appointments' reform, the processes he implemented left space for diversity considerations to be a real factor in the selection of judges. Tellingly, the government's formal publication outlining those processes referred to them as leading to a selection that was 'based on merit'.[39] That is obviously not at all the same as appointing 'solely on merit', and suggests instead a 'minimal' or 'threshold' approach to merit.[40] This is consistent with the fact that the reforms imposed no meaningful constraint upon the Attorney-General. Indeed, the discretion retained by that office holder may be starkly contrasted with the curtailment of the traditional powers of the Lord Chancellor (and now also the other appropriate authorities) under the Constitutional Reform Act.

First, the Advisory Panel established under the new system would assess the expressions of interest and nominations for vacant judicial positions before presenting the Attorney-General with a report listing those candidates that it viewed 'as being highly suitable for appointment'.[41] The provision of a shortlist of possible

34 Ibid.

35 See M. Thornton, '"Otherness" on the Bench: How Merit is Gendered', *Sydney Law Review* 29, 2007, p. 391.

36 Rackley, *Women, Judging and the Judiciary*, p. 193.

37 Gageler, 'Judicial Appointment', p. 160.

38 K. Malleson, 'Gender Quotas for the Judiciary in England and Wales', in U. Schultz and G. Shaw (eds), *Gender and Judging*, Oxford: Hart Publishing, 2013, pp. 481, 492–493.

39 Attorney-General's Department, *Judicial Appointments*, p. 1.

40 See Handsley and Lynch, 'Facing up to Diversity?', pp. 207–208.

41 Attorney-General's Department, *Judicial Appointments*, p. 2.

appointees from which the Attorney-General made the final selection may be distinguished from the requirement in England and Wales that the Lord Chancellor, the Lord Chief Justice or Senior President of Tribunals – depending on the vacancy in question – is initially provided with just a single name from the JAC or, for senior appointments, a specially convened commission.[42] The argument that use of a shortlist would create 'open space' for the executive to promote 'greater diversity … while maintaining selection on merit'[43] was dismissed by the House of Lords Select Committee on the Constitution in 2012. It said the use of shortlists to enable political responsiveness to diversity concerns 'would undermine judicial independence and be contrary to the principle of appointment on merit'.[44] By contrast, the 2009 Australian Senate Committee inquiry on the Australian judiciary shared no such anxiety with the use of shortlists *per se*.[45] But the Committee was dissatisfied by a lack of clarity as to how the Attorney-General proceeded to identify the 'preferred candidate'[46] from amongst the names on that list forwarded by the Advisory Panel.[47] The extent to which diversity considerations guided the Attorney-General's ultimate selection was unstated, but there is reason to suggest they enjoyed some significance in appointments made under the McClelland system.[48]

Second, quite aside from the capacity to choose from the names on the shortlist, the McClelland reforms to federal judicial appointments left the Attorney-General free to select a person not amongst those recommended. In this regard, the nature of the panels as merely *advisory* in nature was abundantly clear. What is more, there was no requirement that the Attorney-General explain – or even publicly acknowledge – a decision to appoint someone not recommended by the Advisory Panel. Consequently, it is unknown whether and to what extent Labor's Attorneys-General limited their appointments to those persons recommended by the Advisory Panels. By contrast, although the Lord Chancellor or appropriate authority in the United Kingdom need not accept the first or even the second recommendation made by the JAC or special selection commission, one of them or a third and final recommendation must be appointed.[49] A refusal or request for

42 The Supreme Court (Judicial Appointments) Regulations 2013 (UK), reg. 19; and The Judicial Appointments Regulations 2013 (UK), regs. 7, 13, 19, 25, and 31.

43 K. Malleson, 'Taking the Politics Out of Judicial Appointments?', *UK Constitutional Law Association Blog*, 21 February 2012. See also K. Malleson, 'Selecting Judges in the Era of Devolution and Human Rights', in A. Le Sueur (ed), *Building the UK's New Supreme Court: National and Comparative Perspectives*, Oxford: Oxford University Press, 2004, pp. 295, 313.

44 House of Lords, Select Committee on the Constitution, *Judicial Appointments*, 25th Report of Session 2010–12, para 37.

45 Senate Legal and Constitutional Affairs References Committee, *Australia's Judicial System*, p. 14, para 3.24. The Committee did recommend that the number of persons on the shortlist should be made public.

46 Attorney-General's Department, *Judicial Appointments*, p. 2.

47 Senate Legal and Constitutional Affairs References Committee, *Australia's Judicial System*, p. 14, [3.20].

48 See Handsley and Lynch, 'Facing up to Diversity?', pp. 211–215.

49 *The Supreme Court (Judicial Appointments) Regulations 2013* (UK), reg. 20; and *The Judicial Appointments Regulations 2013* (UK), regs. 8, 14, 20, 26, and 32.

the reconsideration of the first or second recommendation must be accompanied by written reasons.[50] Additionally, rejection or the request for reconsideration is limited to stipulated grounds.[51]

The preservation of the executive's discretion over appointments in Australia needs to be understood as the result of more than the political reluctance to cede power, although that should certainly not be discounted.[52] It is universally accepted that the requirement under section 72 of the Commonwealth Constitution that federal judges be appointed by the Governor-General means there is a limit to just how independently of government it is possible to make the appointments process. Even the advocates of reform that adheres most closely to the English model favour the use of a shortlist of recommended candidates, not only because they recognize that 'there will rarely be a uniquely "best qualified" person',[53] but also to respect the constitutional requirement of ensuring that the executive, although constrained, will continue to enjoy a meaningful role of selection. This avoids the Attorney-General's role being portrayed as merely 'the selection panel's messenger', as has been alleged in respect of the Lord Chancellor.[54] A Commonwealth scheme of that character would run a real risk of constitutional invalidity.

But from considering debates about reform at the level of the States and Territories, where greater constitutional flexibility exists, it is also clear that the principles of political accountability and diversity are frequently used in tandem to justify the executive's retention of the final say over judicial appointments in Australia. There is an obvious tension here with maintaining the traditional rhetoric about appointments being on 'merit alone' – but that is increasingly giving way to merit as the threshold, after which other factors may legitimately enter the equation. For example, Justice Ronald Sackville defended the Attorney-General's freedom to appoint a person not shortlisted for 'legitimate reasons' that might include the need of the relevant court for some particular expertise or to attain 'geographic balance', not an uncommon consideration in federal systems.[55] In recommending a new Protocol for judicial appointments to the Northern Territory government, a committee headed by the former Chief Justice of South Australia, John Doyle QC, was more explicit. Although the committee insisted that 'the sole criterion for assessing suitability for appointment is merit', it recommended an advisory panel send 'the names of at least two persons' to the Attorney-General for forwarding to the Cabinet so as to 'permit the Executive

50 *The Supreme Court (Judicial Appointments) Regulations 2013* (UK), reg. 21(3); *The Judicial Appointments Regulations 2013* (UK), regs. 9(3), 15(3), 21(3), 27(3), and 33 (3).
51 *The Supreme Court (Judicial Appointments) Regulations 2013* (UK), reg. 21(1) and (2); *The Judicial Appointments Regulations 2013* (UK), regs. 9(1) and (2), 15(1) and (2), 21(1) and (2), 27(1) and (2), and 33(1) and (2).
52 Sackville, 'The Judicial Appointments Process in Australia', p. 136.
53 Evans and Williams, 'Appointing Australian Judges', p. 321.
54 Rackley, *Women, Judging and the Judiciary*, p. 86.
55 Sackville, 'The Judicial Appointments Process in Australia', p. 136.

Government to make a choice'.[56] In making that choice, the committee explained that:

> Cabinet may legitimately take into account other factors. These could include matters such as the specialist skills of the person in question, the needs of the court for particular skills, achieving balance in the age of those on the court to avoid a number of retirements based on age occurring at the same time, gender balance and diversity of background.[57]

As with Gageler's earlier suggestion, the use of other considerations to guide the selection of one individual from among a group of persons all identified as suitably meritorious is not to depart from a model that is described as merit-***based***. But unlike the McClelland changes, judicial reform proposals have not been coy about the limitations of merit and the significance that may be accorded to diversity as a factor in deciding who should be appointed. That difference is most likely explained by a perhaps understandable sensitivity around the political messaging of a government appointing judges for reasons that might be deemed by some to be beyond merit. But it nevertheless inhibited the extent to which McClelland's reforms were able to deliver on his aspiration of greater transparency.[58]

That complaint must, however, be seen as a relative one. As has been noted, after the Coalition assumed power at the Commonwealth level in 2013, the new Attorney-General, Senator George Brandis QC abandoned the reforms that had been instigated by the Labor government and maintained by the two Attorneys-General who had succeeded McClelland. The traditional practice of essentially unadorned executive discretion in the appointment of federal judges was resumed. As for diversity as something even to be encouraged, let alone actively pursued, the new government's position was encapsulated in Brandis' response when asked just prior to the 2013 election what he would do to improve judicial diversity. His answer was simply: 'The Coalition believes judicial appointments should be based on merit'.[59]

Judicial diversity – outcomes

The problem of a fluctuating political commitment to judicial diversity was acknowledged by the House of Lords Select Committee when it rejected calls to afford the Lord Chancellor greater discretion than currently exists under the Constitutional Reform Act by enabling selection of a name from a shortlist of candidates recommended by the JAC. The Committee was unconvinced because, as it said, 'unless a Lord Chancellor is committed to the promotion of diversity,

56 J. Doyle, J. Schafer and M. Grant, *Review of the Processes for the Appointment of Judicial Officers in The Northern Territory*, December 2014, p. 16.
57 Ibid., p. 13.
58 Handsley and Lynch, 'Facing up to Diversity?', pp. 213, 215–216.
59 '*Dreyfus v Brandis*: Federal Election Q&A', *Law Institute Journal* 87(7), 2013, pp. 18, 19.

the use of shortlists could have the reverse effect of reducing the diversity of the judiciary'.[60] But the obvious retort is that while one political decision-maker may be uninterested or hostile to the diversification of the bench, another may not be; so even if diversity waxes and wanes as a consideration in the appointment of individual judges there are good reasons to anticipate it is more likely to be advanced over time than if the means of doing so is placed out of reach of elected representatives.

This is not hard to understand – politicians are held to account for their decisions in a way that the judiciary and legal profession are not. Community standards about inclusiveness, while not necessarily held consistently throughout the population, and even less likely to be so for different attributes, are nevertheless a pressure point for politicians. The courts' comparative remoteness from the public means the underrepresentation of women in the judiciary, for example, may be less likely to elicit the same level of public attention as gender inequalities in the political branches of government. But a general indifference to the issue of judicial diversity is even less likely. The story of the High Court of Australia over the last decade clearly illustrates the capacity for the executive to be responsive to concerns about the homogeneity of the bench. In 2003, the High Court's only ever female member in a century, Justice Mary Gaudron, retired and was replaced by Justice Dyson Heydon. The federal opposition expressed dismay at the return of the High Court to an exclusively male membership,[61] and prior to his own retirement in 2006 Justice Michael McHugh gave two speeches in which he pointedly discussed the possible benefits to judicial deliberation and public confidence in the courts produced by the appointment of women judges.[62] Justice McHugh was indeed succeeded on the Court by a woman, Justice Susan Crennan, with two more following in swift succession. As Rackley reported, in 2012 amongst national final courts, only Greece, Rwanda, Croatia and Canada had a higher percentage of women judges than Australia's High Court.[63] That was a remarkable reversal of fortune; going from an entirely male court to being near the top of the international leader board in just a few years.

What is more, there are positive signs this will hold. Although the Court dipped to two female judges out of seven in early 2015, this lasted just a few months until Justice Michelle Gordon was appointed in June of that year. Some, alarmed by the temporary reduction in the number of women judges, called for a minimum 40

60 House of Lords, Select Committee on the Constitution, *Judicial Appointments*, para 36.

61 N. Roxon, 'Gender, Geography and Philosophy – What Gets a Look-in for the Next High Court Appointment?', Women's Lawyers' Association, Australian Capital Territory, 7 September 2005; Commonwealth, *Parliamentary Debates,* Senate, 8 October 2003, 15973 (Linda Kirk).

62 Justice Michael McHugh, 'Women Justices for the High Court', High Court Dinner, Western Australian Law Society, 27 October 2004; and Justice Michael McHugh, 'Working as a High Court Justice', Women Lawyers Association of New South Wales and the Law Society of Newcastle, 17 August 2005.

63 Rackley, *Women, Judging and the Judiciary*, p. 21, table 1.5.

per cent representation of either gender.[64] But the quick return to a 4:3 gender split on the nation's final court suggests that this may be effectively maintained by way of convention. One might even see the brief retraction to a 5:2 gender composition as helpfully signalling that there are not 'women's chairs' and, by correlation, 'men's chairs' on the Court. The flexibility also admits the clear potential for a majority of female Justices on the Court – the last remaining milestone following the appointment of the first female Chief Justice of Australia in January 2017. That said, it is understandable that some feel unease that 'with no formal importance of diversity in appointments, these steps remain at the whim of the government of the day'.[65] However, it seems preferable to address this not by a quota but through, as discussed above, a more explicit recognition of the value and role of diversity in the selection process – something that has been conspicuously denied or absent in the announcement of all five female appointments to the Court.[66]

The Australian government's willingness to appoint women to the nation's highest court must be, at least in part, in response to political and community expectations that a stark gender imbalance on that institution is no longer acceptable. By contrast, are we really to believe that Lady Hale would still be the only woman on the United Kingdom Supreme Court if the elected government had the means to bring an end to her gender isolation on that body? The enduring near-homogeneity of the UK Supreme Court – despite several opportunities to appoint another female member in the eight years since its establishment – is frankly baffling to an outside observer and cannot but reflect negatively on the reforms of 2005.

The JAC justifiably points to a fairer process for the appointment of women and BAME candidates.[67] But the view remains that change has been 'slower than expected and has been largely in the lower ranks, with the upper ranks remaining substantially untouched'.[68] It seems difficult for gains made by the JAC to offset the potent impression conveyed by a lone female member of the UK Supreme Court – especially when gender is also far from equal at the intermediate level. Just eight of the 39 judges in the Court of Appeal are currently women, and none occupy any of the five ex officio judicial offices of the Court of Appeal. There are 22 women judges of a total of 106 in the High Court of Justice – or 20.8 per cent.[69]

64 K. Rubenstein, 'Rethink Needed as New High Court Justice Appointment Seems to Maintain Gender Imbalance', *Canberra Times*, 12 December 2014; H. Hobbs, 'Finding a Fair Reflection on the High Court of Australia', *Alternative Law Journal*, 40, 2015, pp. 13, 17.

65 K. McLoughlin, 'The Politics of Gender Diversity on the High Court of Australia', *Alternative Law Journal* 40, 2015, pp. 166, 170.

66 Ibid.

67 See Judicial Appointments Commission, *Annual Report and Accounts 2015–2016*, 21 July 2016, pp. 15–17.

68 Gee *et al*, *The Politics of Judicial Independence*, p. 182.

69 Lord Chief Justice and Senior President of Tribunals, *Judicial Diversity Statistics 2016*, 28 July 2016, p. 5, fig. 1.

But if we look below the High Court, the Australian situation is not dramatically better.[70] The Federal Court of Australia has just 23.9 per cent female judicial membership (11 of 46 judges). At the state and territory level, things are, as one might expect, varied. The Supreme Courts of Queensland and Victoria are the better performers with female judicial members at 29.6 per cent and 25 per cent respectively, but the largest such court, the Supreme Court of New South Wales, has 11 female judges to 40 male – just 21.6 per cent. The Supreme Court on which women are fewest is that of Western Australia with only three females out of a total of 21 judges, or 14.3 per cent. While the overall rates of gender diversity in each jurisdiction are higher, this is attributable, as in England and Wales, to a greater proportion of women sitting in lower level courts. The federal judiciary is 36 per cent female and Victoria has the most female judges of any Australian jurisdiction with women occupying 40 per cent of judicial positions. It should be noted that Victoria has increased the percentage of its female judiciary by three per cent in the two years since the Premier of that state announced a 50 per cent quota for the appointment of women to all public offices, including the courts.[71] The worst performing jurisdiction is Western Australia with women comprising 28 per cent of the judiciary.

Despite the impression conveyed by the composition of the High Court, and acknowledging that female presence on the bench is steadily improving,[72] gender equality in Australian courts clearly still has a long way to go. Yet, the topic has excited comparatively modest mainstream political or professional disquiet; there certainly has not been a succession of government reviews and parliamentary inquiries into judicial diversity in Australia as there has in England in recent years. It seems reasonable to attribute the different intensity accompanying the issue in the two jurisdictions to the stark disparity in the gender balance of their respective highest courts. This sets the tone for the discussion at a very different pitch. So despite progress the JAC may be making in broadening the profile of the junior judiciary, the composition of the UK Supreme Court is inevitably emblematic of the persistent underrepresentation of female judges in the upper courts – and the challenges women face within the profession more generally. Conversely, in Australia, the High Court's near equal gender mix appears to have muffled the extent to which the same issues are publicly recognized, let alone the subject of purposeful attention.[73]

70 All statistics for Australian courts are from Australian Institute of Judicial Administration, *Judicial Gender Statistics 2017*, 3 March 2017.

71 D. Andrews, *Speech Presented at State Labor Conference 2015*, 28 March 2015.

72 S. Kiefel and C. Saunders, 'The Independence of a Meritorious Elite: the Government of Judges and Democracy', *XIX International Congress of Comparative Law*, Vienna, July 2014, p. 11; Opeskin, 'The State of the Judicature', pp. 511–512.

73 This is not to ignore efforts to address women's experience at the Bar: M. Perry, 'Women at the Bar: Aspirations and Inspirations', *Federal Judicial Scholarship*, 2014, p. 8; see also Law Council of Australia, *National Attrition and Re-engagement Study (NARS) Report*, Urbis, 2014.

Interestingly, the issue has started to receive greater attention now that it is possible to assess the impact of the Coalition's abandonment of the McClelland reforms. In December 2015, it was reported that, 'Attorney-General George Brandis has appointed as many graduates from Oxford University's Magdalen College – where he obtained a Bachelor of Civil Laws – as he has females to the federal judiciary.'[74] Up to that time, since winning office in 2013, the Coalition had appointed 17 judges just three of whom were women. By comparison, Brandis' immediate predecessor in the office, Labor's Mark Dreyfus QC, also made 17 appointments, of whom 10 were female.[75] In almost six years in power, females accounted for 42 per cent of the judges appointed by the Labor government.[76] Dreyfus, now the Opposition's Shadow Attorney-General, slammed Brandis' record – and also his use of the 'merit alone' justification to explain it:

> The merit of a candidate for the bench cannot be measured or quantified in some crude, reductionist way … An attorney-general must carefully consider a range of factors, of which the diversity of the judiciary is but one, though undoubtedly significant. Even if we accept Senator Brandis's argument at face value, does he really maintain that he was unable to find even a half a dozen women of sufficient 'merit' for appointment to our federal courts? … Though there is certainly more work to be done in ensuring women are properly represented at all levels of the legal profession, no one can seriously doubt there are meritorious candidates among all the women at the Bar, let alone the many more practising as leading solicitors in their field, or working as eminent academics or even state judges.[77]

Dreyfus argued that the government's performance was at least partly due to the abandonment of 'our system of open and transparent appointments' that 'helped ensure that the government properly considered all suitable candidates'.[78] During the 2016 election campaign, Dreyfus kept up pressure on the Attorney-General about his use of 'an appointment method that you can only describe as a black box', and maintained it was 'a conceit for the Attorney-General to believe he had sufficient knowledge of all potential candidates for federal judicial office – even with the assistance of political and departmental staff'.[79] Dreyfus insisted that the existence of a high quality, talented judiciary, reflective of Australian society, depended on 'a relatively transparent and formalized system' of appointments.[80] This is important because it suggests that the opportunity, taken up at various

74 N. Berkovic, 'Female judges at low under Coalition', *The Australian*, 18 December 2015, p. 8.
75 Ibid.
76 Ibid.
77 M. Dreyfus, 'Brandis has failed the test on appointments to the bench', *The Australian*, 18 December 2015, p. 23.
78 Ibid.
79 Merritt, 'Mark Dreyfus', p. 27.
80 Ibid.

times by some state Attorneys-General,[81] to use the traditionally unbounded discretion of the executive simply to make a concerted drive to put more women on the bench is not sufficient. Instead, the policy of the federal Labor party is to preserve that unlimited discretion but to guide its use by an anterior process of some sophistication.

Judicial diversity – next steps?

The Labor opposition says it will reinstate the McClelland reforms to federal judicial appointments when it returns to power. But there are three enhancements it should consider when doing so. First, it should protect the system from the vicissitudes of political fortune by enacting it. Second, it should diversify the composition of the Advisory Panels which were typically comprised of just the head of jurisdiction; a retired judge or senior member of the federal or state judiciary; and a senior member of the Attorney-General's Department.[82] The addition of lay people has been advocated by numerous commentators as necessary to counter any unconscious bias against non-traditional candidates.[83] Third, it should require some public justification by the Attorney-General of a decision to appoint an individual not amongst those shortlisted by the Advisory Panel.[84] Dreyfus has said that the use of the Advisory Panels 'would prevent the system becoming politicized',[85] but this is an inadequate assurance so long as the Attorney-General's discretion remains at large and its use is not subject to any requirement of public acknowledgment, let alone explanation.

The divide between the main Australian political parties on the need for processes supporting the executive to identify persons appointable to the federal judiciary is one that in large measure appears to turn on the different value they ascribe to diversity on the bench. But neither side has any appetite for reducing the traditional power of the executive, and certainly not to the extent achieved by the 2005 reforms in England and Wales. Reflecting on this difference, Justice Sackville surmised that the low incidence of partisan appointments in the United Kingdom after World War II 'may have made it relatively easy for the government to relinquish a power that it had chosen never to exercise in an ideological manner'.[86] The reluctance may be further explained by Australian judicial recognition that a 'democratic deficit' in appointment would have negative implications for the

81 B. Hamilton, 'Criteria for Judicial Appointment and "Merit"', *Queensland University of Technology Law Journal* 15, 1999, p. 10; Thornton, '"Otherness" on the Bench', pp. 398–399. See also Andrews, *Speech Presented at State Labor Conference 2015.*

82 Senate Legal and Constitutional Affairs References Committee, *Australia's Judicial System*, p. 14, para 3.17.

83 For direct reflection on the Advisory Panels used under the McClelland system, see Kirby, 'A Darwinian Reflection', p. 33.

84 See Brennan, 'The Selection of Judges', pp. 14–15; Sackville, 'The Judicial Appointments Process in Australia', p. 136; and Williams, 'High Court Appointments', p. 169.

85 Merritt, 'Mark Dreyfus'.

86 Sackville, 'The Judicial Appointments Process in Australia', p. 134. See further Malleson, 'Appointment, Discipline and Removal of Judges', p. 119.

judiciary's exercise of its power,[87] as well as the aforementioned constitutional constraints at the Commonwealth level.

A commitment to judicial diversity rather than a particular priority of depoliticizing appointments dampens the appeal of embracing reform along the lines of the Constitutional Reform Act. The most obvious rationale for establishing a JAC-style body that operates at arm's length from government and makes recommendations that are, in practice, very difficult to depart from, is to curb partisan influence over the selection of individuals for the bench. The processes ushered in by the Constitutional Reform Act have virtually eradicated political influence over English judicial appointments.[88] But as former Lord Chancellor Jack Straw reflected, '[i]n solving one problem (too much executive power) we went too far the other way …'.[89] The political independence of judicial appointments is an entirely valid and desirable reform objective, the importance of which has been highlighted in Australia by recent controversy.[90] However, the English experience strongly suggests that an excessive regard to depoliticization in the design of judicial appointments processes may risk inhibiting the achievement of a more diverse judiciary. That trade-off may be deliberate and even conceivably worth making – but surely only if a strong corrective is needed to a dominant norm of political patronage in the selection of judges.

Yet, there is another way entirely of thinking about the contrast between Australia and England and Wales and the case for preserving executive discretion. When the executive holds the reins the focus is on *its* inclination (or otherwise), to advance judicial diversity, largely letting the legal profession off the hook. But when the judiciary is formally empowered in the selection of candidates for appointment, it may feel much greater responsibility to effectuate meaningful cultural change.[91] There are real signs that this is occurring in England and Wales, with the Lord Chief Justice having outlined seven 'concrete achievements' of the Diversity Committee of the Judges' Council in its efforts to 'widen the pool' of possible appointments.[92] These include schemes for judicial mentoring and work shadowing, the appointment of over a hundred Diversity and Community Relations judges, efforts to provide flexible working conditions, and removing the requirement of prior judicial experience for appointment to the High Court of

87 A. Mason, 'The Appointment and Removal of Judges', in H. Cunningham (ed.), *Fragile Bastion – Judicial Independence in the Nineties and Beyond*, Judicial Commission of New South Wales, 1997, p. 7.

88 M. Bevir, *Democratic Governance*, New Jersey: Princeton University Press, 2010, p. 163; and V. Bogdanor, *The New British Constitution*, Oxford: Hart Publishing, 2009, p. 67.

89 Straw, *The Hamlyn Lectures*, p. 59.

90 See R. Ananian-Welsh, G. Appleby and A. Lynch, *The Tim Carmody Affair – Australia's Greatest Judicial Crisis*, Kensington: NewSouth Publishing, 2016.

91 Indeed, Gee *et al* argue that this is increasingly important for the self-protection of the English judiciary under the United Kingdom's new constitutional settlement: *The Politics of Judicial Independence*, pp. 192–193.

92 Lord Thomas, 'Speech for the Temple Women's Forum', Leeds, 19 October 2015, p. 4.

Justice.[93] By contrast, judicial initiatives to enhance diversity on the bench in Australia appear both less ambitious and lacking co-ordination. So while it is possible to see the emphasis of the Constitutional Reform Act on the 'encouragement' of diversity as a flimsy aspiration, a feeble alternative to the capacity of government to select judges on the basis of diversity considerations, ultimately a lot depends on execution. At the moment, the English judiciary is making increased efforts to respond to the challenge of diversity while in Australia the executive at the Commonwealth level will not even pay it lip service. Obviously, governments change and the executive can always change tack but that possibility should not lead us to dismiss the attractions of a system under which the judiciary grasps the impetus for diversity. That may well be the slower path towards change, but it may also prove to be the more effective and sustained, bringing lasting benefits to the professional culture of legal practice.

Conclusion

Australian interest in judicial appointments reform was undoubtedly stimulated by the passage of the Constitutional Reform Act 2005 and the dramatic changes it made to the traditional method of unaccountable executive discretion in appointing judges to the English and Welsh courts. Attorney-General McClelland's initiation of a more transparent and consultative system of federal judicial appointments in Australia was a response, but it was both limited and short-lived reform.

The primary lesson from a contrast of these two jurisdictions appears to be that in the desire to achieve maximum independence from the political arms of government, a model may underperform against the objectives of accountability and judicial diversity. Preserving a sufficient degree of political responsibility for the composition of the courts seems prudent for the attainment of a more diverse bench – the rapid transformation of the High Court's gender profile offers a strong illustration, as does the record of the three Labor Attorney-Generals who appointed judges under McClelland's reforms. But the executive can be inconsistent in its focus on diversity, while the judiciary and legal profession, spared any formal responsibility for appointments, may be complacent about the issue and any action they might initiate to address it.

There are several good reasons, many of which were appreciated a decade ago, why Australia should not attempt a 'carbon copy' of the English reforms.[94] But it seems simplistic, or just still too early, to conclude that an executive *capacity* to pursue judicial diversity with vigour when so minded will prove to be the better of a *responsibility* upon the judicial class to create a more open, flexible and supportive professional culture so as to achieve the same end. An ideal model would, of course, attempt to capture both potential strengths.

93 Ibid., pp. 4–6.
94 Evans and Williams, 'Appointing Australian Judges', p. 311.

7 Diversity, transparency and inclusion in Canada's judiciary

Samreen Beg and Lorne Sossin

Introduction

'Of 100 new federally appointed judges 98 are white, Globe finds'.[1] This arresting headline from the *Globe and Mail* in 2012 created waves in the legal community and beyond. While it was known that the Canadian judiciary – particularly federal judicial appointments[2] – suffered from problems related to diversity and inclusion, the extent of the problem had not been explicitly laid out in the past. The headline and report that followed not only highlighted the fact that the judiciary was not seeing any progress with respect to representation, but that it was actually *regressing* from gains that had been made in previous years.

Canada is one of the most culturally, ethnically, religiously, and linguistically diverse countries in the world. However, at a time when one in five Canadians identifies as a member of a visible minority (a figure that rises to 50 per cent in Canada's largest cities), the Canadian judiciary has remained remarkably homogenous – or to put it bluntly – overwhelmingly white. While appointments are no longer dependent on finding candidates from an English, Scottish, Irish, or French background with Protestant or Catholic roots, the appointments do not reflect the heterogeneous composition of Canada's society – especially as the cultural and ethnic makeup of the legal profession becomes more reflective of wider society.[3]

The Canadian judicial appointment process suffers from a number of issues that contribute to the largely homogenous nature of the appointments, but there

1 K. Makin, 'Of 100 New Federally Appointed Judges, 98 are White, Globe finds', *The Globe and Mail*, 17 April 2012.

2 Canada's judicial system is subject to a Constitutional division of powers set out in the Constitution Act 1867 and subsequent statutes relating to the creation of specific courts. Under this scheme, the Federal Cabinet (through the Governor General) appoints members of the Supreme Court of Canada, the Federal Courts, and the 'superior' courts of the Provinces and Territories (including trial level and appellate courts). Provincial 'inferior' courts which are responsible for less serious criminal matters and regulatory offences set out in provincial statutes are appointed by the provinces.

3 The minimum standard for federal judicial appointment is one year of residency in the province or territory of the appointment (except for the Federal Court) and 10 years of experience at the Bar.

are two key problems that should be mentioned at the outset. The first is transparency and accountability, particularly in the federal judicial appointment process. Legislation is skeletal with much of the decision-making process left up to administrative processes dictated by politicians. This decision-making is often ad hoc and continuously changing. There is also a dearth of data available to track the kinds of candidates that apply for judicial positions and those candidates that are ultimately unsuccessful. Data is essential to figure out whether the problem of low representation in the judiciary is related to a shortage of diverse candidates applying for these positions, lack of policies and procedures ensuring capable candidates from diverse backgrounds are appointed, or whether there is simply a complete disregard for diverse candidates.

The second key problem is that there have been few institutional processes put in place to encourage diverse appointments. The judicial appointment process for the Supreme Court of Canada is the only federal appointment process that has institutionalized diverse appointments – unfortunately this institutionalization has remained wedded to conceptions of regional diversity and representation for the provinces, particularly Quebec. This is not to say that these conceptions of diversity are archaic or no longer important, but they are not the *only* representation considerations that exist today – especially at a time when there has never been an Indigenous judge on the Supreme Court of Canada and the number of women judges on the Court is not guaranteed. The lack of institutional processes encouraging diversity for other federal appointments is at odds with an increasingly diverse society where a high number of litigants are unlikely to encounter judges that look like them.

The purpose of this chapter is to provide a high level overview of some of the issues and stumbling blocks Canada has encountered in building a diverse judiciary. It begins by providing a brief overview of the heterogeneous makeup of Canadian society compared with the homogenous makeup of the judiciary. This will provide a helpful backdrop from which to explore conceptual questions related to the bigger question of why a diverse judiciary matters. It then goes on to examine some of the historical questions and milestones in the judiciary related to diversity before summarizing the judicial appointment processes and taking a look at Canada's recent history related to judicial appointments and judicial diversity – specifically judicial appointments under Prime Minister Stephen Harper's Conservative government and recent moves by the new Liberal government led by Prime Minister Justin Trudeau. The chapter wraps up with our thoughts on reforms that might signal greater commitment to diversity and inclusion as essential elements of an effective and independent judiciary.

Canadian diversity and conceptual approaches to judicial diversity

'Canada was born of diversity' remarked Canada's Chief Justice Beverley McLachlin to an audience in Edinburgh, Scotland in 2012. 'We continue to be a country of immigrants, and all signs suggest that diversity in Canada will only increase in the years to come.'[4] While this may be true, why should it matter for the purposes of judicial diversity? The idea that the judiciary should reflect society is not an automatic one, and the purpose of this section is to look at some of the conceptual reasons for a reflective judiciary that have been presented by Canadian academics and commentators. Before those conceptual rationales are addressed however, this section will provide more details on the nature of Canada's increasing diversity and largely homogeneous judiciary.

Canadian heterogeneity vs judicial homogeneity

Historical diversity in Canada and the Canadian 'mosaic'

Canada is largely understood to have had three 'founding peoples': the Indigenous peoples, the British, and the French. However, for a large part of Canada's history the population was primarily composed of people from British or French descent. The trend of Europe being the largest source of immigrants to Canada began to change in the 1960s with major changes to Canada's immigration policy,[5] resulting in a noticeable increase in the presence of 'visible minorities' in Canada in the 1970s. By the 1980s, declining birth rates coupled with a steady influx of immigrants saw the population of those from British and French ancestry sharply decline.

The results from Statistics Canada's 2011 National Household Survey[6] illustrate how the immigration trends of the 1970s, 1980s, and beyond resulted in a 'mosaic' of individuals within Canadian society. Over 20 per cent of the population was foreign-born with more than 200 ethnic origins reported and roughly 19 per cent of the population – or nearly one in five of the Canadian population – identifying themselves as a member of a visible minority group. The three largest visible minority groups were South Asian, Chinese, and Black, accounting for 61.3 per cent of the visible minority population. Two-thirds of the Canadian population reported that they were affiliated with a Christian religion, Roman Catholics being by far the largest Christian group. The respondents that identified as Muslim represented 3.2 per cent of Canada's population, followed by Hindu at 1.5 per cent, Sikh at 1.2 per cent, Buddhist at 1.1 per cent, and Jewish at 1 per cent. National statistics can sometimes belie local realities – Toronto, Canada's largest city, for example, now counts over 50 per cent of its population as foreign born.[7]

4 The Right Honourable Beverley McLachlin, Chief Justice of Canada, 'Judging: the Challenges of Diversity', Judicial Studies Committee Inaugural Annual Lecture, Edinburgh, June 2012, p. 2.

5 P. S. Li, 'Cultural Diversity in Canada: The Social Construction of Racial Differences', Department of Justice Canada, 2000, p. 3.

6 Statistics Canada, *Immigration and Ethnocultural Diversity in Canada*, National Household Survey, 2011.

7 Toronto Vital Signs, *Report 2015*, Online, Available <http://torontosvitalsigns.ca/#> (accessed 30 August 2016).

Judicial diversity in Canada

The judiciary in Canada has a story largely opposite to the statistics outlined above, especially among appointments by the federal government to 'federal courts'.[8] In May 2016 there were no visible minority or Indigenous judges on the Supreme Court of Canada or the Federal Court of Appeal. There were also no visible minority judges on the Federal Court and no Indigenous judges on the Tax Court. Whereas women comprised four of the nine judges on the Supreme Court of Canada, women were very under-represented on other federal courts, though not to the same extent as visible minority and Indigenous judges.

With respect to federally appointed judges to the provincial courts, there was better representation from visible minority, Indigenous, and women judges, though still far below the corresponding population shares for these groups. Meanwhile, provincially appointed judges on provincial courts appeared to fare better from a diversity perspective, though there was still under-representation among visible minority, Indigenous, and women judges.

While the federal judicial appointment process has been recently revamped, it has never included any proactive outreach for or institutional valuing of diversity and inclusion. It is not that issues of diversity and inclusion are absent from this process, but there is little evidence that these issues are viewed as priorities, or valued as commensurate with other aspects of judicial qualifications.

Why do we need judicial diversity?

Why is the lack of judicial diversity necessarily a problem? At its core, diversity matters because judicial appointments ought to involve a merit based process in a system committed to judicial independence, democracy, and the rule of law. Although some may argue that a merit based system is premised on the view that the race, ethnicity, or gender of a well-qualified candidate should not matter, the reality is that a person's qualifications are shaped by who that person is and what perspectives on society and justice he or she brings to the bench. A diverse and inclusive judiciary is what enables the judiciary to be both independent and impartial.[9]

Despite these pressing questions and rapidly growing diversity in Canadian society, attention to the question of whether and to what extent the judiciary is reflective of Canadian society is a relatively recent phenomenon of the last decade (with the exception of gender representation, which is a longer standing concern – at least since the 1980s). As scrutiny of this question intensifies, a number of rationales for enhancing judicial diversity and inclusion have surfaced. Below, we canvass a selection of these rationales (though our review is far from exhaustive).

8 The Supreme Court of Canada, Federal Court and Tax Court.

9 For discussion, see A. Griffith, 'Diversity Among Federal and Provincial Judges', Policy Options, 4 May 2016.

Practical reasons

'As a law student,' Chief Justice McLachlin said in her Edinburgh speech, 'I never dreamed that I would be called upon to decide whether a religious Muslim woman may be permitted to wear a Niqab while testifying, or whether same-sex couples should be allowed to marry, or whether children can refuse life-saving medical treatment on religious grounds'.[10] The values, perspectives, and experiences of people appearing in courts are increasingly different from those judging them, which can 'impact on the ability of the judges to appreciate their circumstances, assess their credibility, and craft appropriate remedies.'[11]

Although judges are capable of making fair decisions for members of minority communities, for the Chief Justice, the increasing numbers of women on the bench has been instructive in demonstrating how a heterogeneous bench can lead to enhanced judicial decision-making:

> My personal experience has led me to the conviction that women on the bench do make a difference. I have seen deliberations take a new turn because of the perspective brought by a woman to an issue involving a woman. And I have seen court culture change ...[12]

According to the Chief Justice, there needs to be a recognition that judges are human beings and that there is a subjective element to judging. What is required for impartial judging is better understood by recognizing subjectivity since judging 'is not an exercise of cold reason, uncontaminated by personal views and preconceptions'.[13]

Other commentators have echoed and expanded on these ideas over the years. The main reason judicial diversity is needed according to these commentators is practical:[14] the more diverse the bench, the better the quality of decisions. Rosemary Cairns Way states that one primary reason for having a diverse bench is to increase the range of available perspectives and experiences. This can make decisions more impartial since it avoids 'unintentionally [replicating] at a systemic level the perspectives and values of a limited subset of human experience'.[15] Having a diverse bench with more widened life experiences opens up what has traditionally been a 'constrained' set of perspectives, and increases the chances that the experiences of litigants will be understood more accurately.[16] Other commentators have noted that judicial diversity is important because a judge's background can influence his or her

10 McLachlin, 'Judging: the Challenges of Diversity', p. 4.
11 Ibid., pp. 3–4.
12 Ibid., p. 18.
13 Ibid., p. 7.
14 R. Cairns Way, 'Deliberate Disregard: Judicial Appointments under the Harper Government', *Supreme Court Law Review* 67, 2(d), 2014, p. 43.
15 Ibid., p. 52.
16 Ibid., p. 52.

choice and the 'particular experiences of a judge can even affect her or his view about the appropriate forum for raising a legal issue'.[17]

The importance of a judiciary that reflects Canada's diverse communities was highlighted in the 1997 Supreme Court of Canada judgment *R.D.S. v The Queen*.[18] The case involved an African-Canadian trial judge who heard a case involving an African-Canadian youth charged with assaulting a police officer. The only two witnesses at trial were the accused and the police officer. The police officer alleged that the youth resisted arrest and became violent with him. The youth alleged that he had been the subject of threats of violence at the hands of the police officer. Because their accounts of the relevant events differed widely, the case focused on credibility. The trial judge indicated that she had reasonable doubt about the accused's guilt and that the Crown did not discharge its evidentiary burden to prove the accused's guilt beyond a reasonable doubt. In particular, the trial judge stated the following:

> The Crown says, well, why would the officer say that events occurred in the way in which he has relayed them to the Court this morning. I am not saying that the Constable has misled the court, although police officers have been known to do that in the past. I am not saying that the officer overreacted, but certainly police officers do overreact, particularly when they are dealing with non-white groups. That to me indicates a state of mind right there that is questionable. I believe that probably the situation in this particular case is the case of a young police officer who overreacted. I do accept the evidence of [R.D.S.] that he was told to shut up or he would be under arrest. It seems to be in keeping with the prevalent attitude of the day.[19]

The case reached the Supreme Court of Canada on the issue of whether the comments of the trial judge (who was the first African-Canadian woman appointed to the bench in the Province of Nova Scotia) gave rise to a reasonable apprehension of bias.[20] Writing for the majority, Justice Cory observed that the 'requirement for neutrality does not require judges to discount the very life experiences that may so well qualify them to preside over disputes'.[21] He went on to say that

> True impartiality … requires that the judge nevertheless be free to entertain and act upon different points of view with an open mind … The sound belief behind the encouragement of greater diversity in judicial appointments was

17 R. Devlin, W. MacKay and N. Kim, 'Reducing the Democratic Deficit: Representation, Diversity and the Canadian Judiciary, or Towards a "Triple P" Judiciary', *Alberta Law Rev*, 2000, p. 734, para 39.

18 [1997] 3 SCR 484.

19 *R.D.S v The Queen*, para 4.

20 Four separate sets of reasons were issued in the case.

21 *R.D.S v The Queen*, para 119.

> that women and visible minorities would bring an important perspective to the difficult task of judging.[22]

The two female members of the Court at that time, Justice McLachlin (as she then was) and Justice L'Heureux Dubé, concurred with Justice Cory, but went even further in their reasons to condone the comments of the trial judge. They wrote: 'An understanding of the context or background essential to judging may be gained from testimony from expert witnesses in order to put the case in context ...: A reasonable person far from being troubled by this process, would see it as an important aid to judicial impartiality.'[23]

While *R.D.S.* highlights the importance of judges bringing their own experiences to bear in their role, the case also reflects ambivalence about certain challenges in operationalizing inclusion. Jennifer Nedelsky has questioned, 'if the solution is to have a judiciary that reflects the full diversity of Canadian society, how can any given person be guaranteed a judge who shares her experiences, assumptions and affective starting points?'[24] Her answer is that judging needs to encompass an 'enlargement of the mind' since 'the more views we are able to take into account, the less likely we are to be locked into one perspective ... It is the capacity for "enlargement of mind" that makes autonomous, impartial judgment possible.'[25]

Sonia Lawrence suggests that a truly independent judiciary is dependent on the larger judicial community as a part of the context informing each individual member's decision making.[26] Lawrence points out that to the extent judges' dining rooms, libraries, and training sessions are homogenous, they do not offer many opportunities to encounter different beliefs, and as a result, 'the range of beliefs, experiences, and attitudes is narrower than that found in society as a whole'.[27]

The introduction of the Canadian *Charter of Rights and Freedoms* in the *Constitution Act, 1982* has bolstered the argument that a reflective judiciary is necessary to increase the quality of judicial decisions. The *Charter* has required an increased amount of judicial intervention into subjective areas that touch upon individual liberty, values, and policy. Balancing individual rights 'against the reasonable limits of a free and democratic society is a value laden process that involves the courts in making public policy and choosing between conflicting interests in society'.[28] A judiciary that appropriately reflects Canadian society is necessary

22 Ibid., para 119.
23 Ibid., paras 44–45.
24 J. Nedelsky, 'Embodied Diversity and the Challenges to Law', *McGill Law Journal* 42, 1997, p. 91, para 107.
25 Ibid., para 107.
26 S. Lawrence 'Reflections: On Judicial Diversity and Judicial Independence', in A. Dodek and L. Sossin (eds), *Judicial Independence in Context,* Toronto: Irwin Law, 2010, p. 200.
27 Ibid., p. 201.
28 Devlin, MacKay and Kim, 'Reducing the Democratic Deficit', p. 16.

because 'fair adjudication requires it'.[29] With an increase in subjective determinations, it is essential that these determinations reflect the community's mix of identities and experiences since 'fairness in a pluralist society … requires pluralist decision-making'.[30] The expectation is that with more diversity, there will be more voices and perspectives that ultimately adjudicate with more empathy, compassion, and effectiveness.[31]

Legitimacy of the judicial system

The second broad reason that commentators have given for necessarily having a judiciary reflective of Canadian society is that the legitimacy of the judicial system depends on it. Entry into the judiciary is a 'tangible sign of enfranchisement for minority groups … it is also a tangible conduit of social mobility for many groups who confront discrimination, exclusionary requirements or other barriers in society'.[32] Conversely, the current institutional nature of the judiciary, according to Cairns Way, reflects the ongoing existence of systemic discrimination since the appointment process has 'disproportionately denied opportunities to Indigenous peoples, racialized individuals,[33] persons with disabilities, women, and other members of equality-seeking groups'.[34] It is vital that in a democratic society 'with an aversion to discrimination, we should expect the Court to reflect society'.[35]

According to Canada's Chief Justice, a diverse bench in a diverse society is necessary for fostering public confidence in the administration of justice.[36] Representativeness is about ensuring that the public sees itself reflected in the judiciary, as some of those who belong to minority groups may not have complete trust in a system 'composed exclusively or predominantly of middle-aged white men in pinstriped trousers'.[37] Lack of confidence in the system inevitably leads to questions about whether a court can appropriately reflect the viewpoints and values of a pluralistic society, with these individuals feeling 'unwelcome and

29 L. Sossin, 'Should Canada Have a Representative Supreme Court?', in N. Verrelli (ed.), *The Democratic Dilemma: Reforming Canada's Supreme Court*, Kingston: The Institute of Intergovernmental Relations, 2013, p. 31.
30 Ibid., p. 31.
31 Ibid., p. 32.
32 Ibid., p. 33.
33 The terms 'racialized person' or 'racialized group' has been adopted by the Ontario Human Rights Commission over terms such as 'racial minority', 'visible minority', 'person of colour' or 'non-white', because the Commission believes it better reflects the recognition that 'race is a social construct.' See Ontario Human Rights Commission, *Racial Discrimination, Race and Racism (Fact Sheet)* Online, Available www.ohrc.on.ca/en/racial-discrimination-race-and-racism-fact-sheet (accessed 13 December 2016).
34 Cairns Way, 'Deliberate Disregard', p. 54.
35 Sossin, 'Should Canada Have a Representative Supreme Court', p. 32.
36 McLachlin, 'Judging: the Challenges of Diversity', p. 20.
37 Ibid., p. 21.

outnumbered in the courtroom – a space where no one should feel excluded on account of gender or background'.[38]

Sonia Lawrence expands upon these points by linking diversity on the bench to judicial independence. She states that because the judiciary has strong social connections to powerful identity groups, in an unequal society this 'sets the judiciary up as a symbol of social exclusion that may harm the democratic legitimacy of the institution (particularly in the perception of excluded groups)'.[39] In this sense the judiciary may become another symbol of hierarchy, as well as a symbol of persistent exclusion that fails to attract the confidence of those under-represented groups.[40] Ultimately, a homogenous bench may include 'a loss of faith in the ability of the courts to deliver fair and impartial injustice … [creating] a clear and important role for diversity on the bench in establishing and maintaining judicial independence'.[41]

Is judicial diversity necessary?

Is judicial diversity in Canada necessary? Based on the above commentary, the answer would be yes. There is growing sentiment that a Canadian judiciary largely drawn from a homogenous elite is problematic. If an independent judiciary is an essential feature of our democracy, attention needs to be paid to the characteristics that make the judiciary independent in practice – not just characteristics that have traditionally been associated with judicial independence. Judicial diversity and representation is more than just a goal in and of itself. It is a way to ensure, in Canada's increasingly diverse post-*Charter* society, that judges are armed with the appropriate tools to effectively deliberate and make decisions, and that the public's confidence in the ability of judges to do this is increased.

In other words, 'Who the judges are matters to what they do'.[42]

Historical developments related to judicial diversity

The history of 'judicial diversity' in Canada has typically referred to two different conceptions of representation, both of them involving the Supreme Court of Canada. The first is the process of ensuring regional representation on the Court. The *Supreme Court Act* has contained provisions since 1949 requiring there to be three judges on the Court who have served on Quebec's Court of Appeal, Superior Court, or are 'from among the advocates of that province'.[43] These

38 Ibid., p. 21.

39 Lawrence, 'Reflections: On Judicial Diversity', p. 197.

40 Ibid., p. 197.

41 Ibid., p. 198.

42 Cairns Way, 'Deliberate Disregard', p. 51.

43 *Supreme Court Act*, RSC 1985, c s. 26 s. 6. Peter McCormick points out that between 1875 and 1928, there was a requirement for two Quebec judges on a six-judge court, and between 1928 and 1949, there was also a requirement for two Quebec judges on a seven-judge court. P. McCormick, 'Selecting the Supremes: The Appointment of

provisions have led to the six other judges also being selected using a regional representation model (though this is established practice, not stipulated in the *Supreme Court Act*). Specifically one judge must be selected from British Columbia, one judge from Alberta, Saskatchewan or Manitoba, three judges from Ontario, and one judge from Canada's Atlantic provinces.[44]

The second historical conception of representation involving the Supreme Court of Canada was the practice of ensuring that among the regional appointments, specific linguistic and religious denominations were included. For example, for a time there was a practice to have one of the three Quebec judges represent the Anglophone, Protestant community (as opposed to the Francophone, Catholic community), while at least one judge from outside Quebec was a Catholic. The basic characteristics of judges at the time could be summarized as consisting of 'middle-aged (or older) white professional males of British or French ethnicity'.[45]

While the first historical conception of representation has remained largely intact, the second form of representation began to undergo changes in 1970 with the appointment of Bora Laskin, the first Jewish judge on the Supreme Court of Canada – and the first judge who was not Catholic or Protestant. In 1973, Bora Laskin was appointed as Chief Justice of the Supreme Court of Canada. Since then, attention to the religious origins of the judges has faded, with the number of Jewish judges on the Court peaking at three between 2006 and 2013. Laskin was also the first judge that did not come from the traditional English/Scottish/Irish/French background. This trend continued in the 1980s and 1990s with the appointment of John Sopinka in 1988 – the first Ukranian-Canadian named to the Court, and Frank Iacobucci in 1991 – the first Italian-Canadian appointed to the Court. More recently, the appointment of Andromache Karakatsanis in 2011 was a first for a judge of Greek origin.

A significant barrier for women was overcome with the appointment of Bertha Wilson in 1982, the first ever woman to serve on the Supreme Court of Canada. The appointment of Wilson heralded in permanent change from the previous era of the Court being an 'all-male society',[46] leading to a steady stream of female judges subsequently being appointed. Currently, four out of nine judges serving on the Court – including the Chief Justice – are women, a milestone that was originally reached in 2004.

Other levels of courts have also slowly seen some 'firsts' with respect to judicial appointments. In 1969, Maurice Charles became the first black Canadian judge

Judges to the Supreme Court of Canada', *Journal of Appellate Practice and Process* 7 (1), Spring 2005.

44 The late 1980s and early 1990s witnessed the 'Meech Lake Accord' negotiations. The Meech Lake Accord proposed that the federal government be required to appoint Supreme Court judges from lists submitted by the provinces. The Accord was subsequently defeated.

45 McCormick, 'Selecting the Supremes', p. 21.

46 P. C. Weiler, *In the Law Resort: A Critical Study of the Supreme Court of Canada*, Toronto: Carswell, 1974, p. 18.

after he was appointed to the Ontario Provincial Court, but it was not until 2012 that a black judge – Michale Tulloch – was appointed to the Ontario Court of Appeal (after being elevated from the Superior Court in 2012). It also took many years for an Indigenous judge to be appointed to an appellate court in Canada (or the Commonwealth), until Harry LaForme was named in 2004 to the Ontario Court of Appeal.[47]

Progress has generally been made with federal appointments of women judges since the beginning of the 1980s, when only 3 per cent of federal judicial appointees were women. This percentage rose to 10 per cent by 1990 and 25 per cent by 2002.[48] In Ontario, the Judicial Appointments Advisory Committee (JAAC) was created in 1989 (which will be discussed further below), whose 'employment equity' mandate saw the percentage of provincially appointed women rise from 3 per cent to 22 per cent between 1989 and 1995.

Despite the 'judicial firsts', there have been serious gaps in appointments of visible minority and Indigenous judges. This is particularly noteworthy considering the fact that Canada has committed itself quite expansively to institutional multiculturalism and has also ensured that protections for 'aboriginal and treaty rights of the aboriginal peoples' were enshrined in section 35 of the *Constitution Act, 1982.* Most glaring is the absence of an Indigenous or visible minority judge on the Supreme Court of Canada.

There have been repeated calls from prominent organizations and academics for an Indigenous judge to be named to the Court. Writing in 2014, Rosemary Cairns Way discussed the under-representation of Indigenous judges among federal judicial appointments generally. She observed that 'fifteen years after the Supreme Court of Canada decided in *R v Gladue* that the overrepresentation of Aboriginal peoples in the criminal justice system qualified as a "crisis", the likelihood of an Aboriginal person facing an Aboriginal judge is virtually unchanged. The number of federally appointed Aboriginal judges in Canada hovers at less than one per cent.'[49]

While Canada's judiciary is certainly not as homogenous as it was a hundred years ago, what is viewed by many today as homogenous is different from the conception of homogeneity present a hundred years ago. The appointment of a judge who was born to Ukranian parents might have been unheard of at the beginning of the last century, but this type of appointment does not carry the same weight it once did with respect to diversity and representation in the judiciary. What would make the judiciary less homogenous today is the increasing

47 S. Lyon and L. Sossin, 'Data and Diversity in the Canadian Justice Community', Osgoode Legal Studies Research Paper Series, 2014, pp. 3–4, subsequently published as 'Diversity and Data in the Canadian Justice Community', *Journal of Law and Equality* 11, 2014.

48 F. L. Morton, 'Judicial Appointments in Post-Charter Canada: A System in Transition', in K. Malleson and P. H. Russell (eds), *Appointing Judges in an Age of Judicial Power: Critical Perspectives from Around the World*, Toronto: University of Toronto Press, 2006, p. 68.

49 Cairns Way, 'Deliberate Disregard', pp. 54–55.

appointment of judges from non-white populations or from non-Christian religious groups. The 'judicial firsts' outlined above were certainly important at the time; however, the short history of diverse judicial appointments in Canada demonstrates that increasing diversity in the judiciary has not moved quickly enough, or kept pace with demographic realities in Canada.

Judicial appointment processes, controversy, and the current debate

Reform of the judicial appointment process and diversity of the judiciary has been an issue for many years under both Conservative and Liberal governments. However, it is doubtful whether a government has received more attacks from the legal community and public at large on its handling of judicial appointments and judicial diversity than the Conservatives led by Stephen Harper between 2006 and 2015. The purpose of this section is to first summarize the legislative and administrative framework present up to that point, outline some of the issues that appeared during the 'Harper years', address the commitments and actions of the Liberal government led by Justin Trudeau, and consider the 'way forward' in identifying problems and potential solutions.

Constitutional, legislative, and administrative standards

The federal and provincial government's appointment processes are governed by separate provisions of the *Constitution Act, 1867*, with each level of government enacting its own legislation and developing administrative processes related to judicial appointments.[50]

Constitutional and legislative framework

Under section 92(14) of the *Constitution Act, 1867* each provincial government in Canada is responsible for appointing all judges for its provincial courts. These courts are typically referred to as 'lower' courts or courts of first instance for matters related to civil, criminal, and family law. Under section 96, the federal government is responsible for appointing judges to the provincial superior courts – which serve as 'higher' trial courts and courts of appeal for cases originating out of section 92 provincial courts. Under section 101 of the *Constitution Act, 1867* the federal government is also responsible for appointing judges to federal courts. All judicial appointments are made by the Governor General in Council – in practice the federal cabinet – on the recommendation of the Minister of Justice. The

50 Unfortunately, at the federal level there has been a huge discrepancy between the lack of commitment to diversity in the appointments process and the federal government's institutional commitment to multiculturalism and diversity. For more on official Canadian multiculturalism see M. Dewing, *Canadian Multiculturalism*, Library of Parliament, 2009, Online, Available www.lop.parl.gc.ca/content/lop/researchpublications/2009-20-e.pdf (accessed 13 December 2016).

exceptions are appointments of Chief Justices and judges to the Supreme Court of Canada, which are made on the recommendation of the Prime Minister.

Noteworthy legislation that has governed the appointment of judges are the federal *Judges Act* and *the Supreme Court Act.* Although the *Judges Act* sets minimum qualifications for appointment to a section 96 or 101 court (for example, having practised in a province for a minimum of ten years), it is fairly skeletal with respect to other criteria relating to qualifications or areas of proficiency.[51] The *Supreme Court Act* contains a similar story. As a result, both of these Acts are 'perhaps more noteworthy for what they do not include'[52] since they say 'little or nothing about the actual system [of appointments] in place. Frequently, what is in place is the consequence of policy directives or guidelines that are ad hoc and informal.'[53]

The case can be different at the provincial level. For example, in Ontario in 1995 the *Courts of Justice Act* formally established in 1995 the Judicial Appointments Advisory Committee (JAAC) – though the programme actually began as a pilot project in 1988. According to section 43(8) of the Act, the purpose of the JAAC is to 'make recommendations to the Attorney General for the appointment of judges'.

The JAAC receives applications for judicial positions, evaluates candidates, conducts interviews, and provides a ranked list of recommended appointments to the Attorney General, who makes the final selection. The *Courts of Justice Act* states that the Attorney General 'shall recommend to the Lieutenant Governor in Council for appointment to fill a judicial vacancy only a candidate who has been recommended for that vacancy by the Committee' and that the 'Attorney General may reject the Committee's recommendations and require it to provide a fresh list'.[54] The JAAC is often cited within Canada and internationally as an example of a transparent, non-partisan appointment process.[55]

Administrative processes

Judicial appointments are heavily reliant on administrative processes and at the federal level in particular, have suffered from a lack of accountability and transparency. Changes were made to the federal process in 1988 in order to create a more streamlined application process. The system – which continues to exist today – consists of a vetting process by an advisory committee ('Judicial Advisory Committee' or JAC, at least one in each province or territory) to provide advice on candidates' qualifications for appointment. This process is administered by the Commissioner of Federal Judicial Affairs, who provides administrative support for each of the advisory committees.

There are issues with this system of appointment. For example, the establishment of the advisory committees and Commissioner's Office has not necessarily excluded

51 L. Sossin, 'Judicial Appointment, Democratic Aspirations, and the Culture of Accountability', *University of New Brunswick Law Journal* 58, 2008, p. 11.
52 Ibid., p. 9.
53 Devlin, MacKay and Kim, 'Reducing the Democratic Deficit', p. 41.
54 *Courts of Justice Act*, ss. 43(11) and (12).
55 Morton, 'Judicial Appointments in Post-Charter Canada', pp. 69–70.

political factors from the judicial appointment process or ensured that a candidate's political past is not considered.[56] Furthermore, there is no enforceable remedy if the government breaches the recognized practice of not recommending to Cabinet a candidate not previously recommended by an advisory committee. Practically speaking, the committees typically find a broad range of candidates at least 'qualified' which provides 'little meaningful constraint' on the federal government's appointment power (and, worse than that, suggests that the committees serve an accountability function that they have neither the authority nor the will to perform).[57]

Appointments to the Supreme Court of Canada have worked differently. Historically very little was known about appointments to the Court since much of the process was secretive and took place behind closed doors. More may have been 'known about the process for electing a new Pope than about the process for selecting a new Supreme Court justice.'[58] An attempt at disclosure and changing the process was made between 2004 and 2005 by Minister of Justice, Irwin Cotler, who served under the Liberal government of Prime Minister Paul Martin.

Specifically, Colter revealed a 'permanent reform' process where: 1) the Minister would conduct consultations to form a long list of five to eight candidates; 2) an Advisory Committee would provide a list of three names to the Minister after an assessment with a commentary of strengths and weaknesses; 3) The Prime Minister would select a candidate on the recommendation of the Minister; and 4) The Minister would appear before a committee to explain the process and selection.[59] When Justice John Major of the Supreme Court of Canada subsequently announced his retirement, Minister Cotler began implementing this process. However, the Liberal government soon fell and they were unable to complete the appointment.

Appointment processes under Stephen Harper's Conservatives

Seven of the nine Supreme Court justices sitting on the Court today were named by Stephen Harper during his nine years as Prime Minister.[60] The government

56 P. Bryden and L. Sossin, 'Judges', in A. M. Dodek and J. G. Hoskins (eds), *Barristers and Solicitors in Practice*, Toronto: Butterworths, 1998, para 11.32.

57 Sossin, 'Judicial Appointment', p. 11. In addition, the roles of these committees were revised under the Harper Conservatives, so that rather than determining whether candidates were 'not recommended', 'recommended', or 'highly recommended', judicial advisory committees would only determine if candidates were 'not recommended' or 'recommended'. Those who were deemed to be 'recommended' were then passed on to the Minister of Justice who would, in consultation with Cabinet and the local judiciary and Bar, determine the candidates to be appointed, with the final decision being made by the government. The Trudeau Government subsequently reversed these changes and reverted to the prior standard. See S. Fine, 'Liberals Overhaul Judicial Appointments Process to Boost Diversity', *The Globe and Mail*, October 20, 2016.

58 A. M. Dodek, 'Reforming the Supreme Court Appointment Process 2004–2014: A 10 Year Democratic Audit', SCLR 67, 2014, (2d) pp. 111–117, 4.

59 Ibid., p. 7.

60 From 2006 to 2015.

named eight Supreme Court judges in total[61] and over half of the current federal judiciary.[62] The number of appointments is noteworthy not only because of the volume of judicial appointments that occurred over the course of nine years, but because of the negative publicity, reaction, and controversy that the judicial appointments received during this time.

Supreme Court of Canada appointments under Stephen Harper's Conservatives

When the Conservatives won a minority government in 2006, one of the first matters of business was to fill the judicial vacancy on the Supreme Court following the retirement of Justice John Major. Prime Minister Stephen Harper chose Marshall Rothstein from the list of three candidates provided to the previous Liberal government. However, the Conservative government deviated from the Liberal plan by having the future Justice Rothstein appear before an ad hoc parliamentary committee – a first for a Supreme Court justice. Two days after the hearing, the Prime Minister named Justice Rothstein as a Supreme Court judge.[63]

Two years later, in order to fill a vacancy left by Justice Bastarache, Minister of Justice Rob Nicholson completed consultations and submitted a list of candidates to a selection panel of five MPs who were to provide an unranked list of three candidates. When the selection panel was overtaken by partisan bickering, the Prime Minister bypassed the list and named Thomas Cromwell as a nominee.[64] Cromwell did not appear at a Parliamentary committee before he was officially appointed because an election was soon triggered followed by a prorogation of Parliament by the Governor General (at the request of the Prime Minister).

In 2011, Prime Minister Harper filled two more vacancies (replacing Justices Ian Binnie and Louise Charron with Michael Moldaver and Andromache Karakatsanis) through the selection panel process used to appoint Justice Cromwell. The process included the involvement of a selection panel of MPs and the appearance of the nominees before a parliamentary committee. The same process was followed in 2012 to appoint Richard Wagner.[65] The government hit a major stumbling block and controversy in 2013 when they named Federal Court Justice Marc Nadon to the Supreme Court to replace Justice Morris Fish. In terms of

61 Justice Rothstein who was named in 2006, retired in 2015.
62 Cairns Way, 'Deliberate Disregard', p. 44.
63 For more, see Dodek, 'Reforming the Supreme Court Appointment Process'; Sossin, 'Should Canada Have a Representative Supreme Court'; and Sossin, 'Judicial Appointment'.
64 Dodek, 'Reforming the Supreme Court Appointment Process', p. 8.
65 By replacing Justice Marie Deschamps, the number of women on the Supreme Court dropped from four to three. Justice Deschamps herself subsequently stated 'Numbers do count … I was sad that I was not replaced by a woman. We are looked at not just as a model for the courts in Canada, but around the world – and I think it's very important that the Supreme Court of Canada remains a model.' See K. Makin, 'Supreme Court Needs More Women Departing Judge Says', *Globe and Mail*, 2 February 2013. The government appointed Suzanne Côté in 2013, once again bringing the number of women on the Court up to four.

process, the government followed the same method as the previous appointments. However, Nadon's appointment gave rise to a series of issues. First, Nadon was the first supernumerary judge named to the Supreme Court. (He had already elected to take partial retirement from the Federal Court of Appeal.) Second, Justice Nadon was not well known outside of the Federal Court where he served for twenty years, and the legal profession did not view him as a 'legal light'.[66] As one prominent Quebec legal academic observed, 'He was on nobody's short list … or on anybody's long list.'[67] The judgment of Justice Nadon that attracted the most attention was a dissent in *Canada (Prime Minister) v Khadr*,[68] in which he sided with the Harper government in a high profile decision involving a Canadian held at Guantanamo Bay.

But the most significant concern was whether Justice Nadon met the criteria to be one of three Quebec judges named to the Supreme Court pursuant to the *Supreme Court Act*. A Federal Court judge had never been named to the Supreme Court as one of the three Quebec judges in the past (the relevant section of the *Supreme Court Act* specifically referred to eligible candidates belonging to the Quebec Bar, the Quebec Superior Court, or the Quebec Court of Appeal).

Shortly after Nadon was appointed in October 2013, a constitutional challenge was initiated by a Toronto constitutional lawyer, while a separate challenge was launched by the province of Quebec. These actions led the federal government to send a reference to the Supreme Court of Canada regarding Justice Nadon's appointment and the Court's interpretation of the Quebec provisions of the *Supreme Court Act*. In an unprecedented 6–1 decision, the Supreme Court ruled that Nadon's appointment was contrary to the Quebec specific provisions of the Act, which were meant to ensure that the Court had civil law expertise 'and that Quebec's legal traditions and social values [were] represented on the Court *and* that Quebec's confidence in the Court [was] maintained'.[69]

On May 1, 2014, just as the drama over the Nadon judgment was subsiding, a headline in the *National Post* stated, 'Tories incensed with Supreme Court as some allege Chief Justice lobbied against Marc Nadon appointment.' John Ivison reported that 'senior Conservatives' advised that Chief Justice Beverley McLachlin may have lobbied against Nadon's appointment. Chief Justice McLachlin released a reply statement to the press through her executive legal officer stating that she had wished to ensure that the government was aware of the eligibility issue but at no time did she express opinions regarding that issue. The Prime Minister's Office issued its own follow-up statement, asserting that the Chief Justice initiated the call to the Minister of Justice, who

66 S. Fine, 'Supreme Court Rejects Harper Appointee Nadon', *The Globe and Mail*, 21 March 2014.

67 T. Hopper 'Marc Nadon caught Stephen Harper's attention with dissent Khadr ruling in 2009', *National Post*, 21 March 2014.

68 2009 FCA 246.

69 See *Reference re Supreme Court Act*, ss. 5 and 6, 2014 SCC 21 (the 'Nadon Reference') para 18.

advised that 'taking a phone call from the Chief Justice would be inadvisable and inappropriate'.[70]

The opposition, legal community, and many political observers were stunned by the allegations. The Canadian Bar Association Presidents (past and present) and the Canadian Council of Law Deans condemned the Prime Minister's conduct directed toward the Chief Justice. Hundreds of lawyers, academics, and concerned citizens signed an open letter deploring the Prime Minister's 'baseless insinuation'.[71] University of Manitoba professor Gerald Heckman and other legal academics brought a complaint to the International Committee of Jurists in Geneva.[72] Ultimately, neither the Prime Minister nor the Chief Justice backed down. A new Justice was appointed to the Court (Justice Clément Gascon, a well-known appellate judge with no ties to the government or track record of supporting its priorities) and both the Chief Justice and Prime Minister moved on (albeit with lingering unease) to other priorities.

Later in the year, Montreal lawyer Suzanne Côté was named as Justice Louis LeBel's replacement after the latter also stepped down from the Court. In both appointments that year, the government chose not to use a parliamentary committee to narrow down the list of candidates nor to hold a parliamentary hearing to question the judge (as had been done previously by the Conservative government), completing a new trend of appointment 'by news release'.[73]

In August 2015, on the eve of the federal election campaign, Stephen Harper announced that Russell Brown would be appointed to the Supreme Court to replace the retiring Justice Rothstein. What troubled commentators and the legal community about the appointment of Justice Brown – in addition to the continued lack of transparency or process – was that he was a 'prolific blogger' at the University of Alberta before he was appointed as a judge in 2013. During this time, he criticized the Supreme Court of Canada and Justin Trudeau, and was a vocal supporter of Stephen Harper. As respected scholar Adam Dodek wrote at the time:

> In Canada, we are not used to the appointment of judges who have said much of anything interesting, let alone controversial. While this surely should not disqualify Justice Brown from appointment, it would be reassuring for Canadians to hear directly from him that he will hear each case with an open mind.
>
> What Canadians really need, however, is to hear from the Minister of Justice or from the Prime Minister as to why they chose Justice Brown over

70 See 'Beverley McLachlin, PMO Give Duelling Statements on Nadon Appointment Fight', CBC, 1 May 2012.

71 T. MacCharles, 'Legal Community Demands Stephen Harper Withdraw Criticism of Beverley McLachlin', *Toronto Star*, 13 May 2014.

72 The ICJ responded that the Chief Justice's conduct was appropriate and that 'the criticism [by Harper] was not well-founded, and amounted to an encroachment upon the independence of the judiciary and integrity of the Chief Justice'.

73 A. Dodek, 'Accountability Needed: Why was Justice Russell Brown Appointed to the Top Court?', *Globe and Mail*, 5 August 2015.

many other supremely qualified candidates in Alberta, Manitoba and Saskatchewan. Some have expressed the view that Justice Brown was chosen precisely because he had expressed such strong pro-Conservative and anti-opposition views.[74]

Federal appointments to other courts under Stephen Harper

While the Supreme Court of Canada appointments and process accompanying it garnered the most headline grabbing attention, there were significant developments made under the Conservative government with respect to other federal appointments. As stated by Cairns Way, 'I worry that the (understandable) public and intellectual preoccupation with the Supreme Court has the effect of distracting from the arguably more significant implications of the government's approach to sections 96 and 101 appointments. Trial judges are the face of justice for ordinary Canadians. And the face they present, as noted above, is noteworthy for its homogeneity.'[75]

The *Globe and Mail*'s report from April 2012 found that in the previous three and a half years the Conservative government had appointed 100 new judges in various provinces, but that 98 of these appointments were white.[76] The report was startling since 'the lack of diversity among judges raises searching questions in a country where one in five citizens belongs to a visible minority and where many people can expect to see a bench that does not reflect them'.[77] What made the trends even more concerning was the 'opaque nature' of the appointment process and the fact that judges with vast powers of interpretation under the *Charter* were still being appointed behind closed doors.

Another *Globe and Mail* report found that the appointment of female judges under the Harper Conservatives had 'diminished to a trickle'.[78] In 2011, only eight women were appointed to federal judicial positions compared to 41 men. In addition there were 356 female judges among the total 1,117 federally appointed judges – despite the fact that parity had been within reach when the Conservatives came to power in 2006.[79] Professor Elizabeth Sheehy was quoted in the article as saying,

> If anything there is a larger pool of brilliant and exceptionally qualified women lawyers to draw upon since 2005. If the current process of selection cannot deliver anything approaching a representative bench ... then it is clear that something is broken.[80]

74 Ibid.
75 Cairns Way, 'Deliberate Disregard', p. 47.
76 Makin, 'Of 100 New Federally Appointed Judges'.
77 Ibid.
78 K. Makin, 'Appointment of Female Judges Slump Under Harper's Tories' *Globe and Mail*, 11 November 2011.
79 Ibid.
80 Ibid. Rosemary Cairns Way subsequently examined judicial appointments under the Harper Conservative government between April 17, 2012 and May 1, 2014 – a total

Other controversies

In June 2014, Canada's Justice Minister, Peter MacKay, became embroiled in controversy after an appearance at an Ontario Bar Association session. At the event MacKay was asked at the event what steps the government would take to address the lack of diverse federal judicial appointments, particularly with respect to visible minorities on the bench. According to multiple reports, Minister McKay responded by stating that the dearth of women and visible minorities on the federal courts was the result of people from these groups not applying. He then 'went on to say women fear an "old boys" network on the bench would dispatch them on circuit work to hear cases in courthouses across the region – a prospect he described as unappealing for women with children in the home.'[81]

MacKay's comments caused an uproar.[82] Criticism directed toward MacKay challenged the factual basis for his claim that qualified minority candidates were not applying, since the federal government does not keep statistics relating to the backgrounds of candidates.[83] MacKay's claim also led to a response from at least one prominent visible minority lawyer who stated that she and others she knew of had applied for federal judicial positions without any success.[84] Further, the idea that women lawyers were hesitant to apply for judicial positions was disputed by commentators who pointed out that judicial positions were actually highly coveted, in contrast to the abysmal appointment rate of aboriginal judges (1 per cent) and visible minority judges (0.5 per cent).[85] This controversy further highlighted the concern that 'ensuring that the judiciary reflects the community it serves … [was] not a priority for this government.'[86]

Movement toward reform

New government, new promises, new processes

On October 21, 2015 Canadians elected a Liberal majority government headed by Justin Trudeau, ending almost a decade of Conservative-led government under Stephen Harper (and reversing the fortunes of the Liberals from the previous election, where they were reduced to third party status). Transparency and

of 107 initial appointments. She found that 40 per cent of these were of women, while 90 appeared to be white and only one was confirmed as 'racialized' (she was unable to find sufficient identifying information for the other 16): see Cairns Way, 'Deliberate Disregard'.

81 T. MacCharles, 'Peter MacKay Tries to Explain Lack of Diversity on Federal Courts', *Toronto Star*, 18 June 2014.

82 Ibid.

83 T. MacCharles, 'Peter MacKay uses Facebook to Rebut "Inflammatory" Media Reports', *Toronto Star*, 23 June 2014.

84 T. MacCharles, 'Lawyer Disputes Peter MacKay's Claim that Women, Visible Minorities Don't Apply to be Judges', *Toronto Star*, 19 June 2014.

85 R. Cairns Way and others, 'Forget MacKay, A Woman's Place is on the Bench', *Globe and Mail*, 20 June 2014.

86 Ibid.

inclusion were key planks of the Liberal campaign. On judicial diversity, in particular, the Liberal platform included 'restoring dignity to the relationship between the government and the Supreme Court' and ensuring that the process of appointing Supreme Court Justices was 'transparent, inclusive, and accountable to all Canadians'.

In May 2016, after months of inaction on judicial appointments, stories began to surface that delays in reforming the appointment process for Trial and Appellate Courts[87] was placing stress on clogged courts and a judiciary that was already stretched thin (not to mention the Supreme Court of Canada, where a vacancy had been created when Justice Thomas Cromwell announced his intent to retire in 2016).[88] The first set of judicial appointments and promotions were finally made on June 17, 2016 using pre-existing processes. Of 15 appointments and promotions, ten were of women and two of visible minorities. These initial appointments and promotions were 'hardly revolutionary in 2016, but ... a welcome change from the trend of the past few years'.[89] The Liberal government also has introduced changes to the Judicial Advisory Committee mandate, which emphasize a judiciary that reflects the diversity of Canada and for the first time will require training for JAC members on diversity and inclusion, and will ask judicial applicants to self-identify by race, gender identity, Indigenous status, and physical disability.[90]

The most dramatic move by the Trudeau government came on August 2, 2016 when the government announced a new process for appointments to the Supreme Court of Canada. Under the new process, candidates can nominate themselves or be nominated by a newly created 'Advisory Board'.[91] Although the government retains exclusive discretion to select the justices, it must do so on the basis of a short list provided by the Advisory Board. The Board provides the 'nonbinding, merit-based' recommendations of three to five qualified and 'functionally bilingual' candidates to the Prime Minister for consideration. The Advisory Board must 'seek to support the Government of Canada's intent to achieve a Supreme Court of Canada that is gender-balanced and reflects the diversity of members of Canadian society.'

Once the Board recommends the short-listed candidates, it must explain how each candidate meets the publicly available criteria. Parliamentarians (through the House of Commons Standing Committee on Justice and Human Rights) have

87 A. Crawford, 'Justice System Can't Wait for Judicial Appointments Review, say Judges', CBC, 7 May 2016.

88 S. Fine, 'Supreme Court Vacancy a Chance for Trudeau Government to Reform Appointment Process', *The Globe and Mail*, 22 March 2016.

89 'A Good Start on Making Judges more Diverse: Editorial', *Toronto Star*, 22 June 2016.

90 S. Fine, 'Liberals Overhaul Judicial Appointments Process to Boost Diversity', *The Globe and Mail*, 20 October 2016.

91 The seven member advisory board includes the following: a retired judge nominated by the Canadian Judicial Council; two lawyers – one nominated by the Canadian Bar Association, the other by the Federation of Law Societies of Canada; a legal scholar nominated by the Council of Canadian Law Deans; three members (including two non-lawyers) nominated by the Minister of Justice. All members are appointed to renewable terms of six-months. The current Chair of the Advisory Board is former Conservative Prime Minister Kim Campbell.

opportunities to question the Minister of Justice and the Chair of the Advisory Board on the candidate ultimately selected, and become acquainted with the candidate in a session moderated by a legal academic. Interestingly, the Board is not required to recommend candidates from a particular region to replace an outgoing Supreme Court justice who is from that same region, as has been the norm.

Much of the criticism of the new process has focused on the failure to make this custom of 'regionalism' in Supreme Court appointments a requirement.[92] The Attorney General clarified in relation to the criticism that (at least) the shortlist for the upcoming appointment to replace retiring Justice Thomas Cromwell (from Nova Scotia) would include a potential appointment from the Atlantic region. Given Canada's constitutional history, regional representation has a clear logic and a compelling history – whether it captures understandings of what it means for the Court to 'reflect' Canada remains to be seen, especially in light of cross-cutting distinctions (urban/rural, north/south) that also define Canadians' sense of themselves and what they share. Additionally, Indigenous representation on the Court might focus less on provincial and regional boundaries, and more on Treaty territories or ancestral territories of specific First Nations (which, of course, cross provincial and regional boundaries in many cases). For all of these reasons, while regional representation remains significant, it alone cannot answer the questions around what a diverse and inclusive Supreme Court requires.

That said, the Liberal government's intent to move away from regional representation sparked a threatened lawsuit[93] as well as a non-binding Parliamentary resolution introduced by the Opposition calling on the government to 'respect the custom of regional representation' (which received unanimous approval).[94] Against the backdrop of the new process and the competing pressures over regional representation, functional bilingualism, and diversity, on October 17, 2016, the Prime Minister announced the nomination of Malcolm Rowe, a white, male Justice of the Court of Appeal of Newfoundland and Labrador, to the Supreme Court of Canada.[95] Justice Rowe will become the first person from the Bar of Newfoundland and Labrador (which joined Canada in 1949) to sit on the Court, and in that sense, represents a historic broadening of the representative reach of the Court. Justice Rowe demonstrated proficiency in both French and English during the friendly Parliamentary hearing held in Ottawa on October 25, 2016.

There are two additional questions related to diversity that need to be addressed. First, the introduction of a nomination process (including self-nomination), together with proactive outreach by an Advisory Committee with a mandate to

92 See Letter from Canadian Bar Association President Janet M. Fuhrer to the Prime Minister and Minister of Justice, 10 August 2016.

93 The Canadian Press, 'Atlantic Canada Lawyers Challenge Trudeau on Changes to Supreme Court Appointment Process', CBC, 19 September 2016.

94 K. Simpson, 'MPs Unanimously Support Regional Representation for the Supreme Court', CBC, 27 September 2016.

95 Justin Trudeau, Prime Minister of Canada press release, 'Prime Minister Announces Nomination of Mr. Justice Malcolm Rowe to the Supreme Court of Canada', 17 October 2016.

highlight inclusion, are intended to broaden the pool for Supreme Court appointments. Whether these procedural changes will contribute to the diversity of the Court remains to be seen, but from a design perspective, they are linked directly to the stated goal of doing so. Second, the new requirement that candidates for a Supreme Court appointment be 'functionally bilingual' may pose a barrier to other forms of diversity and inclusion in the appointment process.[96] Following the announcement of the new process, the Indigenous Bar Association called on the government to revisit the functional bilingualism requirement.[97] From their perspective, the new process would prioritize a candidate who speaks English and French over a candidate who speaks English and one of Canada's Indigenous languages, and a candidate who is bilingual and white should be preferred over one who is unilingual but reflects an ethnic community that is otherwise under-represented on the Court. As Canada evolves, a number of leaders of culturally diverse organizations have noted, so must its notions of diversity and inclusion.[98]

The way forward: identifying problems and possible solutions

Reforms to judicial appointments cannot solely depend on whether a particular government of the day is committed to a diverse judiciary. Canada has seen sharply diverging political discourse on federal judicial appointments between the Harper and Trudeau Governments. Political leadership inevitably shifts according to electoral fortunes. The quality of guardianship over the rule of law and the protection of minority rights ought not to change with the partisan winds.

There are a number of issues that need to be addressed in any potential reform – the current Liberal government has addressed some of these in revamping Canada's Supreme Court appointment process. However, the new system is far from perfect. It is clear that the conversation about what diversity and representation mean in Canada today must continue. While more transparent processes and diverse appointments are certainly welcome, it is essential that certain conceptions of diversity – whether cultural or otherwise – not be emphasized to the detriment of other conceptions of diversity.

Substantive changes to judicial appointments in Canada may also be required. To take just one example, the fact that the *Supreme Court Act* requires three judges from Quebec but no Indigenous judges is not sustainable. Not only has the Indigenous Bar called for such reform,[99] but reforms involving Indigenous judges

96 See L. Sossin, 'The Supreme Court's Long Road to Transparency and Inclusion', *Policy Options*, 9 August 2016.

97 'Indigenous Bar Association Calls upon the Government of Canada to Reconsider its Requirement of "Functional Bilingualism" As It Applies to Indigenous Candidates for Appointment to the Supreme Court', Nation Talk, 22 August 2016.

98 See M. Draaisma, 'New Supreme Court Justice Selection Process Won't Lead to Diverse Bench: Toronto lawyer' CBC, 3 August 2016.

99 Indigenous Bar Association, 'Indigenous Bar Association Appeals to Harper Government to Appoint an Aboriginal Justice to the Supreme Court of Canada', 19 July 2011.

are also consistent with the federal government's stated intentions on adopting the Truth and Reconciliation Commission's Call to Action#42, which commits Canadian governments to 'the recognition and implementation of Aboriginal justice systems in a manner consistent with the Treaty and Aboriginal rights of Aboriginal peoples, the Constitution Act, 1982, and the United Nations Declaration on the Rights of Indigenous Peoples, endorsed by Canada in November 2012.'[100]

Furthermore, if inclusion and transparency are the key prongs for reform in Canada (as the Trudeau government has claimed), then the following specific reforms should follow:

1 Engage in a consultative and public process to determine the various aspects of 'merit' which should inform judicial appointments, including the professional, social, and personal traits and background that candidates bring to the position;
2 Collect and disseminate data on judicial applications (including age, gender, ethnicity/culture, race, language, and socio-economic status in addition to educational credentials and professional background);
3 Adopt a plan with clear goals and benchmarks on what it means for Canada's judiciary to reflect Canadian society;
4 Proactive recruitment of qualified judicial candidates from historically underrepresented communities in the judiciary;
5 Development of an appointment commission process with a mandate for inclusion and clear criteria for merit; and
6 Enhance and clarify the practice for ensuring that the Minister of Justice is accountable to a Parliamentary committee for judicial appointments.

Reforms must correct systemic issues and put transparent processes in place that will outlast a particular party or leader. As set out earlier in this review, valuing diversity in the judiciary includes a fair and inclusive appointment process in addition to a culture of transparency.

Conclusion

Canada's federally appointed judiciary has underperformed with respect to diversity and inclusion, particularly during the recent period of Conservative governments. Although this situation is poised to change dramatically during the tenure of the current Liberal government, it is clear that Canada has a long way to go in seeing a diverse judiciary that accurately reflects Canada's population and employs appropriate processes to ensure this. What is less clear is how the structural aspects of Canada's judiciary and the appointment process itself will continue to evolve. At the moment, the amount of diversity and inclusion flows directly and entirely from the political leadership of the specific government in power at any particular moment.

100 Truth and Reconciliation Commission, *Calls to Action* (2015).

With respect to the Supreme Court of Canada, Chief Justice McLachlin recently suggested that indigenous and other minorities should not be catapulted to the highest court without members of those communities having had the chance to develop experience in the lower courts: the solution to the dearth of diversity at the highest court would therefore be increased diversity in the lower courts.[101] While increased diversity in the lower courts is extremely important, the idea that there may not be enough capable candidates – particularly indigenous candidates in the lower courts, law faculties, and among practising lawyers – is problematic in ensuring more diverse representation in the short-term.

There are no objective guarantees that Canada's judiciary will come to reflect Canadian society in the future. As a result, entrenching the goal of a reflective judiciary needs to be a shared enterprise across the various branches of government. For example, the judiciary itself needs to reflect further on the role of the appointment process as a condition of the constitutional principle of judicial independence. Parliament must also consider the potential role of diversity and inclusion criteria in the *Supreme Court Act*, *Federal Court Act*, and related statutes, and give statutory imprimatur to the judicial advisory committee structure. The Executive should consider how to provide enduring facets to the appointment process that will counter the tendency for each government to approach appointments according to shifting political priorities. While the Executive must remain meaningfully accountable for judicial appointments, that process must remain free from political interference and partisan considerations. The goal of a diverse and inclusive judiciary is to reflect democratic aspirations and serve as a bulwark protecting the rule of law and the constitutional protection of minorities and the disenfranchised. Canada appears at last to be moving more deliberately in this direction, but has some ways to go before this goal is fully recognized.

101 T. MacCharles 'More Indigenous Judges Needed in Lower Court to Develop Skills for Supreme Court: Beverley McLachlin' *Toronto Star*, 10 August 2016.

Reflection

Frances Kirkham CBE

Her Honour Frances Kirkham CBE served as a judicial member of the Judicial Appointments Commission between 2006 and 2011. She was a Senior Circuit Judge in the Technology and Construction Court in Birmingham until her retirement in 2011. She is a founder member of the UK Association of Women Judges.

The first five years of the JAC were exciting and successful. These things stand out.

The excitement of creating a new approach

There may have been some, especially in government, who thought that the JAC would simply continue what the Department for Constitutional Affairs (DCA) had been doing: that we would take over the DCA staff and adopt their procedures. There was no question of that. We quickly developed a completely new approach.

One of the earliest tasks was to define merit and good character, so that we could be confident that we would comply with the requirements of section 63 of the Constitutional Reform Act 2005. We drafted definitions of each, consulted widely and took account of points raised. It was important that our processes be as transparent as possible. So we published the criteria for merit and good character: all could see the standards we would apply.

At an early stage we decided to consider only those candidates who had applied for appointment. We would not continue the old tap-on-the-shoulder approach. We also introduced a requirement that candidates write a self-assessment including evidence to demonstrate how they met the merit criteria. It was puzzling that this proved controversial: it is common practice in so many other areas of work.

For some posts the number of those applying was high. In the selection exercise for Deputy District Judge (Magistrates Court) in 2008/2009 we received 817 applications for 26 posts. In the same period for one of the Recorder exercises we received 983 applications for 128 vacancies. We needed to find a way to manage these fairly. It was difficult to be confident that short-listing for such large numbers by reference only to paper applications and references would be fair. So we introduced written tests as a short-listing tool. Detailed work was undertaken to create test papers which would probe the range of behaviours and skills which we had identified as demonstrating merit. The JAC was helped by practitioners who took time to try out and review test papers for us. In addition, for those posts which would, for most applicants, be their first judicial post (for example, Deputy District Judge and Recorder) we introduced role-play as part of the selection process. This helped identify candidates who were likely to be able to work effectively and courteously with court users and staff.

We identified at an early stage that selection of Deputy High Court judges lay outside the remit of the JAC.[1] As experience of sitting as a Deputy High Court judge was likely to be advantageous to those who aimed at High Court appointment, it was important that the selection of deputies should be as fair and transparent as possible. The senior judiciary worked with us to develop procedures which made the process more transparent and which, we hoped, would make it more likely that candidates from non-traditional backgrounds would be considered.

Before the inception of the JAC, the previous practice in relation to some junior posts had been to create a pool of appointable candidates, then select from that pool when vacancies arose. This approach had resulted in some candidates waiting for years, not knowing whether they would ever be appointed. The JAC successfully challenged continuation of that practice.

We recognized that it was necessary for some of the post requirements to be relaxed if we were to be able to encourage candidates from non-traditional backgrounds to apply for appointment. For a short period we persuaded the Ministry of Justice (MoJ) to do this. For example, they agreed that candidates for appointment as a District Judge need not have previously sat as a deputy. However, our success in that example was short-lived. And we were unsuccessful in our suggestion that the sitting requirements for a High Court judge be reviewed to make the office more attractive for example to those who would find it difficult to spend long periods away from home. Work patterns made it difficult to encourage candidates from diverse backgrounds to apply for senior posts.

Outreach

Prior to the creation of the JAC, people from non-traditional backgrounds generally considered that they would never even be considered for appointment. It was a joy – and a matter of satisfaction – to realize when talking to people at outreach events that many took the view that, if they applied, the JAC would take their application seriously and the selection process would be conducted fairly.

The privilege and pleasure of working with other Commissioners and JAC staff

From the first meeting Commissioners worked well and happily together. Although lay members had to catch up fast, they learned very quickly and

1 This exclusion was widely criticized. Deputy High Court Judge appointments were brought within the remit of the JAC in 2014.

developed a genuine feel for the demands of the work of a judge or tribunal member. Lay and non-lay members learned from each other. Non-lay members appreciated the contribution made by lay Commissioners on all aspects of the selection process, including whether a candidate met the standards for legal competence and intellectual ability. Of course, we did not always all agree, but discussions were always thoughtful and courteous. Persuasive arguments were acknowledged.

The JAC staff welcomed the involvement of and interest taken by Commissioners and worked hard and imaginatively to implement new processes and cope with the large numbers of applicants.

The JAC were making major changes which impacted on others. Our first Chairman, Baroness Usha Prashar, exercised great skill in maintaining good relationships and working cooperatively with outside bodies, often in difficult circumstances. She fought the hard battles with the senior judiciary, ministers and MoJ (and from which the JAC currently benefits). Baroness Prashar ran a happy and effective team and did so with authority, grace and good humour.

The hostility

Perhaps it was not surprising that we experienced so much hostility. The JAC's fresh approach was widely and publicly criticized, especially by those who perceived their interests to be threatened. Barristers were critical: they would face more competition from others – such as solicitors and academics. Many judges were vocal in their opposition to what we were doing. We were criticized for most of our innovations including doing away with the tap on the shoulder, requiring candidates to write a self-assessment to explain why they merited appointment and introducing written tests.

In the early days there was still a strongly-held view that a successful advocate would make a good judge. Our tough selection criteria took us away from that idea, but the view persisted. Senior judges sometimes complained that their favoured candidate had not succeeded (and therefore concluded that the JAC's process was flawed). When we looked at the performance of the supposed star candidate we generally found that he or she had performed badly, often having taken little trouble to prepare properly.

We worked with judges to encourage them to write useful and fair comments in references and in responses to requests for statutory consultation. In the early days we read comments to the effect that the referee knew X's father, who was a jolly good chap, so his son would of course make a splendid judge. It was distressing to read in references, or on statutory consultation, of behaviour by a man described as assertive and confident, and the same behaviour in a woman described as aggressive and strident. Gradually, this changed and we began to receive fair, considered, evidence-based comment which was of genuine help. But we still had to manage the imbalance of information. For example, a successful barrister might be known to a number of supposedly influential judges whereas a solicitor might know none. Commissioners – and especially lay Commissioners – were alive to the potential unfairness that might result.

There was unfair criticism of the JAC in relation to delays. The JAC's procedures were as streamlined as we could make them. The delays came from other parts of the system over which the JAC had no control. In our first year of operation, it often took eight weeks for the MoJ to clarify its vacancy request (the trigger for action by the JAC) then four to six months for the JAC to complete the entire selection process, from advertising the post to sending its recommendation to the Lord Chancellor. Thereafter it could take up to eleven months from the time when the MoJ accepted the recommendation until the successful candidate took up the post. But the JAC, unfairly, was blamed for all the delays.

A learning organization

We recognized that a successful organization is one which learns. We wanted to be able to assess our effectiveness. Had we selected the right people? Were the candidates we selected good at the job? The absence of appraisal or other form of job assessment for most judicial posts made it impossible for us to measure our effectiveness. We could do little more than listen to anecdotal evidence.

Interference and threats to existence

Most of the first Commissioners were appointed for terms of either four or five years, with the intention that there would be some continuity as Commissioners completed their term of office and were replaced by new Commissioners. This careful pattern was abandoned. It was difficult to understand the why. The result was a serious lack of continuity.

The threat to abolish the JAC and bring appointments back into government in 2010 was astonishing, and deeply depressing. How could it be seriously be thought right put the independent genie back in the bottle?

Conclusion

As inaugural Commissioners we were very conscious of our responsibility and made every effort to ensure that we laid strong foundations and established precedents which would stand the test of time. The last ten years have shown that they have. Together, the first Commissioners changed the world of judicial appointments. It was a huge privilege to have been part of that.

Reflection

Noel Lloyd CBE

Professor Noel Lloyd CBE has been a lay member of the Judicial Appointments Commission since 2012. An academic mathematician, he has held a number of academic positions, and was Vice-Chancellor of Aberystwyth University from 2004 until his retirement in 2011. He served as a member of the Commission on Devolution in Wales (the Silk Commission). He was a board member of Jisc and Chair of High Performance Computing Wales; he is Chair of Fair Trade Wales. The views expressed here are his own.

I have been a Judicial Appointments Commissioner since 2012. My background is as an academic mathematician who, as a university Vice-Chancellor and in previous roles, became very familiar with appointments processes generally and with issues of governance. I was also embedded in the life of Wales, both through my involvement in Higher Education and in other ways. The Constitutional Reform Act 2005, and the Judicial Appointments Regulations under the Crime and Courts Act 2013, require there to be, as far as is practicable, a Commissioner with 'special knowledge' of Wales. The work on the Judicial Appointments Commission (JAC) fitted neatly with my membership of the Commission on Devolution in Wales (the Silk Commission) and there was a helpful confluence of interest. This Commission completed its work in 2014, and its work is described in two reports.[1]

I describe my particular engagement with Welsh matters later, but I shall first include some general reflections on the JAC and its work. I then comment on the role of Assigned Commissioner and, finally, I emphasise the importance of attracting diverse candidates for judicial office.

Personal reflections

I have greatly valued – and enjoyed – my experience as a Commissioner: it has been thoroughly satisfying. My over-riding thoughts are of the importance of the

1 *Empowerment and Responsibility: Financial Powers to Strengthen Wales* (November 2012); *Empowerment and Responsibility: Legislative Powers to Strengthen Wales* (March 2014).

appointments for which we make recommendations, naturally, but also of the care and attention with which the Commission conducts its business. We take much for granted in this country in terms of the independence of the judiciary. We must guard this jealously, of course. But it is also important that appointment to judicial positions be made independently, openly and transparently, and on the basis of merit and merit alone.

I have throughout my time found the Commission itself to be an extremely stimulating – and pleasant – group of people. Members come from a range of backgrounds and bring their own particular skills and experience. The judicial members contribute from their particular knowledge but it is a group in which everyone's views have equal status.

One of the things that struck me early on was the sheer number of appointments being processed. In my first years I recall, there were over 700 recommendations out of about 5,500 applications. In recent years it has been more like half these numbers.

The JAC staff also play an exceedingly important role, and are committed to their tasks. Things occasionally go wrong, of course, but I have been impressed with the instinct for public service which I have seen. In common with most other public bodies, there has been a significant reduction in resource over recent years. The JAC is no exception to having to do more with considerably less; inevitably, as a result, the large number of individual transactions places strain on administrative procedures and, more especially, on those who apply them and on candidates in using them.

On a personal level, I have appreciated involvement in panels for senior appointments. The constitution of these panels is laid down in legislation, and though some are chaired by members of the senior judiciary, they are formally committees of the JAC and have a majority of lay commissioners. In addition to the intrinsic interest of the task, I have found the panels to be extremely well balanced, with the lay members playing a full part in proceedings. Judicial members bring particular knowledge, of course, but the views they express are challenged vigorously by the lay members and have to be explained fully to them.

The particular requirements of Wales

The Commission is very much aware of its responsibilities in relation to the requirements of Wales. As a result of the devolution of responsibilities from the Westminster Parliament following successive Government of Wales Acts (1998, 2006, 2014 and now the Wales Act 2017), the law applicable in Wales is diverging to an increasingly significant extent from that applicable in England,[2] and this divergence is certain to increase further.

There is a comment in the second report of the Silk Commission that judges and members of tribunals serving in Wales should have an awareness and understanding of the particular requirements of Wales. The JAC responded to these, and the Lord Chief Justice was strongly supportive.

2 See, for example, the recently published report by the Law Commission *Form and Accessibility of the Law Applicable in Wales* (Law Commission Report No. 366, 2016).

For positions which require working in Wales, the JAC has developed mechanisms to ensure that successful candidates demonstrate an understanding of the administration of justice in Wales or have the ability to acquire that understanding. I should emphasize that it is awareness that is required, rather than detailed knowledge of devolution arrangements and the divergence of the law. The use of the Welsh language in courts and tribunals is also an important feature.

We have developed a pattern of how to test for the required understanding, and though it is a learning process, it is being established as part of 'business as usual'. The detailed approach depends on the requirements of the position under consideration. A separate element of the interview is devoted to these matters, appropriately moderated. The assessment of this part does not contribute to the overall assessment of merit, but is a requirement which must be satisfied separately. It requires a modicum of preparation – I venture to say that this is not always apparent to the extent that perhaps one would expect. Some give excellent responses – others less so!

The process starts with briefing the panels – essential in multi-panel exercises – and the preparation of indicative responses. Often candidates apply for positions in several circuits, so it is not possible to isolate the candidates for Wales for the attention of one panel.

We also now have experience of recommending members of some of the Welsh Tribunals, in this case to the Welsh Government as the appropriate authority. I have been very pleased that the JAC has taken on this work. These have been interesting selections, and the experience is one which can be built upon in future.[3]

As a public body which operates in Wales, the JAC must fulfil the statutory requirement that the Welsh language be treated no less favourably than English. Until recently, the JAC was covered by an 'umbrella' scheme, that of the Ministry of Justice. It became clear to me that this was not satisfactory in that much of it was not directly relevant. It would be better to develop a bespoke scheme applying to the JAC and the specific range of work which it does, thereby also ensuring that responsibility rests closer to the point of implementation.

The Commission agreed, and we set about developing a scheme. Following a constructive period of consultation, the scheme was endorsed by the Welsh Language Commissioner in May 2016. In matters relating to Wales generally, I have found the Commission and JAC staff very supportive of the importance of responding appropriately and proportionately.

The right to use the Welsh language in courts and tribunals is well-established, and derives from the Welsh Language Act 1993, which requires that the English and Welsh languages be treated on the basis of equality in the administration of justice in Wales. Thus enough judges and tribunal members are required who can

3 See, in a slightly different context, the recent statement by Carwyn Jones, the First Minister ('Written Statement – Publication of the legacy report of the Committee for Administrative Justice and Tribunals, Wales and the Welsh Government's response' August 2016).

operate professionally in the Welsh language. Whether an individual post requires the ability to operate in Welsh is included in the Vacancy Request and determined by the Judicial Office and HM Courts and Tribunals Service following consultation with the court or tribunal concerned. In such cases, the JAC will prepare the selection materials and advertise bilingually. Applications in Welsh are welcome. Candidates are asked to describe their experience of operating professionally through the medium of Welsh and their competence is assessed at selection time. This is done in various ways, depending on circumstances. Welsh speaking panellists have been recruited, and if necessary simultaneous translation is used in interviews. This works well – the standard of simultaneous translation is always very high, and it is unobtrusive.

I have been the Assigned Commissioner in exercises requiring competence in Welsh and as part of the quality assurance role I am in a position to give reassurance in relation to the outcome. I am pleased with the way in which this is working, and look forward the process becoming firmly embedded.

The role of an Assigned Commissioner

The JAC's role is to respond to 'Vacancy Requests'. For all selection exercises up to (but not including) the High Court, the hard work of sifting and interviewing is done by panels. The JAC appoints and trains a pool of panellists (about 60 of them); generally an individual panel consists of a lay chair, one other lay member and a judicial member. Selection decisions are taken by the Commission sitting as the Selection and Character Committee (SCC), making recommendations to the 'appropriate authority', as laid down in legislation.

One of the slightly frustrating aspects of the process is the tendency for late changes in vacancy requests (as regards the number of appointments to be filled, for example). When this occurs late in the planning process, or, worse, after an exercise is launched, problems can, and do, arise; though not of its doing, the JAC is in the front line for criticism!

For each selection exercise, one commissioner is 'assigned' to it (for large exercises there may be two). The Assigned Commissioner role is essentially one of quality assurance. They are involved in the exercise throughout, from the earliest planning stages, through to selection and reporting to the SCC. The Commissioner is involved in deciding on the appropriate selection tools, is present at panel preparation events, observes the sift and some interviews and, importantly, attends the various moderations. The Assigned Commissioner also has an important role in relation to diversity – contributing to discussion of outreach and monitoring the diversity of candidates at each stage.

I think that all Commissioners find the role of assigned commissioner to be an interesting one – I certainly do. You feel very much involved in the nuts and bolts of the work which the JAC was established to undertake. At the same time, one has to be careful about respecting the separation of the responsibilities of the commissioner and of JAC staff, who take day-to-day decisions and communicate with candidates.

Selection often consists of responses to a number of scenarios together with a structured interview. For most fee-paid positions, role play is used, in which actors are used in a scenario to test a candidate's responses to a simulated court environment, testing instinctive 'judgecraft'. This is interesting and, in my experience, provides valuable information.

Some selection exercises receive a very large number of applications. For fee-paid roles such as Recorder and Deputy District Judge, there have been well over 1,000 applications. The first task then is to reduce the number through some kind of objective qualifying test to a manageable number to be interviewed. Various approaches are used, depending on the nature of the position and the number of candidates, and the JAC is currently reviewing the range of mechanisms available to it, taking into account their efficacy and their impact on the candidate experience.

Considerable thought is given to the measures necessary to assure consistency. Even when there is only one panel, one must guard against drift over time. Reports on sift and interviews are compiled at the time and against the specific competencies required in the position under consideration. The challenge is all the greater when there are several panels – as there have to be for very large exercises. Interviews, for example, can extend over several weeks and can involve up to eight or so panels for the largest exercises.

The preparation and briefing of panels is obviously key to the process, and in order to establish consistency, a very careful process of regular calibration and moderation is used. The Assigned Commissioner has a role, but the burden falls on JAC staff. The effect of putting in place these measures to optimize consistency is that the whole process can appear burdensome and time consuming. But fairness and consistency are paramount, and come at a cost. One of the continuing challenges is to maintain fairness and the perception of fairness, while at the same time improving the candidate experience and ensuring a high degree of confidence in the process.

Attracting diverse candidates

The JAC takes its statutory duty to encourage diversity in the range of those available for selection very seriously. Within what is permissible under statute, it also seeks to ensure diverse outcomes in the appointments it makes. Society generally expects that the composition of the judiciary reflects the diversity of the communities which are served to a greater extent than currently.

The Commission has developed and implemented a comprehensive diversity strategy, and works closely with key partners in the judiciary and the professions through the Judicial Diversity Forum. However, my fellow Commissioners and I are very much aware of the challenges that remain.

Good progress has been made on increasing the proportion of women at most levels (for example, in 2015/16, 44 per cent of recommendations to legal positions were women) but there has been limited progress so far at the most senior levels. The under-representation of black and minority ethnic individuals remains a significant challenge at most levels, and it has been frustrating that the rate of progress has not been greater.

For my own part, I am also particularly keen to see high quality applications from candidates working in Wales and those wishing to work in Wales. This includes, but is by no means limited to, candidates who have the Welsh language skills required for some positions.

There is also an opportunity for high quality applicants from different parts of the legal sector. I would particularly like to see more academics applying for judicial positions in the Courts and Tribunals. I believe that such work can enhance their work in teaching and research.

Finally, I should like to encourage anyone who is considering applying for judicial positions to consult the JAC's on-line *Am I Ready?* tool and especially to urge applicants not to be discouraged if initially their applications are unsuccessful.

8 Judging the JAC

How much judicial influence over judicial appointments is too much?

Graham Gee[1]

Introduction

Judicial involvement in judicial appointments is valuable. Judges possess unique perspectives on the qualities required for judicial office as well as the needs of the judicial system. Such perspectives should help to shape individual selections as well as the aims, priorities and structures of the selection regime as a whole. Hence, the pertinent question is not whether judges should exercise influence, but how much, what sorts and at which stages of the appointment process. To my mind, these are amongst the most challenging questions with which those responsible for designing, operating or scrutinizing a judicial selection regime must grapple. Questions such as these will give rise to rival and opposing views, not only at the time at which a new appointment regime is introduced, but also periodically thereafter, as and when experience suggests that judges exercise too little influence or too much. During the Judicial Appointments Commission's (JAC) first decade, however, there has been only relatively muted discussion of these questions. A handful of academics have argued that judges today exercise too much influence.[2] However, their concerns are not

1 This chapter draws on confidential interviews conducted between 2011 and 2014 with many of those involved in the judicial selection process in England and Wales. These interviews were part of a project funded by the Arts and Humanities Research Council (AH/H039554/1). These were augmented by a further round of interviews conducted between 2015 and 2017 with senior judges, officials at the Ministry of Justice and officials and commissioners at the JAC. The Society of Legal Scholars' Research Activities Fund supported this second round of interviews. I am very grateful to the interviewees and for comments on this paper from participants at the following conferences: *The Paradox of Judicial Independence* at the Institute of Government (July 2015); *Judicial Appointments in an Age of Diversity* at the University of Birmingham (November 2015); and the *International Legal Ethics Conference VII* at Fordham Law School (July 2016).

2 See e.g.: G. Gee, R. Hazell, K. Malleson and P. O'Brien, *The Politics of Judicial Independence in the UK's Changing Constitution*, Cambridge: Cambridge University Press, 2015; and A. Paterson and C. Paterson, *Guarding the Guardians: Towards an Independent, Accountable and Diverse Senior Judiciary*, London: CentreForum, 2012. Concerns were also hinted at in S. Shetreet and S. Turenne, *Judges on Trial: The*

widely shared by judges, politicians, officials or lawyers.[3] Or more bluntly put: several stakeholders – and the JAC and the senior judiciary in particular – seem wholly unconvinced by academic critiques that judges now possess too much sway over appointments.[4]

Reactions to a book that Robert Hazell, Kate Malleson, Patrick O'Brien and I published in 2015 are emblematic. Drawing on interviews with over two dozen individuals closely involved in JAC-run processes, our book identified the basic dynamic at the heart of the selection regime instituted under the Constitutional Reform Act 2005: the Lord Chancellor's relative retreat from both individual appointment decisions and the day-to-day running of the appointment regime as a whole has been offset by the growing influence of judges, and senior judges in particular.[5] We explained how, in addition to seven judicial commissioners who serve on the 15-member JAC, judges perform vital roles from the very beginning to the very end of the selection process. They shape job descriptions, design qualifying tests and role-playing tasks, supply references, sit on selection panels, provide views as statutory consultees on shortlisted candidates, and – for 95 per cent of vacancies – make the ultimate decision whether to appoint the person recommended by the JAC. We argued that the high levels of judicial influence that are engineered by statute throughout the appointments regime are reinforced in practice by the fact that judges, as repeat players, are adept at using additional selection criteria[6] and

Independence and Accountability of the English Judiciary, Cambridge: Cambridge University Press, 2013, p. 116.

3 There have been at least eight formal reviews of judicial appointments over the last ten years, but not one contained a sustained discussion of the possibility that judges now exercise too much influence. The eight reviews are: (i) the Nooney Review (2007), an internal review of the JAC processes with the stated intention of increasing efficiency (ii) the LEAN Review (2008), a further internal review of JAC's processes with the stated goal of increasing efficiency; (iii) the Constitutional Renewal Bill (2008), later the Constitutional Reform and Governance Bill, where draft clauses sought to give the Lord Chancellor further controls over the JAC but were later dropped; (iv) the Advisory Panel on Judicial Diversity established by Jack Straw and led by Baroness Neuberger; (v) an End-to-End Review of the Appointments Process (2010) established by the Ministry of Justice; (vi) the House of Lords Constitution Committee's Inquiry into Judicial Appointments (2011–2012); (vii) the Ministry of Justice's consultation on judicial appointments (2011), culminating in the Crime and Courts Act 2013; and (viii) the Ministry of Justice's Triennial Review of the JAC (2014–2015).

4 It is not only the JAC and senior judges who have given these academic critiques short shrift, but civil servants as well. See e.g. Ministry of Justice, *Triennial Review: Judicial Appointments Commission* (2015) paras 119–120. Practitioners are generally unmoved by the critique as well, but for a contrary perspective see the essay in this collection by Karon Monaghan QC.

5 Gee *et al*, *The Politics of Judicial Independence*, pp. 159–193.

6 That is to say, additional criteria not stipulated in statute relating to the experience or qualifications that applicants for a given post should possess. Typical is a requirement that candidates for a salaried judicial office should have fee-paid judicial experience (i. e. experience sitting in part-time, fee-paid judicial roles while continuing in their day jobs).

statutory consultation[7] to ensure that considerable weight is attached to their preferences. Our critique was that progress on diversifying the judiciary risks remaining fairly slow in a system with high levels of judicial influence given that judges might favour – whether consciously or not – candidates from conventional professional backgrounds (e.g. the Bar and commercial practice). One reason for this is that judges might attach more weight to the professional experience that a candidate has accrued and less weight on his or her potential to develop into an excellent judge. My co-authors and I were in little doubt that most judges today accept that the lack of diversity is a problem and are genuine in their concern to remedy it,[8] but we argued that despite this they had resisted or diluted initiatives that might have led to faster transformation of the bench. Following the book's publication, the JAC, several senior judges and a number of officials made it very clear to us that they viewed our critique about judicial influence and its implications for diversity as wrong. Several did not mince their words when conveying just how wrong they considered it.

These reactions have given me considerable pause for thought over the last two years. It would be odd if they had not. I have reflected, in particular, on the difficulties of conducting research in this area.[9] It is tricky for outsiders such as academics to capture accurately and then to make sense of all of the various institutional dynamics at play in the long and formal processes run by the JAC, where a changing cast of characters participate in different types of vacancies. It is true that the post-2005 processes managed by the JAC are now much more transparent than the traditional 'tap on the shoulder' approach associated with the Lord Chancellor's Department,[10] but inevitably all of the most important interactions still occur out of sight and behind closed doors. Rendering research even more challenging are the very fluid dynamics between judges, ministers, civil servants and lay people,[11] with relationships ebbing and flowing over even fairly short timeframes as pivotal officeholders enter and

7 That is to say, a requirement imposed on the JAC to consult with certain officeholders (usually senior judges) before it selects a candidate to recommend to the appointing authority.

8 The need for a more diverse judiciary has 'become a truth almost universally acknowledged' even whilst progress remains slow: E. Rackley, 'Rethinking Judicial Diversity', in U. Shultz and G. Shaw (eds), *Gender and Judging*, Oxford: Hart Publishing, 2013, pp. 501, 503. For a more sceptical take, see H. Sommerlad, 'Judicial Diversity: Complexity, Continuity and Change' in this collection.

9 Similar difficulties are discussed in A. Paterson, *Final Judgment: The Last Law Lords and the Supreme Court*, Oxford: Hart Publishing, 2013, pp. 5–9.

10 For a comprehensive account of the pre-2005 approach to judicial appointments, see Lord Mackay, 'Selection of Judges Prior to the Establishment of the Judicial Appointments Commission in 2006' in Judicial Appointments Commission, *Judicial Appointments: Balancing Independence, Accountability and Legitimacy*, London: Judicial Appointments Commission, 2010; D. Woodhouse, *The Office of Lord Chancellor*, Oxford: Hart Publishing, 2001, pp. 133–163; and P. Darbyshire, *Sitting in Judgment: The Working Lives of Judges*, Oxford: Hart Publishing, 2011, pp. 90–95.

11 For an overview, see S. Turenne, 'Judicial Independence in England and Wales since the Constitutional Reform Act 2005', in A. Seibert-Fohr (ed.), *Judicial Independence*

depart the stage.[12] Any analysis of the influence of this or that actor can therefore quickly become out of date. Complicating matters further is that the ways in which actors exercise influence, as well as the degrees to which they do so, can reveal contradictory patterns. For example, actors whose interests are assumed to conflict might find that their interests coalesce at certain points in a selection process,[13] or actors might have excessive influence over some, but not all, levels of appointments.[14] It follows that critiques about overly high levels of influence might hold true for some vacancies but not others, or might have been true at one point in time, but not now. All of this is to acknowledge the real risk that academic critiques of judicial influence might be outdated, overstated or simply wrong, whether in whole or in part.

This is one possible explanation for why the JAC and some senior judges have rejected academic concerns about judicial influence over judicial appointments. There are others of course, including individual and institutional incentives that might lead some stakeholders to neglect, dismiss or downplay such concerns. In particular, senior judges might not wish to disturb a regime under which they exercise significant say over the composition of the bench, while the JAC might not wish to acknowledge the limits on either the ability or willingness of its lay and legal commissioners to counteract the high levels of judicial influence that statute weaves throughout the appointment process.[15] I will not dwell on these explanations, even if some weight ought to be ascribed to them. I will consider instead another explanation: namely, the lack of shared understandings about what it means to talk of 'judicial influence'. My suspicion is that this contributes to a mismatch between how some academics on the one hand and some judges and the JAC on the other assess judicial involvement in the selection process. A lack of shared understandings about the meaning of judicial influence has made it

in Transition – Strengthening the Rule of Law in the OSCE Region, Berlin: Springer, 2012, p. 147.

12 Since the JAC's creation in 2005 there have been seven Lord Chancellors (Lord Falconer, Jack Straw, Ken Clarke, Christopher Grayling, Michael Gove, Liz Truss and David Lidington), three Lord Chief Justices (Lords Phillips, Judge and Thomas), three JAC chairs (Baroness Prashar, Christopher Stephens and Lord Kakkar) and two acting chairs (Lords Toulson and Burnett), with the JAC's relations with the judiciary and the government shaped in part by the occupants of these offices.

13 Tensions have often run high between the Ministry of Justice, the Courts Service and the judiciary on a range of issues relating to the funding of the judicial system as a whole (e.g. court closures), but they each share an interest in ensuring that the people appointed to judicial office are able to 'hit the ground running'. For example successive Lord Chancellors and Lord Chief Justices had had a shared interest in stipulating non-statutory eligibility criteria concerning the expertise and experience needed for a given vacancy. See Gee *et al*, *The Politics of Judicial Independence*, pp. 171–173.

14 Particular concern has been expressed about levels of judicial influence over senior appointments: e.g. Paterson and Paterson, *Guarding the Guardians*.

15 See generally the discussion of the complex motivations and attendant relationships between the stakeholders involved in the new selection processes: E. Rackley, *Women, Judging and the Judiciary: From Difference to Diversity*, London: Routledge, 2013, pp. 76–105.

challenging to foster a constructive debate about whether judges now exercise excessive influence. Part of the problem is that there has been no sustained examination in England and Wales or (so far as I am aware) any other common law jurisdiction of what is meant in this context by judicial influence.[16] We need an account of influence that covers the manifold and sometimes subtle ways in which judges are involved in shaping individual appointment decisions and the overarching appointments regime. We also need a basic framework to help us to evaluate how much and what sorts of influence judges should exercise and at which stages of the selection process. Absent such a framework, we are reduced to making claims about there being too much, too little or just the right amount of influence on the basis of little more than mere intuitions.[17]

This chapter represents the first attempt to identify a broad framework within which to assess judicial influence over appointments in England and Wales. It applies to other jurisdictions in proportion to the degree to which their selection processes and – more significantly – their political and legal cultures resemble those found here. I divide the chapter into three parts. First, to structure debate about such an intricate phenomenon, I suggest that influence is understood to include both *conduct-shaping* (i.e. affecting individual decisions) and *context-shaping* (i.e. affecting the environment in which decisions are made). Conduct-shaping and context-shaping are variable and relational, which in turn can make it very difficult to determine the actual levels of influence that judges exercise. Second, I explain how reflecting on the *inputs, outputs* and *throughputs* of an appointments regime provides a basic framework for determining when judicial influence becomes too high. Such a framework must recognize the indispensable insights that judges have to share about individual selection decisions and the working of the selection regime as a whole, and which by extension justify some measure of influence over judicial appointments. At the same time, it should also identify appropriate limits on the amount of influence that judges enjoy. In doing all of this, it must help us to assess whether the inputs, outputs and throughputs of the selection regime work to adequately promote core values such as transparency, accountability and inclusiveness. Third, it is against this background that I then offer five presumptions to help to assess whether, all things considered, judges enjoy too much, too little or just the right amount of influence. Informing these presumptions is the belief that judicial involvement in the appointments regime must be, so far as possible, structured, open and subject to effective safeguards. I use these presumptions to assess the JAC regime. Developing, deepening and in

16 In continental systems there is slightly more (albeit still relatively scant) discussion of how judicial influence over promotions are heightened through Judicial Councils: see e.g. N. Garoupa and T. Ginsburg, 'The Comparative Law and Economics of Judicial Councils', *Berkeley Journal of International Law* 27, 2008, p. 52; and C. Guarnieri, 'Appointment and Career of Judges in Continental Europe: The Rise of Judicial Self-Government', *Legal Studies* 24, 2004, p. 169.

17 See e.g. Sophie Turenne's review of our book which rightly hinted at the lack of an explicit framework against which to evaluate claims of disproportionate judicial influence: S. Turenne, 'Review', *Cambridge Law Journal* 75, 2016, p. 437.

some respects departing from the critique that my co-authors and I advanced in 2015, I point to important progress made on structuring several instances of judicial involvement. However, I argue that judicial influence within the regime managed by the JAC nevertheless still far exceeds what is desirable.

What is judicial influence?

At one level, judicial influence has an obvious meaning. It denotes the capacity of judges to shape individual appointments, overarching policies or otherwise to ensure favourable treatment of their interests within the appointments regime. At another level, however, careful reflection reveals judicial influence to be an intricate phenomenon not reducible to a snappy and straightforward definition. Part of the reason for this is that judicial influence is likely to manifest in a great variety of different ways. Influence is likely to exhibit many different patterns, with a wide range of judges (tribunal judges and court judges, low-level judges and senior judges) contributing in different capacities (as referees, interviewers, commissioners, the appointing authority) and at various stages of the selection process (short-listing, interview, final decision and so forth). Over and above this, there is good reason to suppose that the professional authority enjoyed by judges, and especially senior judges, transfigures into powerful social forces that significantly shape the actions and decisions of other actors in the appointments regime, such as ministers and civil servants at the Ministry of Justice or the legal and lay commissioners on the JAC.[18] A comprehensive account would address a number of related questions such as: which judges, or groups of judges, exercise influence? Over whom or what? Through what means, channels or processes? To the extent that judges exert influence over other actors, do those actors resist or acquiesce? Do those other actors identify themselves as subject to judicial influence? Are judges conscious of the many ways in which they can and perhaps do exercise influence? What factors shape the ways in and degrees to which judges do so? And to what ends do judges exercise influence? In addressing questions such as these, it is helpful to view influence as extending to both conduct-shaping and context-shaping.[19]

Most people when referring to judicial influence likely have in mind the former. Conduct-shaping refers to the capacity of judges to translate their preferences into concrete decisions. On issues where there is broad consensus, judges might have to exert little or no influence to ensure that their preferences are reflected in actual decisions. On other issues, it might involve convincing other actors to decide something at odds with their own interests in order to vindicate strongly held

18 On the important relationship between authority and influence, see R. Cialdini, *Influence: The Psychology of Persuasion*, London: Collins, 2007, (revised edn). First published in 1984. On the social impact of influence, see generally B. Latane, 'The Psychology of Social Impact', *American Psychologist* 36, 1981, p. 343.

19 I borrow the distinction between conduct-shaping and context-shaping from Colin Hay's work on power: C. Hay, 'Divided by a Common Language: Political Theory and the Concept of Power', *Politics* 17, 1997, p. 45.

judicial preferences. In its strongest expression, in other words, conduct-shaping influence embraces judges' capacity to affect directly the decisions and behaviour of other actors. Conduct-shaping is an important aspect of influence, but it is far from straightforward to evaluate the ability of judges to convert preferences into real world decisions. There are, after all, multiple decisions to make in any one selection exercise (specifying the job description; designing qualifying tests; short-listing applicants; deciding whether to provide a reference and what to include in it; picking the questions to pose during the interview; and so forth).[20] These decisions will not be of equal significance, with important decisions the responsibility of different decision-makers or, in some instances, different combinations of decision-makers. As I explain towards the end of this chapter, most (albeit not all) of the key decisions in the JAC's processes involve one or more judges. In addition, preferences are not necessarily uniform. They might vary between judges at different levels of the bench, and even between judges who sit on the same court. Even a relatively homogenous group such as the senior judiciary might have multiple preferences that are held with varying strength.

Context-shaping is judges' indirect influence, and covers their capacity to shape the context in which individual selection decisions are made. This includes, but is not limited to, the ability of judges to fashion the general policy environment relating to appointments. It also extends to less concrete influence such as the ability to create the values deemed essential for a well-functioning appointment regime in ways that condition and limit the range of decisions that can be made. Closely related to what elsewhere in this collection Alan Paterson terms the judiciary's 'soft power',[21] context-shaping encompasses the ability to mould the assumptions that inform and underpin the decisions and actions of the main stakeholders in the selection regime. Influence is not only about direct impact on decisions, in other words. It is also about an indirect, systemic impact that shapes the issues that will arise for decision in the first place.[22] Examples of judicial influence as context-shaping include the ability of judges to mould how other actors determine the weight to ascribe to legitimacy, accountability and diversity within the overall selection regime. It might also include the ability to shape the tenor of policy debates about – and, by extension, other stakeholders' views on – issues such as whether to further dilute ministerial involvement in individual selection

20 These are examples of only the most obvious *formal* (and the more visible) decisions in a selection process. There is also a range of *informal* (and the less visible) decisions. An example of the latter is the need for the JAC to decide how much weight to ascribe to the judicial views on shortlisted applicants that have been obtained during statutory consultation.

21 A. Paterson, 'Power and Judicial Appointment: Squaring the Impossible Circle' in this collection.

22 See generally S. Lukes, *Power: A Radical View*, London: Palgrave Macmillan, 2nd edn, 2005.

decisions[23] or how 'merit' relates to the experiences that an applicant should possess prior to appointment to the bench.[24]

Of particular note is that the context-shaping influence that judges enjoy might be a byproduct of forces that neither they nor other stakeholders fully recognize or understand.[25] At the same time, it might be the most important and perhaps even insidious form of influence inasmuch as it prevents significant issues from being seen as appropriate or pressing topics of debate. The judiciary's context-shaping influence might be presumed to be especially powerful given that, more so than other stakeholders, judges (and especially senior judges responsible for the deployment and performance of the judicial workforce) are likely to have a clear sense of how the selection regime should work and the outcomes that they want it to generate.[26] On top of this senior judges are often in office for longer than their counterparts at the Ministry and JAC, with this continuity enabling them to become very effective 'repeat players' who are adept at ensuring that their preferences are secured through the working of the selection processes. As accomplished advocates, judges are also likely to be effective in communicating their concerns to other stakeholders – and, indeed, might succeed in convincing other actors of the supposed soundness of otherwise ill-founded concerns. In its strongest expression, context-shaping influence might involve co-opting other stakeholders to further the judiciary's self-interest to the detriment of the public interest. An example would be if judicial commissioners on the JAC succeed in persuading its lay and legal commissioners to accept uncritically the judiciary's stance on contentious questions of policy.[27] Another example would be where judges succeed in 'cultivat[ing] sympathy or support'[28] among political

23 It is notable, for example, that concern about curtailing ministerial and legislative involvement seems to loom large in most discussions of judicial appointments in the Commonwealth. See generally J. van Zyl Smit, *The Appointment, Tenure and Removal of Judges under Commonwealth Principles*, London: Bingham Centre for the Rule of Law, 2015.

24 See Morison's discussion of the concern of many stakeholders in Northern Ireland that judges have an 'undue' influence over appointments, arising in part because of their 'indirect' role in validating certain understandings of merit: J. Morison, 'Finding Merit in Judicial Appointments: NIJAC and the Search for a New Judiciary in Northern Ireland', in A.-M. McAlinden and C. Dwyer (eds), *Criminal Justice in Transition: The Northern Ireland Context*, Oxford: Hart Publishing, 2015, p. 131.

25 T. Benton, '"Objective" Interests and the Sociology of Power', *Sociology* 14, 1981, p. 161.

26 See Paterson, 'Power and Judicial Appointment: Squaring the Impossible Circle' in this collection.

27 As discussed later in this chapter, judicial influence has been cited as a possible reason for why the JAC adopted a very narrow 'equal merit' policy after the Crime and Courts Act 2013 clarified that, where there are two candidates of equal merit, there is nothing preventing the JAC from recommending a person for appointment on the basis of improving diversity on the bench. See also G. Gee and K. Malleson, 'Judicial Appointments, Diversity and the Equal Merit Provision', *UK Constitutional Law Blog*, 6 May 2014.

28 Paterson, 'Power and Judicial Appointment: Squaring the Impossible Circle', in this collection.

elites.[29] Arguably, the fact that there has been such little debate during the JAC's first ten years about judicial influence over appointments could itself be an example of the judges' context-shaping influence.[30]

Conduct-shaping and context-shaping are related, and indeed often mutually-reinforcing. Judges' capacity to shape policies can reinforce their influence over discrete decisions, whilst the ability to shape concrete decisions can mould how other actors evaluate the policy context in which those decisions are made. The best example is, perhaps, the potential for judges to ensure – both at the level of discrete decisions and the level of general attitudes amongst key stakeholders – the dominance of traditional understandings of merit that emphasize advocacy, seniority, private practice at the Bar and appearances before the higher courts. Merit, constructed in this way, not only unfairly advantages certain privileged groups;[31] it also ensures considerable influence for senior judges inasmuch as it ascribes weight to experiences and skills visible primarily to judges in the higher courts, rather than other actors who participate in the selection process. Judges' ability to insist via concrete decisions on traditional understandings of merit (i.e. conduct-shaping) reinforces the dominance of that understanding within the selection regime (i.e. context-shaping), which in turn will make it easier for the senior judiciary to serve as de facto 'gatekeepers' of merit, and therefore of the selection regime and entry into the judiciary more generally.

Judicial influence: variable and relational

Judicial influence is likely to be both variable and relational. It is variable to the extent that both conduct-shaping and context-shaping will fluctuate depending on factors such as: the vacancy in question; the prevailing statutory framework; the personalities of officeholders; and the institutional relationships between the JAC, the Ministry of Justice and senior judiciary. That patterns ebb and flow over time and from vacancy to vacancy makes it challenging to reach a settled view on

29 Examples might include the way in which judicial leaders persuaded parliamentarians that the 2003 reform proposals would imperil judicial independence unless augmented with greater judicial involvement. See Lord Windlesham, 'The Constitutional Reform Act 2005: Ministers, Judges and Constitutional Change: Part 1', *Public Law*, 2005, p. 806; and 'The Constitutional Reform Act 2005: The Politics of Constitutional Reform: Part 2' *Public Law*, 2006, p. 35. Arguably, senior judges were also effective in co-opting the House of Lords Constitution Committee during its 2013 review of the appointments process, with its final report barely acknowledging the risk of excessive judicial influence over the new selection processes. See House of Lords Select Committee on the Constitution,*Judicial Appointments*, HL 272, 2012.

30 It is worth emphasizing the limited claim that I make in this respect. After all, the fact that few stakeholders seem perturbed by the new arrangements might be a sign that judges do not have excessive influence. My point is simply that if there are high levels of context-shaping influence one consequence could be to render it much less likely that there is any debate about the levels of judicial influence.

31 K. Malleson, 'Rethinking the Merit Principle in Judicial Selection', *Journal of Law and Society* 44, 2006, pp. 126, 135–136.

whether judges enjoy too much, too little or just the right amount of influence. This might lead to fairly fine-grained assessments. Several academics have expressed particular concern, for instance, about the high levels of judicial influence over senior judicial appointments (i.e. to the UK Supreme Court and leadership roles such as the Lord Chief Justice, Senior President of Tribunals and the heads of division).[32] Even in respect of senior appointments, however, levels of influence have varied over time. An example is the dilution of judicial involvement following changes in 2013 to appointments to the Supreme Court. The Court's Deputy President was removed from the commissions specifically constituted for appointments to the Court, whilst the President and Deputy were removed from the process of selecting their successors.[33] Another example is how the influence of senior judges over recruitment to lower level courts grew between 2010 and 2012 during Kenneth Clarke's tenure as Lord Chancellor after he indicated that he would only appoint candidates recommended by the JAC who had been first approved by the Lord Chief Justice during statutory consultation.[34]

In addition to being variable, judicial influence is also relational; that is to say, the influence of any one actor is related to and partly shaped by the influence exerted by other actors. This is especially important given that a striking feature of the post-2005 selection regime is its inclusiveness.[35] The pre-2005 regime – although mixing political, judicial and practitioner influences, and while judges enjoyed significant sway through secret soundings – was dominated by the Lord Chancellor and a handful of officials.[36] In a stark departure, the JAC oversees an open and inclusive regime that involves a variety of other actors. The Lord Chancellor and the Lord Chief Justice, assisted by officials from the Ministry of Justice and HM Courts and Tribunals Service, determine the job description for

32 See e.g. A. Paterson, *Lawyers and the Public Good: Democracy in Action?*, Cambridge: Cambridge University Press, 2012, pp. 148–152.

33 See Schedule 13 of the Crime and Courts Act 2013 and the Supreme Court (Judicial Appointments) Regulations 2013. For a discussion of these reforms see: P. O'Brien, 'Changes to Judicial Appointments in the Crime and Courts Act 2013', *Public Law*, 2014, p. 179 and E. Delaney, 'Searching for Constitutional Meaning in Institutional Design: The Debate Over Judicial Appointments in the United Kingdom', *International Journal of Constitutional Law* 14, 2016, p. 752.

34 See Gee *et al*, *The Politics of Judicial Independence*, p. 175.

35 See G. Gee, 'Judicial Policy in England and Wales: A New Regulatory Space', in R. Devlin and A. Dodek (eds), *Regulating Judges: Beyond Independence and Accountability*, Cheltenham: Edward Elgar Publishing, 2016, p. 145.

36 Admittedly, by the mid-1990s, the appointment process was becoming increasingly formal and somewhat more inclusive, with for example candidates being interviewed by a panel comprising a senior civil servant, a sitting judge and – for the first time – a lay person. See generally Lord Mackay, 'Selection of Judges Prior to the Establishment of the Judicial Appointments Commission in 2006' in Judicial Appointments Commission, *Judicial Appointments: Balancing Independence, Accountability and Legitimacy*, 2010. By 2001, a Commissioner for Judicial Appointments had also been created to audit the appointment procedures and to investigate complaints. See generally Sir Leonard Peach, *Independent Scrutiny of the Appointment Processes of Judges and Queen's Counsel*, London: HMSO, 1999.

each vacancy. The panel that interviews and ranks candidates comprises a mix of judges and lay people, with the panel's precise composition depending on the office. For certain appointments, senior judges must also be consulted, as required by statute.[37] On the JAC a mix of lay, legal and judicial commissioners determine which candidates to recommend to one of the three decision-makers who have the final say whether or not to appoint (i.e. the Lord Chancellor for all appointments to the High Court and above; the Lord Chief Justice for all lower level courts; and the Senior President of Tribunals for most tribunal posts).[38] The fashioning of policy is also a much more collaborative enterprise, with roles for judicial associations, practitioner associations and Parliament. That the appointments landscape is so densely populated, with contributions from multiple stakeholders, reflects the fact that no one actor has a monopoly on all of the skills, information, resources or expertise necessary to reach well-rounded assessments of an applicant's suitability for a judicial career or, more generally, the effective pursuit of policy. The type and degree of influence that judges enjoy in an inclusive regime such as this necessarily depends on and is conditioned by the type and degree of influence enjoyed by other stakeholders.

The suggestion, then, is that influence is a variable and relational phenomenon that encompasses conduct-shaping and context-shaping. The complexity of this phenomenon is one factor that renders it challenging to cultivate constructive debate about judicial influence over judicial appointments. It should already be plain that it can be difficult to reliably calibrate actual levels of conduct-shaping and context-shaping. To determine how effectively judges translate preferences into decisions (conduct-shaping influence) requires identifying those preferences and tracing them through each of the various decision points in the selection process. Both parts to this assessment might be hazardous. There are, as noted earlier, multiple decision points, with some more important than others, whilst preferences might vary between different judges, with some more effective in translating their most strongly held preferences into actual decisions. Difficulties with gauging judges' levels of influence are compounded in respect of context-shaping, where the extent to which judges mould the general environment in which individual decisions are made, as well as the ways in which other actors regard that broad environment, is essentially unobservable, at least to outsiders. Furthermore, evaluating the conduct-shaping and context-shaping influence of judges in an inclusive selection regime involves evaluating the extent to which other actors contribute, with those contributions also likely to embrace context-shaping and conduct-shaping, with all of the same evidential difficulties. In an inclusive regime that involves contributions from multiple actors it can be tricky to fillet out the influence of any given one of them. In line with this, since it is difficult to isolate influence over individual selection decisions (conduct-shaping) from their influence over the regime (context-shaping), it is necessary to arrive at an all-

37 See e.g. regs. 6, 12, 18 and 30 of the Judicial Appointments Regulations 2013.

38 See the changes made to the Constitutional Reform Act 2005 by paras 30–40 of Schedule 13 to the Crime and Courts Act 2013.

things-considered assessment that almost inevitably is no more than a rough approximation of the actual levels of judicial influence. All of this could be read as a counsel of despair, with any assessment of the influence exercised by judges so complicated that debate is not profitable. But it should not be read in this way. It should be read instead as underlining the importance of fostering informed, reflective and structured debate that is sensitive to this complexity.

A framework for debating judicial influence

One way to structure the debate about judicial influence is in terms of inputs, outputs and throughputs.[39] Each provides a focus for reflecting on some of the core components of a normatively attractive appointments process. Inputs, in this context, direct us to reflect on the relationship between judicial influence and the decision-making processes that lead to individual selection decisions or the policies and structures of the selection regime.[40] It encourages us to explore judicial involvement in light of who else contributes to decision-making and the quality, degree and weight of their various contributions. Outputs encourage us to explore the relationships between judicial influence and the outcomes of the appointments regime. These include whether talented individuals from diverse backgrounds are appointed to judicial office and, more generally, whether the regime fosters confidence in the courts and tribunals. Throughputs overlap with and build on inputs and outputs as well as shining a light on what occurs 'in the space between' the two.[41] This directs us towards the governance of the regime and, more particularly, the interaction amongst stakeholders when assessed in terms of accountability, openness, checks and balances and the independence of the JAC. This encompasses both the participation-orientation of inputs and the results-orientation of outputs in order to help us to evaluate the degree to which a set of institutional arrangements – and, more particularly, the roles of judges within them – can be justified. In brief: the question of how much and what sort of influence judges should exercise can be structured by referring to those inputs, outputs and throughputs that ought to shape a well-designed and well-functioning selection regime. In this section, I reflect on some of the ways that judicial influence can translate into inputs, outputs and throughputs, taking care to identify the many valuable contributions that judges make as well as the concerns that flow from

39 This distinction is elucidated by Vivien Schmidt in the context of the legitimacy of the European Union. See e.g. V. A. Schmidt, 'Democracy and Legitimacy in the European Union', in E. Jones, A. Menon and S. Weatherill (eds), *The Oxford Handbook of the European Union,* Oxford: Oxford University Press, 2012, p. 661. See also M. Zürn, 'Democratic Governance Beyond the Nation-State', *European Journal of International Relations* 6, 2000, p. 183; and K. Dingwerth, *The New Transnationalism: Transnational Governance and Democratic Legitimacy*, London: Palgrave, 2007, p. 15.

40 See the seminal work by Scharpf on the distinction between input and output legitimacy: F. Scharpf, *Governing in Europe: Effective and Democratic?*, Oxford: Oxford University Press, 1999.

41 V. A. Schmidt, 'Democracy and Legitimacy in the European Union Revisited: Input, Output *and* "Throughput"' *Political Studies* 61, 2013, pp. 2, 5.

those contributions. As will become clear, the inputs, outputs and throughputs of a selection regime (as well as the relationship of judicial influence to each) are interconnected.

Inputs

The starting point is to acknowledge the sound reasons that justify a measure – and perhaps even a large measure – of judicial input into the selection regime. Judges have a legitimate interest in the composition of the judiciary that justifies their involvement in individual appointments and the crafting of policies on the selection regime. They are well positioned to assess the potential judge-craft of applicants for judicial office. They bring first-hand knowledge of day-to-day life in courts and tribunals, and in this way can help to ensure that the changing demands of litigation are reflected in the blend of professional, administrative and personal qualities necessary for particular vacancies. Equally vital is judicial input into the policies on and the governance of the selection regime. Involving judges can help to foster their confidence (and that of the legal community) in the integrity of the selection regime. Importantly, it helps to ensure that judges have a stake in that regime, including shared responsibility for recruiting from under-represented groups.[42] Their involvement also minimizes the danger that other actors – and most obviously: ministers – enjoy too much influence.

For all of these reasons, it is unsurprising that judges are 'anxious'[43] to exercise influence. However, it is no reflection on the judiciary if the rest of the polity is equally anxious to ensure that the judiciary has an adequate influence, but not a 'predominating influence'.[44] Judicial influence is something to be optimized, not maximized, given the risks associated with judges being too involved in the selection regime. These include the risk that a largely self-selecting judiciary will be self-replicating, which irrespective of the quality of the individuals appointed might undermine public confidence in the appointments regime as well as the judiciary as a whole. Judges might, in particular, seek to promote and police an understanding of 'merit' that over-emphasizes experiences and skills which are found chiefly in candidates who resemble themselves. It is not inevitable that self-replication will follow from high levels of judicial influence, but the burden should rest on the judiciary to satisfy the rest of the polity that no connection exists given that it is generally assumed in merit-based selection processes that involving current office-holders risks a cloning effect.[45] Of particular concern is that judges might seek to

42 See s. 139A of the Constitutional Reform Act 2005, which provides that each of the Lord Chancellor and the Lord Chief Justice 'must take such steps as that offer-holder considers appropriate for the purpose of encouraging judicial diversity'.

43 G. Palmer, 'Judicial Selection and Accountability: Can the New Zealand System Survive?' in B. D. Gray and R. B. McClintock (eds), *Courts and Policy – Checking the Balance*, Wellington: Brookers, 1995.

44 T. Legg, 'Judges for the New Century', *Public Law*, 2001, pp. 62, 73.

45 See L. Peach, *Report on the Scrutiny of Judicial Appointments and Queen's Counsel Selection Procedures* (1999).

influence the selection regime in ways that lead to differential weight being placed on diversity for different sorts of vacancies, with more permissive approaches towards diversifying focused on the lower courts and tribunals.[46] A related risk is that high levels of influence might result in appointments on the basis of seniority rather than merit,[47] with an emphasis on attributes unrelated to judicial office, such as whether a person seems a 'good chap'.

There are, then, sound reasons to involve judges in the selection regime, but there are difficult questions about just how much involvement judges should have and at which stages of a selection exercise. It is necessary to discern proper boundaries on judicial involvement not merely to reduce the risks associated with disproportionate influence, but also because there exists broad consensus across the UK that judicial selection regimes should be inclusive and draw on the perspectives of the many other actors with a crucial stake in the work of the courts and tribunals. As noted earlier, well-informed assessments of candidates' suitability for a judicial career should draw on the expertise, experiences and perspectives of a range of stakeholders. The same holds for policy decisions as well. Especially important is to involve ministers, lay people and lawyers.

The limits on judicial inputs should be considered in light of and by reference to ministerial inputs, amongst other things. It is not fashionable to say as much but there are good reasons for ministers to have a meaningful role in individual selections. This is especially so in respect of leadership roles (where judges work closely with ministers and civil servants on the management and funding of the judicial system) and the top courts (where judges often enjoy significant powers over public policy). Such reasons include that ministers can inject an important degree of democratic legitimacy and accountability into the selection regime – and, by extension, into the judiciary as an institution of government. Ministerial involvement can also help to foster the executive's trust and confidence in the courts as well as buttressing ministerial understanding of the constitutional roles performed by judges. Ministerial involvement can also furnish the political will necessary to advance the diversity agenda. Insofar as they tend to view courts in a wide political and social context, ministers are very well placed to understand the importance of diversity and the need to make rapid and visible progress on appointing a judiciary more reflective of society at large.[48] As Andrew Lynch notes elsewhere in this collection, popular concern about diversity might not be evenly distributed throughout the electorate, and hence ministers might have an inconsistent focus

46 R. Hunter, 'Judicial Diversity and the "New Judge"' in H. Sommerlad, S. Harris-Short, S. Vaughan and R. Young (eds), *The Futures of Legal Education and the Legal Profession*, Oxford: Hart Publishing, 2015, p. 79; See also Sommerlad, 'Judicial Diversity: Complexity, Continuity and Change' in this collection.

47 See generally the evidence from other legal systems in J. Bell, *Judiciaries Within Europe*, Cambridge: Cambridge University Press, 2006.

48 For a contrasting view made by Justice Ronald Sackville in light of the Australian experience, see R. Sackville, 'The Judicial Appointments Process in Australia: Towards Independence and Accountability', *Journal of Judicial Administration* 16, 2007, p. 125.

on it, but there is nevertheless good reason to believe that diversity can be 'a pressure point' for politicians.[49] It is also true that ministers can be held to account for the failure to make such progress in ways much less true of judges. This is not to deny that risks flow from ministerial involvement. These include, above all else, the risk that ministers might seek appointments on the basis of partisan factors. Ministers may also place too much weight on the need for selection processes to represent value for money, with the persons appointed able to begin judicial work immediately without long and expensive training.

Questions about the appropriate levels of judicial input should also be weighed alongside lay and legal involvement in the selection process. With backgrounds in commerce, industry, academia and recruitment, lay people can bring fresh perspectives to judicial appointments. This has the potential to limit the scope for judges to exert disproportionate influence. Lay people might, for example, insist on initiatives that strengthen and further formalize selection processes in the face of judicial opposition.[50] They could also challenge tacit understandings of merit by encouraging judges to acknowledge that judge-craft requires competences beyond the technical legal and advocacy skills associated with excellence at the Bar, but also includes the communication and management skills that are especially relevant for a successful career as a solicitor.[51] Involving lawyers also ensures that the concerns of the legal professions are embedded in the selection regime; for example, the solicitor commissioner on the JAC is able to remind the other commissioners of the importance of recruiting judges from diverse professional backgrounds. However, just as involving other actors can counter the influence that judges exert, so too can their involvement actually intensify high levels of judicial influence. Most obviously, the involvement of lawyers on the JAC could encourage a cosy consensus, where lawyers' interests align with judges' interests leading to a 'self-selecting lawyerly caste of judges'[52] characterized by 'too little heterogeneity of outlook'.[53] Barristers, solicitors and legal executives will often have different interests and perspectives, but they might share broadly similar impulses on some

49 A. Lynch, 'Diversity without a Judicial Appointments Commission – The Australian Experience', in this collection.

50 An example is the important role lay people on the JAC played in successfully arguing for interviews to form part of the process for appointments to the Court of Appeal: see Gee *et al*, *The Politics of Judicial Independence*, p. 184.

51 K. Malleson 'Introduction', in K. Malleson and P. H. Russell (eds), *Appointing Judges in an Age of Judicial Power: Critical Perspectives from Around the World*, Toronto: University of Toronto Press, 2006, pp. 3, 9.

52 J. Allan, *Democracy in Decline: Steps in the Wrong Direction*, London: McGill-Queen's University Press, 2014, p. 81.

53 J. Allan, 'Judicial Appointments in New Zealand: If It Were Done When 'Tis Done, Then 'Twere Well It Were Done Openly and Directly', in K. Malleson and P. H. Russell (eds), *Appointing Judges in an Age of Judicial Power: Critical Perspectives from Around the World*, Toronto: University of Toronto Press, 2006, p. 117. See also G. Gee, 'The Politics of Judicial Appointments in Canada', in Judicial Appointments Commission, *Judicial Appointments: Balancing Independence, Accountability and Legitimacy*, 2010, pp. 99, 114.

issues that are a partial product of their similar socialization by legal education and practice. For example, they might share similar views on the question of whether ministers should have any real involvement in selection decisions. The involvement of lay people could similarly sharpen rather than shrink judicial influence where judges succeed in persuading lay people to advance judicial interests that are at odds with the public interest. For example, judges might succeed in persuading the JAC's lay commissioners of the need to select candidates with extensive experience in a fee-paid judicial role who require little on-the-job training from the resource-strapped Judicial College, even although one consequence of this might be to disadvantage candidates from non-traditional backgrounds who tend to be less well placed to take on fee-paid judicial work alongside their day job.[54]

Outputs

The inputs into a selection regime should be determined (at least in part) by the outputs sought from it. The primary outputs of a selection regime are of course the appointments made under it. Underlying the inclusive approach to judicial appointments now found across the UK lies emerging recognition of the fact that the objective is not merely to appoint well-qualified judges. For sure, the regime must ensure that high quality individuals with the array of attributes necessary to excel in judicial office are appointed, with the appointment process sufficiently rigorous to test the professional competence of applicants, but it must do so by drawing on a wide range of perspectives to render it more likely that judges are recruited from a diverse pool, including from underrepresented groups. In other words, the people appointed to the bench should be very well qualified and also reflective of society at large, with the inputs into the selection process designed with this aim in mind. A well-functioning regime should also generate a number of secondary outputs. It should promote the independence of judges and the rule of law, in part by fostering confidence in the judicial system among key stakeholders. It is important to note that there might be a disjuncture between the inputs into the selection regime and the outputs to be secured from it. Limits on the capacity of actors who contribute to the selection process to achieve a more diverse bench might result from, for example, the statutory framework or the structure of the legal professions.[55] It is notable that though valued as an output,[56] diversity does not feature anywhere in the initial assessment of a

54 See generally Gee *et al*, *The Politics of Judicial Independence*, pp. 171–173.

55 See L. Barmes and K. Malleson, 'The Legal Profession as Gatekeepers to the Judiciary: Design Faults in Measures to Enhance Diversity' *Modern Law Review* 74, 2011, p. 245.

56 Part of the Government's justification for introducing the JAC was that it would help 'to make our judiciary more reflective of the society it serves': Department for Constitutional Affairs, *Constitutional Reform: A New Way of Appointing Judges*, CP 10/03, 2003, para 21.

candidate's 'merit' in the JAC-managed regime.[57] It is also of course very difficult to determine the quality of those ultimately appointed, especially where, as in England and Wales, there is no comprehensive appraisal system for reviewing the performance of serving judges.[58]

When thinking about how levels of judicial influence might relate to the desired outputs of the selection regime, it is important to acknowledge, once again, that judicial input is essential for ensuring the selection of high calibre individuals who will be able to handle the demands of a judicial career. At the same time, it is necessary to examine how judicial interests correlate with the public interest. One concern is that if they make multiple, important inputs into the selection process, judges may repeatedly succeed in prioritizing judicial self-interest over the public interest. It might be that most of the time judicial interests and the public interest are aligned, but there might also be occasions where judges resist initiatives that promote the common good. For example, some judges might resist initiatives that reflect best recruitment practices and which are designed to ensure a fairer, more transparent and inclusive process. Or to take another example: even although at some level committed to promoting diversity, judges might obstruct initiatives that potentially lead to faster progress on diversifying the bench where those initiatives imperil traditional understandings of merit.[59] While 'it cannot be in the public interest to marginalize or ignore'[60] the views of judges, it is equally important that the regime ferrets out spurious arguments advanced by judges that are more about entrenching vested judicial interests than furthering the public interest.

Throughputs

Today, the health of a selection regime will be assessed by reference to not only inputs and outputs, but also the quality of governance that results from the way that various key stakeholders interact – or what might be called the throughputs of the selection regime. A central concern, in other words, is that the inputs into that regime, together with the outputs that flow from it, should foster a way of regulating judicial appointments that is transparent, accountable and inclusive, with effective checks and balances to structure the contributions made by the various stakeholders and to ensure that no one actor has excessive influence. The key is to grasp how judicial involvement contributes to the governance of the selection regime; that is to say, to what extent do the multiple judicial inputs foster or frustrate transparency, accountability, inclusiveness, the independence of the JAC

57 G. Bindman and K. Monaghan, *Judicial Diversity: Accelerating Change*, London: Labour Party, 2014, para 3.13.

58 See generally Gee *et al*, *The Politics of Judicial Independence*, pp. 149–155.

59 See G. Gee and K. Malleson, 'Judicial Appointments, Diversity'.

60 J. Sumption, 'The Constitutional Reform Act 2005', in Judicial Appointments Commission, *Judicial Appointments: Balancing Independence, Accountability and Legitimacy*, London: Judicial Appointments Commission, 2010, pp. 31, 39.

and, more generally, an appropriate balance of influence across the various stakeholders?

Particular concerns will focus on the relationship between judicial influence and accountability. Even were it desirable to do so, it is difficult in practice to hold a decision-maker accountable for individual appointments given that judges have security of tenure, and hence are normally in office for much longer than other public officials.[61] There should always remain, however, important measures of both democratic accountability and explanatory accountability for the working of the regime as a whole. Insofar as high levels of judicial influence might come at the cost of ministerial involvement, there is likely be a serious deficit in terms of democratic accountability (in the sense of important decisions being made by someone who is accountable to the electorate, even if only indirectly). At the same time, high levels of judicial influence may or may not be accompanied by an appropriate level of explanatory accountability (in the sense of furnishing an account of their collective contributions to the stewardship of the appointments regime). This depends on the extent to which the judges take steps to explain in what ways and to what ends they exert influence during a selection exercise and, more generally, on policy questions relating to the structure and operation of the selection regime.

Another concern is whether the patterns of judicial influence might work, over time, to undermine the independence of the JAC. Most obviously, the views of the judicial commissioners on the JAC might come to dominate over those of the lay and legal members, with the possibility that the former co-opt the latter. More subtly, the need for the JAC's leadership to nurture the confidence of and maintain constructive relations with the judiciary (and especially senior judges with whom the JAC's Chair works closely) might render it difficult at times for the JAC to distinguish between the public interest on the one hand and judicial interests on the other. It might become difficult for the JAC's leaders to realize the full scope for the JAC's interests and the judiciary's interests to conflict on issues such as how to frame job descriptions, the design of the qualifying tests and role-playing tasks, the use of interviews for senior leadership roles and the application of the equal merit provision.[62] There might also be a lack of clarity about the responsibilities of the JAC's judicial commissioners, and whether they owe their loyalty when discharging their role as commissioners to the JAC, the judiciary or the wider public.[63] For this reason, it is important that, so far as possible, each

61 See generally J. Resnik, 'Judicial Selection and Democratic Theory: Demand, Supply and Life Tenure', *Cardozo Law Review* 26, 2005, p. 579.

62 See generally Gee *et al*, *The Politics of Judicial Independence*, pp. 163–186.

63 The JAC's Commissioners must uphold the Seven Principles of Public Life, which include taking decisions 'solely in terms of the public interest'. As Jan van Zyl Smit notes, it can be inferred from this that individual Commissioners 'must make their own decisions and not prefer the wishes of the constituency whose "seat" they occupy on [the JAC]'. This is not to say, of course, that all will adhere to this requirement. See J. van Zyl Smit, 'Judicial Appointments in England and Wales Since the Constitutional Reform Act 2005', in H. Corder and J. van Zyl Smit (eds), *Securing Judicial Independence: The Role of Commissions in Selecting Judges in the Commonwealth*, Cape Town: Siber Ink, forthcoming.

judicial input into the selection regime is structured by a set of understandings shared by all of the stakeholders as to the purpose and limits of involving judges at specific stages of the selection process. Without such a set of understandings, there is substantial scope for the judiciary to convert their multiple inputs to the selection process into influence that compromises the JAC's independence.

Is there too much judicial influence over the JAC-run selection regime?

As noted as this chapter's outset, the question is not whether judges should have a high level of involvement in judicial appointments, but rather when does such involvement become excessively high? To answer this question, I want to draw on five presumptions that, to my mind, can be extracted from this discussion of inputs, outputs and throughputs. Before turning to those presumptions, I begin by stipulating that judicial involvement in the JAC-run regime is, by design, fairly substantial. This stipulation should be uncontroversial. Few would deny that high levels of judicial involvement are embedded within the JAC regime. That judges are so closely involved with the selection of their colleagues is not surprising insofar as this acknowledges their legitimate interest in the make-up of the bench. Also relevant is that their heavy participation in the new methods of selecting judges was a way of addressing many judges' profound nervousness in 2003 about the proposed abolition (and eventual reshaping) of the office of Lord Chancellor, and the consequent creation of the JAC.[64] Extensive judicial involvement is a product of statute as well as practices that were adopted by the JAC within the statutory framework.[65]

Statute and institutional practice have endowed the judiciary with considerable conduct-shaping influence throughout the appointments process. As mentioned in the introduction, judges are involved at almost every stage of every JAC-managed selection exercise. For vacancies below the High Court, judges are involved from the very beginning (designing job descriptions) to the very end of the selection process (deciding whether to appoint the applicants recommended by the JAC). For vacancies in the High Court, Court of Appeal and leadership roles, judges are involved at every stage save the final decision whether or not to accept the JAC's recommended candidate (although, even here, the very fact that they are involved at all prior stages suggests that the candidates that the JAC or the ad hoc selection panel responsible for senior appointments ultimately recommends to the Lord Chancellor likely reflect the dominant judicial views about who to appoint).[66] As

64 See K. Malleson, 'Creating a Judicial Appointments Commission: Which Model Works Best?', *Public Law*, 2004, p. 102; and K. Malleson, 'The New Judicial Appointments Commission in England and Wales: New Wine in New Bottles?', in K. Malleson and P. H. Russell (eds), *Appointing Judges in an Age of Judicial Power: Critical Perspectives from Around the World*, Toronto: University of Toronto Press, 2006, pp. 39, 51.

65 See generally Gee *et al*, *The Politics of Judicial Independence*.

66 Strictly speaking, the panels for the most senior vacancies (Court of Appeal, heads of division and the Lord Chief Justice) operate as a committee of the JAC, and

one commissioner put it, 'judicial fingerprints' can be found on almost all decisions in selection exercises run by or under the auspices of the JAC. I also stipulate that statute and institutional practice confer significant context-shaping influence on judges. This is a partial product of the status of, and respect for, the judiciary and the legal professions in England and Wales. It also results from a strong judicial presence on the JAC: there are more judicial than lay commissioners, with the number of judges and lawyers outnumbering their lay members to constitute a majority on the JAC. Once again, this stipulation should be uncontroversial. The question is whether their combined conduct-shaping and context-shaping influence gives judges too much say over appointments, bearing in mind the inputs, outputs and throughputs of a normatively attractive selection regime. According to one former JAC commissioner, this represents 'significant but not overwhelming influence'. I disagree, and I now want to point to five rebuttable presumptions that can be taken to indicate that high levels of judicial influence over the JAC regime are in fact too high.

1 Judicial influence is too high if judicial involvement contributes to squeezing out the scope for meaningful ministerial involvement.

Today, the Lord Chancellor has only very minimal involvement in individual appointments.[67] Beyond specifying (in consultation with the Lord Chief Justice) the job description, the Lord Chancellor is no longer involved in appointments below the High Court, i.e. 95 per cent of total appointments. For the High Court and above, the Lord Chancellor sets the job description (again in consultation with the Lord Chief Justice) and, for leadership roles, might also give an oral briefing to the selection panel at the outset of a selection exercise. The Lord Chancellor also has the final say whether to appoint the person recommended by the JAC (or the ad hoc selection panels for the very top appointments), although practice over the last decade suggests that Lord Chancellors almost always accept the names recommended to them. Between 2005 and 2016, Lord Chancellors accepted the candidates that the JAC recommended – literally – 99.9 per cent of the time.[68]

somewhat separate from regular JAC-run selection processes. These panels include very senior judges who are not commissioners of the JAC but who participate ex officio, with other senior judges consulted during the selection process. As a result, the JAC retain an important role in these senior recruitment exercises, but their involvement is less than that for more junior vacancies, with senior judges having more involvement in senior level appointments than on lower level appointments. It is still apt to regard these senior selection rounds as run by or under the auspices of the JAC.

67 It is also relevant, of course, that occupants of this historic office are no longer required to be lawyers or peers and – by virtue of the twinned responsibilities of the Lord Chancellor and Secretary of State for Justice – now juggle a very heavy and politically salient policy portfolio. Viewed in this light, it would be unsurprising if Lord Chancellors' level of interest in individual selections was relatively low, and certainly much lower than pre-2005 Lord Chancellors. See generally G. Gee, 'What are Lord Chancellors For?', *Public Law*, 2014, p. 11.

68 Between 2006 and 2014 (i.e. before the substantial portion of the Lord Chancellor's role as the final decision-maker was transferred to the Lord Chief Justice and the

Under the statute, the Lord Chancellor can depart from a recommendation by the JAC only if he or she is able to provide reasons that raise doubts over the soundness of the JAC's assessment of the candidate's merit.[69] According to one former office-holder, 'the detailed wording [of the statute] and the expectations in practice make it very difficult for the Lord Chancellor to exercise even his limited powers'.[70] This is not to imply that a Lord Chancellor has no influence over individual selections. According to civil servants at the Ministry, Lord Chancellors take an interest in appointments, especially for leadership roles, reviewing substantial evidence compiled during the selection process before deciding whether or not to accept the person that the JAC has recommended. Nevertheless, it is difficult to avoid the conclusion that judicial influence – throughout every stage of the process for lower level appointments and every stage for senior posts except the final decision – has left little if any meaningful scope for the Lord Chancellor to influence individual selections. To put this differently: the conduct-shaping influence of the judiciary within the regime is so pervasive that there remains little room for ministerial involvement, with even the formal powers enjoyed by the Lord Chancellor becoming in practice almost impossible to use, and all of this despite there being several sound reasons (as noted above) for retaining a meaningful ministerial input.

As for policy development, the Lord Chancellor remains an important driver of reform. The reforms introduced in 2013, for example, were initially prompted by Kenneth Clarke's limited interest in lower level appointments.[71] The Lord Chancellor approves the JAC's strategic aims and the performance and policy framework within which it operates.[72] There can be little doubt, however, that policy development is now a collaborative enterprise, with judges possessing a much more significant say than a decade ago. Of note is that the judiciary's considerable conduct-shaping influence arguably intensifies its context-shaping influence, at least insofar as Lord Chancellors appear to accept that the thrust of reforms to the selection regime should be to increase judicial responsibility for selections, rather than decrease it. The overall effect of the 2013 reforms was, for example, to expand the judiciary's influence. Even Clarke's modest proposal that the Lord Chancellor should sit on the panels that recommend candidates for the most senior vacancies was later dropped by his successor, Chris Grayling. Notably, there have been few attempts emanating from Lord Chancellors and the Ministry of Justice to ensure that judicial inputs into the appointments regime are

Senior President of Tribunals), the JAC had made almost 4,300 recommendations, with Lord Chancellors refusing only 5 of them. In other words, Lord Chancellors accepted the JAC's recommendations – literally – 99.9% of the time.

69 See e.g. s. 91 of the Constitutional Reform Act 2005.

70 J. Straw, *Aspects of Law Reform: An Insider's Perspective*, Cambridge: Cambridge University Press, 2013, p. 58.

71 As Clarke put it, the Lord Chancellor's role in lower level appointments had become 'largely ceremonial and ritualistic': House of Lords Select Committee on the Constitution, *Judicial Appointment Process: Oral and Written Evidence*, 2013, p. 424, Q.373.

72 Ministry of Justice, *Framework Document: Ministry of Justice and the Judicial Appointments Commission*, para 3.3.

appropriately structured and underpinned by shared understandings as to the purpose of and limits on those inputs.

2 Judicial influence is too high if it seriously exacerbates accountability deficits in the selection regime.

A democratic accountability deficit was almost inevitable once it was decided in 2003 to move from a ministerial model of appointments to one built around an independent appointments commission. Partial redress can perhaps be found in: the statutory duty on the JAC to publish an annual report;[73] the practice of requiring the person nominated as the JAC's chair to attend a pre-appointment hearing before the Justice Committee of the House of Commons;[74] and the fact that the JAC's Chair, Chief Executive and commissioners have given evidence before select committees from time to time.[75] Lord Chancellors have also from time to time appeared before select committees to discuss, inter alia, aspects of the selection regime.[76] Augmenting this is a statutory duty on the Lord Chief Justice to 'take such steps ... as [the officeholder] considers appropriate for the purposes of encouraging judicial diversity'.[77] All of this might be said to offer a limited, indirect form of democratic accountability – but it pales in comparison to the substantial, direct democratic accountability inherent in the ministerial model.[78] A relevant question is whether, even taking account of these practices, judicial influence on the JAC-run regime is so high as to render the democratic deficit a serious cause for concern. Views will differ on this of course, and some might argue that any such deficit is more serious for some vacancies (top courts) than others (lower courts). A second question explores the extent to which any such democratic deficit is offset by the judiciary's efforts to provide a public account of their input into the selection regime (explanatory accountability).

On the first question, the Lord Chancellor remains formally accountable for the regime as a whole, but now only has very limited levers to shape individual selections, with ministerial input into policy coloured by the judiciary's context-shaping influence. Inasmuch as providing a nexus with Parliament is one of the reasons why Lord Chancellors should have a genuine role in shaping individual selections (as I argued above), and insofar as judicial input has compressed the scope for such a role, then high levels of judicial influence are contributing to a real

73 Constitutional Reform Act 2005, Schedule 12, para 32.

74 See e.g. House of Commons Justice Committee,*Appointment of the Chair of the Judicial Appointments Commission*, HC 416, 2016.

75 See e.g. House of Commons Constitutional Affairs Committee, *The Operation of the Judicial Appointments Commission*, HC 1665-I, 18 July 2006.

76 See e.g. House of Lords Select Committee on the Constitution, *Annual Oral Evidence Session with the Rt Hon Chris Grayling MP, Lord Chancellor and Secretary of Justice*, 2014, pp. 2–3, Q.2.

77 onstitutional Reform Act 2005, s. 137A.

78 There is a danger in overstating this point given that for much of the twentieth century Lord Chancellors were shielded from the full force of democratic accountability in Parliament: see Woodhouse, *The Office of Lord Chancellor*, pp. 165–181.

democratic deficit. Reasons to believe that this represents a serious concern include the scale of the deficit: beyond a role in deciding the job descriptions, there is now no ministerial involvement in 95 per cent of appointments, which in turn raises questions about the appropriateness of requiring the Lord Chancellor to remain accountable to Parliament for the selection regime. More generally, in the face of what some view as the rising constitutional power of the judiciary, it is reasonable to worry about the erosion of the legitimacy that traditionally flowed to the judiciary from the existence of a democratic nexus in the selection regime that resulted from the meaningful involvement of ministers.

On the second question there is reason to doubt whether there are mechanisms in place to ensure the effective scrutiny of the public narrative that judges offer of the ways in which they exercise influence over appointments. To be sure, there is evidence that senior judges take seriously their responsibility to provide an official account of their stewardship of, and contributions to, the selection regime, for example by publishing regular reports and statistics.[79] At the same time, there are few reliable mechanisms for holding judges to account for their considerable influence over the selection regime. For example, the House of Lords Constitution Committee in 2012 made a number of recommendations directed towards the judiciary.[80] It is of course always open for the Constitution Committee, or any other select committee, to invite senior judges to appear before them to discuss actions taken in response to those recommendations,[81] but Parliament's interest in judicial appointments has been sporadic, with select committees not always effective at following up on their recommendations.[82] None of this is the fault of the judges themselves, but rather is in large part an inevitable result of the post-2005 institutional arrangements. What is more, the judiciary's official account of their influence inevitably offers no insight into what goes on behind closed doors. No mention is made in such accounts of, for example, repeated judicial attempts to resist interviews and application forms for appointments in the Court of Appeal and for leadership positions, despite these forming an important and uncontroversial part of most professionalized appointment processes. Similarly, there is little evidence in the official accounts provided by the judiciary of successful judicial lobbying to dilute the JAC's 'equal merit' policy, a matter that I discuss immediately below.

79 See e.g. the Judicial Diversity Committee of the Judges' Council, *Report on Progress 2013–2016*, 2016; the Lord Chief Justice, *The Lord Chief Justice's Report 2016*, 2016, pp. 9–11; and Judicial Office, *Judicial Diversity Statistics 2016*, 2016.

80 See e.g. recommendations that (a) greater stress should be placed within the judiciary on judicial careers, with it easier to move between courts and tribunals and to seek promotion, and (b) a judicial appraisal system should be introduced: House of Lords Select Committee on the Constitution, *Judicial Appointments*, HL 272, 2012, paras 180 and 186.

81 On growing numbers of judicial appearances before Parliament, see R. Hazell and P. O'Brien, 'Meaningful Dialogue: Judicial Engagement with Parliamentary Committees at Westminster', *Public Law*, 2016 p. 54.

82 Gee *et al*, *The Politics of Judicial Independence*, p. 188.

3 Judicial influence is too high if judges repeatedly succeed in ensuring that the public interest is subordinated to judicial interests.

During its first decade the JAC has secured some notable policy developments in the face of judicial opposition. Perhaps the best example is the formalization of the process of appointing members of the Court of Appeal. Another success is assuming responsibility in 2013 for appointing Deputy High Court Judges.[83] However there are also suggestions that, at various points during the JAC's first ten years, judicial interests have prevailed over the public interest. Examples include the successful effort by the senior judiciary to resist the JAC assuming responsibility for the selection of the Senior Presiding Judge (a role with a wide range of management, leadership and governance responsibilities).[84] The most troubling example is, perhaps, the judicial influence that diluted the content of the JAC's equal merit policy. One of the changes introduced by the Crime and Courts Act 2013 was to clarify the meaning of section 63 of the Constitutional Reform Act 2005, which provides that the JAC must select candidates 'solely on merit'. The 2013 Act clarified that, where there are two or more candidates determined to be of equal merit, section 63 does not prevent the JAC from recommending a candidate on the basis of improving diversity on the bench.[85] As a consequence, the JAC had a free hand to devise a policy how best to implement the 'equal merit' provision.

In devising its equal merit policy, the JAC faced two critical questions. First, should the provision apply to all stages of the selection process, including short-listing, or just once at the final stage where the JAC makes its recommendation? Second, to which groups of under-represented applicants should the provision apply? Alas, the JAC answered both questions very narrowly, adopting what its then chair conceded was 'a fairly minimalist' approach.[86] The JAC decided to apply the provision only at the final selection stage, thus blunting its potential to increase diversity. The premise that there might be candidates demonstrating different strengths and weaknesses who are considered of equal merit is relevant to short-listing and at the point at which the JAC decides whom to recommend to the appointing authority. Indeed, it might be thought that it is at short-listing that it is most difficult to differentiate between the best candidates.[87] Applying the equal merit policy at short-listing could help to remove barriers that might prevent non-conventional candidates being invited for an interview. The JAC further limited the provision's potential by applying it only to race and gender. It did so on

83 Judicial Appointments Commission Regulations 2013, SI 2013/2191, Part 8.

84 The selection of the Senior Presiding Judge is seen by judiciary as a question of judicial deployment, not judicial appointment: Gee *et al*, *The Politics of Judicial Independence*, p. 186.

85 Crime and Courts Act 2013, Schedule 13. This is variously known as the 'equal merit', 'tie-break' or 'tipping point' provision and derives from s. 159 of the Equality Act 2010.

86 House of Commons Justice Committee, *The Work of the Judicial Appointments Commission*, HC 1132, 2014, Q31.

87 Bindman and Monaghan, *Judicial Diversity: Accelerating Change*, para 4.8.

the grounds that the equal merit policy should only be invoked where underrepresentation is evidenced by reference to published data. There are practical difficulties related to the availability of reliable data for some of the 'protected characteristics' under the Equality Act. However, the JAC could have been proactive in widening the number of protected groups to whom the equal merit provision can apply. Arguably, a more pioneering and proactive approach would be consistent with the JAC's statutory duty to 'have regard to the need to encourage diversity in the range of persons available for selection'.[88]

What bears emphasis, for these purposes, is that judicial influence accounts for the JAC's narrow equal merit policy. Judges exercised significant sway over the design of the JAC's policy. Over half of the responses to a consultation exercise on the equal merit policy that the JAC ran in 2013 were from judges and their representative bodies. There were also lengthy private discussions between the JAC, senior judges and the Ministry. As the then JAC Chair explained, there was 'serious caution among many [of the JAC's] stakeholders' about the equal merit policy.[89] Confidential interviews with some of those involved in the design of the policy confirm that it primarily was to meet judicial anxiety that the JAC adopted such an anaemic policy. There is also evidence of judicial resistance to the policy in the years following its adoption. According to one interviewee who is closely involved in the appointments process, some judicial commissioners on the JAC fiercely resisted an internal report that recommended that the JAC should extend the equal merit policy to the short-listing stage. In all of this it seems that some judges' attachment to a traditional account of merit – and, in particular, to the view that it will always be possible to distinguish between two candidates – is trumping the JAC's concern for faster progress on diversity.[90] To grasp the potential of the equal merit policy requires a certain attitude about the type of assessments made by selection panels when faced with two or more candidates with different but commensurable judicial qualities – and, more significantly, a change of attitude amongst some judges who serve on or seek to influence the JAC. In short: judicial influence inside the JAC and external pressure brought to bear on it by senior judges and judicial associations has led to a weak policy that 'runs the risk of marking merely another positive headline backed by very little positive impact in terms of addressing the glaring diversity deficit'.[91] The evidence, to date, suggests that judicial influence succeeded in minimizing the impact of

88 Constitutional Reform Act 2005, s. 64.

89 House of Commons Justice Committee, *The Work of the Judicial Appointments Commission*, HC 1132, 2014, p. 13, Q. 31.

90 There are, for sure, some judges who take a different view. See House of Lords Select Committee on the Constitution, *Judicial Appointments*, HL 272, 2012, para 99. Notably, Lady Justice Hallett has encouraged the JAC to consider applying the equal merit policy at short-listing: Judicial Appointments Commission, *Minutes of Meeting*, June 2015, para 5.2.

91 Paterson and Paterson, *Guarding the Guardians*, pp. 47–48.

the equal merit provision: the JAC made 306 recommendations for judicial office in 2015–2016, but invoked the provision a mere 14 times.[92]

4 Judicial influence is too high where this has enabled judicial involvement to be essentially unstructured, lacking transparency and not subject to effective checks.

Arguably, academic critiques about judicial influence over the JAC-run regime – including the critique in the book that I co-authored with Hazell, Malleson and O'Brien – have to date understated the importance of ensuring that, so far as possible, judicial inputs into the selection process are structured, transparent and subject to effective checks. From its inception in 2006, the JAC has sought to ensure a structured selection process; emphasizing, for example, that interviews should follow a set format that enables evidence to be assessed against explicitly stated criteria for appointment, with this designed in part to counter the risk of judges appealing to implicit criteria that form no part of a merit-based selection process.[93] Academic critiques have not always done enough to acknowledge the important work undertaken by the JAC on its creation in 2006 to ensure a structured and open appointment process. A related shortcoming of academic critiques has been to overlook the important steps taken by the JAC and others to structure some of the judicial inputs into the selection process since 2006. For example, the JAC in 2015 sought to address the potential for conflicts that can arise where judges undertake multiple roles in a single selection round (as panel member, statutory consultee, referee and so forth).[94] Similarly, in the face of concern that judicial commissioners tended to enjoy longer terms on the JAC than their non-judicial counterparts, the JAC, the Ministry of Justice and senior judges now share 'an expectation'[95] that there should be consistent tenures for both judicial and non-judicial commissioners alike. These are very welcome developments that should be kept in mind when assessing the degree and nature of judicial influence on the JAC and its selection processes.

Despite these important steps, there is still more work to be done to ensure that judicial contributions are structured and subject to effective checks. A particular problem is the risk that judges will enjoy excessive influence through statutory consultation; that is, where the JAC is required by statute to seek the views of senior judges on the shortlisted candidates before making its recommendation. Evidence that Hazell, Malleson, O'Brien and I collated between 2011 and 2014 suggests that the views of senior judges expressed via statutory consultation carries substantial weight, with that weight increasing with the seniority of the vacancy in

92 Judicial Appointments Commission, *Annual Report and Accounts 2015–16*, July 2016, p. 17.

93 Note, however, Monaghan's essay in this collection which argues that the existence of formally stated criteria is unlikely to substantially reduce the risk of judicial influence: see K. Monaghan, 'Reflection', in this collection.

94 Judicial Appointments Commission, *Minutes of Meeting*, February 2015, para 6.1.

95 Ministry of Justice, *Triennial Review: Judicial Appointments Commission*, 2015, para 118.

question. Further confidential interviews between 2014 and 2017 confirmed continued concerns amongst some inside the JAC about the quality of and weight attached to the judicial views expressed during statutory consultation. My co-authors and I concluded that statutory consultation sometimes operates as a de facto 'veto' for senior judges on the people that the JAC recommends, which led us to worry that statutory consultation gives judges too much influence.[96] As the JAC sees it, however, the weight ascribed to the views expressed in statutory consultation is 'directly proportionate to the quality of those reasons, which is generally high'.[97] What is more, when compared with the typically decisive say that judges possessed via secret soundings under the pre-2005 regime, it could perhaps be suggested that '[t]he relative weight of judicial consultation is bound to be smaller ... and its objectivity easier to assess' in the formal and transparent applications-based regime run by the JAC, where 'the range of information available about candidates is much wider, and largely in the hands of the candidate themselves'.[98] Although there might be something in this, as of 2016, there remains very real (if not always explicitly stated) concern among some in both the JAC and the Ministry about the quality, consistency and relevance of the views that senior judges express during statutory consultation.[99] As one civil servant at the Ministry put it, statutory consultation has a role to play because senior judges 'know the job and they know the people', but the key is to ensure that judges 'give better and more consistent evidence in statutory consultation, and follow a consistent approach'.

5 Judicial influence is too high if judges succeed in co-opting other stakeholders, including in ways that undermine the JAC's independence.

The JAC must be independent not only from the Ministry of Justice, but from the judiciary as well. It is true, of course, that judges have a critical role to play in promoting and protecting the JAC's independence. Indeed, the then Lord Chief Justice, Igor Judge, is credited with robustly defending the JAC in 2010 after tensions with the Ministry became so fraught that there were rumours that the JAC might be abolished just a matter of years after its birth.[100] However, whether by design or otherwise, judges can wield influence that undermines that independence. Judicial influence that undermines the JAC's independence is difficult to detect and calls for constant vigilance. It includes (but is not limited to) co-opting the JAC's leadership, commissioners and staff. In short, the risk of judicial capture

96 Gee *et al*, *The Politics of Judicial Independence*, pp. 172–175.
97 Sumption, 'The Constitutional Reform Act 2005', p. 40.
98 Ibid., p. 39.
99 At a recent JAC meeting, there was a general discussion on statutory consultation and the need for consultees to ensure good quality, evidence-based statutory consultation responses: Judicial Appointments Commission, *Minutes of Meeting*, June 2016, para 3.5.
100 On the JAC's 'near-death experience', see Gee *et al*, *The Politics of Judicial Independence*, pp. 167–170.

of the JAC is real. Over its first decade, this risk has ebbed and flowed, with at least occasional concern inside some parts of the JAC that judicial influence was undermining the JAC's independence. Three issues deserve emphasis.

First, some of those most closely involved in the JAC's work expressed concern in confidential interviews that each of the JAC's first two lay chairs – Baroness Prashar (from 2006 to 2010) and Christopher Stephens (from 2010 to 2016) – sometimes seemed to have been co-opted by the senior judiciary. Ensuring that the JAC's independence is not compromised by judicial capture is among the most important responsibilities of the JAC's leadership (the Chair and the Chief Executive).[101] Of course, the lay Chairs find themselves in an especially delicate position, requiring a range of administrative, diplomatic and political skills to foster and maintain the confidence of multiple stakeholders (ministers, judges, civil servants as well as the various legal professions), each of which might have competing concerns. On his appointment in 2011, Christopher Stephens found confidence in the JAC amongst ministers and senior judges at dangerously low levels. It would be understandable if the Chairs were generally sympathetic to the judiciary's perspectives on contentious questions. After all, the judiciary has an important say in the selection of the Chair,[102] and might be keen to ensure that a suitably sympathetic candidate is selected to lead the JAC. Furthermore, senior judges have ample opportunity to 'lobby' the JAC's Chair and influence his or her mindset. Not only does the JAC's Chair have regular one-to-one meetings with the Lord Chief Justice to discuss the appointments regime, he or she also participates alongside senior judges on panels that select the members of the Court of Appeal, heads of division and judicial leaders such as the Lord Chief Justice.[103] It would be unsurprising if this close and repeated contact with senior judges led some Chairs over time to share the judicial approach on contentious policy questions.

Second, there is some concern that the senior judges who sit as commissioners on the JAC have at times exerted disproportionate influence on both individual selections and the fashioning of the JAC's policies. According to one official, some of the more junior judges on the JAC have seemed at times to 'take their lead' on contentious policy questions from the senior judicial commissioners. An example cited in support of this by the same official was concerted judicial opposition to the JAC's desire to strengthen its equal merit policy. Concern has also been voiced about significant spikes in judicial influence over the JAC that occurred in 2010 and 2016 when the senior judicial commissioner served as the JAC's acting chair pending the appointment of a new lay chair. A particular concern is that these periods of interregnum provided an opportunity for these judges to entrench high levels of judicial influence over the JAC's processes.

101 See G. Gee, 'The Crime and Courts Bill and the JAC', *UK Constitutional Law Blog*, 1 November 2012.
102 See Judicial Appointments Commission Regulations 2013, reg. 9.
103 See Judicial Appointments Regulations 2013, regs. 5, 11, 13 and 23.

Finally, there is concern about whether the JAC's lay and legal commissioners might be deferential to the judicial commissioners, both on decisions relating to individual appointments and policy questions. Similarly, in respect of selection days for lower level vacancies, there are concerns about that judicial members on the interview panels might have an oversized influence. To be clear, in its early days, one of the JAC's priorities was 'to ensure that [the commissioners] worked as a cohesive group' and 'to ensure parity among the commissioners so that there was no distinction between lay and judicial members'.[104] Emphasis was also placed during Christopher Stephens's tenure as Chair to ensure that all decisions were reached by consensus, reflecting the informed view of all of the Commissioners. In several of the interviews that I have conducted with commissioners over the last five years, it has been repeatedly emphasized that every commissioner enjoys the same say, with no discernible difference between how lay, legal or judicial commissioners contribute to the JAC's decisions.[105] There is, according to many of those involved with the work of the JAC, no evidence of any deference to the judicial commissioners. As Geoffrey Bindman QC and Karon Monaghan QC have noted, however, there is reason to be (at the very least) 'a little sceptical of this': by virtue of 'the authority inherent in their status', together with their 'experience of doing the job itself', the judicial commissioners are 'likely in practice to be very influential'.[106]

And, indeed, several interviewees with very good knowledge of the internal workings of the JAC's processes have conceded in private or subsequent to leaving office that it can be exceptionally difficult for the lay commissioners to challenge the views of judicial commissioners and – in particular – senior judges, both on questions of policy and in respect of individual selection decisions. There is usually no suggestion of any outright, explicit deference shown to the judicial commissioners (although at least one interviewee felt browbeaten by some senior judges in one selection round). However, several interviewees have spoken of the role of the lay commissioners in ways that suggests that they perform a limited, secondary role of corroborating the assessments of candidates made by judicial commissioners, with this especially notable in descriptions of selection exercises for senior roles. To be clear, even when performing this corroborating role, lay commissioners can play a vital role in ensuring that fair, open and evidence-based decisions are made. However, a corroborating role is likely to mean that there will be no real difference in the type of appointments made (especially to senior positions), with traditional understandings of merit prevailing.[107] This is significant insofar as the independence of

104 U. Prashar, 'Translating Aspirations into Reality: Establishing the Judicial Appointments Commission', in Judicial Appointments Commission, *Judicial Appointments: Balancing Independence, Accountability and Legitimacy*, 2010, pp. 43, 49.

105 In their report on judicial diversity for the Labour Party, Geoffrey Bindman QC and Karon Monagahan QC make the same point, noting that they 'have been told that the lay members of the JAC are not in any sense deferential to or swayed by the views of the judicial members'. See Bindman and Monaghan, *Judicial Diversity: Accelerating Change*, para 3.18.

106 Ibid., para 3.18.

107 Gee *et al*, *The Politics of Judicial Independence*, p. 185.

the JAC is undermined, in a very real sense, if the lay commissioners become captured by an interpretation of merit that is advanced by judges in the name of their vested interests rather than the public interest.[108] Even strong and impressive lay commissioners with stellar professional careers can lack a coordinated and coherent approach to policy on appointments. The solution is not to dispense with lay involvement on the JAC, but rather to adopt a realistic approach to their ability to act as an effective counter to high levels of judicial influence.

Conclusion

The purpose of this chapter has been threefold. First, it has sought to promote a more structured debate about judicial influence over judicial appointments by providing some tools for assessing when that influence becomes too high. The starting point, I suggested, is to consider influence in terms of conduct-shaping and context-shaping. I then explained how the judiciary's conduct-shaping and context-shaping influence must be evaluated by reference to the inputs, outputs and throughputs of a well-designed and well-functioning appointment regime. From reflecting on those inputs, outputs and throughputs, it is possible to point to five rebuttable presumptions that suggest that the judiciary exerts too much influence. Second, I have sought to use these presumptions to substantiate and add depth to claims made by a handful of academics over the last decade that judges now exercise too much influence under the JAC regime. Third, in all of this, the overriding objective has been less to persuade the main stakeholders in the selection regime that such academic critiques are necessarily correct, but rather to help bridge a gulf between academics on the one hand and judges, the JAC and officials on the other about why it is important to debate the levels of judicial influence. In short: the goal has been to help stakeholders recognize and remedy the fact that this is a debate that has been largely neglected during the JAC's first decade. Moreover, as debates about the need for an independent judicial appointment body heat up in common law countries such as Australia and Canada, there are lessons to be drawn from the experience in England and Wales, both about the levels of judicial influence and – perhaps as importantly – about the difficulty of furnishing a constructive debate about that influence.

I have deliberately framed the five presumptions as rebuttable. This recognizes that debates about influence in the real world are inevitably highly contextual. Abstract propositions about what may or may not constitute excessive influence can only ever be the starting point for debate. It is vital to attend to the unique circumstances in the judicial system at hand, always recognizing that levels of influence will be a product of multiple factors, not all of which directly relate to judges themselves. It might be, for example, that the levels of judicial influence need to be reconsidered if the institutional dynamics in the selection regime do not operate as envisaged. In the JAC regime, high levels of judicial influence are

108 J. Morison, 'Beyond Merit: The New Challenge for Judicial Appointments', in this collection.

mandated by statute, and are thus an important expression of Parliament's will. Yet, in practice, judges exercise much more influence than Parliament intended, partly because successive Lord Chancellors have participated much less fully than anticipated, and also partly because checks on judicial influence are arguably less effective than envisaged (e.g. the scale of judicial involvement on the JAC regime is not counterbalanced by the input of the JAC's lay and legal commissioners). It is also important to keep in mind that the cumulative level of judicial influence might be too high even if no one instance of judicial involvement is objectionable when viewed in isolation. There is of course room to debate whether any instance of judicial involvement is desirable on its own terms (e.g. whether it is desirable for the Lord Chief Justice and the Senior President of Tribunals to have the final say over such a large proportion of selections given that this arguably intensifies an acute deficit in democratic accountability). Yet, even if each and every instance of involvement might be justifiable when viewed in isolation, the combined effect of the involvement that is ingrained throughout the selection regime might lead to the conclusion that judges have excessive influence. Put differently, these presumptions represent a beginning rather than an end to debate about levels of judicial influence. But it is a debate that, in the JAC regime, is long overdue.

9 Judicial diversity and mandatory retirement

Obstacle or route to diversity?

Alysia Blackham

Introduction

A diverse judiciary is essential for a democratic society. While considerable attention has been paid to how judicial diversity can be promoted, most debate has been focused on judicial appointment processes, and the role of the Judicial Appointments Commission (JAC) in securing change. While judicial appointments are fundamental for achieving diversity, the focus on the appointments process assumes that there are judicial posts that need filling. Without substantially expanding the size of the judiciary, diversity can only be achieved through some degree of judicial turnover.

In recent decades, mandatory retirement ages have become a key mechanism for securing predictable turnover in the UK judiciary. However, there has been limited discussion of the potential for mandatory retirement to secure diversity in the judiciary. Even the JAC has little to say about retirement ages, other than that 'the age at which someone is appointed as a judicial officer must allow for a reasonable length of service before retirement' at the statutory retirement age.[1] Despite repeated academic discussion of the role and importance of judicial pensions in securing diversity,[2] and the strong practical overlap between pensions and retirement rules, mandatory retirement has been comparatively neglected as an area of study in relation to the judiciary. As we increasingly move to a holistic understanding of judicial diversity – recognizing the relationship between appointments, working conditions, appraisals, training, career development, travel and deployment in promoting (or hindering) diversity[3] – it is equally important to acknowledge and consider the potential impact of retirement ages on this equation.

The lack of academic discussion on retirement ages for the judiciary[4] stands in stark contrast to the weight of scholarship on retirement ages in relation to other

1 See e.g. Judicial Appointments Commission, *Eligibility for Non-Legally-Qualified Candidates*, London: Judicial Appointments Commission.

2 See G. Gee, R. Hazell, K. Malleson and P. O'Brien, *The Politics of Judicial Independence in the UK's Changing Constitution*, Cambridge: Cambridge University Press, 2015, ch. 4.

3 In Australia, see K. Mack and S. Roach Anleu, 'Entering the Australian Judiciary: Gender and Court Hierarchy', *Law & Policy* 34, 2012, p. 313.

4 Though in Australia, see A. Blackham, 'Judges and Retirement Ages', *Melbourne University Law Review* 39, 2016, 738; in the UK, see A. Blackham, 'Judicial Retirement Ages in the

professions and areas of work.[5] Since the UK government removed the national default retirement age of 65 for the general workforce in 2011,[6] employers have increasingly had to move to a model of workplace relations without fixed retirement ages. Unless employers can show that an employer-justified retirement age is a proportionate means of achieving a legitimate aim, retirement ages can no longer be relied on. Anecdotal evidence suggests that the vast majority of UK employers – bar some outliers, such as the University of Oxford, University of Cambridge and British Airways – are now operating without mandatory retirement. By retaining a mandatory retirement age, the judiciary is the exception to this general trend, and appears to be resisting the broader move towards greater age equality in employment. There is therefore even more need to scrutinize the practical impact of judicial retirement ages, including in relation to their impact on diversity.

The Judicial Pensions and Retirement Act 1993 ('the 1993 Act') imposes a general judicial retirement age of 70 for most judicial office holders, making compulsory retirement a key term of tenure for judicial appointments in the UK. However, as we shall see, the suggestion that requiring older office holders to retire may increase the frequency of judicial appointments, allowing for more diverse appointees[7] is problematic on a number of fronts. Fixed retirement ages may make appointment to judicial office less attractive for individuals with disrupted or non-traditional career paths, particularly women. The concurrent use of

UK: Legitimate Aims and Proportionate Means?', *Public Law* 2017, 196. See generally B. Opeskin, 'Models of Judicial Tenure: Reconsidering Life Limits, Age Limits and Term Limits for Judges', *Oxford J of Legal Studies* 35, 2015, p. 627.

5 See e.g. L. Vickers and S. Manfredi, 'Age Equality and Retirement: Squaring the Circle', *Industrial Law Journal* 42, 2013, p. 61; S. Manfredi and L. Vickers, 'Retirement and Age Discrimination: Managing Retirement in Higher Education', *Industrial Law Journal* 38, 2009, p. 343; S. Manfredi and L. Vickers, 'Pensioning off the Mandatory Retirement Age: Implications for the Higher Education Sector', *Legal Studies* 33, 2013, p. 289; E. Dewhurst, 'Intergenerational Balance, Mandatory Retirement and Age Discrimination in Europe: How Can the ECJ Better Support National Courts in Finding a Balance between the Generations?', *Common Market Law Review* 50, 2013, p. 1333; E. Dewhurst, 'The Development of EU Case-Law on Age Discrimination in Employment: "Will You Still Need Me? Will You Still Feed Me? When I'm Sixty-Four"', *European Law Journal* 19, 2013, p. 517; E. Dewhurst, 'Are Older Workers Past Their Sell-by-Date? A View from UK Age Discrimination Law', *Modern Law Review* 78, 2015, p. 189; C. Barnard, 'Retiring Gracefully', *Cambridge Law Journal* 70, 2011, p. 304; A. Blackham, 'Organisational Responses to the Abolition of Mandatory Retirement: Case Studies of Australian University Practice', *Industrial Law Journal* 45, 2016, p. 144; A. Blackham, *Extending Working Life for Older Workers: Age Discrimination Law, Policy and Practice*, Oxford: Hart Publishing, 2016; and M. Sargeant, 'The Default Retirement Age: Legitimate Aims and Disproportionate Means', *Industrial Law Journal* 39, 2010, p. 244.

6 The Employment Equality (Repeal of Retirement Age Provisions) Regulations 2011, SI 1069/2011.

7 House of Lords Select Committee on the Constitution, *Judicial Appointments*, 25th Report of Session 2010–12, para 193, referring to the evidence of the Association of Women Solicitors, Association of Women Barristers, and Law Society.

retirement ages and fixed pension requirements may therefore actually impede the judicial appointments process, and hinder progress towards diversity, by rendering judicial office less attractive to certain applicants.

While other justifications may also support retirement ages for the judiciary – such as the need to protect judicial independence and 'dignity' by avoiding performance processes; encouraging 'fresh blood', new ideas and judicial renewal; and promoting intergenerational fairness more generally – these arguments are not the focus of this chapter, which focuses solely on the diversity implications of mandatory retirement. However, as I have argued elsewhere, even when taking these arguments collectively, there remain serious questions regarding whether judicial retirement ages can be justified.[8] It is in this context that this chapter scrutinizes the use of diversity arguments as one justification of mandatory retirement ages for judges.

To scrutinize the link between mandatory retirement and judicial diversity, this chapter draws on statistical evidence of the composition of the judiciary, and judicial appointments and retirements, via a survey of Appointments and Retirements announcements posted on the UK Courts and Tribunals Judiciary website spanning from 1 November 2013 to 16 August 2015. I argue that while some (albeit slow) progress on diversity is being made in judicial appointments, this progress would likely be made without compulsory retirement ages: the vast majority of judges leave their role before reaching the retirement age. Thus, natural attrition and judicial pensions are more effective at promoting judicial turnover than compulsory retirement. The use of judicial retirement ages is therefore not an appropriate or sufficient means of increasing judicial diversity.

Judicial retirement ages

Judicial retirement ages were first introduced by the Judicial Pensions Act 1959, which imposed a retirement age of 75 for those appointed to the High Court and above. Later, the 1993 Act introduced a general retirement age of 70 for most judicial office holders in the UK, with the aim of bringing consistency to retirement ages.[9] Section 26 of that Act provides that, upon attaining the age of 70 (or a lower age specified in an Act or other instrument), a judicial office holder shall vacate their office. It follows, then, that most judges must now retire by the age of 70, though for judges appointed to the higher courts before the 1993 Act commenced, the mandatory retirement age is still 75.

The UK is not alone in imposing retirement ages on the judiciary: most jurisdictions (bar the US federal courts) adopt some age or term limits on judicial

8 For discussion of these arguments, and the broader justifications of judicial retirement ages, see Blackham, 'Judicial Retirement Ages in the UK'.

9 The Lord Chancellor, Lord Mackay of Clashfern, *HL Debate*, 16 June 1992, vol. 538, cols 118–126; The Parliamentary Secretary, Lord Chancellor's Department, Mr J. M. Taylor, *HC Debate,* 3 December 1992, vol. 215, col 429.

tenure.[10] Indeed, the UK's retirement age of 70 is comparatively generous when compared with mandatory retirement ages for judges in other Commonwealth jurisdictions.[11] However, there is still a need to consider the practical impact that retirement ages might have, including on judicial diversity.

Retirement ages and diversity

Judicial retirement ages may allow for the appointment of new, more diverse judicial officers by increasing the frequency of judicial appointments.[12] Judicial tenure (and mandatory retirement) 'directly impacts the rate of judicial turnover':[13] shorter tenure facilitates additional judicial appointments.[14] Thus, judicial retirement ages may promote diversity in relation to gender, ethnicity, age and professional background, by making space for more diverse appointees. Arguments about diversity were raised in the parliamentary debates on the 1993 Act.[15] Indeed, the whole process of reform under the Act was described by one MP as a 'scheme to balance the judiciary's gender or racial composition so as to make it more politically acceptable and more in touch with what is supposed to be popular opinion.'[16]

The desire to promote a more diverse workforce may help to justify a fixed retirement age for the judiciary. In the pivotal case of *Seldon v Clarkson Wright & Jakes (A partnership)*[17] the UK Supreme Court (UKSC) considered whether the retirement age of 65 in a law firm's partnership deed was objectively justified as a proportionate means of achieving a legitimate aim. In that case, the Court held that 'intergenerational fairness' (to be achieved through turnover) was a key legitimate aim that might justify a retirement age.[18] This logically also extends to the situation of the judiciary.

To date, there have been a handful of cases relating to judicial retirement ages: intergenerational fairness and diversity feature prominently in most of these.[19] For

10 Opeskin, 'Models of Judicial Tenure', p. 627.
11 J. van Zyl Smit, *The Appointment, Tenure and Removal of Judges under Commonwealth Principles*, London: Bingham Centre for the Rule of Law, 2015, p. 69.
12 House of Lords Select Committee on the Constitution, *Judicial Appointments*, para 188. See also C. R. McFadden, 'Judicial Independence, Age-Based BFOQs, and the Perils of Mandatory Retirement Policies for Appointed State Judges', *South Carolina Law Review* 52, 2000–01, pp. 81, 89.
13 Opeskin, 'Models of Judicial Tenure', p. 657.
14 But might, of course, come at the expense of a loss of experience, which is particularly problematic in a common law system of adjudication.
15 Mr J. M. Taylor, *HC Debate*, vol. 215, col 431.
16 Mr Evans, *HC Debate*, 3 December 1992, vol. 215, col 445.
17 [2012] UKSC 16, [2012] 2 CMLR 50.
18 *Seldon v Clarkson Wright & Jakes (A partnership)* [2012] UKSC 16, [2012] 2 CMLR 50, paras 56–57. The matter was referred back to the Employment Tribunal on the matter of proportionality. The retirement age was ultimately upheld as a proportionate means of achieving a legitimate aim.
19 Though compare *Engel v Transport and Environment Committee of London Councils* [2013] UKET 2200472/2012 (26 April 2013), where a retirement age of 70 was

example, in 2013, in *Lindsay v Department for Employment and Learning*[20] the Employment Tribunal upheld a retirement age of 70 when challenged by a lay member of the employer panel for the Northern Ireland Industrial Tribunals.[21] The Employment Tribunal held that the Department's intergenerational fairness aims were legitimate, including for addressing the disparity in the panel's age profile (72.48 per cent of panel members were aged over 55). The Employment Tribunal also held that the retirement age was a proportionate (and, indeed, the only) means of achieving these aims.[22] If the Department had undertaken a recruitment exercise without a retirement age in place, the age disparity of panel members was likely to endure, and additional members would only reduce the amount of work available for all panel members.[23] Thus, intergenerational fairness was highly influential in *Lindsay*.

Similarly, in *White v Ministry of Justice*,[24] the Employment Tribunal in 2014 upheld the retirement of a circuit judge at age 70. The Tribunal identified five policy objectives underlying compulsory retirement ages for judges:

1 Promoting judicial independence by avoiding assessments about whether an individual remains capable of performing their judicial functions upon reaching a certain age;
2 Preserving dignity by avoiding individual assessments;
3 Maintaining public confidence in judicial health and capacity;
4 Workforce planning; and
5 Sharing opportunities between generations and promoting diversity.[25]

The Employment Tribunal heard evidence that increasing judicial retirement ages to 75 would '[introduce] a permanent and irrecoverable delay in improving diversity of 17 months',[26] as some judges would stay in their position for longer, preventing more diverse candidates from being appointed. Again, intergenerational fairness and diversity were key considerations in this case.

While the case law has largely accepted that judicial retirement ages will promote diversity, it is not so simple in practice. As noted by the House of Lords Constitution Select Committee, adopting higher retirement ages, or removing them entirely, may be 'particularly beneficial to those who started on the career

upheld when challenged by a parking adjudicator. TECLC did not base their case on intergenerational fairness aims. Rather, they emphasized workforce planning and competence issues.

20 [2013] NIET 356/12, [2014] EqLR 180.

21 The provision was challenged under regulation 3(1) of the Employment Equality (Age) Regulations (Northern Ireland) 2006 (NI) SI 2006/261, which is effectively the same as the provisions under the Equality Act 2010.

22 Ibid., paras 19, 22.

23 Ibid., para 17.

24 ET 2201298/2013 (20 November 2014).

25 Ibid., para 19.

26 Ibid., para 32. Note, however, that the decision in *White* may be criticized for its lack of supporting evidence: see *John v Ministry of Justice* ET 3300891/2012 and 1700191/2013 (16 December 2014).

ladder later in life, perhaps after taking a career break to have children.'[27] Thus, primary caregivers (particularly women) may benefit from higher retirement ages. Indeed, retirement ages may prohibit some individuals from '[reaching] the highest levels of the judiciary, however talented or experienced they might be, because their career paths have taken too long.'[28] Thus, retirement ages may disadvantage those with non-traditional career paths. As a result, they directly reinforce the male breadwinner model of work, where men are posited as primary wage earners.[29] As mandatory retirement ages are increasingly removed from other occupations, the presence of a retirement age for judicial appointments may deter those with disrupted or disjointed career paths from considering the judiciary as a career path, particularly women with caring responsibilities. Women may prefer to work beyond the traditional retirement age, either due to lost years in child-rearing, or due to a need for income.[30] Therefore, retirement ages may disproportionately disadvantage more diverse judicial candidates, and inhibit the JAC's work on diversity.

We must also recognize that judges might leave their position for a variety of reasons unrelated to retirement. Thus, imposing a retirement age may be unnecessary in many cases. In *Engel*, the Employment Tribunal heard evidence that most parking adjudicators left their role for reasons other than retirement,[31] which meant that the retirement age was not a proportionate or effective means of achieving turnover. Similarly, in *Hampton v Lord Chancellor*,[32] there was no evidence that recorders would remain in their post until the age of 70,[33] again leading to a finding that the retirement age was not proportionate. This is perhaps unsurprising, given the strain that modern judging can take on individuals, as judicial roles become increasingly onerous.[34] In the 2014 Judicial Attitude Survey, 31 per cent of judges said they would consider early retirement in the next five years, and 22 per cent were undecided, citing limits on pay and benefits and increasing workloads.[35] It is debatable, then, whether judicial retirement ages are necessary to promote more diverse

27 House of Lords Select Committee on the Constitution, *Judicial Appointments*, para 195. See also 'Pennsylvania House Votes to Set Judge Retirement Age to 75', *Washington Times*, 10 February 2015.

28 House of Lords Select Committee on the Constitution, *Judicial Appointments*, para 195.

29 D. Sainsbury, *Gender, Equality, and Welfare States*, Cambridge: Cambridge University Press, 1996, p. 41; A. O'Rand and J. C. Henretta, *Age and Inequality: Diverse Pathways through Later Life*, Boulder: Westview Press, 1999, p. 79; M. Kohli, 'The Institutionalization of the Life Course: Looking Back to Look Ahead', *Research in Human Development* 4, 2007, pp. 253, 258.

30 See S. Campbell, 'Delayed Mandatory Retirement and the Working Woman', *The Gerontologist* 19, 1979, p. 257.

31 Engel v Transport and Environment Committee of London Councils, para 53.

32 [2008] IRLR 258.

33 Ibid., para 51.

34 See generally P. Darbyshire, *Sitting in Judgment: The Working Lives of Judges*, Oxford: Hart Publishing, 2011.

35 C. A. Thomas, *2014 UK Judicial Attitude Survey: Report of Findings Covering Salaried Judges in England & Wales Courts and UK Tribunals*, London: University College London, 2015, pp. 43, 46.

appointments to the judiciary, given many judges may leave their posts well before retirement age. Thus, we need to question the actual impact that retirement ages have on judicial diversity in practice.

The empirical link between retirement ages and diversity

These arguments may be evaluated via the use of statistical evidence about the composition of the judiciary. In 2015, only 25 per cent of judges in England and Wales were women, and 5.9 per cent were black and minority ethnic (BME).[36] This may be compared with the 2001 figures of 14.1 per cent women judges and 1.9 per cent BME judges.[37] This seems to imply that some (albeit slow) progress on gender and ethnic diversity is being made in judicial appointments. However, these general figures cloak the fact that progress on diversity is largely being made in the lower levels of the judiciary and in tribunals: women and BME appointees rarely occupy more senior judicial positions, as illustrated by Table 9.1.

A more compelling picture of the impact of retirement ages emerges when examining judges and tribunal judges by age. As Table 9.2 illustrates, a substantially higher proportion of judges aged under 40 are women (53 per cent), compared with those who are aged 60 and over (13 per cent). However, the picture is less clear cut for BME appointees: while those under 60 are far more likely to be BME, this does not hold consistently across the age bands, with those aged 40–49 more likely to be BME than those under 40. A more consistent picture emerges for tribunal judges.

While this implies that a more diverse pool of appointees is replacing older, retiring judges, it does not provide concrete evidence of this. To prove that retirement ages are having this impact, it is necessary to examine the actual appointments that are being made to the judiciary, and how this compares with the judges who are retiring. To undertake this exercise, I conducted a statistical survey of Appointments and Retirements announcements posted on the Courts and Tribunals Judiciary website,[38] spanning from 1 November 2013 to 16 August 2015 (a total of 485 announcements). Over that period, announcements were made of 237 retirements, five resignations and 243 appointments. In this sample, the average age of appointment was 59.42; the average age of retirement was 66.63; and the average age of resignation was 63.33. Of those that retired, 191 were men (over 80 per cent), and four of those resigning were men. Of those who were appointed, 130 were men (around 53 per cent). Thus, while many retiring judges were replaced with male appointees, over this period 67 more women were appointed to the bench as a result of judicial retirements and resignations. This

36 Courts and Tribunals Judiciary, *Judicial Statistics 2015*, London: Courts and Tribunals Judiciary, 30 July 2015.

37 Courts and Tribunals Judiciary, *Annual Diversity Statistics 2001*, London: Courts and Tribunals Judiciary, 23 March 2010.

38 Courts and Tribunals Judiciary, *Appointments and Retirements*, Online, Available www.judiciary.gov.uk/announcement-type/appointments-and-retirements/ (accessed 11 February 2017).

Table 9.1 Gender and ethnic split by position, UK judges and tribunal judges 2015

Position	*Total in post*	*% Female*	*% BME*
UK judges			
Heads of Division	5	0%	0%
Lords Justices of Appeal	38	21%	0%
High Court Judges	106	20%	3%
Judge Advocates, Deputy Judge Advocates	12	17%	0%
Masters, Registrars, Costs Judges and District Judges (Principal Registry of the Family Division)	35	26%	0%
Deputy Masters, Deputy Registrars, Deputy Costs Judges and Deputy District Judges	55	40%	3%
Circuit Judges	640	23%	3%
Recorders	1,031	16%	7%
District Judges (County Courts)	441	31%	8%
Deputy District Judges (County Courts)	622	37%	6%
District Judges (Magistrates' Courts)	138	31%	4%
Deputy District Judges (Magistrates' Courts)	115	31%	11%
Total	**3,238**	**25%**	**6%**
UK tribunal judges			
First-tier Tribunal	3,969	45%	15%
Upper Tribunal	151	32%	10%
Employment Tribunal – England and Wales	1,200	48%	11%
Employment Tribunal – Scotland	200	48%	1%
Employment Appeal Tribunal	23	35%	17%
Total	**5,543**	**45%**	**14%**

(Source: Judicial Database)

Table 9.2 Gender and ethnic split by age band, UK judges and tribunal judges 2015

	Under 40	*40–49*	*50–59*	*60 and over*
UK judges				
% of office holders who are female	53%	44%	30%	13%
% of office holders who are BME	6%	11%	8%	2%
UK tribunal judges				
% of office holders who are female	56%	56%	52%	29%
% of office holders who are BME	15%	13%	11%	6%

(Source: Judicial Statistics 2015)

implies that progress is being made towards diversity at least partially as a result of judicial retirements.

However, it is important to note that few of these retirements occurred at the judicial retirement age. Of the 233 retirement announcements where an age was specified, only 31 retirements occurred at the age of 70 (13 per cent); and 12 occurred over the age of 70 (in 11 cases, where the judge was appointed prior to the new retirement age of 70 being introduced) (see further Figure 9.1). This raises serious questions as to whether the use of judicial retirement ages is a proportionate means of achieving the legitimate aims of increasing judicial diversity or intergenerational fairness. Rather, as was the case for parking adjudicators in *Engel*,[39] and recorders in *Hampton*,[40] it appears that the vast majority of judges (81.5 per cent) leave their role for reasons other than the retirement age.

These findings are consistent with data from the Ministry of Justice. According to outflow data for the salaried judiciary in England and Wales, 145 office holders (or 7.5 per cent) left their positions in 2014–2015, at an average age of 66.08.[41] These included seven vacancies due to death, two due to medical retirement, two due to removal, and 134 due to retirement.[42] The Ministry of Justice also breaks down these figures according to judicial seniority (see Table 9.3). From Table 9.3 we can see that the age of departure is higher for more senior judiciary: thus, retirement ages will have more impact for those in the higher judiciary.[43] However, these data should be used with a degree of caution: the average age also includes deaths in office ('DIO'), medical retirements ('MR') and removals from

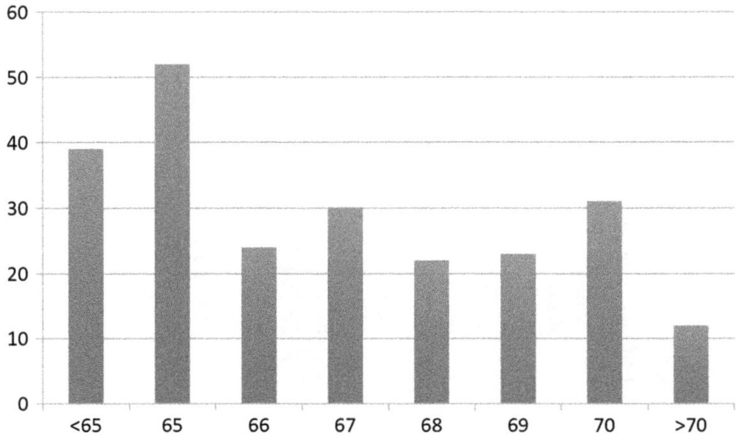

Figure 9.1 Number of judicial retirements by age, 2013–2015

39 *Engel v Transport and Environment Committee of London Councils*, para 53.

40 *Hampton v Lord Chancellor*.

41 Ministry of Justice, *Senior Salaries Review Body: Judiciary: Annual Written Evidence*, London: Ministry of Justice, December 2015, p. 18.

42 Ibid.

43 That is, the High Court and above.

Table 9.3 Departures of Salaried Judges, England and Wales, 2014–2015

Office	*Number of departures*	*50–54*	*55–59*	*60–64*	*65–69*	*70–75*	*Average age*
Higher judiciary	12	0	0	2	3	7	68.58
Circuit bench	47 (2 DIO)	0	1 (1 DIO)	3 (1 DIO)	33	10	67.26
District judges (Magistrates' Court)	9	0	0	4	5	0	64.11
District judges	36 (2 DIO, 1 MR, 1 RFO)	3 (1 DIO, 1 RFO)	1	7 (1 DIO)	22 (1 MR)	3	64.39
Masters and Registrars	5	0	0	1	3	1	65.60
Tribunals	36 (3 DIO, 1 MR, 1 RFO)	1	0	10 (1 MR, 1 RFO)	21 (3 DIO)	4	65.94
Total	145 (7 DIO, 2 MR, 2 RFO)	4 (1 DIO, 1 RFO)	2 (1 DIO)	27 (2 DIO, 1 MR, 1 RFO)	87 (3 DIO, 1 MR)	25	66.08

(Source: Ministry of Justice)

office ('RFO'). Thus, many departures are not instances of voluntary retirement. Unlike the survey above, these figures also clump together all departures after age 70 – thus, it is difficult to determine when the individual was subject to the retirement age of 70 and when they were not, which may distort the average age of departure.

Pensions and diversity

When considering the link between judicial diversity and retirement ages, it is also important to take judicial pension arrangements into account, as pensions may strongly influence judicial retirement behaviour. Until 2015, judicial pensions were provided for by the Judicial Pension Scheme 1993 ('JUPRA'), which was established under the Judicial Pensions and Retirement Act 1993 and associated regulations. Under that scheme, judges were entitled to a contribution-based defined benefit pension, based on a final salary model. The pension scheme had a 20-year restriction on the number of years of service that could be accrued; in other words, judges would achieve their full pension entitlement (an annual pension of half their pensionable pay) following 20 years of service.[44] The scheme had a normal pension age of 65, which would be of most benefit to those appointed at or before the age of 45. The New Judicial Pension Scheme 2015 lifts the 20-year restriction on years of service, imposes higher individual contributions on judges and reverts to a career-average defined benefit pension.[45] This has caused significant discontent among the judiciary, and the transitional provisions have been challenged successfully in the Employment Tribunal.[46]

The combined effect of pension and retirement provisions may deter good candidates from accepting appointment to the bench. Under the 1993 JUPRA pension system, individuals who are appointed to the bench after the age of 50 are unlikely to earn full judicial pension entitlements. This may mean that the 'best people will not accept appointment',[47] as the (comparatively) low pay and lack of a full pension deter practitioners from taking up judicial office. This will be exacerbated by the New Judicial Pension Scheme 2015, which reduces pension entitlements even further. This may lead to a shortage of individuals willing to enter judicial office, with those who do 'putting their duty before their own personal advantage'.[48] Alternatively, this may lead to more wealthy (and often white male)

44 See further Ministry of Justice, *Judicial Pension Scheme 1993: Scheme Guide*, London: Ministry of Justice, November 2014.

45 See Ministry of Justice, *New Judicial Pension Scheme 2015: Policy Papers*, London: Ministry of Justice.

46 *McCloud v The Lord Chancellor* [2017] UKET 2201483/2015 (16 January 2017).

47 Lord Benson, *HL Debate*, 30 June 1992, vol. 538, col 691. See also Viscount Bledisloe, *HL Debate*, 30 June 1992, vol. 538, col 696; Sir Ivan Lawrence, *HC Debate*, 3 December 1992, vol. 215, col 465.

48 Viscount Bledisloe, *HL Debate*, 30 June 1992, vol. 538, col 696.

lawyers 'consider[ing] the High Court as a hobby to pursue for a few years', as they do not need the remuneration or pension provided by a judicial appointment.[49]

The 2014 Judicial Attitude Survey provides a strong indication that pension changes will adversely affect judicial recruitment and retention: 68 per cent of respondents said that reductions in pension benefits would likely lead them to leave the judiciary early (that is, before retirement age),[50] and 76 per cent of respondents said they would discourage suitable applicants from applying for judicial appointment given the likelihood of further pension reductions.[51] This may seriously impede the quality of judicial appointments, including by deterring more diverse candidates. Indeed, the Ministry of Justice has identified an 'emerging problem with recruitment and retention' at the High Court, partly exacerbated by an 'unusual level of early retirements' for senior judges.[52] According to Joshua Rozenberg, a lack of applicants for certain positions has led to the:

> much-criticised 'tap-on-the shoulder' method of recruitment – which the JAC was set up to replace – … [being] discreetly reinstated. What's different is that it's senior judges who are doing the tapping rather than the lord chancellor – and it's now much more like a shove in the back.[53]

The re-emergence of the 'tap on the shoulder' may significantly undermine efforts to increase judicial diversity in the UK. Conversely, the 'tap on the under-represented shoulder' could help to identify and support non-traditional candidates for judicial office, promoting diversity among the judiciary.[54] Thus, it is unclear how recruitment difficulties will play out in relation to diversity.

Beyond general recruitment difficulties, changes to judicial pensions may be a particular deterrent for women applicants, who are more likely to take career breaks to look after children, thereby reducing their overall income prior to being appointed as a judge,[55] and potentially slowing their career progression and ability to be appointed to the bench at an earlier age. Pension changes may disproportionately affect women with lower retirement income or limited pension provision.[56] This challenge was acknowledged in the parliamentary debates on the 1993 Act: 'In many respects, the pension arrangements will make it more difficult

49 A. Jack, 'Empty Benches', *Counsel*, July 2015.
50 Thomas, *2014 UK Judicial Attitude Survey*, p. 46.
51 Ibid., p. 57.
52 Ministry of Justice, *Senior Salaries Review Body*, p. 8.
53 J. Rozenberg, 'Senior Judges Are Hanging up Their Wigs. Replacing Them Won't Be Cheap', *The Guardian*, 4 April 2016.
54 L. Barmes and K. Malleson, 'The Legal Profession as Gatekeeper to the Judiciary: Design Faults in Measures to Enhance Diversity', *Modern Law Review* 74, 2011 p. 245; A. Paterson and C. Paterson, *Guarding the Guardians: Towards an Independent, Accountable and Diverse Senior Judiciary*, London: CentreForum, 2012, p. 78. In Australia, see Mack and Roach Anleu, 'Entering the Australian Judiciary', p. 330.
55 Sir Ivan Lawrence, *HC Debate*, 3 December 1992, vol. 215, col 432, 464.
56 T. R. Klassen and C. T. Gillin, 'Legalized Age Discrimination', *Journal of Law and Social Policy* 20, 2005, pp. 35, 43.

for women who have had a break in their career at the Bar to bring up a family to obtain the pension entitlements normally due to them.'[57]

This will be even more important under the New Judicial Pension Scheme 2015, which places no upper limit on the number of years of pensionable service. Judges will also struggle to return to private practice upon leaving the bench, given the 'no return to practice' rule.[58] Judges with an inadequate pension (and women in particular) may struggle to earn using their legal skills in retirement, except as an arbitrator or mediator. This could pose very real challenges for some judges, and may deter judicial appointments from more diverse groups. In this context, removing or extending judicial retirement ages, and introducing more flexible pension arrangements, may make the judiciary a more attractive career path for non-traditional office holders, like women.[59]

These concerns about the impact of retirement and pension arrangements on the appointments process were categorically rejected by the Government during the debate of the 1993 Act: 'There is little evidence that people accept, or are deterred from accepting, judicial appointment because of the pension arrangements.'[60] According to the Government, pension arrangements are only considered 'collaterally to the main decision' to accept appointment, and a more diverse judiciary will be appointed once 'the reservoir of those available for appointment includes more women and more people of ethnic origins',[61] irrespective of pension entitlements. Judges may also retain their existing pension entitlements, acquired prior to taking up judicial office.[62]

A great deal has changed, however, since the introduction of the 1993 Act: following the 2015 changes to judicial pensions, the arguments advanced by the Government in the early 1990s may no longer be sound. In the survey of judicial appointments and retirements, pensions appeared to have a strong influence on judicial retirement behaviour. Of the 233 retirement announcements where an age was specified, 52 retirements (or 22 per cent) occurred at age 65, the normal pension age under the JUPRA pension scheme. This far exceeded the 31 retirements that occurred at the retirement age of 70 (13 per cent). The vast majority of judges (81.5 per cent) left their role prior to the retirement age, with 151 departures (or 64.8 per cent) between the pension age (65) and age 69.

57 Mr Byers, *HC Debate*, 3 December 1992, vol. 215, col 449.

58 F. Phillips, *The Modern Judiciary: Challenges, Stresses and Strains*, London: Wildy, Simmonds and Hill, 2010, p. 259; Judiciary of England and Wales, *Guide to Judicial Conduct 2013*, March 2013, p. 28.

59 H. G. Genn, *The Attractiveness of Senior Judicial Appointment to Highly Qualified Practitioners: Report to the Judicial Executive Board*, Directorate of Judicial Offices for England and Wales, 2008, p. 29. See also Accent, *Barriers to Application to Judicial Appointment*, London: Judicial Appointments Commission, July 2013, p. 14; House of Lords Select Committee on the Constitution, *Judicial Appointments*, paras 112–17.

60 The Parliamentary Secretary, Lord Chancellor's Department, Mr J. M. Taylor, *HC Debate*, 3 December 1992, vol. 215, cols 432–33.

61 Ibid.

62 Ibid., col 427.

Overall, it appears that judicial pensions might have more impact on retirement behaviour than judicial retirement ages. While progress is being made on judicial diversity, judicial pensions are likely to be more effective at promoting judicial turnover than mandatory retirement. In this context, changes to judicial pension arrangements may have significant consequences for judicial diversity, and are of far more import than mandatory retirement in freeing up judicial posts. This calls into question the usefulness of retaining mandatory retirement ages for the judiciary, and flags the potential risks to diversity of reducing or altering judicial pensions.

That said, a study in Australia has found that women may actually be appointed to the judiciary *earlier* than men, and after less professional experience.[63] In a 2007 survey of the Australian judiciary, the average age of female judges was 54, compared with 61 for men; and 89 per cent of judges and magistrates aged 58 or more were men.[64] On average, women were first appointed as judges at age 45, and 19 years after first being admitted to practice; this was compared with age 50, and 25 years after admission to practice for men.[65]

If these findings also hold in the UK context, concerns about women being disproportionately affected by retirement ages and pensions may be illusory. In the survey of judicial appointments conducted for this study, women were, on average, appointed at an earlier age than men. In the 236 appointment announcements that specified the age or birth date of the appointee, the average age of appointment was 51.19 years of age. For women, the average age of appointment was 49.34, and the median was 49. For men, the average was slightly higher, at 52.79 years of age, and the median age was 53.[66] Thus, like in Australia, women appear to be, on average, appointed to the judiciary at a younger age than men, though the difference is less substantial than in Australia. Further, these statistics reflect appointments to both tribunals and courts: if women are more likely to be appointed to lower-level tribunals, it is unsurprising if they are (on average) appointed at an earlier age. That said, on average women also retired earlier than their male peers, at an average age of 65.24, compared with 66.95 for men. On average, then, retirement ages may actually have *less* impact on women.

Conclusion

In conclusion, it is difficult to argue that mandatory retirement ages are promoting a more diverse judiciary in the UK. While new judicial appointees appear to be more diverse than those who are departing, most judicial departures appear to be linked with the availability of a pension, rather than mandatory retirement ages. This seriously questions one of the key justifications for imposing mandatory

63 Mack and Roach Anleu, 'Entering the Australian Judiciary', pp. 326–327.
64 Ibid., p. 321.
65 Ibid., p. 326.
66 Four announcements of women's appointments did not include an age or date of birth, compared with three for men's appointments.

retirement on UK judges, and prompts a reevaluation of the case law on this topic. Further, it flags the serious risks of changes to judicial pension arrangements. As well as creating significant discontent among the judiciary, reduced pension entitlements may seriously impede progress towards judicial diversity, both by deterring more diverse candidates from appointment, and by reducing the rate of judicial turnover. Thus, governments should approach judicial pension reform with a high degree of caution, and more properly consider the risks for diversity of lowering pension entitlements.

These findings also have consequences for how we regard judges more generally. Discussions of the judiciary often focus on the 'public office' aspect of the judicial role, rather than recognizing that judges, too, are individuals with diverse career paths and professional needs. Re-emphasizing the position of judges as 'workers' entails renewed attention on pay and benefits, judicial career paths, training and development, performance evaluation, flexible working, engagement and job satisfaction. Research on the judiciary is increasingly engaging with these aspects of the judicial role,[67] though there is far more work to be done in this area.

A renewed appreciation of judges as 'workers' also raises challenging questions regarding the retention of judicial retirement ages. If the UK Government has deemed mandatory retirement to be inappropriate for the general workforce, is the judicial role sufficiently unique and special to justify the retention of fixed retirement ages? As judicial careers are increasingly professionalized, and there is a growing move towards performance development and management for judicial officers (at least at the lower levels of the judiciary), we must seriously question the distinctiveness of judicial employment when compared with the general workforce. Progress towards improving the opportunities within and structure of judicial careers may incidentally undermine any justification for mandatory retirement. Future research should engage and grapple with these challenging questions. As the arguments in support of mandatory retirement in the judiciary are called into question, and the nature of judicial careers shifts, the time may come where mandatory retirement for judges (like for the majority of the workforce) should be abandoned.

67 See e.g. Barmes and Malleson, 'The Legal Profession as Gatekeeper'.

Reflection

Karon Monaghan QC

Karon Monaghan QC is a barrister at Matrix Chambers specializing in equality and discrimination law, human rights and EU law. She also sits as a Deputy High Court Judge (Administrative Court) and as a Recorder in the Crown Court. She regularly advises NGOs, public bodies and parliamentary committees on equality and human rights and has published widely in these areas.

In the spring of 2014, Sir Geoffrey Bindman and I were asked by Sadiq Khan MP, then Shadow Lord Chancellor and Shadow Secretary of State for Justice, to prepare a report on the practicable steps that could be taken towards achieving a more diverse judiciary. That report was published in November 2014: *Judicial Diversity: Accelerating Change.*[1]

At that time the senior judiciary was woefully lacking in diversity.[2] Its profile was overwhelmingly White and male and, to the extent that it was possible to deduce, its judges were predominantly from the privileged social classes. It has not noticeably improved. The extent of the failure to make progress on diversity is sometimes difficult to spot. This is because of the Judicial Appointments Commission's (JAC) tendency to present a rosy picture, even when, at best, a more nuanced one is merited. No doubt motivated by a desire to look on the bright side given its own aspirations for change, the JAC is in the habit of press releasing headline statistics which suggest to the reader that progress has been good, in some areas even excellent, when a more granular analysis shows otherwise. Recent widely reported headlines from the JAC included the accurate claim that for the period 1 April 2015 to 31 March 2016,[3] 45 per cent of those recommended for appointment were women and 9 per cent were Black, Asian and minority ethnic (BAME). The JAC also pointed prominently to the (indisputable) fact that the

1 G. Bindman and K. Monaghan, *Judicial Diversity: Accelerating Change*, London: Labour Party, 2014.

2 Our report analyses the data then available at para 5.1ff.

3 When there were in addition to senior appointments, 22 selection exercises which attracted a total of 2,439 candidates. The JAC made 308 recommendations for judicial appointment during this period: Judicial Appointments Commission, *Judicial Appointments Commission Statistics Bulletin: Judicial Selection and Recommendations for Appointment Statistics, April 2015 to March 2016,* 2 June 2016, p. 7.

proportion of BAME candidates was equal to or greater than their level in the eligible pool in four out of the five recruitment exercises (the exception was Circuit Judge).[4] However, these figures conceal a much more disappointing picture.[5]

Drilling down one can see that, for Circuit Judges,[6] while 25 per cent of those recommended for appointment were women when they comprised only 14 per cent of applicants, 42 per cent of the eligible pool[7] were women so the number that applied – and that were ultimately appointed – was relatively small as compared to the number that were eligible.[8] Men, on the other hand, applied and were recommended in greater proportion to their presence in the eligible pool.[9] As for the very senior of judicial appointments,[10] for the period 2012–2015, of the total number of applicants only 5.4 per cent ultimately recommended for appointment were women.[11]

For those who are BAME, the picture is even bleaker.[12] It is true, as the JAC says, that for April 2015 to March 2016, the proportion of *applicants* who declared that they were from BAME backgrounds was equal to or greater than the proportion in the eligible pool in four of the five legal posts.[13] However, the proportion of BAME candidates *recommended* for appointment was significantly smaller (and sometimes very significantly smaller) than their presence in the applicant pool in every one of those competitions.[14] The same is not true for the senior appointments where the proportion of successful candidates who were BAME matched their proportion in the applicant pool: that being precisely zero.[15]

4 JAC, *Statistics Bulletin: April 2015 to March 2016.*

5 Across Council of Europe states, the UK is rock bottom (with only Armenia and Azerbaijan behind them) in the percentage of women among the salaried judiciary: 'European Judicial Systems, Efficiency and quality of Justice',*CEPEJ Studies* 23, 2016, p. 101.

6 JAC, *Statistics Bulletin: April 2015 to March 2016.* The JAC add the caveat that 'the completion rate for gender in the Circuit Judge exercise was low (63%) and therefore any comparisons should be made with caution' (ibid., p. 14). Without any evidence otherwise, one is forced to extrapolate from the completions as they stand. The low return rate is worrying in itself.

7 As to which see, ibid., pp. 13 and 15.

8 Ibid., p. 15.

9 Ibid.

10 Ibid., p. 8: That is, Lord Justices of Appeal, Lord Chief Justice, President of the Queen's Bench Division, Senior President of Tribunals. There are no figures for High Court appointments because the most recent selection exercise was not completed until after compilation of these statistics (ibid., p. 7).

11 Ibid., p. 15.

12 It can be noted that the proportion of candidates who declared they were from a BAME background decreased through the process from application to recommendation in all six reported exercises. This decrease can also be seen in the grouped tribunal and court exercises.

13 JAC, *Statistics Bulletin: April 2015 to March 2016.*

14 Ibid., p. 17.

15 Ibid., p. 17.

The figures for disability overall are even worse[16] and, while the JAC has only just begun to monitor social class and so the results are not yet known, we can safely assume that they will be pretty bad too.[17]

For senior appointments (High Court and above), there is no evidence of sustained significant improvement since the establishment of the JAC.[18] As to the most senior judges, when we prepared our report one member of the Supreme Court was a woman, none were BAME;[19] all heads of Division were men, none were BAME; seven members of the Court of Appeal were women (and an eighth about to be appointed[20]), none were BAME, and 21[21] High Court Judges were women and one was BAME.[22] Two years later, the picture remains the same,[23] notwithstanding further appointments to the senior judiciary,[24] save that 23 High Court judges are now women[25] and two are BAME. On 13 September 2016, it was announced that six new Court of Appeal judges were to be appointed – only one was a woman, none were BAME.[26]

If an increase in the proportion of underrepresented groups in the senior judiciary is to be taken as the measure of the JAC's success, then there is not much to celebrate.

16 Ibid., p. 21. Though the very low reporting rates could, worryingly, demonstrate anxiety about disclosing non-visible disabilities, especially those that have been historically stigmatized such as mental ill-health.

17 Bindman and Monaghan, *Accelerating Change*, paras 5.35–5.41.

18 That there has been no consistent improvement is evident from the JAC's annual reports. This year it shows that while in 2015–2016, 44 per cent of all recommendations for legal appointments were women that represented no increase from 2014–2015 and a worsening of the position as compared to 2013–2014. A similarly patchy picture emerges in the case of BAME and disabled candidates: Judicial Appointments Commission, *JAC's Annual Report and Accounts*, July 2016. See too, Bindman and Monaghan, *Accelerating Change*, part 5.

19 The fact of only one woman Supreme Court judge puts us second to bottom among OECD countries on last reported data: *Global Forum on Public Governance, Women's Leadership in Public Life: Fostering Diversity for Inclusive Growth: Session Notes* (2014) OECD, 15.

20 Bindman and Monaghan, *Accelerating Change*, para 5.7.

21 Of the then 108; Bindman and Monaghan,*Accelerating Change*, para 5.8.

22 Bindman and Monaghan, *Accelerating Change*, para 5.3 *et seq*. See too, Judicial Appointments Commission, *Analysis of the Trends in the Diversity of Applications and Recommendations made by the JAC*, p. 3.

23 Biographies of the Supreme Court Justices and Court of Appeal judges are available online at www.supremecourt.uk/about/biographies-of-the-justices.html; www.judiciary.gov.uk/you-and-the-judiciary/going-to-court/court-of-appeal-home/coa-biogs/ and a list of the current senior judiciary can be found on the Courts and Tribunal website at www.judiciary.gov.uk/about-the-judiciary/who-are-the-judiciary/senior-judiciary-list/ (all accessed 4 December 2016).

24 To the High Court, Court of Appeal and to the position of Master of the Rolls and Chancellor of the High Court of England, at least.

25 Out of a cohort now of 105: Courts and Tribunals Judiciary, *Senior Judiciary*, Online, Available www.judiciary.gov.uk/about-the-judiciary/who-are-the-judiciary/senior-judiciary-list/ (accessed 30 October 2016).

26 Prime Minister's Office Press Release, *Appointment of Lord and Lady Justices of Appeal: September 2016.*

As we observed in our report, there is a constitutional imperative for a diverse judiciary – principally borne out of a need for democratic legitimacy and equality – and that is by now generally understood.[27] However, it has to be recognized that the JAC's failures to significantly improve on the number of women, BAME and disabled judges, especially at senior level, lies not just in its institutional response to the underrepresentation of women and other minorities but to its very constitution and the statutory frameworks in which it must operate.

The majority of the 15 Commissioners who constitute the JAC are judges or lawyers.[28] As to the judges, one must be a Court of Appeal judge and one a High Court judge.[29] Not only are the lay members in the minority then, but also the judicial members include very senior judges, the most senior of whom must be appointed vice-chair.[30]

The JAC is now responsible for selecting candidates for judicial office up to and including the High Court[31] and for convening selection panels[32] in the case of more senior judicial appointments up to but excluding the Supreme Court (namely, the Lord Chief Justice, Heads of Division and Lords Justices of Appeal).[33] In all cases, the selection panels will include very senior judges and other very senior judges will be consulted as part of the selection process.[34] The Lord Chancellor is responsible for convening a selection commission for the purpose of filling a vacancy in the Supreme Court[35] and that commission must be constituted by, inter alios, the President of the Court and a senior UK judge.[36] Designated members of the JACs of the constituent parts of the UK[37] will form

27 *Accelerating Change*, n. 2, Part 1 and citations therein for a very brief discussion on the issues. See too, E. Rackley, *Women, Judging and the Judiciary: From Difference to Diversity*, London: Routledge, 2013, pp. 23–29 and A. Paterson and C. Paterson, *Guarding the Guardians? Towards an Independent, Accountable and Diverse Senior Judiciary*, London: CentreForum, 2012 p. 37ff.

28 Only six in total must be 'lay members', including its chair: Judicial Appointments Commission Regulations 2013 (SI 2013/2191), regs. 3 and 4 and Constitutional Reform Act 2005 ('CRA'), Schedule 12, para 2(1). A 'lay member' is a person who has not held judicial office or practised as a lawyer (or been a member of an Employment Tribunal): Judicial Appointments Commission Regulations 2013, reg. 8.

29 Judicial Appointments Commission Regulations 2013, reg. 4 which also prescribes the offices that the remaining judicial office holders must hold.

30 CRA, Schedule 12, para 11(1).

31 Candidates are then recommended to the Appropriate Authority (Lord Chancellor, Lord Chief Justice or Senior President of Tribunals).

32 Such panels are committees of the JAC and determine their own selection process: ss. 70 and 79 CRA.

33 Section 67, CRA. The JAC is also involved in the selection of the Senior President of Tribunals: The Judicial Appointments Regulations 2013 (SI 2013/2192), reg. 17.

34 Judicial Appointments Regulations 2013.

35 CRA, s. 26.

36 Supreme Court (Judicial Appointments) Regulations 2013 (SI 2013/2193), reg. 11 (having the meaning given in CRA, s. 60(1)(b)-(i)).

37 JAC, Judicial Appointments Board for Scotland and a member of the Northern Ireland Judicial Appointments Commission: Supreme Court (Judicial Appointments) Regulations 2013, reg. 11.

part of any selection panel or commission[38] but the law permits a selection commission to be constituted by a minority of lay members with senior judges in the majority.[39]

While the JAC has a role, then, in all senior judicial appointments, at least because its members will sit on all selection bodies for the senior judiciary, the dominant voices in the recruitment of senior judges are other senior judges who are, in the main, male, White and from privileged social classes. The JAC has no say over that.

The risk that those senior judges who dominate the selection processes will be subconsciously influenced by the perception that the characteristics they possess and they see in their senior colleagues – Whiteness, maleness, privilege – are attributes required of a senior judge of the right calibre, is ever present. The existence of formally stated criteria[40] and any amount of effort by the JAC is unlikely to eliminate that risk.

While there are specific '*diversity*' provisions in the legislation addressing judicial appointments, these are minimal and give little latitude to the JAC even where relevant to the performance of its functions. The JAC is obliged to 'have regard to the need to encourage diversity in the range of persons available for selection for appointments'[41] but this is always 'subject to'[42] its duty to appoint on 'merit'[43] (the assessment of which, of course, is something over which the existing judiciary has significant influence). The JAC has power to prefer a woman candidate over a man and a BAME[44] candidate over a White candidate for the purpose of increasing diversity, but this is exercisable only where the two persons are of equal merit.[45] The JAC has opted to utilize this power only at the point of final selection,[46] following an ultimate ranking of candidates, and not any earlier when it could be used to increase diversity among the pool of shortlisted candidates. It

38 Supreme Court (Judicial Appointments) Regulations 2013, reg. 11.

39 Supreme Court (Judicial Appointments) Regulations 2013, reg. 13. Interestingly, however, when the JACs are nominating a member and the President is nominating a senior judge to sit on a selection commission they must, 'in doing so, have regard (alongside all other relevant considerations) to the fact that it is desirable that the members of the selection commission should include – (a) both women and men; and (b) members drawn from a range of different racial groups (within the meaning of s. 9 (3) of the Equality Act 2010)' and, in the case of the senior judge, the President must have due regard to the territorial composition of the selection commission: Supreme Court (Judicial Appointments) Regulations 2013, regs. 11, 13 and 14. And to like effect in the case of convening selection panels for senior judicial posts (above High Court) see: Judicial Appointments Regulations 2013, regs. 5(16), 11(17) and 23(14).

40 Satisfaction of which must, after all, be assessed and weighed against the selection panels' view of what is required.

41 CRA, s. 64.

42 CRA, s. 64(2).

43 CRA, s. 63(2).

44 The same is true in respect of other groups protected under the Equality Act 2010, s. 4.

45 CRA s. 63(4).

46 See, Judicial Appointments Commission *Equal Merit Provision: JAC Policy*.

also applies a narrow concept of 'merit'. Whether because of a lack of enthusiasm for it or practical impediments to its application in the context of the JAC's chosen approach to selection, this power is rarely put into use.[47]

While the JAC can be criticized for not being more robust in its efforts to secure greater diversity (its minimalist use of the equal merit provision is but one example) and must be called to account for its failures, it has to be acknowledged that it operates under strict limitations. It probably has least power of all involved in the selection processes to effect significant change at the senior end of the judiciary. In our report, Sir Geoffrey and I made a number of recommendations. Most of these (16 out of 20[48]) concerned matters over which the JAC had no relevant responsibility, or had any power to address. These included the removal of barriers which our research indicated were likely to impede access to under-represented groups. For example, we recommended that all posts should be available for part-time work and/or job-sharing unless the Lord Chancellor could transparently justify the need for a full-time appointment; that the circuit system should be abolished and replaced with regional appointments; that, subject to conditions, part-time salaried judges should not be prohibited from continuing in practice and that, subject to conditions, judges should not be prohibited from returning to practice after leaving the bench. We also recommended, inter alia, that the pool from which candidates for very senior judicial office are drawn should be widened to include legal academics. None of these are matters over which the JAC has any power.

The recommendation that attracted the most controversy, and in my view the most important of our recommendations, was that 'a quota system[49] should be introduced so as to achieve as quickly as possible a balance between the proportion of women and men, and BAME and White judges, in the senior judiciary (including in the Supreme Court)'.[50] This would require legislative change.[51] A quota system would, however, bring about change quickly. Anecdotally, it seems that the idea of quotas in the case of appointments to the senior judiciary is increasingly gaining support within the legal profession (though not, it would seem, from within the judiciary). Though the JAC had set its face against quotas (indeed, even targets[52]), its response to our report

47 14 out of the 308 recommendations in 2015–2016: JAC, *Statistics Bulletin: April 2015 to March 2016*, p. 11.

48 Judicial Appointments Commission, *Judicial Diversity: Accelerating Change – Judicial Appointments Commission (JAC) Response to the Report*, 16 February 2015.

49 For illustrations see, Bindman and Monaghan, *Accelerating Change*, para 8.2ff.

50 Ibid., Recommendation 13. For media coverage, see for example, Owen Bowcott, 'Labour party report recommends quotas for appointment of judges', *The Guardian*, 6 November 2014 and Gazette News desk 'Quotas and abolition of circuit in Labour's judicial diversity plan', *Law Society Gazette*, 6 November 2014.

51 Primary legislation would be required to amend the CRA and the Equality Act 2010 (in the latter case because it would prohibit a formal quota system: ss. 50–51).

52 *The Governance of Britain – Constitutional Renewal: Pre-Legislative Scrutiny by the Joint Select Committee on the Draft Constitutional Renewal Bill, evidence from the Judicial Appointments Commission*, June 2008, para 45.

was marginally less disapproving,[53] but it has not initiated any discussions about it so far as I am aware.

Nobody could doubt the genuineness of the JAC's continual expressions of commitment to achieving greater diversity including at senior level in the judiciary. Indeed, one can sometimes sense a degree of frustration (albeit curtailed by institutional loyalty) that their efforts have been largely unsuccessful. The reinforced glass ceiling that serves to keep real or potential women, BAME and other minority candidates outside the judiciary altogether, or certainly downstairs, is one the JAC barely has the tools to crack open. Rather than calling for change, however, the JAC professes an impartiality said to be guaranteed by prescribed criteria for appointment, lengthy and formulaic application forms, scoring systems and what is said to be the all-important involvement of lay people. However, this bureaucratization of judicial appointments does little to mitigate the effects of entrenched discriminatory patterns or, regrettably, to remove the influence of the senior judiciary in the appointments process.

Given the JAC's proven failure to achieve significant change among the senior judiciary, and in the absence of imminent legislative change, perhaps we should look elsewhere. Paradoxically – given that a key impetus for the establishment of a judicial appointments body was the need to separate judicial appointments from the purview of the executive – it is once again the Lord Chancellor to whom we may have to turn. This is because she has the power to send selection panels and commissions back to the drawing board in the event that she is unhappy with their chosen candidates.[54] While quotas are not legislatively mandated, perhaps she could whisper in the ear of the President of the Supreme Court and the Lord Chief Justice that if there isn't greater diversity among those recommended for appointment hereon in, she will exercise her power to insist upon a reconsideration. She might also tell them that if they can't find talented women and minorities to fill the vacancies in their courts, it's because they're mixing with the wrong people.[55]

53 JAC, *Response to the Report.*

54 For details of that the process in the case of the Supreme Court, see Supreme Court (Judicial Appointments) Regulations 2013, regs. 20 and 21. The Lord Chancellor may only reject a candidate on the ground of 'merit' but she may require a reconsideration on the grounds that, in her opinion, 'there is evidence that the person is not the best candidate on merit'. However, it may not be difficult to persuade the Lord Chancellor of this if all the candidates selected are White and male. The provisions also have the effect of permitting the Lord Chancellor to insist upon the de facto quota in the case of judges from Scotland and Northern Ireland (reg. 21). To similar effect in the case of other senior appointments, see Judicial Appointments Regulations 2013, regs. 8, 9, 14, 15, 20, 21, 26, 27, 32 and 33.

55 Paraphrasing the words of Sadiq Khan in an interview with Elle magazine: K. O'Malley, 'When Sadiq Khan Came to Elle: "I've Always Been a Feminist"', *Elle Magazine*, 29 November 2016.

10 Judicial diversity

Complexity, continuity and change

Hilary Sommerlad

Introduction

There is substantial evidence to support the claim that the argument for diversifying the judiciary in the UK has been won.[1] The disjuncture between the judiciary's 'cloistered' and 'aristocratic' traditions[2] and wider society became increasingly untenable following the modernizing and social democratic processes initiated by the post-war social and political settlement. The changes these processes unleashed included the progressive diversification of the solicitors' and barristers' professions and consequent widening of the judiciary's supply base, which, together with the dramatic expansion of the administrative state and hence judicial review, increased and made more evident the 'political' nature of the judicial role.[3] These developments produced in turn a transformation in public opinion about the judiciary, generating pressure to modernize the archaic 'secret soundings' system of judicial appointment.[4] The resulting reform effected by the Constitutional Reform Act 2005 (CRA) has begun to diversify the lower levels of the judiciary. Yet despite the fact that a sizeable pool of eligible female and BAME male lawyers with the level of experience and achievement appropriate for judicial office has now been in existence for many years, progress has been slow, even at the lower levels, and virtually non-existent in the higher courts.[5]

1 See E. Rackley and C. Webb, 'Three Models of Diversity' in this collection.
2 M. Loughlin, *Sword and Scales: An Examination of the Relationship Between Law and Politics*, Oxford: Hart Publishing, 2000, p. 103 and see pp. 71–75.
3 Loughlin, *Sword and Scales*, pp. 102–108. As Kate Malleson notes, the Human Rights Act 1998 further expanded the judge's interpretive role: K. Malleson, *The New Judiciary: The Effects of Expansion and Activism*, Aldershot: Ashgate, 1999, p. 1.
4 This is, inevitably, a crude summary of an extremely complex range of developments which put pressure on the judiciary and the legal profession generally to modernize; see e.g. R. Abel, *English Lawyers Between Market and State: The Politics of Professionalism*, Oxford: Oxford University Press, 2004.
5 Since the CRA, white upper class male dominance of the upper ranks of the judiciary remains largely intact apart from a slight increase in diversity of appointments to the High Court in 2015 (Judicial Appointments Commission, 'Judicial Appointments Commission releases latest diversity statistics', *News Release*, 4 June 2015). See also *Judicial Diversity Statistics 2015*, 30 July 2015, 4 and K. Malleson, 'Prospects for Parity: The Position of Women in the Judiciary in England and Wales', in G. Shaw

This chapter attempts to provide a conceptual framework for understanding this apparent paradox, one that looks beyond the narrow mechanics of appointment procedures to the social, political and cultural contexts in which the judiciary is located. I argue that Sylvia Walby's application of complexity theory to issues of diversity and change and multiple social inequalities provides a useful tool for exploring this context.[6] The basis for Walby's analysis is the conceptualization of the social order as comprising a series of systems, and in particular systematic and self-reproducing relationships. Drawing on scholars such as Niklas Luhmann[7] and Andrew Abbott,[8] she argues that each system, such as the judiciary, exists within an environment consisting of all the other systems with which it is connected, and adapts to changes in the environment constituted by those systems, whilst also forming part of the environment to which other systems must adapt. Change and continuity are then understood as the consequence of the dynamic relationships between complex adaptive systems and their consequent co-evolution. An example of this would be the relationship between the transformation of working practices and organization in the legal professions, including the judiciary, and the diversification of the lower strata of the legal workforce. A further example would be the inter-relationships between globalization and conceptualizations of citizenship and the rule of law. In Walby's account, it would be a mistake to suggest that any of these systems determined the other, but it would be equally false to say there was no causal relationship between them.

There is no space in this chapter to articulate fully the implications of this way of thinking about diversity and the judiciary, but the following should be noted. The co-evolution of systems takes place over time and the speed of change will not be uniform – evidenced here by the fact that, as has frequently been noted,[9] the gendered culture of the judiciary has changed far more slowly than that of the junior branches of the legal profession that feed it. A system may also respond to environmental changes by adapting in such a way as to restore equilibrium ('self-equilibriation')[10] – so one response to the pressure for a more diverse judiciary may be for its powerful members to seek to insulate the system against change.[11] Complexity theory further suggests that at a point where sudden change occurs (such as the rapid increase in the number of women qualifying for law jobs and

and U. Schultz (eds), *Women in the World's Legal Professions*, Oxford: Hart Publishing 2003, pp. 175–190, for discussion of how women (and BAME) candidates are disproportionately appointed to the lower end of the judiciary.

6 S. Walby, 'Complexity Theory, Systems Theory and Multiple Intersecting Social Inequalities', *Philosophy of the Social Sciences* 37, 2007, pp. 449–470.

7 N. Luhmann, *Social Systems*, Stanford: Stanford University Press, 1995.

8 A. Abbott, *Time Matters: On Theory and Method*, Chicago: University of Chicago Press, 2001.

9 See e.g. Malleson, 'Prospects for Parity'.

10 Walby, 'Complexity Theory', pp. 463–466.

11 Beaverstock *et al.* argue that one of the most distinctive features of elite groups is their persistence and social coherence, despite increasing criticism of the social inequalities they generate (J. Beaverstock, P. Hubbard, and J. R. Short, 'Getting Away With It? Exposing the Geographies of the Super-rich', *Geoforum* 35, 2004, pp. 401–407).

becoming available for promotion), a number of potential paths for development may emerge: in a complex environment, quite small influences may produce major transformations. However, Walby draws on a range of writers[12] to point to the phenomenon of 'lock-in', where powerful social and political institutions ensure that possibilities are channelled into one path of development.

In the main body of the chapter, I will draw on these analytical tools to explore some of the principal developments that have shaped the increasingly diverse environment to which the judiciary has had to adapt, commencing with the opposing, but curiously complementary, developments of post-war welfare capitalism and neo-liberalism.

Forces for change: widening access at the base

The increased purchase of diversity ideas and their realization in some areas of the judiciary can be directly linked to the transformation of the state, civil society and labour markets generated by the socio-economic and political changes which have taken place over the course of the last few decades. The source of these changes may be traced to two, fundamentally antithetical, ideologies and the political and socio-economic forces they unleashed: firstly, social citizenship and the subsequent equality struggles conducted by progressive social movements and, secondly, globalization and neo-liberal ideology and policies.

The social democratic form of welfare capitalism[13] which was developed in the UK after the Second World War produced a number of systemic and ideological transformations which re-shaped the legal environment in which the judiciary was situated and expanded the potential for previously excluded groups to participate in professional labour markets. Women[14] were the first such group to enter these markets in considerable numbers,[15] facilitated by the development of both secondary and tertiary education as 'public good' elements of the welfare state[16] and the de-familialization of elements of welfare. At the same time, the expansion of social citizenship vastly increased the extent of discretionary decision-making on

12 Walby, 'Complexity Theory' cites authors writing on technological development (such as B. Arthur, *Increasing Returns and Path Dependence in the Economy*, Ann Arbor: University of Michigan Press, 1994), political developments, (such as P. Pierson, 'Increasing Returns, Path Dependence and the Study of Politics', *American Political Science Review* 94, 2000, pp. 251–268), and historical sociology (e.g. J. Mahoney, 'Path Dependency in Historical Sociology', *Theory and Society* 29, 2000, pp. 507–548).

13 G. Esping-Andersen, *The Three Worlds of Welfare Capitalism*, Cambridge: Polity Press, 1990.

14 The wave of women lawyers who entered en masse from the early 1980s onwards was at first overwhelmingly white and middle class.

15 This also led to the development of segregated lower-paid labour markets in care; see e.g. W. Shelkle, 'Collapsing Worlds and Varieties of Welfare Capitalism: In Search of a New Political Economy of Welfare', LSE Europe in Question Discussion Paper No. 54/2012, London: LSE, 2012.

16 G. Grace, 'Education: Commodity or Public Good?', *British Journal* of *Educational Studies* 37, 1989, pp. 207–221.

the part of agents of the State, and a corresponding development in administrative law and tribunals with quasi-judicial functions. In a way that can be seen as an example of self-equilibriation, this system, intended by the architects of social citizenship[17] as an alternative to formal law, gradually developed to encompass substantial areas of business for private sector firms. Similarly, the suspicion aroused in the judiciary by the existence of this parallel adjudication[18] ultimately led to that element of the Tribunals, Courts and Enforcement Act 2007 which involved the absorption of qualified tribunal members into the judiciary.

The expansion of citizenship to include social and economic as well as political rights also progressively generated a swathe of equality law[19] embracing access to the provision of goods and services and employment, supplemented by positive policies at local and national levels designed to promote equal opportunity and treatment.[20] Parallel changes included a florescence of radical activism and critical thinking (such as feminist and critical race theories) and, generally, the development of an increasingly diverse and irreverent society.[21] The resulting divide between mainstream society and elite male-only institutions such as the judiciary was made glaringly clear by cases such as *Bromley London Borough Council v Greater London Council*[22] (in which the House of Lords' judgment was critiqued as a political and undemocratic) and deeply misogynist judicial pronouncements, most notoriously in rape and provocation cases.[23]

The divide between mainstream society and the judiciary was accentuated by the subsequent development of globalization and revival of classical economic liberalism (generally termed neo-liberalism). The consequent hegemony of the 'market view of society'[24] transformed the democratic, ethical argument for opening up elite institutions into one grounded in commercial, business reasons.

17 T. Humphrey Marshall, *Citizenship and Social Class, and Other Essays*, Cambridge: Cambridge University Press, 1950.
18 Sir Leslie Scarman, *English Law: the New Dimension*, Hamlyn Lectures, 26th series, 1975.
19 Equal Pay Act 1970, Sex Discrimination Act 1975, Race Relations Act 1976, Disability Discrimination Act 1995, Employment Equality (sexual orientation) Regulations 2003, Employment Equality (Age) Regulations 2006, all replaced by the Equality Act 2010.
20 C. Itzen and J. Newman, *Gender, Culture and Organizational Change: Putting Theory into Practice*, London: Routledge, 2003.
21 Lawyers were prominent in the social movements which, from the late 1960s onwards aimed to transform or reconstitute the terms of the social relations of power and citizenship. Subsequently, the usurpationary projects of women (A. Witz, *Professions and Patriarchy*, London: Routledge, 1992) and other 'outsider' lawyers made a major contribution to the public pressure for a more representative judiciary. For critiques, see e.g. J. A. G. Griffith, *The Politics of the Judiciary*, Manchester: Fontana Press, 1977.
22 *Bromley London Borough Council v Greater London Council* (1983) AC 768.
23 An example of such a rape case is 'Holdsworth',*The Economist*, 25 June 1977; 'Blewis',*The Times*, 1983 exemplifies judicial attitudes in homicides of 'nagging' or otherwise 'difficult' women. Both are discussed in S. Edwards, *Sex and Gender in the Legal Process*, London: Blackstone Press, 1996, pp. 352, 397; see too S. Lee, *Judging Judges*, London: Faber & Faber, 1989.
24 K. Polanyi, *The Livelihood of Man*, New York: Academic Press, 1977, p. 258.

As a result, the effectiveness of such institutions came to be viewed as dependent upon obtaining the best merit or 'talent', undermining the legitimacy of those that appeared to be 'reserved' for upper middle class white men. Consequent on this alliance of perspectives, in the UK it has come to be perceived as generally unacceptable to be openly anti-diversity; as Anne Phillips observes, 'equality of opportunity is the default position in liberal democracies, something to which no one could seriously object.'[25]

However, despite the transformative effect of these developments, the social environment within which they took place remained strongly inflected by inherited structures and discourses. Thus neither social democratic nor neo-liberal reforms have extinguished the importance ascribed to a public school and Oxbridge education, nor have they significantly undermined the domination of elite institutions by upper middle class white men; for instance, the proportion of top judges who attended public schools in the late 1980s has only decreased by 2 per cent (from 76 per cent then to 74 per cent today).[26] A further continuity is to be found in the gendered nature of assumptions regarding caring responsibilities. The World Economic Forum's Global Gender Gap Report reports that over the past ten years there has, overall, been either no or minimal progress in women's labour market position in the UK and that, in some respects, it has deteriorated. This period has also seen a resurgence in sexism and misogyny,[27] leading John Beynon to speak of a 'backlash' against feminism and women's rights.[28] Similarly, Critical Race scholars contend that while expressions of overt racism have/had tended to abate, far from being a 'race free' society, a 'new racism' has emerged,[29] characterized by discourses of cultural difference which continue to evoke stereotypical tropes of the (racially inferior) 'other'.[30] In fact, the past few decades have been characterized by

25 A. Phillips, 'Really Equal: Opportunities and Autonomy', *The Journal of Political Philosophy* 14, 2006, pp. 18–32, 18.

26 P. Kirby, *Leading People: The Educational Backgrounds of the UK Professional Elite*, London: Sutton Trust, 2016.

27 There are numerous indicators of this resurgence in misogyny; e.g. the 'lad culture' which now pervades UK universities (A. Phipps and I. Young, 'Neoliberalisation and "Lad Cultures" in Higher Education', *Sociology* 49, 2014, pp. 305–322); see too the Everyday Sexism Project and such movements as Justice for Men and Boys. Further, post Brexit events reveal the tenacity of racism; see e.g. J. Walker 'EU Referendum unleashes wave of hate crime and racism', *Birmingham Mail*, 27 June 2016,.

28 J. Beynon, *Masculinities and Culture*, Buckingham, Open University, 2002. Margaret Thornton also uses the term backlash in her discussion of the difficulties non normative professionals have in achieving recognition as authoritative 'knowers' and how individualization of these difficulties obscures systemic discrimination (M. Thornton, 'The Evisceration of Equal Employment Opportunity in Higher Education', *Australian Universities' Review* 50(2), 2008, pp. 59–70.)

29 R. Miles and M. Brown, *Racism*, Oxford: Routledge, 1989. See also A. Souhami, J. Foster and T. Newburn, *Assessing the Impact of the Stephen Lawrence Inquiry: Home Office Research Study 294*, London: Home Office, 2005; and D. Gillborn, *Racism and Education: Coincidence or Conspiracy?*, London: Routledge, 2008.

30 T. Modood and F. Ahmad, 'British Muslim Perspectives on Multiculturalism', *Theory, Culture & Society* 24, 2007, pp. 187–213.

an increase in inequalities generally, and it appears that social mobility has slowed.[31]

This evidence of the uneven and contradictory nature of the social changes which have taken place in Britain in recent years supports complexity theory's analysis of change as multi-causal and involving complex processes of adaptation, co-evolution and resistance. In the next section, drawing on this analysis, I focus on two developments which have affected the pace and extent of judicial diversification. Firstly, I discuss the role of capitalist rationalization and neo-liberal inspired public sector reforms – commonly termed New Public Management (NPM)[32] – in re-shaping the legal labour market (primarily the solicitors' profession, but subsequently also the Bar and the lower levels of the judiciary) into a pyramid with a broader base but with a more restricted access to the apex of the profession. Secondly, I highlight the impact on the lower courts of the restrictions in access to justice for the ordinary citizen, consequent on the erosion of social citizenship and reconfiguration of the nation state.

Forces for change: restructuring and narrowing opportunities for progression

The ideology and practice of neo-liberal globalization have challenged a range of assumptions that had underpinned the social order, including the significance of social category,[33] the power, size and role of the nation state, the

31 F. Bukodi and others, 'The Mobility Problem in Britain: New Findings from the Analysis of Birth Cohort Data', *The British Journal of Sociology* 66, 2015, pp. 93–117. It is also argued that recent years have seen an erosion of democracy; see e.g. C. Crouch, *The Strange Non-death of Neo-liberalism*, Cambridge: Polity Press, 2011; D. Harvey, *A Brief History of Neoliberalism*, Oxford: Oxford University Press, 2005; and P. Cerny, 'Globalisation and the Erosion of Democracy', *European Journal of Political Research* 36, 1999, pp. 1–26.

32 New Public Management (NPM) is the term developed to denote the (neo-liberal) reconstruction of the public sector, drawing on doctrines of economic rationality and private-sector management techniques. See C. Hood and M. Jackson, *Administrative Argument*, Aldershot: Dartmouth Publishing, 1991; C. Pollitt, *Managerialism and the Public Services*, Oxford: Blackwell, 1993; M. Power, *The Audit Society*, Oxford: Oxford University Press, 1997; and M. Powell, *Modernising the Welfare State: The Blair Legacy*, Bristol: Policy Press, 2008. Applied to the legal aid sector it generated an irresistible pressure towards routinized, poor quality justice. See H. Sommerlad, 'The Implementation of Quality Initiatives and the New Public Management in the Legal Aid Sector in England and Wales: Bureaucratisation, Stratification and Surveillance', *International Journal of the Legal Profession* 6, 1999, pp. 311–343; and H. Sommerlad, 'Managerialism and the Legal Professional: A New Professional Paradigm', *International Journal of the Legal Profession* 2(2/3), 1995, pp. 159–185; and H. Sommerlad, 'Reflections on the reconfiguration of Access to Justice', *International Journal of the Legal Profession* 15(3), 2008, pp. 179–193.

33 According to Beck and Beck-Gernsheim, releasing individuals from rigid, prescribed social positions such as gender roles: U. Beck and E. Beck-Gernsheim, *Individualization: Institutionalized Individualism and its Social and Political Consequences*, London: Sage, 2002.

nature of citizenship and the rule of law. The result has been to undermine 'the coherence, wholeness and unity of individual societies',[34] fragmenting public bodies and unbundling or disarticulating key institutions, their functions and activities.

The legal professions, including the judiciary, are amongst the institutions reshaped in this way. As noted above, the primacy of the free market in neo-liberal thought strengthened the argument for opening up access to privileged professional labour markets, furthering the diversification and feminization which had begun during the social democratic era.[35] The legal field exemplifies this trend: for instance, from being a virtually male only domain, the solicitors' profession is now amongst the most diverse of the UK's traditional, high status occupations.[36] However, as complexity theory's construct of co-evolution would suggest, the professional field into which women and later other marginalized groups were gaining access had adapted to its changed environment, and was consequently very different to that from which they had previously been excluded.[37] A major reason for this adaptation was the neo-liberal assault on the market shelter that had created the profession.[38] In the commercial sector, marketization enhanced competitive pressures, leading to the financialization of larger professional service firms,[39] the decomposition of work and its reconstitution into routine and specialist tasks, increased dependence on less well paid and qualified law workers to undertake this work, and diminution of partnership opportunities. At the other end of the professional spectrum, the application of NPM to the legal aid sector was producing similar patterns. Further, the entry of large numbers of 'non-traditional' lawyers was itself an impetus for ongoing professional transformation, since their lower social status meant that there was now a legal labour force which could be construed as suitable for such work. And this co-evolution of the legal professional systems and the systems of gender and race, which worked to support the naturalness of white male authority, has been replicated in other professional and high level labour markets. The response of all such markets to large-scale influxes of outsiders has been to transform the nature of work and develop career tracks

34 J. Urry and S. Lash, *The End of Organized Capitalism*, Cambridge: Polity Press, 1987, p. 97. The impact of neo-liberal globalization is therefore viewed as not purely economic but also political, cultural and personal; and see Walby, 'Complexity Theory'.
35 For an overview, see H. Bradley, *Men's Work, Women's Work: A Sociological History of the Sexual Division of Labour in Employment (Feminist Perspectives)*, Cambridge: Polity Press, 1989.
36 For instance, women accounted for 70% of the expansion in the solicitors' profession which has taken place over the past 10 years and on 31 July 2015 represented 48.8% of all solicitors with practising certificates (*Annual Statistical Review*, Law Society 2015), and 33.4% of barristers (*Report on Diversity at the Bar 2015*).
37 H. Sommerlad and P. Sanderson, *Gender, Choice and Commitment*, Aldershot: Dartmouth Publishing, 1998.
38 See Abel, *English Lawyers Between Market and State.*
39 J. Faulconbridge and D. Muzio, 'The Financialization of Large Law Firms: Situated Discourses and Practices of Reorganization', *Work, Employment and Society* 22, 2009, pp. 7–25.

segregated by gender, race and class, with related differentials in pay, working patterns and career possibilities.[40]

The justice system generally and the lower levels of the judiciary have been affected in other ways by these changes in the environment and in particular by neo-liberal ideology. In their theorization of the nature of law, Philippe Nonet and Philip Selznick argue that whereas the welfare state was underpinned by a 'thick' version of the Rule of Law which moved beyond delineating the rules of the market and simple constraint of (some) excessive abuses of power to a concern with respect for the dignity, integrity and equal moral worth of all persons and groups, neo-liberal globalization has produced 'a fragmented and impotent polity in which the public interest is emptied of meaning'.[41] And for some time a common theme of scholarship on law and the profession has been the impoverishment of understandings of law, reducing it to technical expertise[42] and the reconfiguration of the legal profession's 'deep' rationality, distorting its moral purpose.[43]

The progressive erosion of access to justice for the private citizen has been fundamental to this process. The neoliberal paradigm which informed New Labour NPM policies was constituted by value for money principles, the individualization and privatization of the social, the de-politicization of material inequality, and the reconfiguration of citizens as agentic consumers – and of those dependent on welfare as 'flawed consumers'.[44] As a result, from being regarded as a key component of post war social citizenship, and, through the tribunal system and legal aid scheme, subsequently expanded into a major facet of democratic justice, access to justice and in particular access to the civil courts has been progressively restricted. This has been achieved by a range of measures such as cuts in

40 Although some professional and high level labour markets (predominantly those in the public sector) have seen greater improvements in levels of diversity in their higher echelons than the legal profession, all are segmented on gender, race and class lines; for instance research into the response of the Christian establishment to the entry of women found that it had developed discrete, ordination tracks which were effectively sex-segregated, with male clergy disproportionately concentrated in high-level positions: P. Nesbitt, 'Dual Ordination Tracks: Differential Benefits and Costs for Men and Women Clergy', *Sociology of Religion* 54, 1993, p. 13. See too L. McDowell, *Capital Culture: Gender at Work in the City*, Oxford: Blackwell, 1997; and L, McDowell, 'Capital Culture Revisited: Sex, Testosterone and the City', *International Journal of Urban and Regional Research* 34, 2010, pp. 652–658 for evidence of pay gaps, separate career paths and explicit sexism in elite City banking.

41 P. Nonet and P. Selznick, *Law in Society: Toward Responsive Law*, New York: Harper Colophon, 1979, p. 103.

42 See e.g. M. Thornton, 'The Dissolution of the Social in the Legal Academy', *The Australian Feminist Law Journal* 25, 2006, pp. 3–18, and M. Thornton, 'The New Knowledge Economy and the Transformation of the Law Discipline' *International Journal of the Legal Profession* 19(2–3), 2012, pp. 265–281.

43 See e.g. G. Hanlon, *Lawyers, the State and the Market*, London: Palgrave MacMillan, 1999.

44 Z. Bauman, 'Collateral Casualties of Consumerism', *Journal of Consumer Culture* 7, 2007, pp. 25–56.

legal aid, court closures, steep hikes in court fees, a drive to divert people from court based solutions to quasi-legal systems and the introduction of case management systems.

Building on the Woolf reform of civil procedure, case management, which now structures both the criminal[45] and civil courts, has been progressively strengthened. For instance, in Public Law Family matters a range of measures have been put in place to speed up the court process, such as: the 26-week limit on the length of cases;[46] tight rules restricting the size of bundles; and the requirement that, prior to the hearing, lawyers bringing an application draft a case summary and management orders. These measures form part of the general application of NPM to lower courts:[47] cumulatively, they have transformed the nature of the legal 'service' that the ordinary litigant can receive in these courts, and, correspondingly, the amount of law contained in what lower level judges do. In place of a bespoke form of justice available to all litigants, there is now a semi-industrialized conveyor belt system in which fast throughput is the priority. As Lucy Welsh argues in her study of the use of case management forms in the Magistrates Courts, the 'increased focus on the perceived need for efficiency over the last two decades'[48] has undermined the position that 'historically … the state's process of … prosecution … was conducted according to a set of rules that led to a fair trial.'[49]

Family law is inevitably more difficult to standardize, but Rosemary Hunter's study of the impact of case management systems on the Family courts[50] supports Welsh's conclusions, revealing how the ultimate goal of judicial control of the process is to minimize the consumption of judicial and court time. Hunter notes how this goal has transformed the judge from the classical, disembodied, impersonal figure into a decision maker who 'is expected to enter into a potentially long term relationship with the parties and to develop a personal familiarity with the details of their case'.[51] This role has been likened to that of a social worker,[52] and this aspect of the judge's work is inevitably strengthened by the increase in litigants in person. Other aspects of the judicial role are technocratic: the

45 Courts and Tribunals Judiciary, *Better Case Management (BCM) Guidance, Criminal*, 10 September 2015.

46 Section 14(2) of the Children and Families Act 2014 amends s. 32(1)(a) of the Children Act 1989 to insert that a case must be concluded: (i) without delay; and (ii) in any event, within 26 weeks, beginning with the day on which the application was issued.

47 Courts and Tribunals Judiciary 'Better Case Management (BCM) Guidance'.

48 L. Welsh, 'Magistrates, Managerialism and Marginalisation: Neoliberalism and Access to Justice in East Kent', Doctoral Dissertation, University of Kent, 2016, p. 173.

49 Ibid., p. 178

50 R. Hunter, 'Judicial Diversity and the "New" Judge', in H. Sommerlad, S. Harris-Short, S. Vaughan and R. Young (eds), *The Futures of Legal Education and the Legal Profession,* Oxford: Hart Publishers, 2014, pp. 79–96; Hunter cites as examples of this development the Civil Procedure Rules, Rule 1.4 and Part 3; Criminal Procedure Rules, Part 3; and Family Procedure Rules, Rule 1.4 and Part 4.

51 Ibid., p. 80.

52 M. Maclean, Personal Communication, 25 August 2016.

introduction of Key Performance Indicators (KPIs) which measure the achievement of desired performance standards, and performance improvement groups,[53] mean that 'many judicial hours (are) being spent on a regular basis poring over court service statistics and developing strategies to improve their KPIs'.[54]

The significance for diversification of this transformation in judicial status is summed up in Hunter's comment that 'Legal knowledge and traditional judicial performance are de-emphasized in favour of a more bureaucratized approach, part administrator, part service worker. This might appear to be a more feminized job description than one requiring traditionally masculine judicial authority'.[55] This observation echoes Baroness Neuberger's report that lower level judges described themselves as 'below the salt', and, moreover, that they felt that they were 'a junior branch where it is normal to be diverse … *but that does not apply further up*'.[56]

However, British justice is a valuable commodity and those who can pay to access the higher courts, which includes non-citizens such as Russian oligarchs, remain entitled to the traditional, Rolls Royce form of justice which requires the judge to play a creative, interpretive role. In fact, this role has been strengthened by the impact of globalization on the international marketability of British law. Barrister David Christie speaks of 'our lead position in dispute resolution. Not just in actual litigation but also in international arbitration and mediation', and argues that it is the reputation of the English legal system on the international stage that attracts wealthy litigants:

> The calibre and integrity of English courts are respected around the world, the consistency of legal decisions affording more legal certainty than can be expected in some other jurisdictions. Judges and legal practitioners are reputed to be, if not the best, then certainly among the best in the world. The structure and stability of the English legal system, its reputation for impartiality and justice, and its freedom from corruption, are second to none … Another attractive aspect is our merged equitable and common law system, believed to provide the versatility and flexibility necessary to hear cases involving all manner of business issues in dispute. It is not just that our courts are well developed, but the fact that London has been a centre for business for centuries. We lead the world as a financial centre and as a centre for capital markets … [English courts] are arguably better equipped than other courts in the world to hear any issue that the business world can throw at them.[57]

53 Hunter specifically questions 'the extent to which KPIs are aimed at producing justice' Hunter, 'Judicial Diversity', p. 82.

54 Ibid., p. 83.

55 Ibid., pp. 83–84.

56 House of Lords Select Committee on the Constitution, *Judicial Appointments: Oral and Written Evidence*, 2010–2012, p. 273 (my emphasis).

57 D. Christie 'Magnates for law: oligarchs in London', *Law Society Gazette*, 12 September 2012.

Maintaining this reputation clearly requires the traditional trappings of justice – not the technocratic or social work role of the lower judge. Christie concludes by contrasting the upper courts' justice with that available to ordinary citizens: 'our new justice secretary[58] may like to consider that without adequate resources the county court, already suffering from poor morale among its staff and unacceptable delays, will only get worse and worse; and this will have a severe effect in the regions where dual High Court (District Registry) and county court centres are the norm'.[59]

In summary, while the role of the lower strata of the judiciary may now be characterized by technical rationality in both recruitment and work practices, it is notorious that its higher levels have been relatively untouched by either NPM or the CRA reforms of the appointment system.[60] Applying the insights of complexity theory, this differential allocation of re-structuring processes should be seen as the result of interactions between a range of complex systems, shaped by, inter alia, inherited institutional frameworks, social networks, cultural practices, policy and regulatory regimes, and political struggles. Within this multiplicity of social phenomena that have encouraged the concentration of NPM initiatives in the lower courts, the impact of neo-liberal globalization on the citizenship system is particularly significant since it has undermined access to justice for the private citizen and hence the role of lower court judges. However, as just noted, a further driver is the increased value to global elites of British justice and the legal profession generally, which, meshed with the traditional status of the higher level of the judiciary, has enabled it to preserve its power. In the following section I will highlight some of the (interlocking) mechanisms which have supported this self-equilibration by the judiciary: specifically, the durability of the gender system; the cultural practices of the elite judiciary and professional closure; conceptualizations of merit and Martin Loughlin's thesis of an 'aristocratic' understanding of judicial office.

Elite reproduction, merit and the classical conception of the judicial role

Complexity theory's comprehension of the social environment as constituted by multiple, interconnected systems which adapt and co-evolve implies that the

58 This was Chris Grayling MP who was promoted to Lord Chancellor and, by convention, Secretary of State for Justice in the UK Coalition Government's Cabinet reshuffle of August 2012.

59 Christie, 'Magnates for law'.

60 In fact the appointment system of higher level judges continues to resemble the secret soundings system in that appointment is conducted by separate, ad hoc appointing commissions on which the incumbents have a dominant role. Of the up to 26 individuals involved in the appointment of a Supreme Court Judge, 20 are members of the senior judiciary and one is a more junior judge. Further, appointments to the role of Deputy High Court Judge – which appears to be a key stepping stone to obtaining salaried appointment to the senior judiciary – are not transparent and depend, in the words of the Association of Women Barristers, on patronage and personalist ties (AWB Evidence to the House of Lords Select Committee on the Constitution Inquiry on Judicial Appointments, p. 24).

processes of change should be seen as simultaneously cumulative and contested. The gender system exemplifies the resulting tension between progress and cultural lag: despite the impact of the social democratic and neo-liberal eras on women's participation in elite institutions, the social environment remains shaped by deeply embedded archaic understandings of gender in socio-structural arrangements and cultural practice.[61] These understandings play a key role in the patriarchal system's capacity to resist deep democratization of institutional power.

Networks of personal relationships are grounded in these understandings and at the same time represent independent mechanisms in the reproduction of power. Writing 30 years ago, Michael Mann described society as 'constituted of multiple overlapping and intersecting sociospatial networks of power',[62] and recent scholarship has argued that this characteristic has intensified as a result of globalization's corrosive impact on state structures, formal hierarchies and rights.[63] The findings of a range of research into high level occupations have underlined the significance for masculine dominance of these networks and the informal cultures they support;[64] for instance, Wes Pue has observed of both the Canadian and English legal professions that: 'professional culture was (and is) formed less in formal correspondence … than in conversations at bars and cafes, gentlemen's clubs, Bar Association dinners, golf games and railways cars'.[65] In the judiciary these networks – which function most effectively in the liminal spaces between public and private realms – develop in the public schools and Oxbridge which continue to provide the majority of elite judges,[66] and are then consolidated in the world of exclusive clubs, through dining rituals and other homosocial practices. The distinctive procedures and protocols which characterize these sites and

61 P. Bourdieu, *Masculine Domination*, Redwood City: Stanford University Press, 2002.

62 M. Mann *The Sources of Social Power*, Cambridge: Cambridge University Press, 1986, Vol. 1, p. 1.

63 K. Eriksson and H. Vogt, 'On Self-service Democracy: Configurations of Individualizing Governance and Self-directed Citizenship', *European Journal of Social Theory* 16, 2013, pp. 153–173, 154. See too M. Castells, *The Rise of the Network Society*, Oxford: Blackwell, 1996; and P. Cerny, 'Globalisation'. Barbara Miztal has noted the significance of informality in ensuring the power of social networks and predicts that globalization will produce a new configuration of informality: B. Misztal, 'Configurations of Informality and Formality in Contemporary Society', in A. Mica, J. Winczorek and R. Wisniewski (eds), *Sociologies of Formality and Informality*, Frankfurt: Peter Lang International Academic Publisher, 2015, pp. 105–127.

64 See e.g. J. Oakley, 'Gender Based Barriers to Senior Management Positions: Understanding the Scarcity of Female CEOs', *Journal of Business Ethics* 27, 2000, pp. 321–334; H. Ibarra, 'Personal Networks of Women and Minorities in Management: A Conceptual Framework', *Academy of Management Review* 18, 1993, pp. 56–87, at 61; G. McGuire, 'Gender, Race, and the Shadow Structure: A Study of Informal Networks and Inequality in a Work Organization', *Gender & Society* 16, 2002 pp. 303–322.

65 W. Pue,*Lawyers' Empire: Legal Professions and Cultural Authority 1789–1950,* Vancouver: University of British Columbia Press, 2016, p. 214.

66 See the Sutton Trust's regular research reports; e.g. P. Kirby, *Leading People London*: Sutton Trust, 2016; Sutton Trust In the News '75% of Judges went to Private School' 24 November 2015 and M. Blackwell, 'Old Boys' Networks, Family Connections and the English Legal Profession', *Public Law*, 2012, pp. 426–444.

practices privilege specific formations of cultural and social capital and tend to exclude women and minorities (either directly or by making outsiders feel unwelcome).[67] Such spaces and the social occasions that take place in them produce a crystallization of social relations, processes, experiences and understanding, leading Doreen Massey to describe them as articulated moments of power, spatialized sites of social reproduction.[68] For the cultural practices which male judges perform[69] in these spaces symbolize the unity of their homosocial community and operate, through repeated citation, to construct their judicial masculinity. As such they represent one of the main barriers to diversity.[70]

The role which these informal, cultural practices play in maintaining the exclusivity of the elite judiciary thus typifies the social closure which, whether viewed from a functionalist or neo-Weberian perspective, is a key feature of professional systems.[71] Whichever theoretical perspective we favour, the construction of the elite judiciary as a system revolves around the making and sustenance of exclusionary personal bonds which 'provide the bases of **durable** inequality'.[72] For in addition to maintaining the existing integrity of the homosocial community, these bonds also ensure its reproduction by providing for successors. As Rosabeth Kanter pointed out in connection with the reproduction of power in corporations, the 'more closed the circle ... the greater the tendency for people to try to

67 A prominent example of such clubs include the Garrick Club which recently voted to maintain its male only character (see A. Gentleman, 'Garrick Club votes to continue with ban on female members', *The Guardian*, 6 July 2015) and also the Travellers Club, Pall Mall which voted in 2014 against allowing in women; one member was cited as saying recently: 'My experience of the club table at the Oxford and Cambridge Club, where one does unfortunately encounter lady members, is that their presence leads to very different and far less enjoyable themes of conversation.' (R. Sanghani 'The real reasons gentlemen don't want women to join their men-only clubs', *The Telegraph*, 10 April 2014).

68 D. Massey, *Space, Place and Gender*, Minneapolis: University of Minnesota Press, 1994.

69 Following Judith Butler, gender is not something that subjects simply have but is also something that must be performed, so that the signs of gender are 'performative' – a term borrowed from J. L. Austin meaning that verbal expressions actually do what they say thereby reproducing patriarchal, classed and raced structures through repetition, or citation, to use Butler's term, of the signs of gender, class and race: J. Butler, *Bodies that Matter: On the Discursive Limits of 'Sex'*, New York: Routledge, 1993, p. 10.

70 H. Sommerlad and others, *Diversity in the Legal Profession in England and Wales: A Qualitative Study of Barriers and Individual Choices*, London: University of Westminster Law Press, 2013.

71 For functionalists (and those who theorized the profession in terms of its 'traits') closure results from the need to distinguish between 'true' professions and other occupations which use the term to refer to themselves but do not possess 'professional' characteristics – that is in order to protect lay people; for neo-Weberians, social closure is viewed as a self-interested strategy to protect monopoly 'rents' and achieve social status. See e.g. M. Sarfatti Larson, *The Rise of Professionalism*, Berkeley: University of California Press, 1977.

72 C. Tilly, *Durable Inequality*, Berkeley: University of California Press, 1998, p. 48 ('bonds, not essences, provide the bases of durable inequality') [My emphasis].

reproduce themselves, the more constraining becomes the emphasis on conformity'.[73] Evidently, as Frederik Barth argues, the correlate of this is the affirmation of the difference/inferiority of outsiders.[74] And the resulting reification of difference is integral to both professional closure and the wider systems of gender and race[75] since it entails the reproduction and naturalization of cultural stereotypes which evoke essentialist, somatic identities, which then undermine the claims of the non-normative subject to recognition as full professionals – as discussed above in connection with the allocation in the solicitors' profession of routine, low level work to 'outsiders'. If we then consider how this system co-exists with neoliberal discourse and practice, we can see that while diversity discourses, which posit difference as something positive, have had some impact on the progress of outsiders, they are counterbalanced by the resilience of the exclusionary practices described above, which are grounded in an homology between merit and masculinity, whiteness and upper middle class identity. As a result, those in the judiciary with the power to allocate rewards and status do not need deliberately to discriminate since the possibility of the majority of outsiders being viewed as capable of achieving significant status on the basis of merit is slight.

But it is not only that traditional practices have survived to blunt the emancipatory potential of democratizing discourses and policies. Neo-liberalism's assault on social and economic rights and its ethos of individual responsibility has, as noted above, resulted in an increase in inequalities:[76] social difference or distinction is inevitably accentuated in a 'free market' for talent. Thus, self-equilibration has been effected by traditional elites in the face of neo-liberal discourses of the irrelevance of social category, through such mechanisms as the hardening of pre-existing hierarchies within the Higher Education (HE) sector. In this way the potential threat posed by the massification of HE to the reproduction of the class system[77] has been countered by the increase in the market value of the

73 R. Kanter, *Men and Women of the Corporation*, New York: Basic Books, 1977, p. 68.

74 F. Barth, *Ethnic Groups and Boundaries. The Social Organization of Culture Difference*, Long Grove, IL: Waveland Press, 1998.

75 An extensive body of research into asymmetrical forms of inclusion and progression in professional labour markets highlights the relationship between the neo-Weberian perspective and systems of gender (e.g. J. Acker, 'Hierarchies, Jobs, Bodies: A Theory of Gendered Organization', *Gender and Society* 4, 1990, pp. 139–158); race and ethnicity (e.g. A. Rafferty, 'Ethnic Penalties in Graduate Level Over-education, Unemployment and Wages: Evidence from Britain', *Work, Employment and Society* 26, 2012, pp. 987–1006), and social class (e.g. S. Vignaendra, *Social Class and Entry into the Solicitors Profession,* Research Study 41, The Law Society, 2001; and L. Ashley and L. Empson, 'Differentiation and Discrimination: Understanding Social Class and Social Exclusion in Leading Law Firms', *Human Relations* 66, 2013, pp. 219–244).

76 See e.g. K. Stone, 'Flexibilization, Globalization, and Privatization: Three Challenges to Labour Rights in Our Time', *Osgoode Hall Law Journal* 44, 2006, pp. 77–104; and M. Bell, 'Between Flexicurity and Fundamental Social Rights: the EU Directives on Atypical Work' *European Law Review* 37, 2012, pp. 31–48.

77 See P. Bourdieu and J. C. Passeron, *Reproduction in Education, Society and Culture*, London: Sage, 1990 for an argument (which resonates with complexity theory) that the complex relationship between the relatively autonomous educational system, the

cultural capital of an Oxbridge degree and other archaic signs of privilege which are read as synonymous with merit.[78] The candidate deemed 'good' or meritworthy is therefore highly likely to resemble current judges, and, if an outsider, to be unlike the cultural stereotype of their particular (non-normative) category (ies).[79] At the same time, the practice of evaluating people according to attributes and performances currently displayed in the judicial arena, legitimates existing hierarchies.[80] Relatedly, work on professional elites has found that merit is conceptualized as innate (rather than stemming in part from social advantage) producing a sense of entitlement amongst incumbents.[81]

Walter Bagehot's phrase 'club government' provides a neat soubriquet for this collective sense of entitlement which characterizes British elites. Loughlin traces its origins to an Aristotelian view of the rule of law as predicated on the 'worthiness of character of those engaged in legislative and judicial decision making',[82] shaped by education, training and experience. His summary of the way in which this ancient conception of the rule of law was inscribed in a very particular view of the judicial role, sheds light on the contemporary polarization between the lower and higher courts:

> not for the English a career judiciary, with its connotations of a purely technical function in the service of the State. The English judiciary are appointed not only because of their exalted status as experienced practitioners of the law in the Inns of Court but also because they are respected members of society ... On the character of this small, closely integrated body of mature practitioners rests the responsibilities of safeguarding and developing the

economy and the social class structure enables the educational system to carry out its function of social conservation.

78 See H. Sommerlad, 'Minorities, Merit, and Misrecognition in the Globalized Profession', *Fordham Law Review* 80, 2012, pp. 2482–2512; H. Sommerlad, 'The "Social Magic" of Merit: Diversity, Equity, and Inclusion in the English and Welsh Legal Profession', *Fordham Law Review* 83, 2015, pp. 2325–2347; and L. Ashley, J. Duberley and H. Sommerlad, *A Qualitative Evaluation of Non-educational Barriers to the Elite Professions*, London: Social Mobility and Child Poverty Commission, 2015.

79 Deborah Rhode writes of the 'well-documented, often unconscious role' played by stereotypes in the profession: D. Rhode, 'From Platitudes to Priorities: Diversity and Gender Equity in Law Firms', *Georgetown Journal of Legal Ethics* 24, 2011, pp. 1041, 1052–1053.

80 These have been termed 'existing conventions of warrant': K. Gergen, 'Warranting Voice and the Elaboration of Self', in J. Shotter and K. Gergen (eds), *Texts of Identity*, London: Sage Publications, 1989, pp. 70, 74. This argument that current conceptualizations of merit are based on existing office holders and encourage selectors to choose people in their own image is also made by A. Paterson and C. Paterson, *Guarding the Guardians: Towards an Independent, Accountable and Diverse Senior Judiciary*, London: CentreForum, 2012, pp. 45–46.

81 See e.g. D. Schleef, *Managing Elites: Professional Socialization in Law and Business Schools*, Lanham, MD: Rowman and Littlefield Publishers Inc., 2006.

82 M. Loughlin, *Swords and Scales*. See also L. Barmes, 'Evidence to House of Lords Select Committee on the Constitution Judicial Appointments Process', pp. 97–103.

> common law tradition ... (this) ancient conception of the rule of law lives on in the twentieth century.[83]

The views of Lord Sumption, a Justice of the Supreme Court, exemplify Loughlin's argument; in the following quotation he echoes the claims made by nineteenth-century English barristers for the pre-eminent importance of their classical education,[84] and, correspondingly, explicitly devalues the worth of a law degree which, he implies, produces an 'uncultured' professional:

> I think it is best not to read law as an undergraduate ... the problem is that we have a generation of lawyers, and this applies to solicitors as well as barristers, who are coming into the profession with much less in the way of general culture than their predecessors. It is very unfortunate, for example, that many of them cannot speak or read a single language other than their own.
>
> Most arguments which pretend to be about law are actually arguments about the correct analysis and categorization of the facts. Once you've understood them it's usually obvious what the answer is. The difficulty then becomes to reason your way in a respectable way towards it. That's why the study of something involving the analysis of evidence, like history or classics, or the study of a subject which comes close to pure logic, like mathematics, is at least as valuable a preparation for legal practice as the study of law.[85]

Or as Lord McNally remarked '(merit) ... is often deployed by people who, when you scratch the surface, are really talking about "chaps like us".'[86]

Conclusion

This chapter has argued that the diversity argument is far from won. Drawing on Sylvia Walby's application of complexity theory to social inequality I have suggested that the 'diversity problematic' should be understood in terms of the judicial system's co-evolution with other systemic transformations of the socio-economic, political and ideological context. Firstly, I identified the positive impact that the social democratic moment of welfare capitalism in the last quarter of the twentieth century, with its enhanced educational opportunities and critique of privilege, produced on the case for the opening up of previously elite occupations, including the judiciary. The expansion of administrative justice consequent on welfare capitalism and the development of the tribunal service also paved the way for the development of a distinct junior branch of the judiciary. Secondly I identified the

83 Loughlin, *Swords and Scales*, pp. 73–74.
84 Pue, *Lawyers' Empire*.
85 Elliott, 'Should prospective lawyers study Law at university?' *Public Law for Everyone*, 25 February, 2013.
86 G. Bindman, 'White male judges: the Supreme Court and judicial diversity' *New Law Journal*, 13 July 2012.

double-edged impact of the neo-liberal hegemony which supplanted social democracy, in its reinforcement of the argument for open labour markets on the one hand, but, on the other hand, its corresponding reinforcement of traditional status markers and role in the stratification and routinization of much professional work, including that of the lower judiciary. This change in the nature of the justice field, together with the evisceration of social citizenship, not only dramatically eroded access to justice for the ordinary citizen but also diminished its nature – and hence the status of professionals practising in the field. Thirdly, this set of systemic changes, in turn, transformed the role of the judge in these courts into one which is primarily managerial and technocratic. As Hunter argues, this new role can be viewed as feminized, and it is therefore in this sector of the judiciary that we see diversification taking place. Thus, as has occurred in other elite professions faced with an influx of 'outsiders', a clear division has developed between 'prestige jobs ... and a new class of more routinized, poorly paid jobs with little autonomy and which are unconnected by promotion ladders to the prestige jobs'.[87] However the higher courts continue to play an extremely high status role which has in fact increased in its significance to the prestige and GDP of the UK. Here the traditional trappings of British justice have a clear value. The existence of an increasingly rigidly stratified judiciary begs the question however of which filters ensure the persistence of the senior branch as a preserve of middle class white males.

Complexity theory suggests the following explanations. The asynchronous nature of systemic and cultural change helps to explain why the erosion of social categories which it is claimed that Neo-liberalism has produced is relatively superficial. Social difference reproduces itself in multiple ways, manifest in the increased significance in recruitment practice of traditional education, accent, cultural preferences on the one hand and, on the other, culturally based assumptions such as who should carry responsibility for social care. In closing off the path to the more diverse judiciary that broader social change might suggest is possible, it is to be expected that elites will practise a form of 'lock-in', through maintenance of control over recruitment channels, and control over the criteria used for appointment. As neo-Weberian sociologists argue, social 'closure' is a defining characteristic of professions. The pressure to modernize has meant that closure no longer consists of a bar at the threshold level but instead becomes significant at later stages of career progression. The bar is constituted by the development of a single opaque and plastic criterion for advancement, 'merit', which the appointing panels can mould to fit their own image and profile.

Finally, complexity theory identifies the significance of multiple networked relationships in affecting the course of change, and the homosocial networks which characterize the upper levels of judicial culture combine with the

87 M. Carter and S. Boslego Carter, 'Women's Recent Progress in the Professions or, Women Get A Ticket to Ride After the Gravy Train Has Left the Station', *Feminist Studies* 7, 1981, pp. 476, 478.

concept of merit to inform who can be deemed to be sufficiently meritworthy to progress – however, in practice, as a senior Immigration Judge commented: 'as regards eligibility, currently it is only one section of the judiciary, the tribunal judiciary, whose judicial appointments eligibility criteria are based fully or largely on merit'.[88]

88 Senior Immigration Judge Hugo Storey, full-time judge of the Upper Tribunal (Immigration and Asylum Chamber) F, 'Evidence to House of Lords Select Committee on the Constitution Judicial Appointments Process' pp. 533–538, 533.

11 Beyond merit

The new challenge for judicial appointments

John Morison

Introduction: towards diversity via merit?

The combination of 'merit' with 'diversity' in judicial appointments has until recently been seen as the best way towards resolving the tension between having the sort of 'representative' (or at least 'reflective') judiciary that is required in a modern legal system, and ensuring that judges remain of sufficient 'quality' to discharge their role effectively. The new appointment systems that grew up across the United Kingdom have been anxious to avoid the more obvious forms of social engineering such as quotas, or schemes of positive discrimination. The result is that 'appointment on merit' has been the supreme governing principle and the pole around which all processes have circulated.[1] Indeed this reflects international best practice and a whole series of international declarations.[2] Every jurisdiction within the United Kingdom has enshrined this in legislation.[3] Originally there may

1 See e.g. Lord Falconer's foreword to the initial consultation paper 'Constitutional Reform: A New way of appointing Judges', Department for Constitutional Affairs, 2003, where he insists that 'of course the fundamental principle in appointing judges is and must remain selection on merit.' (p. 5). See also the response to the consultation by the Judges Council. Online, available at www.webarchive.nationalarchives.gov.uk/ (accessed 11 January 2017). Here the Judges' Council maintains that 'The reputation of our judiciary rests on the fact that it has predominantly been recruited from practising members of the legal profession ... and the fact that all appointments have been based purely on merit' (para 69) and 'the overriding requirement for any appointment body that the best candidates be appointed on merit' (para 80).

2 See e.g. Basic Principles on the Independence of the Judiciary adopted by the Seventh United Nations Congress on the Prevention of Crime and the Treatment of Offenders held at Milan from 26 August to 6 September 1985 and endorsed by General Assembly resolutions 40/32 of 29 November 1985 and 40/146 of 13 December 1985; Recommendation No R (94) 12 of the Council of Europe's Committee of Ministers on the Independence, Efficiency and Role of Judges; see www.wcd.coe.int/ViewDoc.jsp?id=524871&Site=CM; and the Venice Commission (2010).

3 In England and Wales s. 63(2) of the Constitutional Reform Act 2005 provides that 'selection must be solely on merit'. In Northern Ireland, s. 5(8) of the Justice (Northern Ireland) Act 2002, as amended by the Justice (Northern Ireland) Act 2004 provides that 'the selection of a person to be appointed, or recommended for appointment, to a listed judicial office (whether initially or after reconsideration) must be made solely on the basis of merit'. In Scotland, s. 12 of the Judiciary and Courts

have been a number of unresolved tensions for some within the whole project of seeking a judiciary that looks more like the majority of people over whom judgment is to be made. However the idea of 'merit' did seem to allay these fears and suggest that the tensions between diversity and effectiveness could be resolved.

The idea of merit is, however, becoming seen increasingly as problematic. It may even be acting against diversity. Significant figures within the system have expressed dissatisfaction with the idea itself and how it is working.[4] Legislation allowing a candidate from an under-represented minority to be selected when that candidate and another are of equal merit, has attracted suspicion as to its effectiveness.[5] Research is increasingly focusing on the social and cultural conditioning which informs the construction of the idea of merit and suggesting that the idea is narrower than might be hoped. Meanwhile the operationalization of the concept continues to be carried out mainly by those within the system – judges and practitioners – who see themselves as particularly qualified to adjudicate on merit. Of course these are the very people whose background and experience is such that they may hold fast to a culturally created vision of merit that can act contrary to the quest for diversity. The problem for many of the appointment bodies across the United Kingdom is that 'people like us will appoint people like us'. Even ensuring that 'outsiders' are given a place on the bodies appointing judges may not be enough. They may introduce an element of 'independence' – but only of course if their views are heard and they do not become captured by an interpretation of 'merit' that comes from the wider legal profession or, as happened in Scotland, become excluded from crucial aspects of the decision.[6] All of this means

(Scotland) Act 2008 which provides that 'selection must be solely on merit'. See also G. Gee and K. Malleson 'Judicial Appointments, Diversity and the Equal Merit Provision', *UK Constitutional Law Blog*, 6 May 2014. In the Republic of Ireland a high level review of judicial appointments, led by the Chief Justice has recommended that the merit principle be put into law there too. See further Judicial Appointments Review Committee, *Preliminary Submission to the Department of Justice and Equality's Public Consultation on the Judicial Appointments Process*, Dublin: Judicial Appointments Review Committee, 2014 and L. Cahillane, 'Judicial Diversity in Ireland', *Irish Journal of Legal Studies* 6, 2016 p. 1.

4 Much of this debate is usefully summarized in A. Paterson and C. Paterson, *Guarding the Guardians? Towards an Independent, Accountable and Diverse Senior Judiciary*, London: CentreForum, 2012. It has of course been added to since then, most notably by Lord Sumption in an interview with the *Evening Standard* (M. Bentham, 'Rush for Gender Equality with Top Judges could have Appalling Consequences for Justice', *Evening Standard*, 21 September 2015).

5 Deriving originally from s. 159 of the Equality Act 2010 the 'tie-break provision' is now expressed in s. 13 of the Crime and Courts Act 2013. This was originally thought to be impractical to invoke (see e.g. J. Straw, *Aspects of Law Reform: An Insider's Perspective*, Cambridge: Cambridge University Press, 2013, p. 71 and G. Bindman and K. Monaghan, *Judicial Diversity: Accelerating Change*, London: Labour Party, 2014, paras 4.10–4.14). However the Judicial Appointments Commission Annual Reports and Accounts 1 April 2015 to 31 March 2016 maintains that it has been invoked on 14 occasions in the past year (at p. 17).

6 The idea of ensuring a wider interpretation of merit through the involvement of 'outsiders' has been challenged consistently, and within the Scottish Judicial Appointments

that 'merit' as presently constituted can no longer be relied upon to deliver its side of the bargain in the search for a diverse judiciary.

This chapter seeks to unpick this problem, and consider how we might move on. Although the author was a member of the Judicial Appointments Commission in Northern Ireland (NIJAC),[7] what follows does not purport to provide any sort of insider account of what the individual commissioners believed merit to be, or what the Commission as a whole used as any sort of working definition. The criteria used by NIJAC, in common with the other appointment bodies, are clearly set out and are publically available.[8] Rather it draws upon research that NIJAC commissioned into how merit is perceived by the wider legal profession, and how that group believe merit is actually being interpreted by those who make appointments.[9] What is reflected here is a very specific, largely male, hierarchical, Bar-oriented, advocacy-centred, judge-conditioned understanding of merit. Unsurprisingly this is not something that leads inexorably towards the appointment of a diverse judiciary.

After briefly outlining the findings of this research, the chapter then moves to look more closely at the function of merit and what it is actually supposed to deliver in any appointments system, but principally in Northern Ireland where very particular conditions exist. Finally, and in view mainly but not exclusively of the needs of the particular context in Northern Ireland, the chapters sketches out some ideas about what a new concept of merit might address.

The construction of merit – what do the professions think?

This section investigates the understanding of merit, beyond the formal requirements for each post that are held by those who make up the applicant pool. By

Board the role of deciding on important elements of merit has been removed from the lay members. In contrast to the other appointment bodies in the UK the Judicial Appointments Board in Scotland moved away from the practice of giving all its members – lay, judicial and professional – equal status. By means of s. 13 of the Judiciary and Courts (Scotland) Act 2008 now only the judicial and legal members of the board take part in any assessment of an applicant's knowledge of the law or their skills and competence in the interpretation of the law. See further A. Paterson, 'Power and Judicial Appointment: Squaring the Impossible Circle', in this collection.

7 The author served as a commissioner with NIJAC from its inception in June 2003 until June 2012. However, all the views presented here are made in a purely private capacity and should not be attributed to the Commission.

8 See NIJAC website 'Completing Your Application' for details of the generic personal profile and the various key areas of assessment. Online, available at www.nijac.gov.uk/completing-your-application.

9 A research project resulting in a report, *Rewarding Merit in Judicial Appointments?*, NIJAC, 2013, was commissioned by NIJAC to build upon earlier work by P. Leith and others titled *Propensity to Apply for Judicial Office under the New Northern Ireland Judicial Appointments System: A Qualitative Study for the Northern Ireland Judicial Appointments Commission*, NIJAC, 2008. Both research reports can be downloaded from the NIJAC website. The author was involved in the commissioning and on the steering group for the first report and, after completing the role of Commissioner, was the author of the second report, along with P. Leith.

briefly discussing the findings of the research study commissioned by NIJAC, this section explores an understanding of both what merit *should be* and what it is *actually thought to be within the appointment system.*[10]

The NIJAC research originated from a slightly different set of challenges to those facing the other judicial appointments bodies that were founded first in Scotland in 2002, and in England and Wales in 2006. (NIJAC was founded in 2005.) Nevertheless the various pieces of work commissioned by each body in response to their particular circumstances have much in common.[11] There are, however, different emphases in each jurisdiction and unlike in Great Britain, where the initial objective was to ensure an appropriate representation from women and from black and ethnic minorities, in Northern Ireland the focus historically was on recruiting a judiciary that would have the support of all sections of the community (which there means particularly Catholic or nationalists since it was from this section of the population that support was historically missing). However, the results of NIJAC's annual equity monitoring reports which began in 2007, and the conclusions of NIJAC's first research report[12] show, perhaps surprisingly, that the religion theme was not generally particularly problematic.

The first monitoring exercise to take place in Northern Ireland, made public in NIJAC's report from 1997, shows over half of judicial office holders in the Courts were Protestant (54.9 per cent), which is higher than in the legal professions generally (44.4 per cent). However if adjustment is made for the age profile of judicial office holders in the Courts, Protestant representation would be expected to be 52.7 per cent – broadly in line with the actual representation of 54.9 per cent.[13] In contrast, however, in 2007 female representation in the Courts at 21.2 per cent was lower than in the legal profession generally (33.8 per cent). This remains the case in the most recent figures from 2014, where female representation in the Courts at 22.5 per cent is lower than in the legal profession generally (39.3 per cent).[14] The identification of women as a significantly under-represented

10 This part of the chapter draws upon *Rewarding Merit in Judicial Appointments* which was also reported in J. Morison, 'Finding Merit in Judicial Appointments: NIJAC and the Search for a New Judiciary in Northern Ireland', in C. Dywer and A.-M. McAlinden (eds), *Justice in Transition: The Northern Ireland Context*, Oxford: Hart Publishing, 2015, pp. 131–156.

11 See the comparison of the various early research projects under taken by all three bodies provided by the Judicial Appointments Board for Scotland (2009). See also some further possible challenges as identified by the House of Commons Political and Constitutional Reform Committee, *Constitutional role of the judiciary if there were a codified constitution*, Fourteenth Report of Session 2013–14, (2014).

12 Eight years of reports can be found on the NIJAC website. Online, available at www.nijac.gov.uk/publications/reports.

13 NISRA, *The Judiciary in Northern Ireland 2007 Monitoring Report*, NIJAC, 2007. The most recent report, from 2014, has Catholic representation among judicial office holders in Tribunals (40.2%) was lower than in the legal profession generally (53%), and also lower than the representation which might be expected having taken account of the age profile (46.7%) (NISRA, *The Judiciary in Northern Ireland 2014 Monitoring Report,* NIJAC, 2014).

14 Female representation in the tribunal system has been consistently higher but the 2014 figures show that in the higher courts the percentages of women stands at 22.5%

group, particularly in the more senior levels of the court structure in Northern Ireland, is and remains the headline problem in Northern Ireland, notwithstanding the appointment of two women to the High Court in 2015. This issue of course joins concerns about social class – although it is generally difficult to collect data that can reinforce a general perception that senior judges in particular are drawn from within a narrow social compass – and the familiar complaint that solicitors and lawyers working in the public sector remain overlooked.[15]

It was against this background that the NIJAC research project sought to explore further how the potential appointment pool, and a variety legal professionals in general, perceive merit in a judge. A series of interviews and focus groups was carried out by the author with individual practitioners from both branches of the professions and from the public sector at various levels of seniority. There were some women only focus groups and focus groups drawn from lawyers working in different branches of the professions. In all about sixty individuals took part.[16]

A wider view of merit

It was striking that generally those interviewed in the study frequently seemed prepared to see merit in a wider sense than often is traditional in the appointments process. Women respondents, solicitors and those working in the public sector were generally much more favourable towards broader understandings of merit and to non-traditional backgrounds being seen as meritorious. While barristers were most likely to see merit in traditional terms, there was a significant number there too who acknowledged that merit amounts to more than simple technical legal knowledge combined with court experience. As one barrister expressed it,

> knowing the law is just the start … the merit principle needs to be broadly defined to include a wider range of skills, and disentangled from experience in the traditional sense.

Frequent mention was made by many respondents of qualities of empathy and judgement, case management, good listening skills and experience as well as problem-solving. It was thought that merit in this sense could be found in non-traditional candidates and the view was expressed that judicial appointments could

compared to 75.5% men – although two high profile female appointments to the High Court in 2015 have altered immediate appearances significantly.

15 There are no judicial office holders from black and minority ethnic groups in Northern Ireland and although there is some representation among lay magistrates and in tribunals potential applicants are in such small numbers within the eligible pool that no proper conclusions can be drawn here.

16 The other author of the report, Philip Leith, conducted an online survey using various vignettes to explore attitudes towards particular features in a hypothetical application. Details of this, and of the methodology for the interviews and focus groups, can be found in NIJAC, *Rewarding Merit in Judicial Appointments.*

and should be made from a broad range of individuals outside the traditional world of practice at the Bar. As one salaried public sector lawyer put it, 'you need things people from non-traditional backgrounds can bring … case management, managing staff'.

Notwithstanding this general acceptance of merit there was a widespread sense that meritorious candidates may not be recognized within the system as it operates presently. The fact that the wider view of merit was not always reflected in judicial appointments was seen as not necessarily the fault of the appointment processes as such but rather a failing of the wider legal system which has produced and sustains a particular view of merit.

Merit and practice at the Bar

When it comes to detailing and evidencing merit in practice the interviewees generally agreed that merit is more likely to be recognized as existing within a Bar practice, and be based on based on seniority and experience of advocacy in court. This view was not unique to barristers but was noted in a more critical way by those not at the Bar. Judges were thought to reinforce this view of merit and ensure its dominance in the appointment process. Women generally believed themselves less likely to be seen as having this sort of merit or indeed have the opportunities to gain it. From the barristers' perspective, however, it was felt that the high profile of court work brought particular value, and showed merit very clearly. Experience of advocacy in court over a sustained period of time and at a reasonably high level was felt, particularly by some barristers, to be the most effective – if not indeed the sole – way of demonstrating merit for judicial office. One (male) barrister put it simply,

> the most successful practitioners are the most successful judges. They have demonstrated that they know the law … and get on with colleagues … and if females have got on despite the obstacles [then they too must have merit].

Trying to excavate in more detail exactly what this understanding of merit entails and how it might be evidenced proved interesting. For some respondents merit was clearly related directly to the sort of work that an individual might have before appointment. Often interviewees, particularly from the Bar, took the view that a mixed, high-end practice provided the best basis to demonstrate merit. High value chancery work was mentioned as providing an opportunity to demonstrate the necessary skills. Criminal law was mentioned frequently as important and so too was judicial review. If an applicant worked mainly in the High Court with occasional visits to the Court of Appeal or even the Supreme Court or Strasbourg this too was thought to be significant. As a barrister pointed out, 'how else do you demonstrate merit except if you can do the more difficult cases? …'.

However, this linking of merit to particular kinds of work was not universally held. Respondents, particularly those not from the Bar, made a distinction between cases in particular courts which demonstrated merit as opposed to those which had merely some sort of prestige. It was suggested that complexity and difficulty might be found in all sorts of areas of law. A public sector lawyer expressed the view that:

> if you can handle … industrial tribunal cases … equal value … indirect discrimination you can handle anything that is likely to come up in the High Court … you would be very unlucky in the High Court to come up against anything as complex.

Similarly, social welfare law was mentioned as a complex area where skills developed there would be transferable to a senior court appointment, although generally it was not thought to be recognized as such.

This view of merit as being found mainly at the Bar was not universally held. The more senior Bar appeared more willing than juniors to find merit beyond their ranks. One senior barrister told us of 'two examples of judges … who have come from the solicitors' profession and they are excellent judges'. However, the same respondent went on to say, 'the Bar think that we have a particular set of skills that make us good judges … our skills are more transferable'. This view was expressed more trenchantly by younger barristers with one in a focus group insisting:

> There is a difference between a barrister and a solicitor … they [solicitors] routinely sit behind the junior and senior counsel … they have all sorts of opinions but they don't have to ask the questions, put themselves on the line.

Although it was not entirely clear how exactly it translates into the judicial role, barristers generally did represent their work as closer to that of the judge than other lawyers. Of course not all the skills relevant for judicial appointment are developed in a private practice at the Bar, and to see it in this way risks missing other important attributes. As a public sector lawyer pointed out, 'the judicial skill set and the private practice skill set are not necessarily exactly the same'. A partner in a firm of solicitors remarked: 'A lot of them are good advocates but that doesn't make them a good judge … a good judge is the opposite, not a spin doctor …'.

Merit and seniority

There was also a view that merit was most likely to be found with those with many more years of experience than the formal requirement for most judicial posts. This view was fairly widely held but seemed to be particularly prevalent among barristers. Indeed it was a senior barrister who said:

> We need the very best people who have dealt with high value cases, been to the Court of Appeal, Strasbourg, dealt with difficult and complex cases and only if you have done this are you really good enough to demonstrate the sorts of skills [for the High Court].

This view, that experience often far in excess of the minimum required formally is important, reinforced the idea of a 'pecking order' for judicial appointment that was discovered in earlier research.[17] Here again the idea emerged that the Bar (mainly) but the legal profession in general, would have some idea of who was 'worthy' and who should be next on the bench. Views along these lines linked in to more general criticisms that 'outside bodies' could not be expected to be alive to the pecking order. For example, the view was expressed that 'competence based [appointment] works in England and Wales where there are a lot of people ... but we [in Northern Ireland] are still a small enough jurisdiction, and people know each other and know their reputation'.[18]

The research did of course elicit other views which did not directly link age with merit. As one barrister said:

> Does experience equate with age? ... I know people who have done 12 or 13 years of work at the very highest level and others who have been pootering around for 25 years and more and will never do the same level of work.

It may be possible to obtain sufficient experience of work at the appropriate quality in a short period. However it was interesting that several respondents made the point that opportunities now for accelerated experience were diminishing. One interviewee said:

> times have changed. When we started the Bar there were a lot less people there and we got a lot of experience quickly ... you cannot possibly get the experience now in seven years that I got in seven years ...

This seemed to be accepted – at least by some female practitioners surveyed. Another (quite senior) female barrister said, 'we haven't had the breadth of experience that some of our male colleagues have had and we are going to be quite a few years behind them'. A more junior (female) barrister saw the problem simply as 'there are too many of us and we can't get the experience in just a few years'.

There were several respondents who were very aware of the consequences of equating merit with seniority. As one senior practitioner put it, 'there are no High Court judges who are work-shy but there is an expectation that you are going to work harder in your sixties than you did even in your twenties that is unusual'.

17 Leith *et al*, *Propensity to Apply for Judicial Office*, pp. 13–14 and 97–98. It is interesting to note that this view about needing to 'serve time' can be found even at the highest level. Recently Lord Neuberger, lamenting the absence of more women in the Supreme Court, suggested in mitigation that 'this reflects the profile of the pool of people who were eligible for appointment to the High Court 20 or more years ago' – as if 20 plus years of service (rather than the stated 15 years) were necessarily required for such an appointment ('The Role of the Supreme Court Seven Years On – Lessons Learnt', Bar Council Law Reform Lecture, 2016).

18 As the same respondent put it, 'in Northern Ireland, we kind of know who is 'right''.

This was felt to narrow the applicant pool to those who maintained an energy and enthusiasm about continuing the long hours, hard work culture that had put them in the position where they may be seen as meritorious. It was also seen as potentially limiting the pool yet further as it was felt by some that such a decision about extending one's active working life may well be one that men would find easier to take than women for a whole host of reasons relating to caring responsibilities and life patterns.

Merit as male

This view, that merit may most often be associated (at least by some people both within and outside the appointment process) with practice at the Bar, with a particular sort of caseload and obtainable only with a degree of experience, has an obvious implication, and the view was expressed that women were less likely to be able to demonstrate merit of this sort. It was mentioned frequently how women are channelled into family work where it may be more difficult to attain, or at least demonstrate, the necessary experience. As one respondent put it, 'there's not a lot of law in family law' echoing the view found in earlier research about the status often accorded to 'chick law'.[19] However other interviewees took the view that there was rather a different skill set, and it was just as valuable in evidencing merit for judicial appointment. For example, a QC who practiced only rarely in the family court reported an experience of seeing a female barrister in action:

> I was in court and was blown away by her advocacy skills but judges don't see her … I thought it was a lot more difficult … a very limited number of judges see them … and they are held in private.

Indeed, the view was expressed quite strongly that this pigeon-holing of women, combined with the way in which merit is seen in particular types of work and courts, may have the effect that it is difficult for women to present themselves as having the same degree of merit. Indeed female respondents, as well as some males, were very keen to make the point that generally 'female merit' is something different, and does not seem to be transferable. As a member of one focus group put it, 'the requirement to succeed is that you must think just like a man, you must act like a man … be as good as a man'. Several female interviewees reported that it is often particularly difficult for women to emulate this male model of merit. There are wider factors which may make it more difficult for women to progress in the same way. These include not only the diversion of women into family law specialisms and sexist briefing patterns at the Bar, but also some structural factors, some of which may be related to the Bar library set-up in Northern Ireland but which may well have application more widely.[20] There was a view expressed by female respondents, and not generally

19 See Leith *et al*, *Propensity to Apply for Judicial Office*, pp. 23, 56 and 61.

20 Barristers in Ireland – both North and South – are generally organized around a library system which provides working facilities and a referral system rather than in chambers with clerks as in Great Britain.

contradicted by male respondents, that men were better able to pursue the informal networks that can lead to success. For example, one focus group respondent said:

> men can stay on here [the Bar library] and then go home to a cooked dinner, the kids in bed, and go straight into the study ... they can hang around here ... do their work in the library ... networking in an informal way ... they can run into someone in the servery or on the stairs... and get worked passed on.

In contrast, women talked of the difficulties of managing careers and families. As one female barrister put it, 'most of the women at the Bar are juggling not only their practice but also their family life ... I have watched my male peers at the Bar advance far beyond me ... they have good wives at home'.

Some respondents felt that this may be changing – albeit at a very slow pace. There was some mention of the feminization of the legal professions at the lower levels and also mention of the emergence of a cohort of women lawyers who are more ambitious than their predecessors, or at least more impatient about the obstacles. Nevertheless the system itself was thought to have changed little. As one interviewee expressed it, 'the women are adopting a male way of succeeding ... but the system, the way of succeeding, needs to be changed'.

Merit policed by judges

While judges are only part of any appointment panel within NIJAC (which will also contain commissioners appointed from the professions and lay people putting them in a minority), many of the respondents in the research believed that the judiciary maintained a particular influence beyond this by virtue of their role as consultees or referees in the process. The Bar-influenced, male-oriented view of merit was thought to be reinforced as judges play this gatekeeper role. As one barrister respondent reported:

> those on the bench see the skill sets they bring as being the ones that are needed ... it is an advocacy skill set by and large ... Judges have the view that the profile we [barristers] have represents what a good judge is.

From the perspective of some barristers – those doing the right sort of work in the right courts – this was not a problem. But if, like many women, your practice is not at the Bar or not in the areas of particularly visibility to the judges, this may appear as another barrier. Solicitors too in particular often expressed the view that their skills were being overlooked because judges controlled the idea of merit and viewed it mainly in relation to barristers' skills.

Judicial pathways – formal and informal

The existence of a formal career path that might lead to appointment at the higher level was not something that the research was able to uncover to any great degree.[21] There was mention of a few individuals who, it was reported, seemed to have taken on judicial office at a relatively junior level but who were thought to have further ambitions. However this was not seen as a universally available career option, although it was suggested that it might be a good thing in that it, 'would allow a wider range of people to demonstrate the appropriate competencies … [as] the part-time roles have the potential to do this'. As one focus group member put it, 'if you shine in one tier you should have the opportunity to move up'. It was thought that this possibility might even encourage good applicants who would not otherwise think of a judicial career. A senior lawyer from the public sector made the point that, a 'judicial pathway is the *key thing* … I work in a sector where there are some extremely capable women but who have no perception of the possibility to be a part-time judge'. The creation of this possibility was felt to be an important attraction. Indeed there was a view expressed widely that a series of appointments, moving up through the tiers of the judiciary from lower courts, might be an appropriate proving ground, and perhaps of at least equal validity to a career in the Bar. As one respondent put it:

> merit has to be real merit … but if someone is a solicitor, a female in family work west of the [River] Bann … they need a place to show that they can do the hard work. It is the County Court that is the place. They can progress from there.

Although the idea of a formal pathway to a judicial career that might take a judge up the rungs of the career ladder remains an uncertain although interesting possibility, there was very little doubt among research participants about the existence of an informal pathway to judicial preferment. It was widely reported in all the focus groups that there were a number of important attributes and career choices that render a candidate 'meritorious'. Some are straightforward such as being on various panels to undertake government work or appointment as Queen's Counsel. Others are less obvious. As one interviewee remarked that 'it is funny how, irrespective of the existence of NIJAC, there are certain truths that are self-evident … senior crown council will become a judge'. When pressed further on what this informal track might involve it was said, 'you have access to the right sort of work … if you're known in the back corridor [of the High Court], if you're Treasury Counsel, if your father was a judge …'. Another informant characterized

21 A 'Judicial Career' is a concept which appears as Recommendation 44 of the 'Report of the Advisory Panel on Judicial Diversity 2010' in England and Wales: 'The concept of a judicial career is key to achieving progress on a more diverse judiciary … This means identifying clearer career paths so that those considering joining the judiciary understand their options and know how they can develop the skills and experience required to progress from one section of the judiciary to another' (Advisory Panel on Judicial Diversity, 2010). See also the ***Judicial Career Progression Chart with Eligibility Criteria***, updated in February 2016 on the Courts and Tribunals Judiciary website. Online, available at www.judiciary.gov.uk/about-the-judiciary/judges-career-paths/judicial-career-progression-chart/.

a successful candidate as someone who may well have been 'vocal on the Bar Council or served on it … very high profile, everyone would have heard of them'. Much of this idea of a career pathway was seen to be about networking and making the correct contacts, and much seemed to exclude women for structural reasons.

Various events including dinners and lectures were thought to be important. It was here that the necessary impressions can be made and the important contacts fostered. As one informant put it, 'the person who has played at that level is going to have an advantage … you have access to the right sort of work' and, crucially, 'you know the judges'. This latter element – connections with the senior judiciary – is seen as particularly important, mainly in relation to access to appropriate consultees or referees. This was believed by some respondents to be a feature that impacts particularly on women. Women reported themselves to be less likely to network and less willing to ask judges for support. As one interviewee expressed it,

> A fairly homogenous group are describing themselves to themselves, and, although you have a fair and transparent appointment process, the way in which a candidate is described will favour someone who has a traditional, mixed private practice …

The study did uncover some limited praise for NIJAC's efforts at encouraging diversity. One (female) interviewee remarked that 'NIJAC do give a lot of good guidance and if you follow what they say you should be able to get yourself through it … eventually'. Overall, though, there was perhaps a sense of helplessness with regard to what NIJAC can do. As another interviewee expressed it, 'the procedure, the selection process itself, isn't the problem … the problem is the gene pool in the profession itself … how you get yourself into the position where you are the best candidate … there isn't enough diversity in the profession.' As one solicitor remarked, 'to what extent have we really changed or do we now have a very open and transparent organization applying the same old criteria …. you know, let's have somebody who looks exactly like the last guy? …. And [these] criteria don't seem to working to deliver a representative judiciary'.

'Merit' as the problem rather than the solution

In many ways it seems as if 'merit' – at least as it is actually deployed in the appointment system – is part of the problem in preventing a more reflective judiciary because it operates to disadvantage female applicants. It is not that meritorious female candidates do not exist but rather that merit is defined in a way which emphasizes qualities that women may find more difficult to demonstrate. Of course such a finding about the socially constructed nature of merit, and the way in which the concept poses as neutral while being in reality strongly gendered, is not new – either in relation to judicial appointments or more generally.[22]

22 See e.g. K. Malleson, 'Rethinking the Merit Principle in Judicial Selection', *Journal of Law and Society* 33, 2006, p. 126; E. Rackley, *Women, Judging and the Judiciary:*

However what is new from the study is the growing realization among the profession itself, particularly amongst women that 'merit is the problem'. The ways in which merit is defined and operationalized within the appointment system is now subject to a strong degree of scepticism. As one of the interviewees noted, 'the law does not know just how much it has to change … there is a meritocracy but it's *their* meritocracy … that's a fact of life'.

Part of this change must be a move 'beyond merit'. If the present understanding is allowed to remain, and the problem is seen only to be about how to move more women within this definition (whether by judge-shadowing, mentoring, outreach and any of the other worthy activities of, for example, the Judicial Diversity Committee of the Judges' Council[23]), there will be little or no change. Such initiatives may result in a few more female appointments, and so remove the worst appearance, but they will not result in significant change. Lord Sumption's estimation of 50 years before gender equality can be achieved may well prove correct.[24] Discussions of merit in appointments need to be moved beyond gender precisely in order to achieve the sort of gender balance that is appropriate for a modern judiciary seeking the most talented judges. There are many challenges facing the legal system in Northern Ireland as there are elsewhere, and any new concept of merit should address these. Current efforts in the appointment system are aimed at dealing with a single problem (improving diversity in the higher levels of the judiciary) but they are ignoring multiple other problems about access to justice, cost, delay, etc. and the judges' role in tackling these. If these wider issues were addressed as we are thinking about who should be appointed to the judiciary, and the focus moved away from 'merit' as presently constituted, and towards finding the people most able to address the broader aspects of being a judge too, it may well resolve the problem of diversity anyway. Discussion of merit must move away from questions of gender balance, and ways of moderating or even manipulating the system so as to enable a more diverse judiciary on these terms. Only when a new concept of merit, properly considering the needs of the legal system for a changing world, is articulated can the appointment system move on. Paradoxically perhaps, it is only when we leave diversity out of the mix in the recipe for merit (and so leave behind the wider attempts to squeeze increasing numbers of women into the existing definition of merit) that more women will be appointed. A definition of merit that moves on from the current emphasis on legal competence as demonstrated in practice, and focuses on a wider skill set for

From Difference to Diversity, Abingdon: Routledge, 2013; S. Kenney, *Gender and Justice: Why Women in the Judiciary Really Matter*, Abingdon: Routledge 2013; and the collection edited by U. Schultz and G. Shaw (eds), *Gender and Judging*, Oxford: Hart Publishing, 2013; or the classic accounts of C. MacKinnon, *Toward a Feminist Theory of the State*, Cambridge, MA: Harvard University Press, 1989; and C. Gilligan, *In a Different Voice: Psychological Theory and Women's Development*, Cambridge, MA: Harvard University Press, 1982.

23 See Judicial Diversity Committee of the Judges' Council, *Report on Progress 2013–2016.*

24 See above n. 4.

managing the legal system as a public service, will undoubtedly result in more female candidates (and other non-traditional applicants) meeting the standards and so increase the diversity of the judiciary.

Re-engineering merit

Although this discussion so far has privileged the voice of the legal community in articulating what merit is, and it has reported that many there are open to a broader view of merit, it is suggested now that we should look elsewhere to understand what might be involved in any new version of merit. The respondents in the research offered their views, and often these reflected the perspective of individuals building a career and seeking fairness in that process. While this is not a negligible consideration, the legal system is not run for the benefit of legal practitioners.[25] The needs of the users of the legal system, including those who pay for much of it, must be given greater consideration. It may be true, as Malleson has noted, that there has been a process by which 'the judiciary changed from a club to a profession'.[26] If this is to continue a modern judiciary must be developed with the skill set to meet the requirements of this wider group of stakeholders. What exactly are these and how do we uncover them?[27]

Much of this will involve re-conceptualizing the legal system as a *public service* and considering what the public might want or legitimately expect from the judiciary.[28] While the idea of a public legal service, and the related notion of problem-solving courts, have been resisted traditionally, there are signs that change may be

25 At the same time diversity among judges is not to be valued only because it enables more practitioners to attain judicial office. Indeed a more diverse judiciary might well bring many attractive features beyond improving the career prospects of some practitioners. These include reflectiveness of wider society, a reduction in the chill factor for court users, and maybe even a more nuanced way of judging. (On this see the research summarized in R. Hunter, 'More than Just a Different Face? Judicial Diversity and Decision-making', *Current Legal Problems* 68, 2015, pp. 119–141). However, here as more generally in this area, the major gain must surely be the reassurance for the public that if, as must be the case, talent (as opposed to experience) is evenly distributed across all genders and ethnic groups, a diverse judiciary is a sign that the widest possible talent pool in society is being drawn upon.

26 K. Malleson, *The New Judiciary: The Effects of Expansion and Activism*, Aldershot, Ashgate, 1999, p. 163.

27 Further research must be carried out developing the work of, for example, H. Genn, *Paths to Justice: What do People Do and Think about Going to Law*, Oxford: Hart Publishing, 1999 and C. Thomas and H. Genn, *Understanding Tribunal Decision-Making: A Foundation Empirical Study*, London: Nuffield Foundation, 2013.

28 Rosemary Hunter has gone some way to describing what might be required by a 'new judge' at the various levels across the legal system while at the same observing how women are appointed mainly at the lower levels where stereotypical 'feminine skills' seem to be required, leaving the upper levels of appointment to maintain stereotypical 'masculine' associations ('Judiciary Diversity and the 'New' Judge' in H. Sommerlad, S. Harris-Short, S. Vaughan and R. Young (eds), *The Futures of Legal Education and the Legal Profession*, Oxford: Hart Publishing, 2015, pp. 79–96).

underway.[29] If such a move is encouraged it will bring with it a long shopping list. Some of the items on it will include: effective case management and ensuring value for money; a developed and integrated approach to using new technology; improved public relations and making sure that although parties may leave court having lost, they feel they have been heard; assisting litigants in person, and pursuing the various values of justice for everyone in a context of declining legal aid support and increasing costs. There is even an argument that a judge-led, inquisitorial system of justice may be a better way of conducting family and civil cases, especially where litigants are without representation.[30] Such an approach would require very different skills from those usually associated with the judicial role.

At the same time it is also important to look at what judges actually do within the present set-up (rather than what applicants for their posts do). There is some important research here already but more needs to be done.[31] Only when there is a clearer and more fully articulated understanding of the role of the judge in terms of case management, communicating with court users and the public, managing teams and providing leadership can we properly understand what makes a good applicant for judicial office. What skills do judges actually use in the everyday management of cases at various levels? Are these skills generic or do they vary enormously with the type of case and nature of the parties? The idea that judges are inevitably merely referees, deliberating on issues of law and matters of fact from Olympian heights, before descending to give perfectly formed judgments that bring justice to the parties and further embroider the tapestry of the law, must be challenged. Surely some judges in some sorts of cases must have a different role? We can perhaps, following Lon Fuller, accept a definition where in

29 The Lord Chancellor and Secretary of State for Justice and the Lord Chief Justice have established a joint working group to examine models of problem-solving courts and advise on the feasibility of possible pilot models to be taken forward in England and Wales in 2016/17. See Ministry of Justice, 'Problem-Solving Courts Working Group: Terms of Reference' and, more generally, J. Donoghue, *Transforming Criminal Justice? Problem-Solving and Court Specialisation*, London: Routledge, 2014.

30 Indeed this is something that no lesser figure than Lord Thomas LCJ was prepared to consider some time ago (J. Rozenberg, 'Lord Chief Justice helps politicians grasp courts' "hot potato"', *The Guardian*, 4 March 2014.) Dramatically increasing numbers of litigants in person across the system suggest that this approach may find favour more generally.

31 Much of what is known about the judiciary is focused on the USA. See, e.g. N. Meveety (ed.), *The Pioneers of Judicial Behaviour*, Ann Arbor: University of Michigan Press, 2002. In the UK the focus has been mainly on the most senior courts. See e.g. A. Patterson, *Final Judgment: The Last Law Lords and the Supreme Court*, Oxford: Hart Publishing, 2013; or even on particular aspects of their work: e.g. B. Dickson, *Human Rights and the United Kingdom Supreme Court*, Oxford: University Press 2013; or G. Gee, R. Hazell, K. Malleson and P. O'Brien, *The Politics of Judicial Independence in the UK's Changing Constitution*, Cambridge: Cambridge University Press, 2015. There is more limited work on everyday role of the judge. For a relatively rare example, see P. Darbyshire, *Sitting in Judgment: The Working Lives of Judges*, Oxford: Hart Publishing, 2011; and Thomas and Genn, *Understanding Tribunal Decision-Making* (above n. 27).

contrast to an administrative decision, 'adjudication is a device which gives formal and substantive expression to the influence of reasoned argument' and still seek to develop a hierarchy in the forms or nature of adjudication.[32] In some types of cases – perhaps most – there is surely room to allow the judge to develop a more active role in controlling proceedings, limiting the involvement of counsel and experts, and reducing costs and time. Some of this overlaps with the movement towards changing the nature and structure of the courtroom itself, in order to build flexibility into the system, make the court user the focus of any reform and recognize the importance of services which assist litigants – particularly those without representation.[33] Just as there were when the tribunal system was introduced, there will be many in the legal profession who will attack this in terms of allowing a second class service. However, many ordinary users of the legal system who either must fund themselves or pay for others to use legal aid, will undoubtedly favour a low-cost, accessible court system run by skilled, empathetic, 'hands-on' judges over the 'Rolls Royce service' of the more traditional court process.

These challenges occur right across the legal systems of the United Kingdom. In the particular context of Northern Ireland where the initial research was carried out there are additional factors. Some of these relate to what might be termed the 'new legal space' created following the peace process and the devolution of justice.[34] And there are other, particular issues about the cost of legal aid in Northern Ireland too.[35] A recent report on Access to Justice for the Department of Justice in Northern Ireland considered a wider range of issues and many of the conclusions here reinforce more general arguments about a more responsive, consumer-led, public service orientated judiciary.[36] For example, the report contains a call

32 L. Fuller and K. Winston, 'The Forms and Limits of Adjudication', *Harvard Law Review* 92, 1978, pp. 353–409 at p. 368. See also D. Dan-Cohen, 'Bureaucratic Organizations and the Theory of Adjudication', *Columbia Law Review* 85, 1985, pp. 1–37.

33 See further, JUSTICE, *What is a Court?*, 2016 Online, available at https://2bquk8cdew6192tsu41lay8t-wpengine.netdna-ssl.com/wp-content/uploads/2016/05/JUSTICE-What-is-a-Court-Report-2016.pdf (accessed 11 January 2017). See also *Transforming Our Justice System By the Lord Chancellor, the Lord Chief Justice and the Senior President of Tribunals*, London: Ministry of Justice, 2016.

34 See further discussion of this in Morison, 'Finding Merit in Judicial Appointments', pp. 132–135.

35 According to the *Legal Services Agency Northern Ireland Annual Report and Accounts for the year ended 31 March 2016* the legal aid bill for Northern Ireland runs at somewhere between £1.5m and £2m *each week*. Expenditure at this extraordinary level has attracted considerable criticism from which the judiciary along with the legal professions have not been immune (see e.g. the Northern Ireland Public Accounts Committee, *Inquiry into Managing Legal Aid: Department of Justice, Legal Services Agency Northern Ireland, Department of Finance, Northern Ireland Audit Office*, Hansard, 26 June 2016).

36 C. Sutt, *A Strategy for Access to Justice: The Report of Access to Justice (2)*, 2015. Online, available at www.justice-ni.gov.uk/sites/default/files/publications/doj/access-to-justice-review-part-2-report.pdf (accessed 11 January 2017). This report follows on from and develops an earlier version, *Access to Justice Report* published in 2011.

for a more inquisitorial approach from judges, particularly to support the increasing numbers of litigants in person, with additional requirements for parties to engage with each other and the court prior to a hearing.[37] The report encourages judges to develop plain English approaches, again particularly with reference to the experience of the litigant in person.[38] Better case management by judges is a recurring theme with recommendations that more business should be conducted by phone or email rather than in full hearing, and that practices of over-listing where lawyers were left waiting around at public expense should be controlled.[39] The report also encourages judges to explore mediation and various forms of alternative dispute resolution as an alternative to a costly hearing and even suggests involving judges in early neutral evaluation in the context of informal indications to counsel at interim stages in civil, non family, legally aided proceedings with a reporting system to record diversions from trial.[40] Two other important reports, reviewing civil and family justice in Northern Ireland,[41] both reinforce in different contexts, similar ideas about the importance of judges being economically aware, acting in teams to solve problems and offering leadership, seeking alternative resolutions to full court proceedings and being responsive to the increasing numbers of personal litigants. Furthermore each report gives a full chapter to 'Paperless Courts' where judges take a leading role in developing IT.

All of this suggests a very different type of judge in possession of a rather different version of 'merit' than that of the successful former practitioner at the Bar who has a career of high value, prestigious cases listed on his curriculum vitae. As we move beyond merit in the traditional sense, and start to develop a clearer view of what the modern judge should look like, opportunities will undoubtedly open for a more effective, and, at the same time, more diverse, judiciary.

37 Sutt, *A Strategy for Access to Justice*, paras 7.9–7.13.
38 Ibid., para 7.27.
39 Ibid., paras 7.18 and 7.22. To this might also be added issues such as the 'proliferation of authorities' that Lord Carnwath identified recently in Postech v Royal Borough of Kensington and Chelsea [2017] UKSC 36. Here the court found itself presented with a huge range of materials, many of which were described as familiar, uncontentious … [and] unlikely to be more than peripheral', with others falling into a category which the judge described as being 'sufficiently familiar to the court not to require extensive citation' (paras 45–46).
40 Ibid., paras 28.14–15.
41 See *The Review of Civil and Family Justice: The Review Group's Draft Report on Family Justice (August 2016)* and *The Review of Civil and Family Justice: The Review Group's Draft Report on Civil Justice* (The Gillen Report), October 2016 available from the Judicial Studies Board for Northern Ireland website.

12 Problems of scale in achieving judicial diversity

Rosemary Hunter

Introduction

This chapter is an attempt to bridge the gap between differing perceptions of the progress made by the Judicial Appointments Commission (JAC) towards the achievement of greater diversity in the judiciary in England and Wales. For the purposes of analysis two opposing positions are identified, which are called for the sake of brevity 'the JAC position' and 'the critical position'. The JAC position is generally articulated by the JAC itself, although it is shared by supporters in the legal profession, the judiciary and in government and policy circles. The critical position is sometimes understood (by the JAC among others) to be an academic position; however, the label 'critical' is preferred to 'academic' in order to make the point that it is not only academics who take this position. It is articulated, for example, by the Judicial Diversity Initiative (JDI) lobby group,[1] which is made up of both academic and non-academic members, and is also shared by many women and members of minority groups in the legal profession and by other non-academic promoters of greater judicial diversity.[2] These positions as discussed in this paper are 'ideal types', less complex and nuanced than they may be in reality. The benefit of presenting them in heuristic terms, however, is to enable the sources, nature and scope of their differences to be seen clearly, which in turn can be an aid to mutual understanding and also help in finding middle ground between them.

To put the opposing perspectives at their most basic, therefore, the JAC position maintains that the JAC is doing everything it can to achieve greater diversity in the judiciary, and that good progress is being made. The critical position, by contrast, holds that progress towards greater judicial diversity has been minimal, fragile and disappointing. Moreover, each side finds the other's continued maintenance of their respective positions frustrating and irritating.

In seeking to address this divide, it must be acknowledged that I am not a disinterested observer, but a well-known proponent of the critical position. The

1 See the JDI website: http://judicialdiversityinitiative.org/ (formerly the Equal Justices Initiative).

2 See e.g. G. Bindman and K. Monaghan, *Judicial Diversity: Accelerating Change*, London: Labour Party, 2014; JUSTICE, *Increasing Judicial Diversity*, London: JUSTICE, 2017.

objective of this chapter, however, is not simply to re-state that position in an attempt to persuade readers that it is correct. Rather, the following analysis aims to show that both positions are 'correct', when the fact that they start from radically different premises is taken into account. The chapter thus attempts to arrive at a shared understanding of those divergent premises, which might help the two sides to work together more constructively in the future.

The paper is inspired and aided by Mariana Valverde's recent book, *Chronotopes of Law*.[3] Valverde argues that socio-legal scholars need to pay greater attention to issues of scale and jurisdiction when analysing particular governmental ideas, phenomena and preferences. The following analysis is not so focused on the question of modes of governance – although the mode of governance of judicial appointments is surely one of the issues at stake in this discussion – but Valverde's direction of the socio-legal gaze to fundamental issues of scale and jurisdiction is nevertheless illuminating and thought-provoking. Shifting attention to this level of abstraction or meta-analysis enables the transcendence of immediate disagreements to see how the opposing positions configure themselves along scalar and jurisdictional axes, and hence both manage to be 'correct' while effectively talking past each other. In Valverde's account, 'scale' is composed of three elements: spatiality, temporality and 'mood', or affect. These elements are interconnected in spatio-temporal, affective and jurisdictional assemblages which she calls, following the Russian philosopher Mikhail Bakhtin, 'chronotopes'.[4] So instead of opposing positions, we might begin to think of *the JAC chronotope* and the *critical chronotope*. In the following discussion, the chapter attempts to delineate the elements of each chronotope, dealing with them separately for the purposes of analysis while also noting the ways in which they are ultimately interconnected.

Spatiality

At first blush, it might appear that the JAC and critical positions are operating within the same space, since both are concerned with the appointment of the judiciary in one particular national territory, England and Wales. But on further consideration, it can be seen that *space* is configured differently in the two chronotopes. For while the JAC fixes its gaze exclusively on the situation in England and Wales – because that is its jurisdiction – the critical gaze is not so confined; it is, rather, a transnational or global gaze. In other words, for the JAC, the current situation in England and Wales is comparable only on a temporal scale – with what happened in the past, and more particularly before it began its work in 2006 – while for critics, the current situation in England and Wales is also comparable on a spatial scale – that is, how it compares with the situation in other countries and on international courts, as evidenced by this collection which includes

3 M. Valverde, *Chronotopes of Law: Jurisdiction, Scale and Governance*, London: Routledge, 2015.

4 Ibid., pp. 9–14.

contributions from Northern Ireland, Scotland, Australia, Canada, South Africa and the Commonwealth generally as well as from England and Wales.

Indeed, it is a common trope of scholarship on gender and judging to compare the proportion of women on the UK Supreme Court (UKSC) to the proportion of women on other national supreme and constitutional courts and on supra-national courts.[5] Needless to say, it compares badly. Comparisons are also drawn between the overall proportion of women in the judiciary in England and Wales and their proportion in the judiciaries of various European, Anglo-Commonwealth and African countries, where it also compares badly.[6] Apart from the results of these comparisons, the key point to note is that critical conversations about gender representation in the judiciary are international and comparative. Scholars around the world have been talking to each other about this topic and publishing comparative work for at least the last 15 years,[7] including comparisons not only between judiciaries, but also between different judicial appointment systems and their relative performance in producing a more diverse judiciary.[8] Thus, global benchmarking has become an integral element of critical thinking in relation to judicial diversity, but does not form part of the JAC's publicly-articulated consciousness. Consequently, the JAC chronotope and the critical chronotope appear to operate on quite different spatial scales.

Temporality

But while the spatial scale plays a role in the formation of each chronotope, the temporal scale is absolutely central to understanding the differences between the two chronotopes. Discussions of judicial diversity are full of references to temporality, from Lord Taylor's original confident assertion in 1992 that the imbalance between male and female, black and white in the judiciary would be

5 See e.g. E. Rackley, *Women, Judging and the Judiciary: From Difference to Diversity*, London: Routledge, 2013, pp. 20–22; A. Paterson and C. Paterson, *Guarding the Guardians: Towards an Independent, Accountable and Diverse Senior Judiciary*, London: CentreForum, 2012, p. 38.

6 See e.g. U. Schultz and G. Shaw, 'Introduction: Gender and Judging: Overview and Synthesis', in U. Schultz and G. Shaw (eds), *Gender and Judging*, Oxford: Hart Publishing, 2013, pp. 9–13.

7 See e.g. U. Schultz and G. Shaw (eds), *Women in the World's Legal Professions*, Oxford: Hart Publishing, 2003 generally, and in particular K. Malleson, 'Prospects for Parity: The Position of Women in the Judiciary in England and Wales', in U. Schultz and G. Shaw (eds), *Women in the World's Legal Professions*, Oxford: Hart Publishing, 2003. See also international and comparative research listed on the JDI website.

8 See e.g. M. S. Hurwitz and D. Noble Lanier, 'Explaining Judicial Diversity: The Differential Ability of Women and Minorities to Attain Seats on State Supreme and Appellate Courts', *State Politics and Policy Quarterly* 3, 2003, p. 329; Paterson and Paterson, *Guarding the Guardians*, ch. 5; S. Kenney, 'Which Judicial Selection Systems Generate the Most Women Judges? Lessons from the United States', in U. Schultz and G. Shaw (eds), *Gender and Judging*, Oxford: Hart Publishing, 2013; S. Iyer, 'The Fleeting Benefits of Appointments Commissions for Judicial Gender Equity', *Commonwealth and Comparative Politics* 51, 2013, p. 97.

redressed 'in the next five years',[9] to Lord Sumption's recent interventions predicting that gender equality will not be achieved for at least another 50 years, and urging patience in the meantime.[10] In turn, there are three aspects of temporality which can be teased out: the past, the future, and the pace of change.

The past

When discussing the past in relation to judicial diversity, the key issue that arises is: when did the past begin? Or, to put it another way, what is the duration over which progress towards diversity ought to be measured? Here, the JAC chronotope contains a short history. The JAC came into existence in 2006. So in assessing the JAC's performance in achieving judicial diversity, the relevant period to be examined is the last 10 years. In fact, the JAC has been prepared to look a little further back to see whether the diversity of applications and recommendations relating to the courts judiciary during the period of its existence has increased compared to the period preceding its formation from 1998 to 2006.[11] On this basis the general picture is one of improvement for both women candidates and BAME candidates within the courts judiciary.[12] (On a broader spatial scale, it might be observed that the same picture of improvement is generally true in many other common law jurisdictions with different judicial appointment systems).[13]

By comparison to the JAC chronotope's 18 years, the critical chronotope contains a much longer history. Feminists, for example, have been agitating for and striving towards equality for women in all spheres of activity, of which the judiciary represents only one site, at the very least since 1970, when the UK women's liberation movement first articulated its demand for equal education and job opportunities.[14] Or since 1962 when Elizabeth Lane was the first woman judge appointed to the Circuit bench. Or since the passage of the Sex Disqualification Removal Act 1919 which permitted women's entry to the legal profession. Or

9 Lord Taylor, 'The Judiciary in the Nineties', The Richard Dimbleby Lecture, 1992.

10 Lord Sumption, 'Home Truths about Judicial Diversity', Bar Council Law Reform Lecture, 15 November 2012.

11 Judicial Appointments Commission, *Judicial Selection and Recommendations for Appointment Statistics, April 2013–September 2013*, London: Judicial Appointments Commission, 2013, p. 18. See also Judicial Appointments Commission, *Statistical Digest of Judicial Appointments of Women and BME Candidates from 1998/99 to 2008/09*, London: Judicial Appointments Commission, 2010; Judicial Appointments Commission, Diversity trends analysis, Judicial Appointments Commission, December 2014.

12 Judicial Appointments Commission, *Judicial Selection and Recommendation for Appointment Statistics, October 2013–March 2014*, London: Judicial Appointments Commission, 2014, pp. 33–34.

13 See e.g. M. S. Hurwitz and D. Noble Lanier, 'Diversity in State and Federal Appellate Courts: Change and Continuity Across 20 Years', *Justice System Journal* 29, 2008, p. 47; and Iyer, 'The Fleeting Benefits of Appointments Commissions'.

14 *National Women's Liberation Movement Conference*, Ruskin College, Oxford, February 1970.

since the 1850s with the establishment of first wave feminism in Britain and the beginning of campaigns to remove the legal injustices and impediments imposed on women in both private and public life.[15] Black and minority ethnic men and women have sought racial equality in the UK since the waves of post-war immigration from former British colonies began in the late 1940s, or indeed since slaves were brought to Britain by their owners from the colonies in the eighteenth and early nineteenth centuries.[16] On a global scale, women and racial minorities have been denied equal status and equal representation since time immemorial, and their under-representation in the judiciary in England and Wales and in other countries is just one of the many indicators that equal status and equal representation have not yet been achieved. Thus, from a critical perspective, equality has been a very long time coming.

The future

The discussion of the past also points to different conceptions of the future within the JAC and critical chronotopes. The critical vision of the future is an outcome, an ideal state to be realized: that is, gender parity and proportionate representation for currently under-represented groups in the judiciary. The JDI defines gender parity to mean there should be no fewer than 40 per cent and no more than 60 per cent of women and men from diverse backgrounds at all levels of the judiciary.[17] Moreover, the JDI was set up in 2010 with the explicit aim of working towards the achievement of gender parity in the judiciary by 2015. The rationale for this end-date is set out on the JDI website:

> By the mid-1990s women and men were equally represented amongst newly qualified lawyers. In recent years women have increasingly outnumbered men in the qualifying cohorts of both barristers and solicitors. By 2015 the balance of women and men in the legal profession will therefore be such that there will be no legitimate justification for the continued over-representation of men on the bench.[18]

This introduces another common trope within critical discussions of judicial diversity, which of course has to be understood within the context of the critical

15 See e.g. H. Taylor Mill, 'The Enfranchisement of Women', *Westminster and Foreign Quarterly Review*, July 1851; B. L. Smith Bodichon, *A Brief Summary in Plain Language of the Most Important Laws Concerning Women, Together with a Few Observations Thereon*, London: John Chapman, 1854; and C. Norton, *English Laws for Women in the Nineteenth Century*, London: Printed for Private Circulation, 1854. These publications were, of course, preceded by M. Wollstonecraft's *A Vindication of the Rights of Woman*, Boston: Peter Edes, 1792.

16 See e.g. *R v Allan* (1827) 166 ER 179 ('The Slave, Grace').

17 'About JDI' Online, Available http://judicialdiversityinitiative.org/about/ (accessed 23 February 2017).

18 Ibid.

view of the past just outlined – that is: when will we get there? How much longer will it be before our ideal end-state is achieved? And here, against the background of a long history, the critical chronotope would like the future to be short. Consequently, any projections which anticipate a long future are greeted with dismay. This includes trend analyses such as that undertaken by the Equality and Human Rights Commission, which estimated in 2011 that at the current rate of progress it would be 45 years before there would be an equal number of women in the senior judiciary.[19] And it includes contentions such as Lord Sumption's, noted above, that it may take 50 years to achieve a fully diverse judiciary,[20] a figure not based on trend analysis but which he acknowledged to be a guess, and which appears to have been arbitrarily selected in order to place the event at what would appear to be, for him, a reassuring distance from the present. Within the critical chronotope, however, it follows that if the current system is likely to produce a long future, then it needs to be changed.

The JAC chronotope, by contrast, as evidenced by its official statements and publications, appears to contain no vision of the future at all. There is no ideal end-point to be realized with regard to the composition of the judiciary as a whole or at any particular level. The JAC's statutory role is to select candidates for judicial appointment solely on merit,[21] and to 'have regard to the need to encourage diversity in the range of persons available for judicial selection'.[22] In these terms, therefore, the JAC has no statutory concern for the diversity results of its selection processes. The only point at which it has such a concern is where it considers two candidates to be of equal merit. In this circumstance, it may prefer one of them over the other 'for the purpose of increasing diversity' on the court or in the office to which the selection process relates.[23] The statutory wording makes it clear that the JAC is not required to exercise a preference in these circumstances, but is 'not prevented' from doing so. The limits of this mandate are clear in the fact that the equal merit provision was applied in relation to only 14 out of 308 recommendations (fewer than 5 per cent) in 2015–16.[24]

Beyond this, the JAC is also subject to the public sector equality duty under the Equality Act 2010, and pursuant to this duty it has established equality objectives which include 'to monitor the diversity of candidates selected for judicial appointment (against the eligible pool where available) and take remedial action where available'.[25] This implies that the candidates selected should reflect the

19 Equality and Human Rights Commission, *Sex and Power 2011*, London: EHRC, 2011, p. 10.
20 Lord Sumption, 'Home Truths', p. 14; M. Bentham, 'Rush for gender equality with top judges "could have appalling consequences for justice"', *Evening Standard*, 21 September 2015.
21 Constitutional Reform Act 2005 (CRA), s. 63.
22 Ibid., s. 64.
23 Ibid., s. 63(4).
24 Judicial Appointments Commission, *Judicial Selection and Recommendations for Appointment Statistics, April 2015–March 2016*, London: Judicial Appointments Commission, 2016, p. 11.
25 Judicial Appointments Commission, *Equality Objectives 2012–2016*, Judicial Appointments Commission, Objective 3.

proportions of relevant identity-groups in the eligible pool of candidates. But this is an end-point that relates to each individual selection exercise rather than to the composition of the judiciary as a whole. The JAC's concern is with the achievement of diversity within its own processes rather than with the achievement of diversity in the judiciary per se.

It follows that within the JAC chronotope, the future stretches only as far as the end of the next selection exercise, or at most, the publication of the next Statistical Bulletin. At that point the JAC takes stock of whether its end-points have been achieved. In the latest reported statistics at the time of writing (April 2015–March 2016), the proportion of women and BAME candidates recommended for appointment was mostly at or above their proportions in the relevant eligible pools, and if not, only slightly and not statistically significantly below.[26] The same applied to religious and sexual minority candidates overall, substituting Census or Integrated Household Survey data in the absence of data concerning eligible pools.[27] No pool or population data was apparently available for candidates with a disability, although the proportions of recommended candidates generally reflected the proportions of applicants with a declared disability in each exercise.[28] Younger applicants (45 or under) tended to be somewhat over-represented and older applicants (46–65) somewhat under-represented in recommendations, but whether that was interpreted as a good or a bad thing was not made clear.[29] There were two exceptions to these patterns. First, in the selection exercise for Circuit Judges, lower proportions of women (25 per cent) and BAME candidates (6 per cent) were recommended for appointment than their proportions in the eligible pool (42 per cent and 11 per cent respectively).[30] Secondly, solicitors were consistently under-represented in recommendations compared to their proportions in the eligible pools for each exercise.[31]

On this analysis, the JAC achieved its diversity objectives and provided a fair process for all groups of candidates other than solicitors, or those who applied to be Circuit Judges. All it needs to do for most groups, therefore, is to keep up the good work. This helps to explain the upbeat JAC press-releases which accompany each statistical bulletin, and which highlight the proportions of women and minority candidates recommended for appointment and the instances in which recommendations exceeded a group's representation in either the eligible or the applicant pool. Although solicitors are always under-represented in recommendations compared to the eligible pool, here again the JAC chronotope contains no vision of the future. There is no horizon or time-frame set for improving the proportion of solicitors recommended, suggesting that the current pattern may continue indefinitely.

26 Judicial Appointments Commission, *Judicial Selection 2016*, p. 15, Table iii; p. 17, Table iv.
27 Ibid., pp. 23–24.
28 Ibid., pp. 20–21, Table vi.
29 Ibid., pp. 22–23, Table vii.
30 Ibid., Tables iii and iv.
31 Ibid., p. 19, Table v.

The pace of change

The final temporal aspect of the two chronotopes relates to the pace of change, the respective expectations about how, and how quickly, change in the overall profile of the judiciary will occur. These are connected to their respective views of the future: the JAC chronotope has no particular view on the pace of change, although by implication, overall diversity will be achieved by the incremental sum of however many merit-based and diversity-monitored selection exercises it takes (in the case of solicitors, this is likely be very slow indeed), while the critical chronotope wants change to occur as soon as possible. In this respect the difference between the two chronotopes may be analogized to the difference between common law and legislative approaches to law reform. The JAC chronotope is like the common law – a process of incremental development which broadly moves the law in line with social change while maintaining significant continuities with the past. The critical chronotope favours legislation – a means of bringing about a specific end by decisive and imperative legal change.

Mood

The dimension of 'mood' relates to the affective and aesthetic elements of scale. Here, again, the two chronotopes can be clearly contrasted. The views of spatiality and temporality within the JAC chronotope result in a mood of optimism and confidence. This was well illustrated, for example, in the riposte by Alexandra Marks, one of the members of the JAC, to Lord Sumption, reported in the *Guardian* on 1 October 2015. Marks was reported as saying that 'The rate at which women are being appointed judges is gathering momentum in a "snowball effect", ensuring gender equality on the bench is not that far away', that Sumption's comments were 'unduly pessimistic' and that '[t]he pace of change is accelerating'. According to the report, '[t]here will come a time – fairly soon, she believes – when we reach a tipping point, when the Supreme Court and [Court of Appeal] will suddenly begin to fill up with female judges'.[32] The JAC chronotope considers the current system to be effective. Its 'three-pronged approach to placing diversity at the heart of everything it does' incorporates 'fair and non-discriminatory selection processes', 'advertising and outreach' and 'working with others to break down barriers'.[33] All stages of the selection process are quality assured and equality proofed to ensure there is no discrimination or unintended bias, equality impact assessments are conducted on all changes in the selection process, and reasonable adjustments are provided for candidates who need them.[34] Everything that can be done is being done.

The critical views of spatiality and temporality, on the other hand, result in quite a different mood – one of urgency and impatience for change and, when

32 O. Bowcott, 'Number of female judges in UK "snowballing" despite equality row', *The Guardian*, 1 October 2014.

33 Judicial Appointments Commission, *Diversity Strategy*.

34 Ibid., and Judicial Appointments Commission, *Judicial Selection 2016*, p. 4.

faced with the slow pace of actual change and the lack of urgency demonstrated by other actors, of profound pessimism about the prospects for any real progress under the current system. The critical chronotope asks why the judicial appointment system is failing to produce greater judicial diversity and engages in analysis to identify the problems and structural changes that may produce better results.[35] It sees the road to equality impeded by multiple barriers representing entrenched interests, which need to be actively combated and overcome. From the perspective of the critical chronotope, Marks's predictions about the forthcoming advent of gender equality on the bench sound as unrealistically optimistic as Lord Taylor's assertion in 1992 quoted above.

Jurisdiction

The issue of jurisdiction is also crucial in explaining the difference between the JAC and critical chronotopes. This was hinted at above when discussing the JAC's lack of future goals concerning the composition of the judiciary as a whole. The JAC is technically responsible only for that section of the judiciary which it has played a role in selecting. This involves not only a temporal limitation but also a jurisdictional limitation. Importantly, the JAC's regular jurisdiction extends only as far as the High Court. The Court of Appeal and UKSC have separate selection processes,[36] and so when the JAC refers to the increasing numbers of women and BAME judges, it means increasing numbers within the lower courts and tribunals judiciary rather than within the senior judiciary.

By contrast, within the critical chronotope, 'the judiciary' primarily means the senior judiciary. It is the senior judiciary who are most visible, who have the greatest influence on the law, who carry the greatest authority and prestige, who are most important symbolically when it comes to measuring progress towards judicial diversity, and whose diversity has the greatest effect on the attitudes and aspirations of potential future candidates.[37] As the *Guardian* article referred to above astutely observed, '[a] few, judiciously chosen appointments in the next round of selections to the UK's Supreme Court could change public perceptions rapidly'.[38] The fact that women and BAME candidates are appointed as District Court judges, tribunal judges, and (sometimes) Circuit judges at or above their proportions in the relevant eligibility pools, or even that the overall proportions of women and BAME judges on those courts and tribunals may be increasing, is

35 See e.g. Bindman and Monaghan, *Judicial Diversity*; JUSTICE, *Increasing Judicial Diversity* and K. Malleson, 'The Disruptive Potential of Ceiling Quotas in Addressing Over-Representation in the Judiciary' in this collection.
36 CRA ss. 25–27B (Supreme Court), 76–79 (Court of Appeal).
37 See e.g. G. Goelzhauser, 'Diversifying State Supreme Courts', *Law and Society Review* 45, 2011, pp. 761, 773–774, who notes that the appointment of Black and women justices to the US Supreme Court created heightened attention to the issue of judicial diversity and, in the USA, increased the odds of States appointing their first Black or women judges.
38 Bowcott, 'Number of Female Judges in UK'.

perceived to be of little consequence while there remains only one woman on the UKSC, only eight women on the Court of Appeal, no women Heads of Division, and no BAME judges in any of those positions. Comparatively, it is well known that women and racial minorities are clustered at the lower ranks of judicial hierarchies, just as they are clustered in the lower ranks of the legal profession and other occupational hierarchies.[39] Increased representation would probably occur at lower levels under any appointment system. The real hard work, as in other occupations, lies in getting women and racial minority candidates to the top. In a very real sense then, their different jurisdictional orientations mean that in discussions about judicial diversity, the JAC and critical chronotopes are often talking about different things.

In *Chronotopes of Law*, Valverde discusses the way the mundane technicalities of jurisdiction have a depoliticizing effect. By hiding contradictions between different legal chronotopes and preventing incommensurable processes from clashing, they avoid awkward encounters which might tend to undermine the legal system's appearance of coherence and legitimacy. A similar argument might be made in the context of judicial diversity. The way the JAC's jurisdiction is constructed means that responsibility for appointments to the Court of Appeal and the UKSC, and hence for lack of progress towards greater diversity at those levels, is located elsewhere.

The question of jurisdiction bears further examination, however. The JAC does, in fact, have direct jurisdiction over appointments to the Court of Appeal, albeit not in the same way as over lower level appointments. The process and the composition of the selection panel are different, and governed by statute, but the Constitutional Reform Act 2005 as amended in 2013,[40] now makes it clear that Court of Appeal selection panels are convened by the JAC and constitute committees of the JAC.[41] Thus, Court of Appeal selection panels are presumably also subject to the JAC's public sector equality duty. And indeed, the JAC's 2016 Statistical Bulletin does include for the first time a report on the selection exercise for the Court of Appeal in 2012, together with grouped selection exercises for senior appointments including the Court of Appeal in 2013–2015. The results of these exercises were that women were recommended for appointment at or above their levels of representation in the applicant pool (10–15 per cent), while no BAME candidates or candidates with a disability, aged under 46 or with a background as a solicitor applied for these posts.[42]

But that is far from the end of the story. Diversity monitoring at lower levels includes comparisons between applications and recommendations, and also between the eligible pool and applications. For the Court of Appeal and other senior appointments, however, eligible pool data is not provided, making it impossible to gauge the relationship between the proportions of the relevant

39 See e.g. Schultz and Shaw (eds), *Women in the World's Legal Professions.*

40 Crime and Courts Act 2013 Schedule 13(4).

41 CRA, s. 79.

42 Judicial Appointments Commission, *Judicial Selection 2016*, pp. 15, 17, 19, 21–22.

groups in the eligible pool and their proportions applying. Yet the eligible pool may fairly readily be identified. In relation to lower level appointments, the JAC adopts the fiction[43] that everyone who meets the statutory criteria is eligible, that is, all those who have the specified number of years' post-qualification experience as a solicitor, barrister or CILEX as the case may be.[44] For the Court of Appeal therefore, the eligible pool would be all those who have seven years' post-qualification experience as a barrister or solicitor.[45] According to the 2016 Statistical Bulletin, at least 40 per cent of this pool are women, at least 9 per cent are from a BAME background, and at least 85 per cent are from a professional background of solicitor.[46] Eligible pool data are not available by disability or age, but it might be expected that a substantial proportion of the pool was aged under 46. If one follows the logic of diversity monitoring applied at lower levels, therefore, there is a serious disparity between the proportions of women, BAME groups, solicitors, and people aged under 46 in the eligible pool for the Court of Appeal and their representation in the applicant pool. Since the JAC's statutory duties include having regard to 'the need to encourage diversity in the range of persons available for judicial selection',[47] this ought to be a matter for concern. The JAC's general strategy for bridging gaps between the eligible and applicant pools is to engage in targeted outreach and awareness raising and to challenge unnecessarily restrictive selection criteria in order to increase the diversity of the applicant pool. The apparent lack of action in relation to the applicant pool for Court of Appeal appointments would suggest that this aspect of the JAC's Diversity Strategy is failing.

In practice, though, the issue here is a rather different one. It is generally understood that only judges with experience on the High Court will be appointed to the Court of Appeal.[48] Thus, the de facto eligibility pool for Court of Appeal appointments is the current High Court, which at the time of writing contained 106 judges, 21 per cent of whom were women, two were BAME, one was a former solicitor, and none were aged under 46. Thus, although there is a possibility that women are under-represented among applicants to the Court of Appeal, the real problem is the lack of diversity of the High Court, considered as an eligibility pool for the Court of Appeal. It follows that the only effective way to increase the diversity of applicants to the Court of Appeal is to increase the diversity of the High Court. This is clearly within the JAC's jurisdiction. In turn, the only effective way to increase the diversity of the High Court is to increase the

43 It is a fiction because candidates meeting the statutory criteria must, in practice, also meet other non-statutory criteria in order to be considered seriously for appointment; in particular, for salaried judicial posts, the requirement that candidates have gained at least two years' judicial experience in a fee-paid post prior to appointment. Since it is more difficult to obtain data on the actual eligible pool, the notional eligible pool is reasonably used as a proxy.

44 Judicial Appointments Commission, *Judicial Selection 2016*, p. 13.

45 Senior Courts Act 1981, s. 10; Tribunals, Courts and Enforcement Act 2007, s. 50.

46 Judicial Appointments Commission, *Judicial Selection 2016*, p. 13.

47 CRA, s. 64.

48 See e.g. Courts and Tribunals Judiciary, 'Court of Appeal judges', Courts and Tribunals Judiciary website.

diversity of the pools from which High Court judges are in practice drawn, that is, the ranks of Recorders and Deputy High Court judges. These are also squarely within the JAC's jurisdiction. Here again, the JAC's Diversity Strategy falls short. When it comes to increasing the diversity of eligibility pools, its strategy is to work with other organizations, including the Bar Council and the Law Society, 'to identify ways of improving judicial diversity'.[49] While this may help to diversify the eligibility pool for entry-level positions (including Recorders), it is only an indirect means of increasing diversity further up the judicial hierarchy. At higher levels, it is the JAC itself which has the major capacity to achieve greater diversity in eligibility pools by means of its selection processes for the roles and courts which constitute those pools, yet as explained above, it considers the courts and positions for which it undertakes selection exercises only as receivers of recommendations, not as sources of applications. Arguably, this is a question of jurisdiction. The JAC interprets its jurisdiction as being over the selection process and the outcomes of selection but not over the inputs to selection, that is, eligible pools above entry level. This is a matter of choice rather than a statutorily-imposed limitation.

The same argument applies in relation to appointments to the UKSC. Appointments themselves are clearly beyond the JAC's jurisdiction. UKSC selection commissions are convened by the Lord Chancellor, and must only include one member of the JAC, alongside members of the equivalent commissions for Scotland and Northern Ireland and representation from the Supreme Court itself.[50] But for most Supreme Court appointments (other than those of Scottish and Northern Irish justices), the JAC again has jurisdiction over the de facto eligible pool – which in this case is constituted by members of the Court of Appeal – and over the pipeline leading into that eligible pool.

Apart from the issue of eligibility pools, diversity monitoring in the case of Court of Appeal and UKSC appointments is complicated by the fact that for each selection exercise there may be only one appointee, which makes it difficult to compare the profile of recommended appointees with that of the applicant pool. One response to this difficulty would be to make comparisons over time rather than only in relation to individual selection exercises. Thus, if women currently make up 21 per cent of the High Court and 18 per cent of the Court of Appeal, one would expect around one in five Court of Appeal and UKSC appointments to be women. If five or more recommendations were being made in a single selection process, one would see whether that was the case for the single process. For example, there will shortly be a number of vacancies on the UKSC, with six justices due to retire by the end of 2018, and the argument for engaging in an aggregate selection process for these six vacancies is compelling.[51] But if only one

49 Judicial Appointments Commission, *Diversity Strategy*.
50 CRA, ss. 26–27.
51 The Supreme Court announced on 11 July 2016 that 'recruitment for these vacancies will be grouped together in joint selection exercises to take place over the next two years'. Further details were provided in February 2017, indicating that there would be

recommendation is made per selection process, then it would alternatively be possible to determine whether proportional representation is achieved over the course of five selection processes. This would require a shift within the JAC chronotope in relation to temporality as well as jurisdiction.

In fact, the JAC's policy is not to report on any selection exercise for which there are fewer than 10 recommendations in order to maintain candidate confidentiality.[52] It deals with this by grouping small selection exercises and reporting on their results in aggregate. For example, as noted above, the 2016 Statistical Bulletin reports on grouped Court of Appeal and other senior appointments for the period 2013–15. This grouping – which does include aggregation over time as well as within year – makes the numbers up to 11 recommendations for appointment, thereby enabling observance of the confidentiality policy. But the nature of the grouping then becomes a reason not to provide statistics on the eligible pool for these appointments, since 'proportions in the eligible pool may differ due to eligibility criteria and when the exercise was run'.[53] While this is technically true, in reality, differences over time and between the eligibility criteria for different appointments will have made a negligible difference to the proportions of relevant groups in either the de jure or de facto eligibility pools for these appointments, and approximately accurate figures would be more valuable for the purposes of diversity monitoring than no figures. Moreover, the confidentiality policy itself is difficult to fathom. Successful applications become public knowledge when judges are appointed, so concerns to maintain the confidentiality of those recommended for appointment are unnecessary. Candidate confidentiality would be at risk if the *eligible pool* was so small that applicants would in practice be identifiable. But this is not the case for women on either the High Court or the Court of Appeal. It is the case for those with BAME or solicitor backgrounds on the High Court, but this would be so due to their extremely low numbers in the eligible pool, regardless of the number of recommendations to be made. Indeed, to state that no candidates who applied for senior judicial posts declared they were from a BAME background or had the professional background of solicitor[54] might be seen as a breach of confidentiality for the tiny number of judges from these categories on the High Court. Thus, the best way both to protect confidentiality and to promote diversity is to increase the numbers of under-represented groups in relevant eligible pools. It is not a matter of one consideration yielding to another but of both aims working in the same direction.

In summary, while at first glance the JAC and critical chronotopes simply appear to operate on the basis of different jurisdictions, further analysis suggests that it is the JAC's diversity strategy which is limited rather than its jurisdiction. The JAC's diversity monitoring does not extend to the disparity between eligible

two selection processes, one to appoint three Justices in 2017 and the second to appoint a further three Justices in 2018.

52 Judicial Appointments Commission, *Judicial Selection*, p. 8.

53 Ibid., p. 15, Table iii, Note 1.

54 Ibid., pp. 16, 18.

pools and applications at the most senior levels of the judiciary where it does have jurisdiction, it does not acknowledge responsibility for the composition of those eligible pools, and it too readily avoids diversity monitoring at senior levels by reference to claims of time and eligibility differences and confidentiality requirement which do not stand up to scrutiny. While the JAC does not have jurisdiction over UKSC appointments, it does have jurisdiction over everything that leads up to a UKSC appointment, and thus cannot entirely distance itself from critical concerns about the lack of diversity on the UKSC.

Conclusion

To summarize the features of the two chronotopes, the JAC chronotope is focused on the lower courts and tribunals judiciary, and on providing fair selection processes for appointments to those positions. On its own terms, the current situation is good. Candidates (other than solicitors) are applying and being recommended broadly in proportion to their representation in the relevant eligible pools, and there is confidence that this state of affairs can be maintained. Although the JAC does not formally articulate a future vision for the judiciary as a whole, when specifically asked, it is optimistic about increasing diversity at all levels. The critical chronotope, on the other hand, is essentially concerned with the composition of the senior judiciary. From its comparative and historical perspective the current situation is poor and moving too slowly. It has a clear vision of an ideal future and would like that vision to be achieved with some urgency. It is, however, pessimistic about the prospects of that occurring under current arrangements, and therefore believes the current arrangements need to be changed, drawing upon international experience on the relationship between judicial appointments systems and increasing judicial diversity.[55]

Through a chronotopic analysis, I hope to have shown that both of these positions are, for the most part, rational and defensible. But they exist on fundamentally different planes in terms of scale – spatial, temporal and affective. They represent entirely different ways of apprehending the same set of circumstances; effectively they speak a different language. For the most part, therefore, it is not possible to adjudicate in any meaningful way between them. The exception is in relation to jurisdiction, where there is more commonality than might at first sight appear, and where some of the differences appear to be a product of self-imposed restrictions by the JAC which may not be defensible.

Where genuine differences exist, the analysis does suggest some possibilities for finding middle ground between the two chronotopes. One is for critics to be more understanding of the JAC's temporal limitations, and for the JAC to be more

55 See Bindman and Monaghan, *Judicial Diversity*; Kenney, 'Which Judicial Selection Systems'; Hurwitz and Lanier, 'Explaining Judicial Diversity'; Iyer, 'The Fleeting Benefits of Appointments Commissions'; Hurwitz and Lanier, 'Diversity in State and Federal Appellate Courts'; Goelzhauser, 'Diversifying State Supreme Courts'. While JUSTICE's *Increasing Judicial Diversity* report does not draw on international experience with judicial appointment systems, it draws instead on experiences of increasing diversity in other industry sectors and professional occupations.

understanding of the critical sense of historical injustice and related expectations. Another is for critics to be more appreciative of the work of the JAC within its core jurisdiction. At the same time, the JAC could respond to the widely-held concern with the composition of the senior judiciary by developing ways of monitoring and reporting on diversity within the senior judiciary commensurate with its jurisdiction at that level and in relation to eligible pools. Finally, critics could direct some of their attention away from the JAC towards others with statutory responsibility for judicial diversity.[56] As well as the rather limited duties imposed on the JAC in relation to encouraging diversity in the selection process, the Constitutional Reform Act 2005, as amended by the Crime and Courts Act 2013, provides that both the Lord Chancellor and the Lord Chief Justice 'must take such steps as [they consider] appropriate for the purpose of encouraging judicial diversity'.[57] It follows that some of the critical focus in relation to judicial appointments might be turned towards the Lord Chancellor and the Lord Chief Justice and the steps they have (or have not) taken to encourage judicial diversity.

At the same time, critics must acknowledge the regrettable fact that no-one has statutory responsibility for achieving a more diverse judiciary and hence, no-one can be held to account for failing to do so.[58] The deliberately limited mandate given to the JAC and to the Lord Chancellor and Lord Chief Justice, the pervasive language of 'encouragement' rather than goals, purposes or achievement, is a political problem for which the statutory actors cannot be blamed. As noted above, the only point at which anyone may have the 'purpose' of increasing judicial diversity is in the application of the equal merit provision. This points to the importance of the scope of the JAC's policy on when the equal merit provision will be applied,[59] and critics have argued that the policy is 'disappointing cautious' in this regard,[60] but this is a slender basis on which to build a more diverse judiciary. As a matter of governance, the careful diffusion of bounded roles and powers in relation to judicial appointments between the JAC, the Lord Chief Justice, the Lord Chancellor and UKSC selection commissions enables the goal of judicial diversity to disappear between the cracks. When critics call for systemic change, therefore, their criticism should be directed not so much at the JAC for failing to fulfil a function it does not have, but at the current statutory arrangements which leave that function inadequately addressed.

56 Those who have done so include Paterson and Paterson, *Guarding the Guardians*, and G. Gee, R. Hazell, K. Malleson and P. O'Brien, *The Politics of Judicial Independence in the UK's Changing Constitution*, Cambridge: Cambridge University Press, 2015, both of whom are critical of the judiciary's role in hampering faster progress towards judicial diversity.

57 CRA, s. 137A.

58 JUSTICE, *Increasing Judicial Diversity*, Part III includes proposals to address this issue.

59 Judicial Appointments Commission, *Equal Merit Provision*.

60 G. Gee and K. Malleson, 'Judicial Appointments, Diversity and the Equal Merit Provision', *UK Constitutional Law Blog*, 16 May 2014.

Reflection

Cordella Bart-Stewart

Cordella Bart-Stewart is a solicitor and a fee-paid judge of the First Tier Tribunal (Immigration and Asylum Chamber). She is also the Executive Director of the Black Solicitors Network, which works to support and facilitate students and solicitors of African and African-Caribbean heritage entry into, and progression through, the legal profession and judiciary. Formed in 1995, the BSN has over 7,000 members in England and Wales and is the primary voice of black solicitors in England and Wales.

In introducing the Judicial Diversity Statistics in 2016, after commenting on the improved position as regards gender, the Lord Chief Justice said:

> [t]he percentage of BAME judges under 50 years of age has increased from 12 per cent to 16 per cent which provides some encouragement for the future … [but] we are disappointed that there has been no improvement in either courts or tribunals in the total percentage of judges from a Black Asian and Minority Ethnic background.

Recent statistics from the Judicial Appointments Commission (JAC) and the Judicial Office show that the number of judges of known black and minority ethnic origin at both Court and Tribunal level have remained almost static over the past few years. The man or woman on the Clapham omnibus might reasonably conclude that the appointment *process* is broken and needs fixing – and yet the solutions currently applied are more about fixing the *candidate*.

It is often said that the reason for the low numbers of BME judges is their failure to apply. I decided to apply to be an Immigration Adjudicator in an open competition in the dying days of the so-called 'tap on the shoulder' – although I received no obvious tap on my shoulder and had no idea who did whatever tapping did occur. As a middle-aged black woman who came to the UK as a child, was educated in state schools then a Polytechnic, who set up and grew a successful small business, was involved with various community organizations and most importantly was a good lawyer, I was confident that I had the required skills and experience to be a good judge. I completed an application form where I was able to demonstrate this. There was no qualifying test but a fairly robust interview which I felt I handled well. Many months later I was informed that I had been recommended for appointment. This was 1999–2000. I think at that time the right balance had been struck. The Lord Chancellor understood and encouraged diversity. A number of BME contemporaries made successful applications to the Courts and Tribunals around that time and this is the base from which the JAC started and was expected to improve.

I am a founder member and Executive Director of the Black Solicitors Network (BSN). The BSN was established in 1995. Its core aim is to help students and solicitors of African and African-Caribbean heritage access and progress in the profession which includes the judiciary. From 1997 I have been representing the BSN on the issue of better diversity in the judiciary including drafting responses to consultations, being part of focus groups and workshops and giving evidence. I have also had a couple of meetings with the JAC's Commissioners. I left each meeting disappointed and feeling we were being patronized. There was a growing feeling that the JAC did not understand the inherent barriers facing black solicitors. There was a focus on encouraging applications from solicitors in the city of London as if this is where all the talent lies. Also, at the time, the tap on the shoulder still existed for some appointments.

In December 2008 the *Law Society Gazette* ran on its front page an article in which I called for an independent review of the appointment process and indicated that BSN would not take part in further roadshows, which I considered to be mere marketing exercises. An invitation came for a further meeting which was much more convivial and a good working relationship with the JAC developed. The JAC was persuaded to fund a number of roadshows co-hosted by the BSN for BME lawyers. As well as a Commissioner, a number of JAC staff attended including competition managers who were able to break down and explain in detail the application process and what was being sought from the candidate at each stage. The first was at the JAC offices and was oversubscribed. Two others were held in London and one in Birmingham. All were highly successful and the format was incorporated in future JAC roadshows.

From speaking with solicitors I learned they were also wary of the introduction of role-play exercises as part of the selection process fearing this favoured the Bar. At that time there were few Solicitor-Advocates. I was able to put this to the JAC and, working with Law Society, a role-play video was produced to appear on the JAC and Law Society websites. I was consulted on the redesign of a more informative and user-friendly website for the JAC and persuaded the Law Society to commission and fund application workshops for aspiring BME candidates as part of their commitment to increase the diversity of the judiciary.

These initiatives were undoubtedly successful as the number of *applications* from those declaring BME ethnicity increased substantially. The fact is that BME lawyers apply in the same proportion – and often in proportionately higher numbers – than the proportion of the ethnic population in the UK and eligible BME pool. However, this has not followed through to recommendations and *appointments*.

In recent years the JAC has not had anywhere near the same level of engagement with BSN or other special interest groups as it did its early years.

Communication is limited and sporadic and for the last few years, non-existent. The focus is on funding roadshows, but without any real consideration of their effectiveness, or at least so it seems to many outsiders. It was from having those at times testy conversations that we were able to show the JAC where the barriers were and come up with solutions. Having raised awareness amongst BME lawyers, there has not been the opportunity, or it seems interest, to discuss with us initiatives that might help to turn more applications into sound appointments.

JAC figures often include competitions for non-legal tribunal members. There has been success in that area. However, if these are excluded, the number of BME judges is exceptionally poor. It is far lower than their proportionate number in the legal profession and society as a whole. This is a concern. As stated by the Advisory Panel on Judicial Appointments chaired by Baroness Neuberger in 2010 'Failure to appoint well-qualified candidates from diverse backgrounds to judicial office represents exclusion from participation in power'. A visibly diverse judiciary is a tangible expression of inclusion and vital to a stable, cohesive society.

The JAC success in appointing non-legal members from BME backgrounds is evidence that an independent commission can work well for non-under-represented groups. There should be questions asked about why the JAC is so successful at appointing non-legal members of BME ethnicity but not legal members. Is there a different concept of merit, conscious or otherwise when it comes to lawyers? Is there a higher threshold?

One explanation often offered by the JAC, without any supporting evidence, is that BME candidates are applying too early in their career. Again, the fault is seen to be with the candidate. Such an explanation is at odds with the JAC having reduced the minimum number of years in practice that is required before being eligible to hold judicial office. Further, the evidence is that the age at which judges are appointed has reduced, significantly in some areas.

Even before the JAC, the view of many was – and remains – that one of the biggest barriers is the concept of 'merit'. It is difficult to define or measure objectively and evidently militates against changing the status quo. The actual test applied to BME legal candidates (not just confined to the JAC) would seem to be *exceptionally* good and *exceptionally* worthy. Potential is not measured.

In 2013 the JAC consulted on the definition of merit and the 'ability to understand and deal fairly' quality now encompasses an awareness and understanding of diversity of the communities which the courts and tribunals serve, commitment to justice, independence, public service and fair treatment and willingness to listen with patience and courtesy. It is welcome recognition that candidates must have an awareness and understanding of diversity but unclear how this can lead to an increase in the appointment of candidates from under-represented groups. It is no different to a requirement to have in place a diversity policy. It does not evidence structural change. Merely tinkering with words does not change ingrained attitudes.

If there were emphasis on a judicial career this might have an effect on the type of people selected and improve diversity. The greatest trial lawyer is unlikely to be the best manager of people, have any idea of running a business or organization or be a good and effective leader, all the qualities that should be essential skills in a modern judiciary. There must be proper continuous training and professional development, a system of mentors and appraisal at all levels of the judiciary. An effective appraisal system should be taking forward those with potential for higher office and not leaving them to stagnate.

Whilst there have been various initiatives to look at the issue of improving the diversity of the judiciary, as with increasing the number of women on boards, it is unlikely that there will ever be a proportionate number of BME lawyers without imposing targets for selection of candidates from certain groups. The JAC has a general duty to have regard to diversity. 'Regard' is not an obligation to achieve diversity. It is time that the JAC is set specific targets for the delivery of measurable objectives.

The impact and consequence of a system that excludes large sections of the community is real and diversity does matter. There is a lot of focus on higher court appointments, which is good, however for the majority of the black and ethnic minority population engagement with the justice system is more likely to be at the local Magistrates, County Court and Tribunals. Black men are disproportionately arrested, charged, convicted and sent to prison. It should be a matter of great concern that the number of BME District Judges (Magistrates Court) are in single figures when the Magistrates Court may be the only interface they, their family and peers have with the judiciary and court system. The Judicial Office figures reveal that London has one of the lowest percentages of BME Judges in England and Wales although its ethnic minority population is over 55 per cent. Until these disparities are taken seriously and addressed the perception of large sections of the population that judges are remote, do not reflect society and that the system is unfair, will persist.

My closing thought, however, relates to the role of the professions. They need to do better. The Law Society publication *Earnings and work of private practice solicitors in 2007*, published in February 2009, is an in depth survey focusing on the various types of solicitor in private practice. The survey revealed that:

- On average BME solicitors earn 17 per cent less than their white counterparts (after taking account of gender, grade, firm size and all other variables)
- 34 per cent of BME solicitors are more likely to take on legal aid work in comparison to 23 per cent white solicitors.
- 77 per cent of these solicitors will spend over 50 per cent of their time doing legal aid in comparison to 54 per cent of white legal aid practitioners.

And yet, the authors concluded '[s]uch differentials, though large do not in themselves provide evidence of discriminatory or unfair practices in the case of gender or ethnicity'.

There lies the problem. There are numerous studies limited to moments in time but no real interest in rooting out and tackling what may be '*discriminatory or unfair practices*'. There is much hand wringing but until BME lawyers are considered as worthy and as competent as their white counterparts the prospects for a truly diverse judiciary remains ever remote.

13 The disruptive potential of ceiling quotas in addressing over-representation in the judiciary

Kate Malleson

Introduction

It is widely agreed that greater diversity is needed in the composition of the senior judiciary in the UK, and that reforms to date have not brought about change which has gone far enough or moved fast enough. The official explanation for the continued homogenous make-up of the judiciary has framed the problem in terms of the under-representation of certain groups; most notably women, BAME lawyers, LGBT+ lawyers, and those from less wealthy backgrounds.

Drawing on Rainbow Murray's work on gender quotas in legislatures,[1] this chapter argues for a shift in the conceptualization of the problem away from the under-representation of marginalized identity groups to the over-representation of dominant identity groups; most notably white male barristers from affluent backgrounds. This shift is not purely semantic. It has a radical effect on how we understand the 'problem' of judicial diversity and its potential solution. In particular, it reveals the disruptive potential of quotas when reframed as a 'ceiling' to cap the over-representation of dominant identity groups.

The effect of this change is to shift the burden of proof from under-represented groups to demonstrate that their inclusion will not disrupt the merit principle onto over-represented groups to demonstrate why they should continue to enjoy preferential treatment which, prima facie, undermines merit. Reframed as a ceiling to cap over-representation, quotas are no longer a temporary special measure which has the potential to damage a merit-based system but an intrinsic, essential and ongoing requirement of a merit-based appointment system. This reframing also changes the design of the optimum quota system in relation to its subjects, levels and time-frame.

Despite the slow pace of change and the fact that much of it remains confined to the lower echelons of the judiciary, there remains considerable resistance (especially amongst officials and judges) to reforms that would lead to real and rapid change, such as quotas.

1 R. Murray, 'Quotas for Men: Reframing Gender Quotas as a Means of Improving Representation for All', *American Political Science Review* 108, 2014, 520–532.

Homogeneity, merit and under-representation

The strikingly homogenous composition of the senior judiciary in England and Wales and the UK Supreme Court may be more extreme than is found in many other countries, but it is not unique. All higher courts around the world, whether in democratic countries or otherwise, are drawn from narrow identity groups which mirror the power relations of their society; most notably, but not exclusively, in terms of gender, ethnicity, religion, socio-economic background, age, disability and sexual orientation. Despite widespread expressions of official commitment to greater diversity and the institution of varied reforms across different judicial appointments processes, no country has achieved reflective diversity in even one of these identity characteristics across all ranks of judges let alone diversity across the full range.

In England and Wales this problem has been the subject of increasing scrutiny and criticism over the last two decades, with a consensus emerging as a result amongst politicians, lawyers and judges on the need to increase judicial diversity. A wide variety of different explanations have been put forward in both official and academic discourse for the continued lack of progress. Although these explanations differ in detail they share a common approach which envisages the problem in terms of barriers to entry faced by certain identity groups leading to their under-representation.[2] The particular characteristics of the groups identified as under-represented has changed over the last 20 years. Originally limited to gender and ethnicity, it now includes age, disability and sexual orientation. Nor are these current categories definitive, as the President of the UK Supreme Court, Lord Neuberger has acknowledged: 'we should not limit minorities to the well-known categories ... people with approaches, beliefs and mindsets which are not typical of a particular walk of life may well be wrongly under-represented in that walk of life.'[3]

Just as the recognized categories of under-representation have expanded so too has the range and location of the barriers to inclusion. Some are identified as located in society generally and include: socio-economic disadvantage inequalities in the education system, the gendered division of labour as well as direct and indirect discrimination. Others are seen as the consequence of the individual choices, preferences and confidence levels of potential candidates from under-represented groups, their career patterns, the effects of 'ghettoization' in the legal profession, the judicial application process, judicial working arrangements and the judicial career structure.

The responses to these varied explanations for under-representation have been equally diverse and extensive. Since 1999 at least sixteen official inquiries and reports have been produced, generating an array of proposals for reform, many of which have been implemented.[4] The different policy responses share a common

2 See e.g. Lord Neuberger, 'Rainbow Lecture 2014 on Diversity', House of Commons, 12 March 2014.

3 Murray, 'Quotas for Men', para 4.

4 The most recent report being The General Council of the Bar, *Snapshot: The Experience of Self-Employed Women at the Bar*, London: The Bar Council, 2015.

goal of seeking to dismantle the barriers both in the legal profession and the judicial appointments process and to encourage and support those from under-represented groups to meet the qualification criteria and to apply for judicial office in greater numbers. These policies have included institutional reform such as the creation of the Judicial Appointments Commission (JAC) in 2006 and procedural changes to the application and assessment processes such as the development of merit-based competencies and the use of assessment centres. Other initiatives have sought to change the priorities and attitudes of under-represented identity groups, for example through outreach programmes, mentoring and shadowing, flexible working arrangements, the creation of diversity networks and diversity officers, diversity road-shows and 'myth-busting campaigns'.[5]

The underlying and generally uncontested assumption which underpins these policies and initiatives is that the problem is essentially operational rather than structural; if the right reforms (whether internal to the judiciary or external to the legal profession and beyond) can be implemented so as to dismantle the myriad barriers which disadvantage under-represented groups, the appointments process can then fulfil its duty to select on merit alone whilst also transforming the make-up of the judiciary.

Moreover, the early years of that reform process were marked by a sense of optimism. Lord Taylor, when Lord Chief Justice in 1992, confidently expressed the view that real change would be seen within five years. However, as time went by and change proved elusive, this confidence evaporated. Lord Sumption, a Supreme Court Justice and former member of the JAC, argued in 2012 that expectations had been unrealistic concluding that it would take around fifty years to achieve a fully diverse judiciary.[6] Even more pessimistically, a review of women's progress at the Bar in 2015 concluded that: 'current trends suggest that with the present model of practice at the Bar a 50:50 gender balance among all practising barristers is unlikely ever to be achieved'.[7]

The general response to the fact that the problem is more intractable than originally thought has been to argue that efforts need to be redoubled to tackle the more widespread, diffuse and entrenched barriers faced by under-represented groups. This approach has included a new willingness to engage with more proactive measures to address the barriers. Where originally it was hoped that Lord Irvine's rallying cry 'don't be shy, apply!' would be sufficient to bring about change, more recent recommendations include the creation of a judicial career path and the introduction of positive action measures in the form of a 'diversity support initiative' specifically for candidates from under-represented groups who might be applying for deputy High Court posts (women, BAME lawyers and those coming from less advantaged social or educational backgrounds).[8] This last

5 For full details, see Judicial Diversity Taskforce, *Improving Judicial Diversity – Annual Report*, London: Ministry of Justice, 2013.

6 Lord Sumption, 'Home Truths about Judicial Diversity', Bar Council Law Reform Lecture, 15 November 2012, p. 14.

7 The General Council of the Bar, *Momentum Measures: Creating a Diverse Judiciary*, London: The Bar Council, 2015, para 2.3.

8 www.judiciary.gov.uk/about-the-judiciary/judges-career-paths/diversity-support-initiative/

initiative, introduced in 2015, involved designated posts for candidates with no previous experience of sitting as a part-time judge (which often includes lawyers from non-conventional social and professional backgrounds), and were attached to a tailored programme of mentoring and support.

These more radical initiatives represent a substantive ratcheting up of the response to the problem of a lack of judicial diversity and reflect the increasing pressure which the judicial appointments process is under as a result of the lack of progress. What has not changed is the underlying approach to the problem in which the focus remains on the under-representation of certain groups and where the solution lies in tackling the barriers faced by these groups. This approach also elides into a focus on the ways in which members of these groups can be helped to adapt in order to more closely resemble candidates from over-represented identity groups both in relation to appointment and promotion. Rosemary Hunter has described this as the 'remedial model' in which those from diverse backgrounds 'are to be properly acculturated, assimilated, inculcated with appropriate norms of behaviour and steered in the right direction so they are able to overcome their unpropitious origins and made capable of progression.'[9] The remedial model which focuses on the under-representation of traditionally marginalized group underlies and informs most official and academic responses to the problem of judicial diversity in the UK since the early 1990s. If real and rapid progress is to be made, an alternative and more radical approach is required.

Homogeneity, merit and over-representation

The alternative approach advocated here is to reframe the problem as one of *over*-representation. This change is more than semantic; it has a radical effect on how we understand the lack of judicial diversity and its potential solution. If the ongoing homogeneity in the judiciary is understood in terms of over-representation, the spotlight moves from the barriers to appointment which keep under-represented groups *out* and falls instead on the ways in which the current system keep members of certain identity groups *in*. It draws attention to the fact that while the precise composition of the included and excluded groups may change over time, they consistently correspond to the most powerful groups in the legal profession which, in turn, correspond to the most powerful identity groups in society at large. As the composition of those powerful groups changes so the judicial appointments process, in turn, adapts to meet their interests.[10] It reveals that the judicial appointments process, even if it functions at its optimum, is merit-based only to the extent that it can select the best candidates from a pool of the

9 R. Hunter, 'Judicial Diversity and the "New" Judge', in H. Sommerlad, S. Harris-Short, S. Vaughan and R. Young (eds), *The Futures of Legal Education and the Legal Profession*, Oxford: Hart Publishing, 2015, pp. 79–96.

10 See K. Malleson 'Rethinking the Merit Principle in the Judicial Appointments Process', *Journal of Law and Society* 33, 2006, pp. 126–140.

most powerful identity groups of the day not from the total pool of the strongest potential candidates.

In the early years of the judicial diversity debate, it was the relationship between merit and diversity per se which was seen as problematic and it was common for objections to be raised to efforts to increase diversity on the grounds that they would undermine the merit-based system. Today such claims are generally recognized as conceptually flawed and it is normal to hear that diversity 'is not merely consistent with merit: it reinforces merit'.[11] But while the alleged tension between merit and diversity has been reconciled in mainstream diversity discourse, a much more serious, though less commonly articulated dilemma remains: How is it possible to claim that an appointments system which produces ongoing and systematic homogeneity in those appointed is essentially merit-based without concluding that the current appointees are somehow more fit to be judges than those from other groups? Although few commentators would now (publicly at least) claim that white, male barristers from affluent backgrounds are inherently more intelligent or morally suited to be judges, this dilemma inevitably gives rise to ambivalent expressions about the extent to which the current system, if genuinely merit-based, is a reflection of the distribution of potential judicial quality. This ambivalence is illustrated by two recent statements by Lord Sumption. On the one hand that; 'any group of the most talented people of their generation is going to be unrepresentative'[12] and on the other that: 'ambition and talent (actual or potential) are randomly distributed through the population'.[13]

The increasing tendency is for judges, lawyers and politicians to support the latter view (again, at least publicly) and to reject the claim that talent is more often found in white, wealthy male barristers.[14] There is also an increasing willingness to acknowledge that the ongoing homogeneity casts doubt on the extent to which the system is fully merit-based. As Lord Neuberger has noted, if, for example, women would make equally good judges as men then the fact that 80 per cent or 90 per cent of judges are male '... suggests, purely on a statistical basis, that we do not have the best people because there must be some women out there who are better than the less good men who are judges'.[15] What is true of women must be equally true of members of every other under-represented identity group, most notably those from the majority of the population who come from family backgrounds outside the wealthiest proportion of society. If it is generally

11 Neuberger, 'Rainbow Lecture', para 15.

12 W. Steavenson, 'Jonathan Sumption: The Brain of Britain', *The Guardian*, 6 August 2015.

13 J. Sumption, 'The Constitutional Reform Act 2005' in Judicial Appointments Commission, *Judicial Appointments: Balancing Independence, Accountability and Legitimacy*, London: Judicial Appointments Commission, 2010, 36.

14 Karon Monaghan and Geoffrey Bindman described this view 'as both offensive and unsupportable on any rational test of merit' (G. Bindman and K. Monaghan, *Judicial Diversity: Accelerating Change*, London: Labour Party, 2014 p. 12).

15 Lord Neuberger, Oral Evidence to the House of Lords Select Committee on the Constitution Inquiry into the Judicial Appointments Process, 16 November 2011, Q.251.

acknowledged that judicial ambition and talent are randomly distributed in society and that the judicial appointments process remains closed to many, if not most people who might make good judges it becomes difficult to maintain the claim that the system is merit-based in a meaningful sense. At the very least it must suggest that the system is only partially merit-based.

The standard official response to this dilemma of focusing on barriers which are extrinsic and pre-existing to the judicial appointments process, amounts to the claim that the judicial appointments process is as merit-based as it can be given the limited material it is given to work with. However, for this to provide even a partial defence of the current selection regime would require the judicial appointments process to be structurally distinct from the legal profession. Yet this claim is unsustainable. In a system in which senior judges are appointed from senior members of the legal profession, the judicial appointments process inevitably reflects the arrangements of the legal profession and the two are structurally interconnected.[16] Moreover, judges continued to play a central role in the judicial appointments process as members of the JAC, in devising the application tests, through writing references for candidates etc.[17] The construction and application of what constitutes merit for the purposes of judicial selection therefore has been shaped, over many years, to fit the career patterns, preferences, skills, qualities and experiences of a small group of barristers who are dominated by certain identity groups. The selection of senior judges from this elite corps of barristers is a consequence of the historical establishment of the Bar as the more powerful branch of the legal profession and, within the Bar, the dominance of a limited number of London chambers. The determining feature of the way the formal and informal merit criteria were formulated, interpreted and applied in practice over the years has been to privilege this sub-set of lawyers. In effect, they have been the beneficiaries of a protracted and honed system of preferential treatment.

There is nothing pre-ordained about the composition of the judicial candidate pool or the construction and application of what constitutes merit in the judicial appointments process. Leaving aside the more radical, though perfectly defensible question of whether judges actually need to be practising lawyers (given that many judges around the world are not – including approximately 21,500 lay magistrates in England and Wales), and even accepting that judicial candidates should be limited to those who fulfil the current eligibility criteria, the potential candidate pool is, and always has been, many times larger and more diverse than the current pool. In practice, most eligible lawyers, however talented, have no real prospect of being appointed to the judiciary, particularly to the senior judiciary.

The construction of merit as a reflection of the interests of the dominant members of the legal profession is clearly illustrated by the age profile of the

16 E. Barmes and K. Malleson, 'The Legal Profession as Gatekeepers to the Judiciary: Design Faults in Measures to Enhance Diversity', *Modern Law Review* 74, 2011, pp. 245–271.

17 See G. Gee, R. Hazell, K. Malleson and P. O'Brien, *The Politics of Judicial Independence in the UK's Changing Constitution*, Cambridge: Cambridge University Press, 2015.

judiciary. Although the formal eligibility rules require only that a candidate must have had seven years of legal experience, senior judges have almost all been appointed in their 50s or 60s. Even if we accept the argument that most candidates would not acquire the skills necessary to be a good judge until they had undertaken some years working in a legal field and also that ability generally falls away with extreme age, a system based solely on merit would expect a distribution of merit amongst an age-range from approximately 30 to 80. The near monopoly of appointees around the age of 55 is a reflection of the close alignment of the judicial appointments process with the career patterns and preferences of the traditional candidate pool rather than an objective search for judicial merit in the widest possible candidate pool.

Given the structural connections between the legal profession, the judiciary and the judicial appointments process, this outcome was inevitable. The segmented and stratified recruitment pools from which different judicial ranks are selected are neither accidental nor the result of a neutral and objective external determination of which people might make the best judges. Instead they are the consequence of gate-keeping by dominant identity groups in the legal profession.[18] Because the candidate pool and the construction of merit have a reflexive relationship to each other, the preferential treatment of these identity groups in judicial appointments is not an aberration or a distortion but an inevitable and in-built consequence of their historical and ongoing dominance within the legal profession.

The system is therefore merit-based only in the limited sense that it seeks to apply the selection criteria between the different candidates who are the beneficiaries of the preferential treatment of a system designed to best fit with their qualities, experiences and expectations. It is not one in which the best lawyer is appointed to the senior judiciary but generally the best white, male, wealthy barrister in late middle-age. It is thus a 'merit plus' system in that other factors operate in addition to merit and is also an 'iceberg' merit system in that the great majority of the system is below the waterline so that the merit system is a small visible part which comes into play at the end of a long process of preferential treatment.

In the past, when the career patterns or demographics of the dominant identity groups in the legal profession have changed, the judicial appointments process has adapted to fit them. When, for example, a period in the army or navy was a normal feature of the education and training of young upper-middle class men, military experience as an officer was identified as evidence of potential judicial competence. As military experience died out so too did the value placed on it by the judicial appointments process.[19] This correlation between military and judicial skills now seems irrational to the point of being absurd. Yet it is likely that the assumption which underpins the current system that evidence of advocacy skills provides good evidence of judicial potential will in time seem equally, if not more perverse given the very different skills required of advocates and judges. If the

18 Barmes and Malleson, 'The Legal Profession as Gatekeepers'.
19 See K. Malleson, 'Rethinking the Merit Principle', p. 139.

earnings of the Bar continue to decline so that the children of affluent elites increasingly choose to become solicitors rather than barristers, the skills and experiences of solicitors (such as case management and client care), will come to replace those of advocates as evidence of judicial merit in the senior judiciary. Indeed, this is already starting to happen.[20]

Moreover, the specific solicitors' skills and experiences which are taken to be evidence of judicial competencies will not reflect those of the majority of solicitors working in high street firms or as in-house lawyers, but will likely be more particularly framed to reflect the experiences of a particular sub-set of solicitors; that is partners in large London commercial firms. It is not coincidental that Lord Collins, the first and, to date, only former solicitor to sit in the UK Supreme Court, had been a partner in the city law firm Herbert Smith and shared the identity characteristics of his fellow judges in all respects other than his choice of legal career path. Although solicitors as a whole are acknowledged as an under-represented group within the judicial appointments process, and efforts are being made to reduce their barriers to appointment and increase their numbers in the candidate pool, in practice it is likely to be the elite partners of city firms who will be the primary beneficiaries of changes in the system to encourage more solicitors to be appointed to the senior judiciary. To date, the system has not yet adapted sufficiently to tempt significant numbers of this sub-group of lawyers to give up their very large incomes in return for the status and security of the judiciary. In time, however, if young lawyers from dominant identity groups continue to choose commercial law firms over the Bar, the fit between the judicial appointments process and the judicial careers will adapt to match their needs and preferences.

The creation of the Judicial Appointments Commission in 2006 established a more independent system in the sense that it further removed the appointments process from the control of elected politicians, but not in the sense of being removed from the control of dominant identity groups. Nor is it easy to imagine how a judicial appointments process *could* be independent in this sense. Even if the judiciary and senior lawyers played a less influential role in the process than they currently do, the construction and application of what constitutes merit in the judicial appointments process will always be formulated and applied by those from dominant identity groups in society generally and therefore closely correlated to the dominant identity groups in the legal profession. Moreover, even if such a structurally independent judicial appointments process which was secure from capture by dominant identity groups could theoretically be constructed, those groups which had more social, economic and political resources would be best able to adapt themselves to fit the requirements of the new system and so reestablish their dominance for as long as the judiciary continued to be their preferred career option.

The value of reorientating the problem towards over-representation is that it keeps the focus firmly on these sorts of patterns which reveal the ways in which the preferential treatment of dominant identity groups is structurally embedded in

20 Hunter, 'Judicial Diversity and the "New" Judge', pp. 79–96.

the judicial appointments process. This identification, both historical and contemporary, of a close correlation between the composition of the judiciary and the dominant identity groups of the legal profession and society more widely is not unique to the UK or any particular legal and judicial system. Preferential treatment in the judicial appointments process for dominant identity groups is replicated in different ways across all judiciaries.

There is nothing surprising about this. All selection processes for powerful institutions are devised and developed by dominant identity groups. The judicial appointments process would be unique if it had been different. It has not been, and cannot be, decoupled from the power relations of the identity groups in the legal profession from which it is drawn or from society more widely. It is sometimes claimed that civil law systems with career judiciaries have broken this pattern in relation to gender because women in those systems make up a much higher proportion of the judiciary. But the participation rates of women in civil law judiciaries is no more than a reflection of the relatively lowly status of their trial court judiciaries. The appellate, constitutional and supreme courts of civil law systems, where judicial status is high, are as much the preserve of an elite (including in some cases non-lawyers) drawn from the dominant identity groups of the society as they are in common law systems.[21] Women are present in these top courts in much lower numbers despite the so-called 'feminization' of the lower courts.

By reframing the problem as one of over-representation the tendency to homogeneity is understood to be inherent in and structural to the existing system. The effect of this realization is to acknowledge that as a structural problem it requires a structural response. Reversing over-representation can only be achieved by reducing the space reserved for those from dominant groups who have traditionally secured office in disproportionate numbers. As Lord Neuberger has acknowledged, this can only be achieved by disrupting the expectations of powerful identity groups:

> … if the top echelon of jobs remains static, it is logically inevitable that the sons and daughters of those at the top will have to go down the snakes in order to enable those from less privileged backgrounds to go up the ladders.[22]

By reframing the problem as one of over-representation the focus shifts away from those groups which cannot climb the ladders to those groups which must go down the snakes. Because it is impossible for the judicial appointments process to be removed from the influence of dominant identity groups, this necessary level of disruption can only be achieved by the addition to the system of an extraneous structural mechanism with the capacity to undermine its inbuilt tendency to provide preferential treatment for dominant identity groups. To date, the only mechanism which has demonstrated this disruptive potential is a quota system.

21 See e.g. the statistics provided on women in the French judiciary in the annual report of the Conseil Supérieur de la Magistrature, *Rapport D'Activé 2014*, Paris: Conseil Supérieur de la Magistrature, 2014.

22 Neuberger, 'Rainbow Lecture', para 10.

Quotas for under-represented groups

The use of quotas to increase diversity, most often but not exclusively in relation to gender, is increasingly common in a growing range of selection processes to public and private institutions. Over half the world's legislatures operate some form of gender quota and seven European countries have introduced them in corporate boards.[23] In Northern Ireland the so-called 50:50 scheme operated successfully in the police service between 2001 and 2011 to increase the number of recruits from Catholic backgrounds. The use of quotas in judicial appointments process is also widespread, although much less widely known. In particular, many selection processes to supreme courts, constitutional courts and international courts operate some form of quota. These may be applied as the result of a constitutional provision, a statutory requirement or a convention. Although judicial quotas are increasingly used to promote gender equality they have historically been more commonly used to ensure that different geographical, regional, provisional or (in the case of international courts) national groupings secure fair representation in the judiciary.

The Supreme Court of Canada, for example, operates under a statutory stipulation that at least three of the judges on the Court must be appointed from Quebec. The Court also applies a convention quota that the remaining six positions are divided geographically: three from Ontario, two from Western Canada, and one from Atlantic Canada.[24] In Belgium, the Constitutional Court has, since its inception, imposed linguistic quotas in judicial appointments: six judges should be Dutch-speaking, and six judges should be French speaking. In India, a convention quota requires that members of the Supreme Court be distributed between the different states.[25]

The UK itself has also historically operated a successful and uncontroversial quota system in its highest court. Section 27(8) of the Constitutional Reform Act 2005 which governs the composition of the UK Supreme Court provides that: 'In making selections for the appointment of judges of the Court [a selection] commission must ensure that between them the judges will have knowledge of, and experience of practice in, the law of each part of the United Kingdom.' This formalizes what has traditionally been a long-standing convention that two judges will be appointed from Scotland and one from Northern Ireland. A practice is now emerging of ensuring that one judge with a Welsh connection will sit on UKSC appeals from or involving Wales, and in time this may come to be formalized as a

23 Others, including the UK, have proposed doing so if voluntary measures do not bring about significant change. See C. Fagan, M. Menendez and S. Anson (eds), *Women on Corporate Boards and in Top Management*, London: Palgrave MacMillan, 2012, p. 33. In addition, over half the legislatures in the world now have gender quotas. See the Global Database of Quotas for Women, at: www.quotaproject.org/aboutQuotas.cfm.

24 Parliament of Canada, 'Supreme Court of Canada': www.parl.gc.ca/Parlinfo/compilations/SupremeCourt.aspx?Menu=SupremeCourt&Current=True

25 A. Chandrachud, 'An Empirical Study of the Supreme Court's Composition', *Economic and Political Weekly*, Jan. 1, 2011, 71.

convention that one Justice must be Welsh.[26] In a recent internal review of the appointments process the former Chief Executive, Jenny Rowe, noted that this emerging convention was linked to the development of Welsh law but also added that there is 'an important question of the Court having the confidence of the communities it serves' in light of the 'asymmetry' between the present requirement to have two justices from Scotland and one from Northern Ireland but not from Wales.[27] If and when greater political autonomy is granted to Wales (and assuming that the Supreme Court continues as a UK-wide court) the pressure for a permanent Welsh seat is likely to grow, irrespective of the extent to which a distinct body of Welsh law develops.

In jurisdictions where religion is a dominant political force, the religious background of the appointments is often the subject of a quota. The Israeli Supreme Court, for example, operates convention quotas for different Jewish groups.[28] More recently, gender quotas have become increasingly common as the pressure for women's representation has moved up the political agenda including on the Newfoundland Supreme Court and the Austrian High Court. In 2015 the Belgian Constitutional Court announced that statutory gender quotas would be introduced for that court,[29] while in the same year the Government of Victoria in Australia announced that gender quotas would be used in selecting the provincial judiciary. Such gender quotas are most commonly found in courts which have been recently created, particularly at international level such as that operated in the International Criminal Court.[30]

Although formal quotas have sometimes provoked controversy, particularly when first implemented, their widespread use is a recognition of the fact that top courts, in particular, require a degree of representativeness amongst their judges to maintain their legitimacy. The question is not whether courts require fair representation so much as which groups need to be represented in order to maintain their legitimacy and authority.[31] Despite the fact that the imposition of quotas inevitably results in the selection of judges from a smaller candidate pool in relation to the quota, the claim that they undermine merit or the impartiality of the

26 Gee *et al*, *The Politics of Judicial Independence*, p. 217; A. Chandrachud, 'Diversity and the International Criminal Court: Does Geographic Background Impact Decision Making?', *Brooklyn Journal of International Law* 38, 2013, 499.

27 *Chief Executive's Review of the Process followed by Selection Commissions making Recommendations for Appointment to The Supreme Court*, London: UK Supreme Court, 2015, 5.

28 See E. Salzberger, 'Judicial Appointments and Promotions in Israel: Constitution, Law, and Politics', in K. Malleson and P. H. Russell (eds), *Appointing Judges in an Age of Judicial Power: Critical Perspectives from Around the World*, Toronto: Toronto University Press, 2006, 241, 250.

29 A. Remiche, 'Belgian Parliament introduces sex quota in Constitutional Court', *Oxford Human Rights Hub*, 21 April 2014.

30 See R. Mackenzie and others, *Selecting International Judges: Principle, Process and Politics*, Oxford: Oxford University Press, 2010.

31 S. Kenny, *Gender and Justice: Why Women in the Judiciary Really Matter*, London: Routledge 2013, p. 126.

court is rarely heard. For example, the selection of two Scottish judges and one Northern Irish judge from two very small jurisdictions has never given rise to claims that the incumbents are less qualified than their English or Welsh counterparts or that they are less impartial because of their explicit labelling as the Scottish and Northern Irish Justices on the Court. Nor has it ever been suggested that they sit only to hear Scottish or Northern Irish cases.[32]

Yet despite the increasingly widespread use of quotas to enhance the legitimacy of the courts, arguments in favour of more extensive use of quotas in the judiciary in England and Wales have, until recently, been firmly rejected. In 2005 Lord Falconer, then Lord Chancellor, stated that 'we won't have quotas'.[33] Five years later the House of Lords Constitution Committee report on Judicial Appointments similarly concluded that there was 'no case' for the introduction of quotas.[34] This conclusion was also shared by the Advisory Panel on Judicial Diversity led by Baroness Neuberger in 2010.[35] In 2015 the first quasi-official proposal for judicial quotas was put forward in a review carried out by two senior lawyers, Karon Monaghan QC and Geoffrey Bindman QC, commissioned by the then Shadow Lord Chancellor, Sadiq Khan. Their report on the judicial appointments process argued that the 'near absence of women and Black, Asian and minority ethnic judges in the senior judiciary, is no longer tolerable'[36] and proposed the introduction of both gender and ethnicity quotas. Yet despite the relatively limited and moderate form of quotas proposed the report was ignored by the incoming Conservative Government and is unlikely to be revisited in the near future.

Quotas versus merit

The explanation for this ongoing and widespread resistance to quotas in the UK, despite the general consensus as to the need for greater diversity and the failure of reforms to date, comes back to the construction of the diversity problem in terms of under-representation.[37] Because quotas to date have been designed to make space for under-represented groups it is assumed that the benefit of the quotas accrues primarily to the under-represented group rather than the judiciary generally or the public which it serves. The effect is to leave quotas open to the claim that they undermine selection on merit. Critics of quotas, even if they

32 Monaghan and Bindman, *Accelerating Change*, para 8.6.
33 Lord Falconer, 'Increasing Judicial Diversity: The Next Steps', Speech at the Institute of Mechanical Engineers, 2 November 2005, p. 6.
34 House of Lords Select Committee on the Constitution, *25th Report of Session 2010–12 Judicial Appointments*, 2012, HL paper 272, para 102.
35 J. Neuberger, *The Report of the Advisory Panel on Judicial Diversity 2010*, London: Advisory Panel on Judicial Diversity, 2010.
36 Monaghan and Bindman, *Accelerating Change*, p. 1.
37 This focus on under-representation is equally evident in relation to quotas for legislatures. See S. Franceschet, M. Krook and J. Piscopo, *The Impact of Gender Quotas*, Oxford: Oxford University Press, 2012.

acknowledge the flaws of the current appointments system, argue that their introduction would reduce the quality of the judiciary by restricting the ability of the appointments process to pick the best possible applicants on merit alone, whatever their identity. In 2012, for example, the House of Lords Constitution Committee accepted the view of many of those who gave evidence that quotas would 'dilute the quality of the judiciary and undermine the merit principle'.[38] More recently, Lord Justice Leveson has stated that quotas 'are the antithesis of appointment on merit'.[39]

A particular and recurring feature of the claim that quotas risk undermining merit is the objection that they would stigmatize those appointed under it as 'quota judges'. The House of Lords Constitution Committee was heavily influenced by this fear, noting that quotas were described by Lord Judge as 'insulting' and by Lady Justice Hallett as 'patronizing'. The Committee concluded that quotas 'would send out the message that candidates had only been appointed because of their sex, race etc.'.[40] This mirrored the conclusion of the Neuberger Report which rejected quotas on the basis of evidence it had received which argued that 'the introduction of quotas would be seen as undermining the position of people from under-represented groups appointed on the strength of their true personal ability.'[41] More recently, Lord Justice Leveson has described the use of quotas as 'demeaning whether to women or those from minority ethnic groups'.[42]

A striking feature of the fear of stigmatization is that it does not appear to be shared by white, male barristers from affluent backgrounds appointed under the current system. If it is the case that the current system is merit-based, and if talent and ambition are randomly spread amongst lawyers, then a judge appointed from a group disproportionately over-represented in the judiciary cannot know that they have been appointed solely on the basis of their own merit. Neither they nor anyone else can know for sure whether or not they were one of the higher quality judges in the over-represented identity group who would have been selected in a fully merit-based system or whether they were one of those who would have been displaced by a more talented candidate from a currently excluded group. The fact that white, male barristers from affluent backgrounds are not concerned about stigmatization under the present system, despite the fact that they are the beneficiaries of a de facto quota system in their favour suggests that the construction of merit is not, in reality, grounded in an empirical assessment of the likely comparable qualities of those appointed in relation to the distribution of talent and ability in the total possible candidate pool. Instead what constitutes judicial merit is

38 House of Lords Select Committee on the Constitution, '25th Report', para 102.

39 Sir Brian Leveson, 'Justice for the 21st Century', *Caroline Weatherill Lecture*, Isle of Man, 9 October 2015, 8.

40 House of Lords Select Committee on the Constitution, '25th Report', para 102.

41 Neuberger, 'Report of the Advisory Panel'; Judicial Diversity Taskforce, 'Improving Judicial Diversity: Progress Towards Delivery of the "Report of the Advisory Panel on Judicial Diversity 2010"', September 2012, para 44.

42 Leveson, 'Justice for the 21st Century', p. 8.

heavily influenced by the assumption that the person who is most likely to make a good judge is the person who most closely resembles the traditional judicial appointee.

The argument that quotas undermine appointment on merit is intuitively powerful if quotas are framed as a 'floor' for artificially reserving space for under-represented groups within an essentially merit-based system. Indeed, supporters of quotas have themselves often conceded that quotas potentially pose a threat to the merit principle. As a result they base the argument for their introduction on the claim that they are a necessary evil required to speed up the pace of change which must be introduced for as short a time as possible and to the most limited degree needed until the system self-corrects itself as a more diverse candidate pool emerges.

The fact that arguments against quotas have often been put by women and BAME lawyers and judges has carried particular weight and has, understandably, had a chilling effect on proposals for their introduction.[43] Because quotas have been framed as targeted at under-represented groups and so implicitly for their benefit rather than for the benefit of society at large, objections from those who are perceived to be the potential beneficiaries of the quotas will inevitably trump arguments in favour of quotas. Because judges and judicial candidates from under-represented identity groups are generally under pressure to prove that they are as good as their peers from more traditional judicial backgrounds, it is unsurprising that they should fear that quotas will lead to the perception that they are less well-qualified and/or less impartial than other judges.[44] These fears are a direct consequence of quotas being framed as a distortion of the merit system; at best a necessary but temporary form of positive discrimination designed to benefit members of under-represented groups rather than to improve the quality of the judiciary for the benefit of society as a whole.

Quotas for over-represented groups

Reframing the problem as one of over-representation rather than under-representation reveals the flawed premise upon which the objections outlined above is based. A fully merit-based system is dependent on securing the largest possible pool of qualified candidates and anything which reduces that pool will potentially undermine the overall quality of those selected. It is therefore the current over-representation of certain identity groups which is instrumental in reducing the quality of the pool and which needs to be addressed. This argument has been developed by Rainbow Murray in relation to the use of gender quotas in

43 This chilling effect is not limited to the judiciary and is evident in many other appointments processes. See C. Bacchi, 'Policy and Discourse: Challenging the Construction of Affirmative Action as Preferential Treatment', *Journal of European Public Policy* 11, 2004, p. 136.

44 S. Chakrabarti, 'The Judiciary: Why Diversity and Merit Matter', in Judicial Appointments Commission, *Judicial Appointments: Balancing Independence, Accountability and Legitimacy*, London: Judicial Appointments Commission, 2010, p. 69.

legislatures. She demonstrates that the lack of gender diversity in legislatures 'requires a solution that focuses on restricting over-representation, rather than redressing under-representation' and that reframing quotas in terms of the over-representation of men rather than the under-representation of women has the potential to increase the quality of representation for all.[45]

Murray's arguments in relation to the use of gender quotas in the electoral system are equally applicable to other forms of quotas and for other institutions, including the judiciary. If judicial merit was objectively only found disproportionately amongst white, male barristers from affluent backgrounds, then placing a ceiling on their numbers would reduce the quality of the judiciary. But if potential judicial talent and ambition are randomly distributed amongst the population generally and the legal profession more specifically, then capping the proportion of appointments from the dominant identity groups will increase the quality of the judiciary by making space for the talented potential candidates who are currently excluded. The effect of redesigning quotas as a ceiling will therefore be to enlarge rather than reduce the pool of qualified candidates and so drive up the quality of the judiciary. By reframing judicial quotas in this way, their rationale changes dramatically. Instead of being understood as a floor to allow in a minimum number of under-represented identity groups (who might not be as good as the existing judges), they become a ceiling designed to cap the over-representation of dominant identity groups (who by the law of statistical averages will not all be as good as the best of those excluded). In this way, the reconceptualization of the problem of homogeneity in terms of over-representation reveals not only that quotas can promote rather than undermine selection on merit but, more radically, that they are a pre-requisite of a merit-based judicial appointments process. When quotas are designed as a ceiling rather than a floor, their purpose is to *keep out* weaker candidates who are currently the beneficiaries of the preferential treatment built into the system rather than *allow in* weaker candidates who are currently excluded. Quotas thus become an intrinsic and essential feature of a merit-based appointment system.

The effect of this shift in approach is to expose the flaws of both the quality and impartiality concerns associated with the concept of 'quota judges'. Where the subject of the quota is the over-represented identity group, a judge who is appointed from an under-represented identity group is no longer occupying a 'reserved' seat but simply competing equally on merit in a system which no longer allows preferential treatment for certain dominant identity groups. Moreover, this shift also, paradoxically, benefits well-qualified judges who come from groups which are currently over-represented. As the new 'quota judges' appointed in proportion to their distribution within the full candidate pool, such judges can now be confident – for the first time – that they have been appointed on merit alone.

This logic also serves to dispel the fears which have been expressed that quotas might discourage potentially strong applicants from currently over-represented

45 Murray, 'Quotas for Men', p. 521.

groups, who might fear the system is stacked against them. On what basis could, for example, a man object to applying for judicial office under a system which has allocated 50 per cent of the positions to men? If the quota directly reflects the proportion of the population to which a candidate belongs, and if talent is randomly spread between women and men, any such objection would amount to a claim to the right to be the beneficiary of a system of preferential treatment. Lady Hale has suggested that the judiciary would be 'better off without prima donnas who might not apply for such reasons …'.[46] While she may be right to suggest that this attitude in itself might raise questions about the suitability for judicial office of the candidate, the substantive basis of the objection also disappears if the quota itself is designed to cap the disproportionate participation of such groups.

The same rationale also serves to counter the claim that the introduction of a quota system potentially undermines judicial impartiality, or at least the appearance of such. If the quota is designed to cap the participation of over-represented groups rather than to reserve space for under-represented groups, there can be no suggestion that a judge appointed in a system which applies quotas is there to represent any particular group. Indeed, the only sense in which the identity of a judge from an under-represented group has relevance in a ceiling quota system relates to the fact that they are *not* a member of the capped identity group. Nor could it be claimed that there is any danger that judges from over-represented groups appointed under the ceiling quota might be seen to be there to represent their identity group. Given that there is currently no suggestion that white, male barristers from affluent backgrounds have been appointed to represent their identity group in a system in which they are over-represented, there is no logical reason why this claim should be made for the first time when they are appointed under a system in which a ceiling quota has been introduced to cap their over-representation.

Although these arguments have not yet been systematically articulated in the existing discourse on judicial diversity, the potential value of ceiling quotas has already begun to be recognized in practice in some judicial appointments processes. The statute of the International Court of Justice, for example, applies a quota which does not reserve seats for any particular nationality but instead provides that no two judges on the court can belong to the same nationality.[47] Similar provisions exist in the selection processes to the International Criminal Tribunal, the International Criminal Court,[48] the International Criminal Tribunal for the former Yugoslavia and the International Criminal Tribunal for Rwanda.[49] These ceiling quotas are designed to ensure that no one nationality dominates the

46 Lady Hale, 'Women in the Judiciary', *Fiona Woolf Lecture*, 27 June 2014, p. 19.
47 Statute of the International Court of Justice, June 26, 1945, 59 Stat. 1031, 33 U.N. T.S. 993, Art. 3, para 1.
48 Rome Statute of the International Criminal Court, July 17, 1998, 2187 U.N.T.S. 90, Art. 36 (7).
49 See A. Chandrachud, 'Diversity and the International Criminal Court: Does Geographic Background Impact Decision Making?', *Brooklyn Journal of International Law* 38, 2013, p. 495.

court. Although they are limited in scope and ambition and do not seek to use quotas to create a fully merit-based system, the shift in approach which they represent is significant. By focusing on the potential over-representation of powerful nations they highlight the threat posed to the quality and legitimacy of courts if one identity group occupies a disproportionate space on the bench.

The design of judicial quota systems

The shift from floor to ceiling quotas not only changes the way we understand the relationship between the composition of the judiciary and the construction of merit, it also affects the design of the quota system. Three key questions must be addressed when designing a quota system: Which groups should the quota apply to? What level should the quota be set at and for how long should it be applied? The answers will be very different depending on whether the quota system is a ceiling or a floor.

Quota subjects

Identifying the most appropriate subject(s) of a quota will often be difficult and controversial, whatever the quota system. It will depend on the particular context of time and place and the distribution of power amongst different identity groups. Both types of system must engage with the challenges of intersectionality since people do not divide neatly into over-represented and under-represented identity groups. All of us are a mix of identities, some more and some less well represented, and as a wider range of identities secure political recognition the complexity and variety of our identities increases. If the primary aim of the quota system is to improve the quality of the judiciary, then the basis for identifying the most appropriate quota subject will be the one which most effectively increases the candidate pool and reduces preferential treatment which undermines merit.

The extent to which floor quotas can achieve this is limited by the fact that the system is perceived as a temporary special measure which must be minimized to avoid undermining the pre-existing merit-based system. The most appropriate quota subject for a system of floor quotas will therefore be the under-represented group whose exclusion is extracting the highest political cost and whose inclusion will have the least substantive impact on the judiciary or the judicial appointments process. In practice, this will usually mean the under-represented identity group which has the greatest capacity to mobilize and lobby for inclusion.

The particular identity of this group or groups will change over time as social and political conditions change. The dynamic nature of the creation of quota subjects is evidenced by the changing historical patterns of judicial quotas in the US Supreme Court, which has one of the longest historical experience with informal quotas. In its early years, from the founding of the Court until the late nineteenth century, geography was the dominant quota category since state representation on the Court by less powerful states was a key political issue at the time.[50] This changed as religion, race, and gender secured higher priority in the struggle for representation. By the late nineteenth century a 'Catholic seat' had emerged on the Court which continued through the twentieth century when a 'Jewish seat' was added from 1916 to 1969.[51] These two convention quotas disappeared as the political significance of religious identities receded. Today, gender and ethnicity are the most significant identity characteristics in the judicial diversity discourse and geography has all but disappeared as a quota subject for the Supreme Court. In other courts, noted above, the increasing use of gender quotas, whether statutory or by convention, is evidence of the increasing mobilization of women in demanding political representation in institutions of power. Although inclusion of women in courts through quotas will undoubtedly increase the quality of the judiciary by widening the candidate pool to include half the population previously excluded, this is not the driving rationale behind the identification of women as subject quotas in systems applying floor quotas.

By contrast, in any one jurisdiction, the subject of ceiling quotas should be identified by each judicial appointments process as the identity group which is most heavily over-represented and therefore has most effect on reducing the candidate pool and undermining selection on merit. By focusing on over-representation, ceiling quotas are less prone to become embroiled in the dilemma of how to rank each particular intersectional under-represented identity group in order to determine which should be included as a quota subject. Instead, by focusing on the dominant identity groups, and by seeking to cap their over-representation, they allow space for a wide range of under-represented groups in a variety of intersectional forms. Which of these particular identity groups in which particular intersectional configuration are represented at any one time will be determined by the random distribution of talent amongst different people from under-represented identity groups at any one time. This approach also ensures that there is space for those men who are a 'minority in a majority' because of some aspect of their identity which does not conform to the dominant identity group.[52]

The subjects of ceiling quota systems will change in the same way as they do under a floor system in response to changing social and political conditions. But the basis for determining which subjects are given priority will be very different. The degree to which an under-represented group can lobby to secure recognition of its right to be included will have no relevance. Quota subjects will be identified, instead, with reference to the current composition of the judiciary. The process for determining the subject of ceiling quotas starts by identifying which groups are dominant in the judiciary so as to identity the extent of the discrepancy, if any, between these identity groups and their proportion of the potential candidate pool. Those groups which are most heavily over-represented when the two

50 Chandrachud, 'Diversity and the International Criminal Court', pp. 496–498.

51 Ibid., pp. 502–504.

52 R. Murray, 'Defining and Measuring Men's Interests', WIP Paper prepared for presentation at the European Consortium of Political Research (ECPR) Joint Sessions Workshop on *The Causes and Consequences of Male Over-Representation*, Warsaw, 30 March–1 April 2015.

categories are compared, and so most seriously undermine the merit-based system will be prioritized as the subject of a quota. The default quota subject will therefore be those identity groups which are over-represented in proportion to the population as a whole. The onus will shift to the appointments body to demonstrate that the over-representation of that group can be justified on objective merit grounds, that is, that they are inherently more capable of being judges.

The different approach to socio-economic disadvantage provides a good illustration of the different outcome in practice which arises when quotas are framed as a ceiling rather than a floor. The disproportionate dominance of judges from the most affluent groups in society is, empirically, the aspect of the judicial appointments process which most undermines selection on merit given the quantitative gap between the proportion of potential candidates from very wealthy backgrounds in the population (both generally or in the legal profession) compared to the judiciary. Yet to date, no judicial appointments process has created quotas subjects based on socio-economic disadvantage despite the fact that this is the least representative element of the judiciary. If the extent of the effect of homogeneity on the quality of the judiciary were the determining factor in the selection of quota subjects this identity group would be prioritized above gender and ethnicity. The explanation for the absence of quotas for judges from socio-economically disadvantaged backgrounds in the current system of floor quotas is that members of this identity group have less capacity to mobilize and lobby for recognition than other under-represented groups. Those lawyers and judges who come from disadvantaged socio-economic backgrounds have, by definition, moved out of that identity category by virtue of their successful legal career. While it is, of course, possible for individuals to be committed and effective advocates on behalf of other identity groups, a group which is reliant on the endeavours of another group to lobby on its behalf will never be as effective in securing political capital as one in which the members of the identity group mobilize on their own behalf.

Similar arguments can be made in relation to age as an identity group. The under-representation of younger people in the judiciary has only recently started to be recognized as a problem which needs to be addressed. Until recently the appointment of judges in their late 50s and 60s was accepted as a necessary and inevitable consequence of the merit system in which those in that age group make inherently better judicial candidates. Lawyers in their 20s, 30s and even 40s were regarded in much the same way as women once were, as automatically, inherently and collectively unqualified to be judges. The construction and interpretation of the merit criteria in such a way that only candidates towards the end of their legal careers could, until recently, hope to succeed in applying for higher judicial office was accepted as a neutral requirement, rather than one which met the needs and preferences of senior barristers who wish to pursue a lucrative and successful career at the Bar for 30–40 years before taking the pay cut (albeit traditionally offset by a generous pension) that comes with judicial office.

The contention that at least *some* younger candidates would make better judges than *some* older appointees is one which most objective observers would accept. One reason why this relatively uncontentious claim has not resulted in active efforts to increase the age range of the judicial candidate pool so as to improve the quality of the judiciary is that there are fewer younger people in sufficiently powerful positions to lobby for their interest compared to other under-represented groups. The pressure for the recognition of younger people as an under-represented quota category in a floor system, in common with those from poorer backgrounds, is dependent on the lobbying of older, richer people, either altruistically or inspired by the fact that they were once themselves younger and/or poorer.

In contrast, women, those from BAME backgrounds, disabled or LGBT+ lawyers, do not generally leave their identity group as they move through a legal career and up the hierarchy of power. Indeed, in the case of disabled lawyers and judges and some sexual orientations, they might in fact acquire their under-represented status later in life. Some individual judges and senior lawyers may not personally feel a commitment to advance the interests of other members of their under-represented identity group or groups but those who do will be in a much stronger position to lobby from the inside for the recognition of the groups to which they belong.[53]

The quota subjects of both floor and ceiling quotas will therefore change over time on the basis of the changing political capital of different identity groups. The key difference between the two systems being that ceiling quotas will change in response to the increasing dominance of different identity groups within the judiciary and therefore will be seeking to correct the empirical imbalances as they arise whereas floor quotas will be responding primarily to the changing relative effectiveness of political lobbying and mobilization of different identity groups in society.

Quota levels and timeframes

Just as the quota subjects in a floor quota are selected to minimize damage to the assumed pre-existing merit-based system, for the same reason the level at which the floor quota is set may legitimately be lower than the presence of the identity group in the population. This explains why quotas for women judges are, for example, often set at below 50 per cent.[54] In contrast, a ceiling quota system is driven by the fact that the highest quality outcome is achieved with selection from the widest possible candidate pool most closely resembling the diversity of the population at large. Therefore the default quota level of ceiling quota for an over-represented group will be set at the level of their presence in the population as a whole. The ceiling quota level will only be increased if there is convincing empirical evidence to show that it needs to be higher as a result of very specific and intrinsic skills or abilities which are disproportionately found in the dominant

53 See Kenny, *Gender and Justice*, for a full analysis of the importance of the mobilization of women's groups in securing the appointment of more women judges.

54 K. Malleson 'Gender Quotas for the Judiciary in England and Wales', in U. Shultz and G. Shaw (eds), *Gender and the Judiciary*, Oxford: Hart Publishing, 2013.

group. The onus will be on the appointing body to demonstrate objectively that these skills or abilities are disproportionately possessed by that over-represented group. Increasing the default ceiling quota to a level higher than that of the population as a whole would itself constitute a 'special temporary measure' which would need to be justified and limited because of its inherent incompatibility with a fully merit-based system. For example, in setting the quota level for a ceiling gender quota, the quota level for men would, by default, be set at 50 per cent and only increased if there was evidence to show that men disproportionately possessed skills or abilities which made them better judges. The onus would be on those arguing for a higher than 50 per cent quota level to demonstrate why this increase was necessary on merit grounds.

Moreover, if a ceiling quota level needed to be set at a level which was higher than that of the proportion of the identity group in the population at large, this would be prima facie evidence the system was not fully merit-based and so was losing well-qualified candidates. It would therefore indicate that changes would be needed to the way in which the candidate pool was constructed in order to ensure that this distortion was addressed so that the system could be fully merit-based. In this way, ceiling quotas do not take the construction of the candidate pool as a given. Every eligibility rule which limits the candidate pool has the potential to create preferential treatment for certain identity groups and limit the pool in a way which reduces the merit-based nature of the system. A ceiling quota would therefore place the onus on those supporting all pre-existing selection criteria which limit the candidate pool to justify the claim that such limits enhance rather than restrict merit. For example, the requirement that judicial candidates must have prior advocacy experience or experience sitting as part-time judges, either as a formal or informal requirement, would need to be justified with evidence to show that candidates without such experience *cannot* (as opposed to *might* not) be as good as judges as those who have had that experience. All aspects of the system which favour the current over-represented groups would be subject to scrutiny in determining the largest possible candidate pool so as to secure the most qualified candidates.

Setting the default quota for over-represented groups also ensures that when political and social conditions change, formerly under-represented groups do not come to dominate. For example, if over time women continue to qualify as lawyers in higher numbers than men and come to form a dominant identity group in the legal profession they may one day come to form over 50 per cent of the judiciary. This would then trigger their categorization as an over-represented group and a cap of 50 per cent would be imposed irrespective of the fact that they constituted over 50 per cent of the legal profession. Action would then need to be taken to ensure that men were being included in the candidate pool to the same proportions as the population at large so as not to reduce the quality of the judiciary. In this way, ceiling quotas do not benefit one group over another but seek to ensure the widest possible candidate pool to ensure the highest possible quality of judges appointed.

Similar differences in outcome between ceiling and floor quotas arise in determining the point at which quotas should be applied in the appointments process and for how long they should remain in place. Floor quotas are almost always understood as temporary measures, even by those who support their use. For example, in 2015 the Committee on the Elimination of Discrimination against Women (CEDAW) – a body of independent experts established under the auspices of the UN High Commissioner for Human Rights – produced a general recommendation on women's access to justice which included a proposal that, where necessary, states should take 'temporary special measures' to ensure that women are equally represented in the judiciary.[55] A number of different mechanisms are used which reflect the fact that quotas are classed as temporary special measures quotas. These include 'sunset clauses' in which the quotas expire after a certain period or when under-represented groups reach a certain level of appointment. The introduction of the quotas may also be deferred, introduced gradually over time or once the numbers reach a certain threshold. The purpose of these different limitation mechanisms is to minimize the danger of less well-qualified candidates being appointed.[56]

In contrast, because ceiling quotas focus on the damage caused to the quality of the judiciary by the current over-representation of dominant identity groups, their goal is to reduce that over-representation as quickly and fully as possible and to maintain this check on the tendency towards over-representation. If over-representation is understood to be a normal and inevitable tendency of all appointments systems, the default position will be to assume that ceiling quotas will be an ongoing, intrinsic and necessary feature of a merit-based appointment system rather than a temporary special remedial measure. Once again, the onus shifts to those who argue for the removal of the ceiling quota to demonstrate that without it the system will select candidates from identity groups as closely as possible in proportion to society at large so as to be able to claim that the system is fully merit-based.

This same logic means that ceiling quotas should also be applied as early in the process as possible so as to widen the candidate pool as much as possible since limiting the over-representation before the formation of the candidate pool will drive up the degree of competition between candidates from different identity groups. Floor quotas, on the other hand, often seek to limit the application of a quota to the later stages of the process so as to reduce the disruption of the quota system to the current process on the assumption that the effect of quotas is more likely to be to keep out well-qualified candidates than to let them in. The decision by the Judicial Appointments Commission to limit the application of the 'tipping point' provisions of section 159 Equality Act 2010 to the last stages of the selection process rather than to the earlier short-listing stage is evidence of this approach towards even very limited positive action interventions falling short of quotas. The application of the same approach to a quota system would have the effect of reducing its capacity to increase the merit-based system.

55 Committee on the Elimination of Discrimination against Women, *General Recommendation on Women's Access to Justice*, 23 July 2015.

56 Malleson, 'Gender Quotas'.

Conclusion

Hopes that the judiciary will, however slowly, come in time to reflect the diversity of identity groups in the population of England and Wales are misplaced. The evidence to date suggests that this change will not come about without the implementation of a mechanism to counter the inevitable tendency of the appointments process to privilege those from dominant identity groups and so undermine the merit system. Quotas can provide this mechanism provided they are reframed as a ceiling to check over-representation. As long as quotas continue to be constructed as a means of making space for under-represented groups they will, understandably, be resisted on the grounds that they undermine merit and the appearance of impartiality. Whereas as a cap for checking over-representation it is clear that their effect is to benefit society as a whole in driving up the quality of the judiciary by ensuring that weaker candidates from dominant identity groups do not secure judicial office as a result of non-merit based factors. The creation of ceiling quotas would shift the burden of proof away from under-represented groups to demonstrate that their inclusion will not undermine the quality of the judiciary and onto over-represented groups to demonstrate why their continuing disproportionate participation is justified.

This shift is dependent on the political will to create a fully merit-based system. Since this can only be done by breaking the near monopoly of dominant identity groups in the judicial appointments process the disruptive effect of this change will be considerable. Most obviously, the less talented members of over-represented identity groups need to go down the 'snakes' so that their more talented counterparts from under-represented groups can go up the 'ladders'. It will also provoke the unarticulated but powerful fear that if judges are not disproportionately drawn from dominant identity groups the effect will be to weaken the power and status of judges.

This fear is not unique to the judiciary but affects all institutions of power. In 2004, the then president of the Royal College of Physicians, Carol Black, asked how the medical profession, previously dominated by white males, was going to retain its influence in the light of its 'feminization'.[57] More recently, Lady Hale raised the same 'demon' in relation to the judiciary: 'Would a radical increase in the numbers of women and BME judges lead in time to lower pay, lower status and ultimately to a less able judiciary?'[58] Although stressing that she did not hold this view, she expressed the fear that others (privately) did. The flip side of this problem is the question posed by Rosemary Hunter in 2015 in asking whether, if the government succeeded in curtailing judicial review and repealing the Human Rights Act 1998 we would see more judges from diverse backgrounds being appointed to a senior judiciary reduced in power.[59] Such questions are deeply

57 In interview with the BBC: BBC News, 'Women docs "weakening" medicine', 2 August 2004.

58 Lady Hale, 'Equality in the Judiciary', Kuttan Menon Memorial Lecture, 21 February 2013, 7.

59 Hunter, 'Judicial Diversity and the "new" Judge', p. 96.

disquieting. But it is vital that they are articulated because they reveal the underlying basis of an invisible resistance to building the political will needed to create fully merit-based selection systems particularly in relation to the most senior levels in medicine, law, politics and all other institutions of power.

The proposal for ceiling quotas in the judicial appointments outlined in this chapter therefore needs to be understood as just one part of a wider political equality project which seeks to disrupt the automatic identification of institutional status and power with the over-representation of dominant identity groups. This project remains one of the most challenging and important ones for liberal democracies in the twenty-first century. The judiciary, as a body which enjoys high status and public confidence, is well-placed to take up this challenge and to live up to its claim that it is '... perfectly obvious that background, ethnicity, religion, sexuality and gender are utterly irrelevant to the ability of an individual to be a good judge'.[60] If this is true, then there is nothing to fear and much to gain from the creation of a fully merit-based selection system in which no one identity group is over-represented and the random distribution of judicial talent and ambition in the population can be tapped to drive up the quality of the judiciary.

60 Lord Judge, 'Equality in Justice Day', Royal Courts of Justice, London, 24 October 2008, p. 3.

14 Three models of diversity

Erika Rackley and Charlie Webb

Introduction

It might appear that we no longer need to make the case for a diverse judiciary. True, the judiciary as a whole, and the senior judiciary in particular, is not diverse enough. But few, if any, now dissent – openly at least – from the view that, all else equal, a more diverse judiciary would be a good thing.[1] Moreover, it is clear that the judiciary in England and Wales is becoming more diverse. There are more women, BAME and openly gay judges than ever before and, particularly at the lower levels, more judges who haven't taken the standard public school-Oxbridge-Bar route since the Judicial Appointments Commission (JAC) started overseeing the appointments process.[2] Attention has therefore shifted to how we get greater diversity: now we are agreed that diversity is a good thing, what do we need to do to bring it about? Implicit in this is the thought that we no longer need arguments for judicial diversity – those arguments have been made and won – what we need now is action.

But this is too quick. Arguments for judicial diversity remain important and one way to see this is by examining where they take us: What is the diversity we are aiming for? More precisely, how will we know when the judiciary is sufficiently or optimally diverse? Is greater diversity – all other things being equal – always a good thing? In this chapter we shall explore three leading arguments for judicial diversity and the sort of diversity they support. As we shall show, the differences between these arguments, and the models of diversity they offer, matter. They matter strategically: some of these arguments are stronger, some may have greater purchase with relevant audiences. But more importantly they matter because, in the end, they take us in different directions, leading to very different ideas of judicial diversity and differently constituted judiciaries.

1 A point noted by Kate Malleson almost twenty years ago (K. Malleson, *The New Judiciary: The Effect of Expansion and Activism*, Farnham: Ashgate, 1999, p. 106).

2 Of course, there is still much more progress to be made. See further Karon Monaghan's 'Reflection' in this collection. For the latest diversity statistics, see Judicial Office Statistical Bulletin, 'Judicial Diversity Statistics 2016' published 28 July 2016 (revised 2 December 2016).

Three arguments for a diverse judiciary

For many years now, successive Lord Chancellors, senior judges, civil servants, parliamentarians, academics and, more recently, the JAC have acknowledged the importance of ensuring greater diversity among our judges.[3] This sees a diverse judiciary as an end, a goal of a properly functioning appointments system. However, while this way of thinking is understandable and indeed often useful, it is also somewhat misleading. Judicial diversity is better seen not as an end but as a means, valuable for what it contributes or reveals about some other end we value independently. So the answer to the question of why we want a diverse judiciary isn't 'just because'. If judicial diversity is 'a good thing', it is because it serves or instantiates some other, broader good.

But what good? Here views differ. A number of well-rehearsed arguments coalesce around three broad themes: equality of opportunity; democratic legitimacy; and the substantive difference diversity makes to judicial decision-making.[4] The first locates the good of a diverse judiciary in the fact it reflects a commitment to ensuring fairness to would-be judges and, through this, an openness to seeking judicial merit in all quarters: nobody should be excluded from judicial office, or face additional barriers on their path to judicial office, by virtue of their sex, sexuality, race, social background and so on, thus ensuring that our judiciary is open to all talents. The second focuses instead on how the law and the justice system are viewed by the community they serve: a judiciary that better reflects that community as a whole, as opposed to one which appears to privilege some groups over others, enhances public confidence in the judiciary and legal system and, thereby, promotes respect for law. Finally, difference arguments tie the good of diversity to the importance of having a judiciary that is as strong as it can be: our judiciary will be

3 Indeed, increased judicial diversity has cross party support. See generally discussion in E. Rackley, *Women, Judging and the Judiciary: From Difference to Diversity*, London: Routledge, 2013, pp. 69–105. Recent examples include the former Lord Chancellor and Secretary of State for Justice, E. Truss' 'Women in the Legal Industry' speech at the Sparks21 Conference on 9 November 2016; the discussion between John Pugh MP, Elizabeth Truss MP, Mike Wood MP and Richard Burgon MP in the House of Commons in September 2016 ('Legal Professionals', *Hansard* 614, 6 September 2016); and the Labour Party's *Judicial Diversity: Accelerating Change* report authored by leading QCs, Geoffrey Bindman and Karon Monaghan, in November 2014: G. Bindman and K. Monaghan, *Judicial Diversity: Accelerating Change*, London: Labour Party, 2014, discussed further by Monaghan in this collection.

4 As identified by B. Hale, 'Equality and the Judiciary: Why Should We Want More Women Judges?', *Public Law*, 2001, p. 489 and discussed at greater length in Rackley, *Women, Judging and the Judiciary*, pp. 23–29. Arguments for greater diversity are most often made in relation to gender and the potential difference or otherwise women judges will make to the judiciary as an institution and/or substantive decision-making. Nevertheless, while the reasons for the under-representation of different identity groups will vary, the arguments for the importance of having more women on the bench can be extended, with the necessary alterations, to other under-represented groups and/or diversity characteristics.

stronger – that is, better able to do its job – if it can take advantage of the (sometimes) different attributes and qualities possessed by different groups.[5]

Each of these distinct goods gives us reason to bemoan the present lack of diversity and all pull, for now, in the same direction: toward a more diverse judiciary than we currently have. Accordingly, in so far as we are trying to make the case against the status quo, we have not needed to draw them apart. Indeed, it often makes sense not to draw them apart. There is a significant, if limited, overlapping consensus between them which allows advocates of each of these arguments to work in coalition for (to this extent) common cause. Moreover, and in any event, these arguments are not mutually exclusive: endorsing one doesn't preclude us from endorsing the others.

Nonetheless, they do, ultimately, lead to different end points. Indeed, though they all provide arguments for diversity, they provide not so much different arguments for diversity as arguments for different diversities. And so, far from being relics of a debate that has already been 'won', differing arguments for diversity provide differing templates for the form diversity might take – for what a diverse judiciary might look like.

Equality of opportunity

The equality of opportunity argument holds that judicial appointment should be open to all able to do the job well. Accordingly no person or group should stand a better chance of judicial appointment on account of characteristics which are unconnected to their abilities: women should have same opportunity to be judges as men, BAME candidates the same chance as white candidates, and so on. Judicial diversity matters here since it is the likely outcome of such equality of opportunity: given an even distribution of judicial talents or potential across all relevant groups, we should expect that, if members of all such groups have the same opportunity of appointment, all those groups will, over time, be appropriately represented within the judiciary. By contrast, a lack of diversity is indicative that those sub-groups with a disproportionately high number of representatives on the bench have an improper or unmerited advantage over those from sub-groups with disproportionately few.[6] As Lord Neuberger noted in his evidence to the Constitution Committee back in 2011:

> The idea that women are less good judges than men is fanciful ... But if that is right ... why are 80 per cent or 90 per cent of judges male? It suggests, purely

5 There are, of course, other arguments for improving judicial diversity. Rosemary Hunter identifies three additional arguments in the literature for why we should want more women judges: the presence of role-models and provision of active mentoring; the likelihood of greater empathy for women litigants and witnesses and the educational and/or 'civilizing' effect of women judges on their male colleagues: R. Hunter, 'More than Just a Different Face? Judicial Diversity and Decision-Making', *Current Legal Problems* 68, 2015, pp. 119, 123–124.

6 K. Malleson, 'The Disruptive Potential of Ceiling Quotas in Addressing Over-representation in the Judiciary' in this collection.

> on a statistical basis, that we do not have the best people because there must be some women out there who are better than the less good men who are judges.[7]

However, while it is implausible that the attributes of good judging are disproportionately distributed in favour of a small group of white, male barristers, what is less clear is what a judiciary which was the product of true equality of opportunity would look like.

At its most straightforward the answer looks simple. If it's right to assume that judicial talents are (at least roughly) distributed evenly across all sections of our community, diversity on the basis of equal opportunity means that we should have a judiciary which is – more or less and over time – as diverse as the relevant community from which it is drawn. The question we should then ask is what community we're talking about. One answer is to look to the community of possible or plausible appointees. Of course, that all have, in principle, a fair and equal opportunity for judicial appointment does not mean that all wish to take that opportunity or are positioned to avail themselves of it. Nonetheless, we should, on this view, expect a judiciary which is the product of true equality of opportunity to be, in broad terms, no less, though also no more, diverse than the field of candidates as it exists at the relevant time. This frames the relevant community very narrowly. Indeed given attitudes to judicial qualification which have prevailed until very recently (and perhaps continue to prevail in some quarters of the senior judiciary), it would exclude almost everyone but senior barristers; though now it might be extended to solicitors, legal executives and academics. Following this logic, taking equality of opportunity as our reason for diversity, the judiciary will be optimally or appropriately diverse once it reflects the relevant legal community (so conceived), even if – ultimately – that isn't very diverse at all.

The upshot of this line of argument is that equality of opportunity as a model for diversity ends up tied to the diversity of the relevant candidate pool. And this in turn means that, so far as the make-up of that pool does not reflect the make-up of the broader community from which it is drawn, getting a judiciary which reflects that broader community is dependent on first securing greater diversity within that pool of judicial candidates. As the JAC has recognized since its inception, appointments to the judiciary are largely beholden to the diversity, or lack of diversity, of the relevant pool or community. Usha Prashar, inaugural chair of the JAC, noted in 2007

> it is futile to concentrate just on the diversity of the judiciary when the problems are linked so intrinsically with the diversity of the legal profession as a whole … As the legal profession remains unrepresentative, our ability

7 Lord Neuberger, Oral Evidence to the House of Lords Select Committee on the Constitution Inquiry into the Judicial Appointments Process, 16 November 2011, Q.251.

> to change the diversity profile of the judiciary overnight will be limited. Particularly at the highest levels of judicial office.[8]

Now if we take the relevant community as the pool of existing candidates for appointment, such that it is their and only their equality of opportunity we are concerned with, this is just the way it goes. All we can ask is that those in a position to be appointed get a fair chance of appointment.[9] But there is good reason for those concerned with equality of opportunity not to stop there. For one thing, true and full equality of opportunity for judicial appointment entails equality of opportunity for making it into the pool of possible appointees. We don't have equality of opportunity if that equality kicks in only once a number of would-be candidates have been unfairly excluded. This conclusion is strengthened if we ask why we should value equality of opportunity. Ensuring equality of opportunity of appointment is important not only as a matter of fairness to individual candidates but also – again on the assumption that attributes relevant to judicial excellence are distributed more or less evenly (that is proportionately) between all relevant sub-groups – to ensure that our judiciary finds those best suited for the job. Would-be judges aren't treated fairly if they are unfairly prevented from becoming genuine or plausible candidates for appointment and those making judicial appointments will fail to find those best suited to being judges if the candidate pool is unduly narrowed at the outset.[10]

The way forward then is to change the scope and make-up of the pool. One suggestion here is to look beyond the upper echelons of the Bar in order to find merit in a broader range of people. It may well be that this solution would lead to a pool from which a presentably diverse judiciary may be drawn. For example, the proportion of BAME candidates, and in turn the appointment of BAME judges, is likely to be higher, although still not very high, were the 'pool' for senior judicial appointment truly, and not just notionally, expanded to include, say, barristers who have not taken silk, sole practitioners and non-practising academics. Another strategy would involve moving beyond purely formal notions and mechanisms of equal treatment to processes aimed at providing a fuller or more substantive understanding of equality, such as through forms of positive action.[11] In these ways, this broader application of the equality of opportunity argument means that

8 U. Prashar, 'Judicial Appointments: A New System for a New Century', public lecture as part of the 'New Developments in Criminal Justice' seminar series, *Centre for Crime and Justice Studies*, 27 March 2007.

9 Unfortunately, even since the establishment of the JAC, this is not always the case. See Karen Monaghan's 'Reflection' in this collection.

10 See further L. Barmes and K. Malleson 'The Legal Profession as Gatekeeper to the Judiciary: Design Faults in Measures to Enhance Diversity', *Modern Law Review* 74, 2011, p. 245.

11 Malleson, 'The Disruptive Potential of Ceiling Quotas'; K. Malleson, 'Gender Quotas for the Judiciary in England and Wales', in U. Schultz and G. Shaw (eds), *Gender and Judging*, Oxford: Hart Publishing, 2013, pp. 481–500. K. Malleson, 'Diversity in the Judiciary: the Case for Positive Action', *Journal of Law and Society* 36, 2009, p. 376.

it need not take the pool as given but can instead support the widening of that pool so that it provides a truer reflection of the public from which it is drawn.

Nonetheless, it remains true that equality of opportunity arguments often leave those charged with making judicial appointments with their hands tied.[12] If there is to be true equality of opportunity, and thereby a more fully diverse judiciary, this equality needs to exist at a much earlier stage to ensure not only that all who enter the legal professions can progress according to their abilities and qualities, unhindered by prejudice and barriers unrelated to their expertise, but also that those who have the talents and desire to enter into these professions are in a position to do so. This requires intervention at a much earlier stage, notably before career options narrow and career paths are mapped out.[13]

So the end point of equality of opportunity arguments for diversity differs depending on where and when these arguments are applied. Only when rolled out beyond the judicial appointments process itself to all policies and practices which end up contributing to the make-up of the pool of candidates for appointment do these arguments tend to a judiciary which is diverse in roughly equal measure to the general public it serves. Moreover, even then – even, that is, were there to be unqualified equality of opportunity – we should not expect anything like a perfect correlation between the diversity of the judiciary and that of the general public. For one thing, there will be inevitable statistical variations. Though there is no more reason to expect the attributes that make for judicial excellence to be present in one group than in another, it should be no surprise – and no necessary signal of

12 Indeed, more generally, it might be thought that equality of opportunity arguments have only so much to say to those charged with making appointments. They tell them that they should look for and within as broad a pool of possible, so that they don't miss any eligible candidates, and then see that all those candidates are properly considered. But, if we are concerned with equality of opportunity, whether, in the last resort, a particular vacancy ought to be filled by a member of a particular group depends wholly on the merits of the relevant candidate(s). Ensuring that everyone has a fair and equal opportunity for judicial appointment means ensuring that all candidates have their candidacy assessed on the merits, whatever their gender, ethnicity, sexuality and so on. Appointing a member of an under-represented group who is not the strongest candidate on their merits is contrary to equality of opportunity, whether this is viewed as a matter of individual fairness or as a function of ensuring that only those who'll make the best judges are appointed. (Though, as noted, equal opportunity arguments may support certain forms of positive action, so as to ensure that those who have previously been treated unequally are accorded a proper opportunity to develop and display their 'true' merits.) So while equality of opportunity suggests that we should expect a judiciary as diverse as the pool from which it is selected, the diversity it supports is not the product of measures aimed at securing greater diversity or the increased representation of under-represented groups but is rather the likely side-effect of a policy of appointment which is blind to candidates' diversity credentials and made only on merit.

13 This point is not new. See, e.g. Bar Council, *Entry to the Bar Working Party: Final Report*, London: Bar Council, 2007, chapter 3; Advisory Panel on Judicial Diversity, *The Report of the Advisory Panel on Judicial Diversity 2010*, London: Ministry of Justice, 2010, pp. 22–23. And for an example of the form such intervention might take see The Sutton Trust's 'Pathways to Law' programme: www.suttontrust.com/programmes/pathways-programmes-2/pathways-to-law/.

inequality of opportunity – if, at any given point in time, we find more of those people in the one than the other. But more importantly, even if judicial qualities and opportunities to enter the legal professions are evenly distributed across all groups and sections of society, it would not follow that an appetite for a career in the law would be similarly distributed. Not everyone wants to be a lawyer, and not every lawyer wants to be a judge. There is always the possibility that some measure of under-representation of some groups in the judiciary and in the legal profession more broadly derives not from any lack of opportunity but from a form of self-exclusion, which, if freely chosen, rather than the consequence of, say, a longer-standing denial of fair opportunity to (or exclusion of) members of such groups, is – on this argument – largely unproblematic.[14]

Democratic legitimacy

A second argument for judicial diversity is grounded in the importance of the judiciary being democratically legitimate. Here the primary reason for wanting judicial diversity is so that the judiciary as an institution has the respect and confidence of the communities it serves, as is necessary for it to fulfil its function.[15] A judiciary which does not reflect the relevant communities is, so it is suggested, less likely to garner such support. As Lord Neuberger noted in his 2014 Rainbow lecture:

> the more we concentrate power and influence in the hands of a few, the greater the risk of alienation of the many. If, as a black person, you see very few black MPs and peers, no black High Court Judges, hardly any black FTSE 100 company directors, you are much less likely to feel that our society is your society, and you are likely to become disaffected and alienated.[16]

At first blush, this argument may seem to lead us to the same sort of broadly proportional diversity as follow from equal opportunity arguments, though here it is clear that the relevant community to which appointments should be proportional is not the privileged subset of actual or would-be lawyers or candidates for

14 Of course, key here is the extent to which such exclusion is 'freely chosen'. For an insight into the view of those seeking – and rejecting – judicial appointment see: H. Genn, *The Attractiveness of Senior Judicial Appointment to Highly Qualified Practitioners – Report to the Judicial Executive Board*, London: Judicial Office for England and Wales, 2008; and K. Malleson and F. Banda,*Factors Affecting the Decision to Apply for Silk and Judicial Office*, London: Lord Chancellor's Department, 2000.

15 This argument gained prominence in the context of *R (on the application of Miller and Dos Santos) v Secretary of State for Exiting the European Union and associated references* heard on the 5–8 December 2016 (the 'Brexit' case) during which the live streaming revealed in very vivid and visual way the lack of gender and racial diversity on the UKSC bench (and in the courtroom more generally). See, e.g. J. Parkinson, 'White men only? Brexit case and legal diversity', *BBC News*, 6 December 2016.

16 Lord Neuberger 'Rainbow Lecture on Diversity 2014', House of Commons, 12 March 2014.

judicial office but rather the wider public. On this view, so long as there is, at least over time, a broad correlation between, say, the BAME population and the number of BAME judges, it cannot be said to be, on this measure alone, unrepresentative of that community and insensitive to its interests.

However, on legitimacy arguments, proportional diversity should be thought of, at most, a starting point. First, arguments for proportional diversity require us to identify which communities the judiciary should reflect. The desire to ensure public confidence in the judiciary does not require all groups to be present on the bench. As Anne Phillips notes in the context of political representation:

> some divergences are positively beneficial. We do not normally consider the interests of lunatics as best represented by people who are mad … Establishing an empirical under-representation of certain groups does not in itself add up to a normative case for their equal or proportionate presence. It may alert us to overt forms of discrimination that are keeping people out, but it does not yet prove the case for radical change.[17]

It is clear that the judiciary is better off without any lunatics in its number. Now, equality of opportunity arguments will also get us to the same result. The equal opportunity these arguments support is an equality of opportunity for those possessing qualities and attributes relevant for judicial office: equal opportunities arguments count against the appointment of lunatics, not for it. But in respect of other groups, these two sorts of argument come apart. On equal opportunity arguments, the proportional representation of particular groups with particular distinguishing characteristics within the judiciary is an indicator that appointment to the bench is, as we might say, blind to those characteristics. So, assuming that judicial qualities are not disproportionately possessed by certain groups, we should expect a judiciary which succeeds in appointing those who possess such qualities in highest measure to find, roughly and over time, members of all such groups in proportion to their presence within the broader community. For instance, one might expect, again over time, to find judges born on all days of the week represented on the bench and in such numbers as would be consistent with a random allocation of judicial qualities across all birth-days. If it turned out that people born on Sunday were never, or almost never, appointed to the bench, it would indicate that, absent further information, we are missing out on some excellent candidates.

There is here then at least the makings of an equality of opportunity argument for appointing more people born on a Sunday (or at least for ensuring that the judiciary is truly open to those born on Sundays). Nonetheless, it is hard to imagine any explanation for the absence of people born on a Sunday within the judiciary other than innocent and benign statistical anomaly. And if this is the explanation then perhaps we should not worry about equality of opportunity here

17 A. Phillips, *The Politics of Presence: The Political Representation of Gender, Ethnicity and Race*, Oxford: Clarendon Press, 1995, p. 39.

after all: there's no reason to think that those born on a Sunday have had and now have any less an opportunity for judicial appointment; it is just chance that judicial qualities have been unevenly distributed for a period of time or that those born on a Sunday have disproportionately chosen other career paths (and not on account of any sort of discrimination or unequal treatment).

So take another group: Leos. There is no more reason to think that judicial qualities are distributed unevenly across different star signs as across different birthdays. So again, we might expect, roughly and over time, to find as many Leos on the bench as Virgos and Librans, and so on. And if we do not, that would again suggest that the judiciary is not finding all the best talents, raising a presumptive equality of opportunity concern. Here however there is a possible explanation other than statistical anomaly and chance. It is well documented that those born on dates nearer the start of the school year, and who are therefore, on the whole, older and better developed when they start school, have a continuing advantage over those born later and so who start school younger.[18] If those advantages are reflected in secondary school destinations and success, it is also likely to find some echo in university destinations and success and in turn in career choice and progression. And if this is true, then it is far from inconceivable that those born earlier in the school year end up advantaged when it comes to judicial appointment, not because those appointing judges have any preference for that particular characteristic but because those with that characteristic are more likely to be in a position to manifest or develop those attributes which are relevant to judicial office. If so, there is an equality of opportunity issue here: how do we ensure that those born later in the school year are not at any such disadvantage?[19]

But there would be no democratic legitimacy concern. Why? Because there is no history or (other) practice of prejudice or discrimination against Leos, no reason for members of such group to consider that the judiciary or broader legal system may be set against their interests. Indeed it makes little sense to speak of the interests of Leos, in so far as this implies any difference between their interests and the interests of (members of) other groups. Indeed there simply is no Leo identity of this kind.[20] And, on this basis, there is no reason to think that Leos, or indeed anyone else, would think that their relative absence from the judiciary marks some failure of the legal system to represent or respect the interests of that group. It is a different story, however, when we turn to other groups: for instance those defined by gender, race, sexuality, religion. For there is reason to think that, for example, the continuing and complete absence of BAME representation on either of the two appellate courts, when viewed against the backdrop of the

18 A study in 2015 found that 'the youngest children were almost twice as likely to have both language difficulties and behaviour problems relative to older children in the same reception class' (R. Adams, 'Summer-born children in danger of being left behind, says school study', *The Guardian*, 4 June 2015).

19 Of course, this isn't to suggest that it is a particularly pressing equality of opportunity concern, let alone one those appointing judges need to be alive to. The point is to bring out where these various arguments for diversity lead and how they differ.

20 Though Shelley von Strunckel may disagree.

broader treatment of such groups now and in the past, can only be doing increasing damage to the authority of the judiciary and the rule of law more broadly.

Moreover, again in contrast to equal opportunity arguments, the aim of ensuring public confidence in the judiciary will sometimes, as against a particular historical and social backdrop, necessitate more and occasionally less than proportional representation of the relevant groups.[21] Some groups may not need proportional representation in order to have confidence in the justice system and commitment to the rule of law. It is unlikely that the 80.5 per cent of the UK population who identify as 'White British'[22] would feel alienated and disadvantaged, or consider the judiciary to be democratically deficient, were the senior judiciary to be, say, 'only' three-quarters White British. (Though White British candidates for judicial office may complain of a lack of equal/fair opportunities.) Conversely, it may take more than a proportional representation of some minority groups to feel that a justice system that has historically assisted or facilitated their oppression or marginalization now stands up for them too. Here mere proportional representation may not be enough (especially if there is limited equality of opportunity to enter the relevant community/pool). At other times, proportional, representative appointment may seem tokenistic, particularly where numbers are small. Indeed, in such cases, exact proportional representation might not be possible.[23] If a particular minority makes up only, say, 5 per cent of the population, exact proportional representation on a 12-member supreme court at any one point of time is impossible.[24]

Finally, legitimacy arguments have implications for who should be chosen from these relevant groups and what they should do once appointed. In keeping with equal opportunity arguments, they support appointment of members of the relevant groups who are likely to make the best judges, for this in turn is most likely to improve confidence in the judiciary. But legitimacy arguments may take us beyond orthodox understandings of appointment on merit. For instance, if the judiciary is to have the confidence of all sections of the public, then it is important that those appointed from minority and traditionally under-represented groups are seen to make, or at least to be able to make, an equal contribution. By the same token, these arguments also suggest that there is a premium on those who seek to highlight rather than to play down their membership of the relevant group and the significance of these attributes to their position on the bench. It also matters what level these judges are: if judges from a particular group never or disproportionately rarely make it to the top courts, this may cause members of that group to doubt their equal standing within the judiciary. Or, going the other way,

21 For a full exposition of this argument in the context of political representation see Phillips, *The Politics of Presence*, pp. 46–47.

22 Census 2011 figure: www.ons.gov.uk/peoplepopulationandcommunity/culturalidentity/ethnicity/articles/ethnicityandnationalidentityinenglandandwales/2012-12-11 .

23 Phillips, *The Politics of Presence*, pp. 46–47.

24 Though it may be possible in cases where the UKSC utilizes its ability to call on ad hoc judges.

it may be thought to matter – and indeed matter more – that the judges members of public are more likely to see, including magistrates and Crown Court judges, are drawn from diverse backgrounds.[25]

To what sort of diverse judiciary do these legitimacy arguments lead? The short answer is that it will depend. What appointments will improve the legitimacy of the courts will depend not just on the present make-up of the judiciary but also, and more importantly, on the social and political backdrop against which those appointments fall to be made. We can divide up the public in any number of ways in reference to any number of different attributes. For many, indeed most, of these groups, there is simply no legitimacy argument for their representation on the bench. This is, as we have seen, true of the group 'people born on a Sunday', so too of Leos. This is because, while all such groups have a common denominator, the members of these groups have no real common or distinctive identity. It is only groups which have some such distinctive identity, which might then have the sort of distinctive culture or outlook which, it may be argued, a truly legitimate judiciary ought to represent. And it is only these groups which might reasonably feel that the judiciary or broader political system does or does not represent them *as a group*. But which groups have this sort of identity and which of these groups have received the sort of unequal treatment which might support calls for their greater presence on the bench will vary across times and across communities. If we were as blind to gender as we are to the days of the week on which people are born, then one could argue that there would be no legitimacy concern if the judiciary nonetheless happened to be predominantly, or indeed exclusively, male (though there would remain other arguments for greater gender balance and, were this state of affairs to continue, it would go to creating the conditions in which women may come to feel that the judiciary was not properly representative). In those communities, as ours, where there is no such gender blindness and instead long-standing gender inequality, and hence where there is a strong legitimacy argument for the appointment of more women judges, how many women judges it would take for the judiciary to be, on this one measure, representative and legitimate will depend on the identity of those judges and the contribution they (are able to) make and the way they are treated.

Judging differently

A final argument for diversity considers the difference a diverse judiciary might make to how cases are decided. That some measure of diversity is essential if the judiciary is to be best positioned do its principal job of deciding cases well is not seriously doubted. We would not be well served by a Supreme Court populated exclusively by judges from the Chancery Division, and this is so even were the

25 See, e.g. discussion in R. Hunter 'Problems of Scale in Achieving Judicial Diversity' and A. Lynch 'Diversity without a Judicial Appointments Commission – The Australian Experience', both in this collection.

Chancery Division possessed all the finest legal minds.[26] Similarly, a Supreme Court which is to hear appeals from Scotland and Northern Ireland, as well as from England and Wales, benefits from having Scottish and Northern Irish justices.[27]

The diversity in these examples is primarily a diversity of expertise, of technical legal competence: different judges have different specialisms and a judiciary which deals well with a range of different cases requires a selection of judges with specialisms spanning the full range of those cases. But our most senior judges are not just law-appliers but law-makers. Sometimes they must answer questions to which the law provides no answer, where the judge must fill a gap by making new law. At other times, top courts must consider whether to depart from existing law, moving the law in a new direction. The higher the court, the more of these questions the law leaves open. In all such cases, providing an answer requires judges to make their own determinations of what is just and reasonable. For these reasons, good judging involves not just technical legal skills but sound judgement, and a strong judiciary is marked not only by its legal expertise but also, and perhaps more importantly, by its ability to discharge its law-making responsibilities well.

The sort of good sense and good judgement that makes for good judicial law-making is more likely from a judiciary which possesses a broader range of perspectives and insights. This is not because good law seeks to combine all, or all plausible, viewpoints but because decision-making, whether of an individual or a collective, is only likely to be improved by exposure to and consideration of a variety of ideas and arguments: 'Out of the attrition of diverse minds there is beaten something which has a constancy and uniformity and average value greater than its component elements'.[28] This then gives us a different sort of argument for why we might value the increased presence of certain traditionally under-represented groups within the judiciary. In so far as members of such groups have experiences and insights which would better inform judicial decision-making and law-making, and where those experiences and insights have been missing or under-appreciated (at least in part) on account of the lesser representation of such groups from the judiciary, the judiciary would be stronger and judicial decision-making would be enhanced by greater diversity.

26 The best explanation of this point is Paterson and Paterson's: 'a relentlessly individualized concept of merit is entirely inappropriate for [the UKSC] ... In a rough sense, it would be akin to a football manager repeatedly signing high-scoring centre-forwards without any view to the wider needs of his side': A. Paterson and C. Paterson, *Guarding the Guardians? Towards an Independent, Accountable and Diverse Senior Judiciary*, London: CentreForum, 2012, p. 48.

27 This is not to suggest that the only reasons for having Scottish and Northern Irish justices is for their expertise in Scottish and Northern Irish law. For more on the role of Scottish judges in the House of Lords, see A. Paterson 'The Scottish Law Lords of Appeal, 1876–1988', *Juridical Review*, 1988, p. 235.

28 B. N. Cardozo, *The Nature of the Judicial Process*, New Haven: Yale University Press, 1921, p. 177.

What we are looking for is what one may call a diversity of contribution, in one way similar to the diversity of contribution provided by judges with different legal specialisms. Here though the diversity is not of expertise – of technical legal know-how – but of observation and insight. These diverse observations and insights in turn provide, not always but on occasion, a diversity of perspectives which can be brought to bear when addressing those questions which the positive law leaves unanswered. Where are these diverse insights likely to be found? In judges with varied backgrounds and experiences. For though one's background and experiences are not determinative of one's views and values, there's good reason to think that they play their part by setting the conditions to which those views and values are, in part, a response. So the argument this gives for having, say, more women judges is not that women are just as likely to possess the qualities of good judges (though this is true) nor that the legitimacy of or public confidence in our judiciary requires that women be better represented (though this too may be right), but that a predominantly male judiciary, particularly at appellate level, and as set against a common law made almost exclusively by men, is likely to miss out on insights and arguments that women judges would be more likely to provide and which would make for better decisions and better law.[29]

What sort of diversity does this argument support? If our aim in seeking a diverse judiciary is to see that certain neglected positions and arguments are better appreciated, this supports such diversity as is needed for these positions and arguments to be given the recognition and weight they merit. So it is likely that there are insights and arguments that (some) women judges are best, or perhaps uniquely, placed to provide and which, at the very least, merit consideration when it comes to determining how the law should respond to a range of practical problems.[30] What we then need is women judges who will indeed bring in those insights and arguments. But that there are certain insights which women judges are best placed to provide does not imply that these are insights which *only* women judges can appreciate or apply.[31] On the contrary, the ideal is that, once these insights and arguments are introduced, they become woven into the common law, adding to the stock of insights and arguments to which any judge – man or woman – may have recourse.

As such, it is conceivable that, on occasion, all it may take is one enlightened judge to offer a perspective or to see an argument others have missed but which

29 For the full argument, see Rackley, *Women, Judging and the Judiciary*.

30 See, e.g. Lady Hale's comment in relation to *R (on the application of* McDonald*) (Appellant) v Royal Borough of Kensington and Chelsea* [2011] UKSC 33 in which she was the sole dissent that it could be that the 'physical differences between men and women lead them to have different views of what dignity means in this context. So it is not surprising that women take a different view' (quoted in Paterson and Paterson, *Guarding the Guardians*).

31 Nor that all women judges will share the same insights or perspectives. Indeed, in so far as the valuable insights women can provide on some question may be diverse and, where they are, there is then a good of having women judges who can offer the full range of such insights.

those others then recognize and adopt. Certainly there will be times when something less than proportional representation will be sufficient: it is hardly likely that, from where we stand at present, the insights and experiences of white men would be neglected were they to come to be statistically under-represented in the judiciary. But for groups who have been long under-represented, full acceptance of the distinct insights and perspectives they may offer may require their proportional over-representation, at least in the short term. It may only be when such groups acquire what Will Kymlicka has termed a 'threshold presence' that they will be in a position to make a meaningful difference.[32]

Accordingly some arguments will have to be made and remade before they catch on. It may be that there are some issues on which, for instance, judges initially split along gender lines.[33] But this is not because, or at least this need not imply that, there are distinct male and female values, such as require that we stack the judiciary with women to ensure a balance between these distinct values. The sort of gender balance needed for all such insights and perspectives to find not only expression but also the recognition they merit within the case law is not something that can be answered in the abstract. It will depend on the condition in which a legal system and system of laws finds itself, on the range of questions judges must address within that system, and on the identities and attributes of present and potential members of the judiciary. So, on difference arguments, the case for having more women involved in law-making processes is stronger where the laws and law-making of a particular community more often fail to register or factor in insights and arguments which women are more likely to provide, and the case for having more women judges is stronger the more questions the positive law leaves open for judges and the more of those questions are ones on which women judges are likely to provide distinct perspectives. Similarly a community which is in such a position is likely to benefit from, or indeed require, a higher number of women judges where existing judges are less open to new arguments or different insights or where the women judges who would be appointed would, for whatever reason, struggle to get their voices heard.

Similarly context-dependent is what sorts of groups, or 'diversity characteristics', ought to be represented on the bench to ensure that the courts are in a position to benefit from the full range of relevant perspectives and insights. So, on difference arguments, for there to be any case at all for appointment of members of a particular group, *as* members of that group, we need to be able to identify particular

32 W. Kymlicka, *Multicultural Citizenship: A Liberal Theory of Minority Rights*, Oxford: Oxford University Press, 1995, ch. 7 discussed in Phillips *The Politics of Presence*, pp. 47 and 67. This can work either way – so that a small numerical group might be over-represented proportionally and vice versa. On this view, we might only need say 25 per cent women to change discussion – this is not to limit women to 25 per cent but just to argue that it may be that this is all that is needed on this basis. There is also a question about where this threshold presence is located: among the senior judiciary, on the Supreme Court and so on.

33 See e.g. discussion of the so-called wrongful birth cases in Rackley, *Women, Judging and the Judiciary*, pp. 177–185.

insights or perspectives which members of that group are likely to provide (and which are unlikely to be provided by others) which merit consideration when the courts address particular questions. Or at least we need to be able to say that it is likely that members of that group will have valuable insights or perspectives which others are unlikely to provide, even if we cannot yet say what those insights and perspectives will be. Here too then we will find no argument for the appointment of Leos or those born on Sunday. But it does give us an argument for the importance of diversity in relation not only to gender but to sexuality, race, class, disability and various other aspects of one's person or background which are likely to have played distinctive roles (for at least some people) in shaping (at least some of) their perspectives and values.

Conclusion

ANDREW TYRIE MP: What is the desired outcome [of the JAC's appointments process]? …

BARONESS PRASHAR: The desired outcome is that the judiciary becomes more diverse …

ANDREW TYRIE MP: More diverse up to what point? …

BARONESS PRASHAR: I am not willing at this stage to give you figures and numbers.[34]

There are various reasons why Tyrie's question may prove difficult to answer, some more compelling than others. But one good reason is that there is no one-size-fits-all model of an optimally diverse judiciary. Not only do the different arguments for diversity lead us, in the end, in different directions, but the sort of diversity each of these arguments supports will also, to a greater or lesser extent, vary from place to place and time to time. Moreover, these arguments are not mutually exclusive – accepting one does not commit us to denying the others – and the diversity we get when two or more of these arguments are combined will be different still. Finally these arguments for diversity do not exist in isolation but vie with other arguments which properly bear on the judiciary we should want and the judges we choose. That there are good reasons for wanting a diverse judiciary does not mean that this is or should be the sole or overriding objective in judicial appointments. It matters that the judiciary is legitimate, but this is not all that matters; that judicial decision-making is improved when it can call on a diversity of perspectives and insights does not mean that this is all good judicial decision-making involves. In all cases, judicial selectors must weigh these reasons against other reasons, other considerations which may, on the facts, count against an appointment which would improve diversity.

It is easy to assume that the value of diversity is never exhausted; that more diversity – or at least greater representation from traditionally under-represented

34 Constitutional Affairs Committee: *Minutes of Evidence*, 18 July 2006, Q.26–29.

groups – is always a good thing. The arguments we have offered here show why such assumptions may be misplaced. Different arguments for diversity are in truth arguments for different diversities, for differently constituted diverse judiciaries. For now, these arguments for diversity pull together. Each tells us that our judiciary is not diverse enough. It may be tempting, therefore, to leave thinking about what a diverse judiciary might, in an ideal world, look like until its reality is more pressing.[35] But given the significant number of upcoming vacancies on the Supreme Court,[36] and with increasing impatience at the slow rate of change and growing calls for the adoption of quotas and targets,[37] these questions may be upon us – and the JAC – sooner than we think.

35 See e.g. T. Legg's 'Reflection' in this collection.
36 See B. Hale, 'Appointments to the Supreme Court' in this collection.
37 See e.g. Malleson, 'The Disruptive Potential of Ceiling Quotas'; Bindman and Monaghan, *Judicial Diversity: Accelerating Change*; Anon, 'Lady Hale calls for targets to address lack of judicial diversity', *Scottish Legal News*, 23 Feb 2016.

Reflection

Jenny Rowe CB

After a long and distinguished career as a civil servant, including an extended period in the Lord Chancellor's Department, Jenny Rowe CB became the first Chief Executive of the UK Supreme Court in 2008. The Chief Executive has a statutory duty to run 'an efficient and effective administration', under the direction of the Court's President and Deputy President and including oversight of the Court's annual budget. In 2015, the Court had an operating income of £7.98million.

When I took up my appointment as Chief Executive of the UK Supreme Court in May 2008, the issue of appointments to the Supreme Court did not feature in my thinking at all. Indeed I do not recall any mention of the appointment process, and a role for the Chief Executive, in the recruitment material for my post. Not until late 2008 did it dawn on me that this was a major issue where I needed to do some serious thinking in conjunction with Lord Phillips, then the senior Law Lord, but appointed to be the first President of the Supreme Court.

I was not the only person in this position: it soon became clear that Ministry of Justice (MoJ) officials had not given this a great deal of thought. (One of the consequences of that was that I had no budget to support the appointment process!) And later still, officials in the devolved administrations were somewhat bemused when I contacted them about the role devolved politicians and judges had in the process. At the time there were too many practical things to do for me to enable me to spend long considering how this state of affairs had arisen; but reflecting on it after seven years or so it seems remarkable that more time had not been spent on considering the needs of the highest Court in the UK, and one which operated regularly at that crucial nexus between politics and the law.

As a junior official in the 1980s I had worked in judicial appointments under the 'old' system; I had been responsible for civil and public service appointments at a senior level; and I had undertaken a good deal of interviewing and assessing. But the new judicial appointments system introduced by the Constitutional Reform Act 2005 (the Act) was not familiar to me; and Lord Bingham had agreed with the Lord Chancellor that this system would be used on a voluntary basis for any appointments that needed to be made prior to the Supreme Court coming into being, and before the relevant statutory provisions came into force.

The Act sets out a broad framework and some very specific requirements, including consultation with all the senior judiciary and politicians around the UK, and requirements such as selection must be on merit. But the Act also allowed each selection commission to determine its own process. This provided considerable flexibility when we were establishing the first selection commission and working out the approach. We could have been cautious and, for example, adopted the approach of inviting existing senior judges to apply. The Act, however, provided for the eligibility of suitably experienced lawyers who were not judges and Lord Phillips was determined that the process should be as open and transparent as possible. We therefore took what many saw as a radical step of publicly advertising and inviting applications.

Amongst the issues we had to consider/bear in mind were:

- The fact that we were recruiting to the House of Lords initially so that the successful applicants would be made peers, but those that followed might not. (There are wider issues here about the role of the House of Lords and possible reform; the role retired judges can and should play in the legislative process; and indeed the issue of judicial titles for Justices of the Supreme Court);
- The process set out in the legislation was clunky and the statutory consultees were almost exclusively men;
- The challenge of maintaining confidentiality. Towards the end of the process the names of two applicants who were not already judges entered the public domain. This was very concerning for them and a matter of great frustration to me, as it continued to be on every future occasion. My training in recruitment, as well as my personal experiences, made me regard confidentiality as critical in generating confidence in the system, and in encouraging individuals who might lack confidence to apply;
- How to define the job and the skills and experience required. In particular how best to articulate criteria which properly reflect merit, and which differentiate from the skills and experience required of Judges at Court of Appeal/Court of Session level: and which can also apply to non-judicial applicants. This has proved to be a continuing challenge and the criteria have been refined subsequently;
- How to define/assess merit;
- The requirement for geographical representation and the fact that these were UK appointments.

The first of these issues was the only one unique to the first competition and the selection commissions which followed provided opportunities to reflect further on these matters, as well as highlighting other things to be considered. In all seven selection commissions sat in the period from 2008/9 to 2013, including one for the post of President and one for that of Deputy President. The latter was the only one not publicly advertised as we were at the full complement of Justices. Supported by my secretary, I provided the support to all those commissions. I believe this continuity was helpful and made it easier to review and learn lessons from each experience. At the same time officials in relevant departments, and those working for senior Judges, were also able to consider and identify good practice.

I conducted two reviews of the process, one internal review in 2010 and a further review in 2015 which was published, and which can be found on the UK Supreme Court website. These were more formal opportunities to take stock and, on the second occasion in particular to consult a wide range of interested bodies. One of the issues which caused me concern was how to get the best out of the consultation process required by the Act. The most helpful responses for the commission were those specifically addressed to the criteria and backed up by evidence. The quality and nature of the responses inevitably varied, but all helped to build up a picture of individual applicants.

The function and conduct of the interview was another feature we considered regularly. I find it difficult to envisage a process that does not include an interview, but there is always a risk that the interview, coming as it does at the end of the process, might play a disproportionately large part in the decision making process.

I know that the internal dynamics of a selection commission has been a topic of some interest, and no little speculation, from observers of the process. There are some general points it is possible for me to make in an essay of this nature. The suggestion is frequently made that lay members of a selection commission will inevitably give way to the judicial members. Such suggestions tend to overlook the fact that the lay members all came with extensive interviewing and appointments experience, and from a variety of professional backgrounds. The judges were always very respectful of these levels of expertise and welcomed the perspective offered by lay members. Indeed, in a situation where inevitably many of the applicants were known to the judges, the lay members were well placed to identify and probe issues which may not have been so apparent to those more familiar with their day to day work. There was no shortage of lively discussion and debate, and no question at all of the lay members being supine.

Inevitably I have not been able to touch on all relevant issues in the preceding paragraphs. One very important issue is that of diversity and the need to attract the widest range of applicants. Another is the question of what, if any, role politicians should play in the process and the issue of the so called 'democratic deficit'. I will confine myself to saying that if there were easy solutions we would have found them by now!

15 Appointments to the Supreme Court[1]

Lady Hale DBE

'Once we accept that who the judge is matters, then it matters who our judges are.'

So says Professor Erika Rackley in her prize-winning book, *Women, Judging and the Judiciary.*[2] If this is so of the judiciary as a whole, then how much more so must it be of the Supreme Court? The case load of the Supreme Court consists almost entirely of cases raising an 'arguable point of law of general public importance which ought to be considered by the Supreme Court at that time …'.[3] In other words, the point is arguable, because there is no law or what law there is does not give a clear answer. It is a point of law, rather than of practice and procedure, which we usually leave to the appeal courts in each part of the United Kingdom. It is of general public importance, because it matters to a great many more people than the parties to the case, often to the public as a whole, whose interests need to be protected. And the case is a suitable vehicle for the Supreme Court to decide it. These are the hard cases which matter to us all. They are also the cases where the judges have a choice.

It has long been recognized, as Justice Felix Frankfurter of the United States Supreme Court put it, that a person 'brings his whole experience, his training, his outlook, his social, intellectual and moral environment with him when he takes a seat on the supreme bench.'[4] Another famous American Judge, Benjamin Cardozo, argued that this should be seen as a good thing:

> The eccentricities of judges balance one another. One judge looks at problems from the point of view of history, another from that of philosophy, another from that of social utility; one is a formalist, another a latitudinarian, one is

1 This is the text of a keynote lecture given at the University of Birmingham in November 2015, before the appointments of Liz Truss as Lord Chancellor and Lord Kakkar as Chair of the Judicial Appointments Commission and the advertisement of three vacancies in March 2017. The final proofs of this chapter were submitted to the publishers before the announcement that from October 2017 Lady Hale would be President of the UK Supreme Court, joined by the second woman to serve on the Court: Lady Black.

2 E. Rackley, *Women, Judging and the Judiciary: From Difference to Diversity*, London: Routledge, 2013, winner of the Society of Legal Scholars' Peter Birks prize for the best academic law book published that year.

3 UK Supreme Court, Practice Direction 3.3.3.

4 P. Elman (ed.), *Of Law and Men: Papers and Addresses of Felix Frankfurter*, New York: Harcourt, 1956, pp. 40–41.

> timorous of change, another dissatisfied with the present; out of the attrition of diverse minds there is beaten something which has a constancy and uniformity and average value greater than its component elements.[5]

These eminent judges were writing at a time when the United States Supreme Court Justices were all white men. If the attrition of diverse minds is a good thing in itself, then how much better would it be if those diverse minds incorporated diversity in a wider range of parameters than their 'eccentricities', including of course sex, ethnicity, professional and social background. Not only that, if yet another eminent American judge, Oliver Wendell Holmes Jr, was right to say that 'the life of the law has not been logic; it has been experience',[6] then we must have a wider range of experiences contributing to that life. As Professor Judith Resnik has put it:[7]

> A major shared premise [of feminist legal scholarship] is that knowledge of the world is constructed from one's viewpoint and that what has been assumed (by some) as a universal viewpoint is, in fact, a viewpoint of some men, who have articulated a vision of reality and claimed it to be true for us all.

We are talking, of course, of the top appellate court, where the judges sit as a panel. In most of the old common law world, the top courts sit en banc, nine in the US and Canada, seven in Australia, and five in New Zealand. We in the UK are unusual in sitting in panels, usually of five but sometimes of seven or nine. Since moving from the House of Lords, we have sat in larger panels more often than we did there. There are various reasons for this, including our ready access to a larger courtroom, but one is that, the greater the number of justices who agree upon it, the greater authority is given to a decision. Another is the (apparently) reduced risk that the composition of the panel will dictate the result. We do not accept that any of us is sufficiently consistent and predictable in his or her approach for this to be a real problem. But we acknowledge that the public may think it so.

So how are we doing with appointments to our own Supreme Court? I was sworn in as a 'Lord of Appeal in Ordinary' on 12 January 2004. Fifteen people have been sworn in as Lords of Appeal in Ordinary or Justices of the Supreme Court of the United Kingdom since then. Even if we leave out the two who were sworn in the day after me,[8] the Court has more than replaced itself in that time. One might have hoped that the opportunity would have been taken to achieve a more diverse collegium. It has not happened.

5 B. Cardozo, *The Nature of the Judicial Process*, New Haven: Yale University Press, 1961, p. 177.
6 O. W. Holmes Jr, *The Common Law*, Boston: Little, Brown, and Company, 1881, p. 1.
7 J. Resnik, 'On the Bias: Feminist Reconsiderations of the Aspirations for Our Judges', *Southern California Law Review* 61, 1988, pp. 1878, 1906.
8 Lord Brown of Eaton-under-Heywood and Lord Carswell. The editors of the Law Reports assumed, until corrected, that I was junior to them.

All of those 13 appointments were men. All were white. All but two went to independent fee-paying schools. All but three went to boys' boarding schools. All but two went to Oxford or Cambridge. All were successful QCs in private practice, although one was a solicitor rather than a barrister. All but two had specialized in commercial, property or planning law. None had spent much, if any, time as an employee. I share with them the experience of being white and having been to Cambridge. In every other of those respects I am different: I went to a state day school, my profession was University teacher and then Law Commissioner, my specialism was family and social welfare law. How is it that, despite their very different characters and outlooks, they remain such a homogenous group?

The Constitutional Reform Act 2005 (CRA), which set up the Supreme Court, has little to say about the criteria for appointment or the qualities necessary to do the job. Candidates for appointment must of course meet the statutory criteria,[9] but these are very wide. A person must have:

a held high judicial office for a period of at least two years; this means being a judge of the High Court, Court of Session, or above;[10] or
b satisfied the 'judicial-appointment eligibility condition'[11] on a 15-year basis; this means being a barrister or solicitor in England and Wales and having engaged in law related activities, both for 15 years or more; but law related activities are very widely defined, and include acting as an arbitrator or mediator, practice or employment as a lawyer, and teaching or researching law;[12] or
c been a 'qualifying practitioner' for a period of at least 15 years; a qualifying practitioner is either a Scottish advocate or a solicitor entitled to appear in the Court of Session or the High Court of Judiciary or a Northern Irish barrister or solicitor.[13]

Thus there is no requirement that candidates be serving judges or indeed be in independent practice either as a barrister or solicitor, as long as they are professionally qualified and experienced in law. Judicial experience is obviously helpful (academics have the luxury of being able to consider points of principle without having to decide real cases) but there are a great many different kinds of such experience. In a collegiate body where many different voices may be heard, there is no reason why a suitably qualified academic lawyer should not be appointed. Several Justices of the Supreme Court of the United States were academic lawyers before they were appointed directly to federal appellate courts. One Justice had not been any kind of judge before appointment. Only two have ever been trial judges.

9 CRA, s. 25(1).
10 CRA, s. 60(2)(a).
11 As defined in the Tribunals, Courts and Enforcement Act 2007, s. 50.
12 2007 Act, s. 52.
13 CRA, s. 25(2).

The 2005 Act provides that selection must be 'on merit'.[14] But at the same time, the selection commission must ensure that, between them, the judges of the Court will have knowledge of, and experience of practising, the law of each part of the United Kingdom.[15] In practice, this has so far meant that we have followed the usual practice in the House of Lords of having two Justices from Scotland and one from Northern Ireland. This has meant that when there is a vacancy from either place, it has been filled by another Justice from that place. There is obvious good sense in having this geographical quota in a court which is there to serve the whole of the United Kingdom, but it raises some interesting questions.

First, what if the only candidate from the place in question is conspicuously less meritorious than candidates from elsewhere in the United Kingdom? I hasten to say that this has not yet happened. All our ethnic (Celtic) minority are of very high quality indeed. But given the small size of the actual pool in Scotland and Northern Ireland, it is not inconceivable that the problem would arise in future. Second, with, at present, nine Justices likely to come from England and Wales, there is scope for appointing Justices with little or no experience of judging or even legal practice but with all the other qualities required to be a success. But in Scotland and even more so in Northern Ireland, there is little scope for such diversity of professional background.

Third, what is meant by a 'part' of the United Kingdom? Should it now include Wales? At present England and Wales share the same justice system. But we no longer share the same legislative system. Since 2011 Wales has had full legislative competence in relation to devolved matters and increasingly Welsh law is diverging from English law in those areas. The point has been made that it is rare indeed for provinces, states or territories within larger sovereign states to have their own legislatures but not also to have their own justice systems. If Wales were eventually to achieve its own justice system, then the case for a Welsh Justice would be compelling. But even before that, it can be argued that, at least for any case involving specifically Welsh law, there should be a Welsh Judge on the court. At present we have the great advantage that the Lord Chief Justice of England and Wales is a Welshman with a deep understanding of the Welsh context. That may not always be the case. But to increase the ethnic quota when we do not have any other sort of quota or even targets to redress historical disadvantage might make achieving other important forms of diversity even harder.

So how were those 13 appointments made? The first two[16] were appointed in what I assume to be the time-honoured way. The Lord Chancellor consulted the serving Law Lords at a round table meeting in his office in the House of Lords. The senior Law Lord, Lord Bingham, spoke first and it would have taken a bold person to disagree with him. The Lord Chancellor no doubt also consulted the Lord Chief Justice, the Master of the Rolls, and the other Heads of Division. A name emerged and the Prime Minister was advised accordingly. Before advising

14 CRA, s. 27(5).
15 CRA, s. 27(8).
16 Lord Mance and Lord Neuberger of Abbotsbury.

Her Majesty to make the appointment, the Prime Minister checked with the person concerned whether he was willing to accept it. This was presumably (and certainly in my case) the first that he had heard of it.

Things changed after the changes made to other judicial appointments by the Constitutional Reform Act 2005 came into force. It was decided voluntarily to adopt the new model for Supreme Court appointments even before the Supreme Court came into existence. So Lord Collins, Lord Kerr and Lord Clarke were appointed in the new way, as have been all the later appointments.

Under the 2005 Act, the Lord Chancellor must convene a selection commission when it appears that the number of Justices is or will soon be less than the maximum allowed.[17] The maximum is now the full-time equivalent of 12.[18] Thus commissions are convened ad hoc when a vacancy arises, although the same commission may deal with more than one vacancy if they will soon arise. Originally, the members had to include the President of the Court, who would preside, the Deputy President, a member of the Judicial Appointments Commission for England and Wales, a member of the Judicial Appointments Board for Scotland, and a member of the Judicial Appointments Commission for Northern Ireland. Following changes made by the Crime and Courts Act 2013, the Deputy President is no longer a member of the commission. Instead, there must be a 'senior UK judge', nominated by the President, 'having due regard to the territorial composition of the selection commission'.[19] The Deputy President and other Supreme Court Justices do not count as senior UK judges for this purpose.[20] The likelihood is that the Lord Chief Justice, or his equivalent in Scotland or Northern Ireland, will be nominated, depending on the part of the United Kingdom from which the vacancy arises.

The change was explained on the basis that it would improve the prospects of more diverse appointments if the existing Supreme Court judiciary were not two-fifths of the selection commission. It has not gone unnoticed[21] that this change coincided with my own appointment as Deputy President. It is not obvious that increasing the already very substantial influence of the national chief justice will change mattes for the better – although at least he does now have a statutory duty to encourage judicial diversity[22] and the present incumbent in England and Wales is going about this in a vigorous manner.

Apart from the President, who sits ex officio, and the senior UK judge, who is nominated by the President, the other members are normally nominated by the Chairman of the respective appointments bodies. In practice, the Chairmen in England and Wales and Scotland have usually nominated themselves. But the

17 CRA, s. 26(5A).

18 CRA, s. 23(2).

19 Supreme Court (Judicial Appointments) Regulations 2013/2193, regs. 11(1)(e) and 14(1)(b).

20 Reg. 2(f) and 2005 Act, s. 60(1)(b) to (i).

21 For example, by Lord Hope, *HL Debate on the Regulations*, HL Hansard, 23 July 2013, col. GC405.

22 CRA, s. 137A, inserted by the Crime and Courts Act 2013.

Chairman of the Northern Ireland Commission is the Lord Chief Justice, who has not thought it appropriate to nominate himself. At least two of the non-judicial members must be non-legally qualified,[23] and in practice there have often been three non-lawyers. The nominators must also have regard to the fact 'that it is desirable that the members of the selection commission should include (a) both men and women, and (b) members drawn from a range of different racial groups'.[24] In practice, there has almost always been at least one woman on the commission, but since Baroness Usha Prashar ceased to be Chairman of the Commission for England and Wales they have all, I believe, been white British.

The scheme of the Act is that one name goes forward for each vacancy. (Long gone are the days when two names were put up to the Prime Minister for him to choose between.) The Lord Chancellor has three basic options. He can agree to the selection; he can reject it if he thinks the candidate is not suitable; or he can ask the commission to think again if he thinks there is not enough evidence that the candidate is suitable, or there is evidence that this is not the best candidate on merit, or there is not enough evidence that the Court would then have knowledge and experience of the law in each part of the United Kingdom.[25] In practice, he has always agreed to the selection. He has to give reasons for either of the other options,[26] and this raises the possibility of judicial review (although I doubt very much whether any serious candidate would wish to invoke this). Once agreed, the name is forwarded to the Prime Minister who advises Her Majesty accordingly.[27] This means that there is hardly any scope for political influence over the selections. It is interesting that we have gone from a system which was theoretically entirely in the hands of the politicians, although in practice appointments have not been made on political grounds for decades now, to a system which is in reality outside the hands of the politicians.

Is this a good thing? In most other common law countries, the final selection is always made by a government minister. Even when there is a selection commission, the practice can be to submit more than one name, so that the minister may choose. This practice is viewed with alarm by many who value our tradition of a judiciary which is entirely independent of party politics. Does the country really want the minister's political advisers trawling through the judgments of the recommended candidates so as to select the one with whom they are most comfortable? On the other hand, it is noteworthy that we have recently had two eminent journalists raising the issue of whether the public has a right to know the politics of the senior judiciary.

Charles Moore has argued that, 'if they are to decree what is "right" and apply slippery concepts like "proportionality", rather than sticking to strictly legal issues, we need to know their politics'.[28] We can argue about the extent to which such

23 Reg. 13(3).
24 Reg. 11(3).
25 Regs. 20 and 21(1) and (2).
26 Reg. 21 (3).
27 CRA, s. 26(2) and (3).
28 C. Moore, 'We're turning judges into masters of the state, which is not their job', *Daily Telegraph*, 24 October 2015.

'legal issues' have always involved difficult and sometimes politically charged choices. But we also need to think about his assertion that 'The effective removal of the Lord Chancellor from the process (in the name of political impartiality), far from opening up the field, has made the judiciary an even tighter club'. Jeremy Paxman has also argued that we need to know more about precisely who our judges are. He asked 'If the English appointments process is nosy enough to inquire about sexual preferences, why does it not also ask how would-be judges vote in elections?'[29] One answer might be that we ask about sexual preferences because sexual orientation is a characteristic expressly protected by the Equality Act 2010 whereas politics as such are not. The argument which Paxman accepts as 'unanswerable' is that in the UK the Supreme Court is not supreme: Parliament can always trump the judiciary by passing a new law.

But might there be other ways of improving the democratic legitimacy of appointments without exposing them to the risk of party political bias? In Israel, for example, the appointing body is composed of both Parliamentarians and serving Judges. One possibility would be to include senior politicians, one from the government and one from the opposition, on the selection commissions. This might improve the input of elected Parliamentarians into appointments without making them overtly party political. Simply including the Lord Chancellor on the commission might run that risk.

The Act provides that there may be up to 12 Justices – this now includes 12 full-time equivalents, thus making it possible to have so-called 'part-time' salaried appointments.[30] This has been tried elsewhere in the judiciary with a view to making the job more attractive to people with caring and other responsibilities which make it hard for them to take on the role full time. Obviously, thought will have to be given to how this might be accommodated in the next round of appointments. If there is only a single vacancy, the court would lose judge-power unless there were candidates wishing to job-share. This might be less of a problem where there were several vacancies to fill. Another problem might be defining the minimum requirement for a full-time post, whether in terms of days actually sitting in court or in terms of the number of cases undertaken, because we all work in such very different ways.

At present, the selection commissions do not undertake any outreach work with a view to encouraging the widest possible range of candidates to consider applying. Those whom our former chief executive, Jenny Rowe, consulted for the purpose of her recent review of our appointments process agreed that by the time each ad hoc commission is convened it is too late. There were also risks in any member of a selection commission encouraging particular individuals to apply. But most thought that the court itself – the Justices and senior staff – should be engaging in such work – encouraging suitable people and even groups of people to consider putting themselves forward, offering shadowing and mentoring, and the like. One possibility would be to establish an unofficial 'search committee',

29 J. Paxman, 'Who are you to judge?', *Financial Times*, 31 October 2015.
30 CRA, s. 23(2), as amended by the 2013 Act.

keeping an eye open for potential future candidates and giving them appropriate experience and encouragement so that they would be better placed to make an application when the opportunity arose. It occurs to me that this is something where the Deputy President might take the lead, given that she is no longer on the commission itself.

The Act has little to say about how the commissions should go about their work. They do have to have regard to any guidance given by the Lord Chancellor (but so far as I know, none has yet been given).[31] They have developed a set of qualities and abilities against which to measure merit. In the most recent recruitment, these included 'exceptional' ability in the following areas:

- knowledge and experience of the law;
- intellectual ability and interest in the law, with a significant capacity for analysing and exploring a range of legal problems creatively and flexibly;
- willingness and ability to learn about new areas of the law;
- clarity of thought and expression; and
- an ability to work under pressure and to produce work with reasonable expedition.

Candidates also had to show:

- social awareness and understanding of the contemporary world;
- an ability to work with colleagues, respecting their views, but also being able to challenge and debate in a constructive way;
- a willingness to take part in the wider representative role of a Supreme Court justice, for example by delivering lectures, taking part in conferences, meeting student and other groups; and
- vision, coupled with an appreciation of the role of the court in contributing to the development of the law.

And, perhaps above all:

- independence of mind; and
- integrity.

Obviously, these criteria have been developed with some notion of what is entailed in the job of Supreme Court Justice. One of Jenny Rowe's other recommendations is that we establish mechanisms to draw up a more detailed job description for Supreme Court Justices, in consultation with 'external stakeholders' as well as current Justices. This might lead to some revision of the selection criteria. While I can see that this would be a good idea – it might lead us to question some of our current assumptions – I am a bit sceptical about what difference it would make. The qualities listed are the obvious ones, although it is

31 CRA, s. 27(9).

interesting that they do not include that elusive quality, 'judgment'. The more difficult questions are how they are to be assessed and weighted against one another.

The basic process of making selections was established by the first commission and has remained largely unchanged. It begins with open advertisement, although usually not in the print media, because they are so expensive. It continues with letters of application. There is at present no formal application form, but applicants are expected to address themselves to each of the criteria and provide evidence of how they are met. They are also expected to submit examples of judgments of which they are particularly proud and of extra-judicial writings or speeches. They are also asked to name referees. Jenny Rowe has suggested that there should be a formal application form, so that the commission has the same basic data on each candidate, but that candidates should also submit a CV and a short personal statement. Some of the potential candidates may find the whole process of selling themselves in this way off-putting: many have never had to make a job application in their lives. We should be looking for ways to help and encourage the best to apply.

The Regulations require the commission to consult the senior judiciary: that is, the judges of the Supreme Court, the Lord Chief Justice of England and Wales, the Master of the Rolls, the Lord President of the Court of Session, the Lord Chief Justice of Northern Ireland, the Lord Justice Clerk (the second senior Scottish judge), the President of the Queen's Bench Division, the President of the Family Division, and the Chancellor of the High Court.[32] The commission also has to consult the Lord Chancellor, the First Minister in Scotland, the First Minister in Wales, and the Chairman of the Northern Ireland Judicial Appointments Commission. Normally, these people are consulted on all the applications received, before any short-listing (but may be after long-listing). It may be worth pointing out that, at present, all but one of these people are men.

There is at present no set form for referees and statutory consultees. Jenny Rowe has suggested developing a more structured set of questions for them 'with the aim of eliciting the most useful information'. But if so, I do hope that this does not turn into the very rigid form which referees and judicial assessors are expected to fill in for other judicial appointments and allows referees and consultees the freedom to supply narrative references giving the real flavour of the candidate.

Once this information is in, the commission draws up a short list for interview. The general view of Jenny Rowe's consultees was that an interview was inevitable and could be very useful in exploring some of the criteria. It is particularly important for the lay members who would probably not know the candidates personally or by reputation. But there is also concern that the interview can play too decisive a part in the overall process. Jenny Rowe recommends that the commission should have a long meeting in advance of the interviews, going through all the material available, arriving at provisional views on who should be

32 Reg. 18.

recommended and identifying areas to explore with particular candidates. After the interviews, it might be helpful to wait a day or so before taking a final decision, so as to reflect on all the evidence.

At present, before the Lord Chancellor decides whether to accept the selection, he must again consult the statutory consultees.[33] This is very odd, given the limited options available to him. It is particularly odd, embarrassing even, in the case of appointments as President or Deputy President. It means that the other Justices of the court know the result, but the candidates do not (unless they have indiscreet friends who spill the beans).

The next selection commission is also going to have to consider what to do about the so-called 'equal merit' provision. Where two persons are of equal merit, the Equality Act 2010 'does not prevent the commission from preferring one of them over the other for the purpose of increasing diversity within the group of persons who are the judges of the Court'.[34]

The House of Lords Constitution Committee recommended that this should apply to all judicial appointments.[35] Their evidence revealed different views about whether it would make a difference. Some thought that it might do so in the larger selection exercises for the lower ranks of the judiciary, where it could be very difficult to rank all of the candidates in strict order of merit. But for individual appointments at the higher levels, some doubted whether two candidates are ever truly equal, if you drill deep enough.[36] Others argued that the assessment of comparative merit is an inherently subjective exercise – how do you rate each candidate against each desirable quality and how do you rate each quality against the others? So you might well end up with candidates who were equally well-qualified, but for different reasons.[37] I take the latter view, because there is so much room for variation in choosing, assessing and then weighting the various parameters involved in merit. The Constitution Committee were uncertain how often it would be used, but took the view that might enable more candidates from under-represented groups to be appointed and it would 'send out a strong signal that diversity in judicial appointments is important, without undermining the merit principle'.[38]

The next selection commission is going to have to decide what use, if any, to make of this provision, which is optional. One issue is whether it should just be applied to the obvious 'headline' criteria of sex and race, or whether to all the other characteristics protected by the Equality Act 2010. Another is whether it should only be deployed at the final selection stage (as the JAC have decided) or

33 Reg. 19(5).
34 CRA, s. 27(5A)(b), added by the 2013 Act.
35 House of Lords, Select Committee on the Constitution, *Judicial Appointments: 25th Report of Session 2010–2012*, HL Paper 272.
36 Including Lord Sumption, JAC Chair Christopher Stephens, and Baroness Neuberger.
37 Including the then Lord Chancellor, Kenneth Clarke, Lord Neuberger, Lord Justice Goldring and Lady Justice Hallett.
38 House of Lords Select Committee on the Constitution, *Judicial Appointments,* para 101.

whether it could be deployed at the shortlisting stage as well. The JAC's approach has been criticized[39] on the basis that it would obviously be much more powerful if it meant that candidates who were identified as potentially able to benefit from this provision were identified at an early stage and included in the later stages of the selection process. Leaving it to the end means that the selection commission has already narrowed its options before it knows whether the candidates are truly equal.

Another problem is that if the field of choice is narrowed by having regard to the subject matter needs of the court, then the scope for improving diversity would be even further reduced. We already have our ethnic quota, which may well have to go up to four in the foreseeable future. If we start trying to predict our subject matter needs, we may well introduce bias in favour of subject areas where under-represented groups are not strong. Who would have thought that we would have three Justices who started their full-time judicial careers in the Family Division of the High Court?

I believe that anyone who is appointing the Justices of the Supreme Court should be able to look at the body of Justices as a whole and ask how they can collectively best serve the needs of the UK justice system. Excellence is important (though I am embarrassed to claim it). But so is diversity of expertise. And so is diversity of background and experience. It really bothers me that there are women, who know or ought to know that they are as good as the men around them, but who won't apply for fear of being thought to be appointed just because they are a woman. We early women believed that we were as good as the men and would certainly not be put off in this way. I may well have been appointed because the powers that be realized the need for a woman. I am completely unembarrassed about that, because they were right, and I hope that I have justified their confidence in me. I don't think that all the talk about the best women being deterred is a plot to put them off, but I am sure that they should not be deterred by talk such as this. We owe it to our sex, but also to the future of the law and the legal system, to step up to the plate.

The great Lord Bingham seems to have agreed. He pointed out that merit 'is not self-defining'. It 'directs attention to proven professional achievement as a necessary condition, but also enables account to be taken of wider considerations, including the virtue of gender and ethnic diversity'.[40] There will inevitably be six vacancies on the Supreme Court between September 2016 and December 2018 and a further three before the middle of 2020. It is hoped to be able to fill this in groups of three at a time, which may make it easier to achieve a more balanced 'ticket'. If we do not manage to achieve a (much) more diverse Court in the process we ought to be ashamed of ourselves.

39 By the Equal Justices Campaign (now known as the Judicial Diversity Initiative).

40 T. Bingham, 'The Law Lords: Who Has Served', in L. Blom-Cooper, B. Dickson and G. Drewry (eds), *The Judicial House of Lords 1976–2009*, Oxford: Oxford University Press, 2009, p. 126.

Appendix I

The JAC's selection exercise activity (2006–2016)

Year	*Number of selection exercises*	*Recommendations made*	*Applications received*	*Number of times Lord Chancellor, Lord Chief Justice or Senior President of Tribunals rejected or requested reconsideration of JAC recommendation*
2006–2007	The JAC ran 38 exercises in total during 2006–2007, but only seven were launched and run using the JAC's new processes.	In the seven selection exercises run under its new processes, the JAC made **64** recommendations.[a]	2,210	0 (All 64 recommendations that the JAC made using its new selection processes were accepted by the Lord Chancellor).
2007–2008	41	**458**	2,535	0
2008–2009	24	**449**	3,518	1[b]
2009–2010	25	**446**	3,084	1[c]
2010–2011	21	**684**	4,684	1[d]
2011–2012	25	**746**	5,490	2[e]
2012–2013	36	**597**	4,637	0
2013–2014	35	**806**	5,591	0
2014–2015	30	**312**	2,056	0
2015–2016	22	**340**	2,588	1[f]
	TOTAL	**4,902**	36,393	6

a The JAC inherited a large number of transitional selection exercises that commenced under the pre-2006 selection regime. Only 13 selection exercises were launched and run during 2006-07 using the JAC's new processes, and of these only 7 were fully completed during the year.

b The Lord Chancellor asked the JAC to reconsider one recommendation and a new recommendation was subsequently accepted. The need for a reconsideration arose from a lack of clarity about what were essential criteria for a candidate to meet and what were desirable.

c The Lord Chancellor asked for reconsideration of one recommendation. On reconsideration the recommendation was confirmed and was subsequently accepted by the Lord Chancellor.

d The Lord Chancellor rejected one recommendation where he considered the candidate was not suitable for the particular function of the office for which they were selected. In this instance the JAC made another recommendation, which was accepted.

e The Lord Chancellor rejected two recommendations for fee-paid medical members, where the number and range of applicants was limited. The Lord Chancellor considered the candidates did not have the required experience for the particular function of the office.

f The Lord Chief Justice rejected recommendation for a salaried legal post on the basis that the recommended candidate did not have the requisite experience for the office.

Appendix II

Key officeholders during the JAC's first decade

2006–2007				
JAC Chair	*Other JAC Commissioners*	*JAC Chief-Executive*	*Lord Chancellor*	*Lord Chief Justice*
Baroness Prashar (*Lay*)	Lord Justice Auld[a] (*Judicial*) Dame Lorna Boreland-Kelly (*Lay Justice*) Professor Dame Hazel Genn (*Lay*) Mr Justice Goldring (*Judicial*) Lady Justice Hallett (*Judicial*) Sir Geoffrey Inkin (*Lay*) Judge Frances Kirkham (*Judicial*) Edward Nally (*Professional: Solicitor*) Sara Nathan (*Lay*) District Judge Charles Newman (*Judicial*) Judge David Pearl (*Tribunal*) Francis Plowden (*Lay*) Harriet Spicer (*Lay*) Jonathan Sumption QC (*Professional: Barrister*)	Claire Pelham	Lord Falconer[b]	Lord Phillips
2007–2008				
Baroness Prashar (*Lay*)	Lady Justice Hallett (*Judicial*) Dame Lorna Boreland-Kelly (*Lay Justice*) Professor Dame Hazel Genn (*Lay*) Mr Justice Goldring[c] (*Judicial*) Sir Geoffrey Inkin (*Lay*) Judge Frances Kirkham (*Judicial*) Edward Nally (*Professional: Solicitor*) Sara Nathan (*Lay*) District Judge Charles Newman (*Judicial*) Judge David Pearl (*Tribunal*) Francis Plowden (*Lay*) Harriet Spicer (*Lay*) Jonathan Sumption QC (*Professional: Barrister*) Lord Justice Toulson (*Judicial*)	Claire Pelham	Jack Straw	Lord Phillips

a Lord Justice Auld, who had been the JAC's first Vice Chair, retired in September 2007.
b Lord Falconer was replaced as Lord Chancellor by Jack Straw when Gordon Brown became Prime Minister in June 2007.
c Lord Justice Goldring left the JAC in September 2008 following his appointment as a Lord Justice of Appeal.

JAC Chair	*Commissioners*	*JAC Chief-Executive*	*Lord Chancellor*	*Lord Chief Justice*
		2008–2009		
Baroness Prashar (*Lay*)	Lady Justice Hallett (*Judicial*) Lady Justice Black (*Judicial*) Dame Lorna Boreland-Kelly (*Lay Justice*) Professor Dame Hazel Genn (*Lay*) Sir Geoffrey Inkin (*Lay*) Judge Frances Kirkham (*Judicial*) Edward Nally (*Professional: Solicitor*) Sara Nathan (*Lay*) District Judge Charles Newman (*Judicial*) Judge David Pearl (*Tribunal*) Francis Plowden (*Lay*) Harriet Spicer (*Lay*) Jonathan Sumption QC (*Professional: Barrister*) Lord Justice Toulson (*Judicial*)	Claire Pelham	Jack Straw	Lord Judge[d]
		2009–2010		
Baroness Prashar (Lay)	Lady Justice Hallett (*Judicial*) Lady Justice Black (*Judicial*) Dame Lorna Boreland-Kelly (*Lay Justice*) Professor Dame Hazel Genn (*Lay*) Sir Geoffrey Inkin (*Lay*) Judge Frances Kirkham (*Judicial*) Edward Nally (*Professional: Solicitor*) Sara Nathan (*Lay*) District Judge Charles Newman (*Judicial*) Judge David Pearl (*Tribunal*) Francis Plowden (*Lay*) Harriet Spicer (*Lay*) Jonathan Sumption QC (*Professional: Barrister*) Lord Justice Toulson (*Judicial*)	Claire Pelham	Jack Straw	Lord Judge

d Lord Judge replaced Lord Phillips as Lord Chief Justice in October 2008.

2010–2011 [e]				
Christopher Stephens (*Lay*) (For part of 2010, Lord Justice Toulson, Vice Chair, served as the JAC's Acting Chair).	Lord Justice Toulson (*Judicial*) Mr Justice Bean (*Judicial*) Lady Justice Black (*Judicial*) Dame Lorna Boreland-Kelly (*Lay Justice*) Professor Dame Hazel Genn (*Lay*) Sir Geoffrey Inkin (*Lay*) Edward Nally (*Professional: Solicitor*) Sara Nathan (*Lay*) District Judge Charles Newman (*Judicial*) Judge David Pearl (*Tribunal*) Francis Plowden (*Lay*) Harriet Spicer (Lay) Jonathan Sumption QC (*Professional: Barrister*)	Nigel Reeder[f]	Ken Clarke[g]	Lord Judge
2011–2012 [h]				
Christopher Stephens (*Lay*)	Lord Justice Toulson (*Judicial*), Mr Justice Bean (*Judicial*) District Judge Malcolm Birchall (*Judicial*) Lady Justice Black (*Judicial*) Martin Forde QC (*Professional: Barrister*) Alexandra Marks (*Professional: Solicitor*) Professor Noel Lloyd (*Lay*) Judge Alison McKenna (*Tribunal*) Stella Pantelides (*Lay*) Lieutenant General Sir Andrew Ridgway (*Lay*) Ranjit Sondhi (*Lay*) Dame Valerie Strachan (*Lay*) Judge Deborah Taylor (*Judicial*) John Thornhill (*Magistrate*)	Nigel Reeder	Ken Clarke	Lord Judge

e The Commissioners who left during 2010–11: Baroness Prashar (*Lay*); Lady Justice Hallett (Vice Chair, *Judicial*); and Judge Frances Kirkham (*Judicial*).
f Claire Pelham stepped down as Chief Executive in October 2010, with Nigel Reeder appointed as Interim Chief Executive until December 2011, at which point he was appointed Chief Executive.
g After the 2010 General Election, Ken Clarke replaced Jack Straw as Lord Chancellor.
h The Commissioners who left during 2011–12 were: Dame Lorna Boreland-Kelly (*Magistrate*); Professor Dame Hazel Genn (*Lay*); Sir Geoffrey Inkin (*Lay*); Sara Nathan (*Lay*); District Judge Charles Newman (*Judicial*) Judge David Pearl (*Tribunal*); Mr Francis Plowden (*Lay*); Harriet Spicer (*Lay*); and Jonathan Sumption QC (*Professional: Barrister*).

2012–2013				
JAC Chair	*Other JAC Commissioners*	*JAC Chief-Executive*	*Lord Chancellor*	*Lord Chief Justice*
Christopher Stephens (*Lay*)	Lady Justice Black (*Judicial*) Mr Justice Bean (*Judicial*) District Judge Malcolm Birchall (*Judicial*) Martin Forde QC (*Professional: Barrister*) Professor Noel Lloyd (*Lay*) Alexandra Marks (*Professional: Solicitor*) Judge Alison McKenna (*Tribunal*) Stella Pantelides (*Lay*) Lieutenant General Sir Andrew Ridgway (*Lay*) Ranjit Sondhi (*Lay*) Dame Valerie Strachan (*Lay*) Judge Deborah Taylor (*Judicial*) John Thornhill (*Magistrate*) Mr Justice Wilkie (*Judicial*)	Nigel Reeder	Chris Grayling[i]	Lord Judge
2013–2014[j]				
Christopher Stephens (*Lay*)	Lady Justice Macur (*Judicial*) Mr Justice Bean (*Judicial*) Martin Forde QC (*Professional: Barrister*) Professor Emily Jackson (*Lay*) Professor Noel Lloyd (*Lay*) Alexandra Marks (*Professional: Solicitor*) Katharine Rainsford (*Lay-Magistrate*) Lieutenant General Sir Andrew Ridgway (*Lay*) Lucy Scott-Moncrieff (*Judicial-Tribunal*) District Judge Christopher Simmonds (*Judicial*) Dame Valerie Strachan (*Lay*) Debra van Gene (*Lay*) Mr Justice Wilkie (*Judicial*)	Nigel Reeder	Chris Grayling	Lord Thomas[k]

i Ken Clarke was replaced as Lord Chancellor by Chris Grayling in September 2012.

j The Commissioners who left during 2013-14 were: Lady Justice Black (*Judicial*); District Judge Malcolm Birchall (*Judicial*); Judge Alison McKenna (*Judicial Tribunal*); Stella Pantelides (*Lay*); Ranjit Sondhi (*Lay*); Judge Deborah Taylor (*Judicial*); and John Thornhill (*Magistrate*).

k Lord Thomas replaced Lord Judge as Lord Chief Justice in October 2013.

2014–2015 [l]					
JAC Chair	*Commissioners*	*Chief-Executive*	*Lord Chancellor*	*Lord Chief Justice*	*Senior President of Tribunals*
Christopher Stephens (*Lay*)	Lady Justice Macur (*Judicial*) Martin Forde QC (*Professional: Barrister*) Professor Emily Jackson (*Lay*) Judge Usha Karu (*Judicial*) Professor Noel Lloyd (*Lay*) Alexandra Marks (*Professional: Solicitor*) Katharine Rainsford (*Magistrate*) Lieutenant General Sir Andrew Ridgway (*Lay*) Lucy Scott-Moncrieff (*Judicial Tribunal*) District Judge Christopher Simmonds (*Judicial*) Dame Valerie Strachan (*Lay*) Judge Phillip Sycamore (*Judicial Tribunal*) Debra van Gene (*Lay*) Mr Justice Wilkie (*Judicial*)	Nigel Reeder	Chris Grayling	Lord Thomas	Sir Jeremy Sullivan
2015–2016 [m]					
Christopher Stephens (*Lay*) (From April to October 2016, Lord Justice Burnett, the JAC's Vice Chair, served as Acting Chair).	Lord Justice Ian Burnett (*Judicial*) Martin Forde QC (*Professional: Barrister*) Professor Emily Jackson (*Lay*) Judge Usha Karu (*Judicial*) Professor Noel Lloyd (*Lay*) Alexandra Marks (*Professional: Solicitor*) Katharine Rainsford (*Magistrate*) Lieutenant-General Sir Andrew Ridgway (*Lay*) Lucy Scott-Moncrieff (*Judicial: Tribunal*) District Judge Christopher Simmonds (*Judicial*) Dame Valerie Strachan (*Lay*) Debra van Gene (*Lay*) Mr Justice Alan Wilkie (*Judicial*)	Nigel Reeder	Michael Gove[n]	Lord Thomas	Sir Ernest Ryder

l From 2014, the JAC made recommendations to the Lord Chancellor, Lord Chief Justice or Senior President of Tribunals, depending on the vacancy in question.
m Lady Justice Julia Macur stepped down as a judicial commissioner and Vice Chair in 31 October 2015. Christopher Stephens's second term as Chair ended in April 2016.
n Michael Gove was replaced as Lord Chancellor by Liz Truss in July 2016.

Appendix III

Outline of JAC selection processes

Strictly speaking, the JAC recommends candidates for appointment as judges of the High Court and to all of the judicial offices listed in Schedule 14 of the Constitutional Reform Act. The JAC also provides support for selection to fill some other judicial posts that lie outside of Schedule 14. The Lord Chancellor may also request the JAC's assistance in connection with any other appointments that he considers appropriate.

Planning for a selection exercise begins when the JAC receives a vacancy request and eligibility statement from the Lord Chancellor. The JAC may be required to select a candidate for immediate appointment to identify candidates for vacancies that might arise in the future. The vacancy request and eligibility statement specify: the role, number and location of the posts; any minimum eligibility requirements laid down in statute and any additional selection criteria that have been stipulated by the Lord Chancellor; and whether part-time working appointment is possible. On receipt of the vacancy request, the JAC will launch the selection exercise, including by publicizing the selection exercise on its website.

Short-listing

The JAC usually short-lists candidates either by an online Qualifying Test (which is prepared and moderated by judges and which is designed to test a range of qualities and attributes required for judicial office) or a paper-based sift (usually by a JAC panel chair, lay member and a judicial member). Typical is to invite candidates to a selection day on a ratio of two or three people per vacancy. In 2015–2016, the JAC experimented with telephone interviews as a short-listing tool (where candidate were invited to analyse a decision of an appellate court). Short-listed candidates are invited to attend a selection day.

References

References – or what the JAC now terms Independent Assessments – are requested. The JAC uses two types of references: (i) Judicial/Professional References from a range of people designated by the JAC for each selection exercise; and (ii) Personal References from people who are chosen by the candidates.

Selection day

Shortlisted candidates attend a selection day. Overseeing the selection day is a panel, which usually consists of a panel chair, a judicial member and independent member. The selection day may involve only an interview, but can also include a presentation, situational questioning and a role play activity. The selection panel prepare a report that will be considered by the JAC's Commissioners.

Statutory consultation

Statutory consultation requires the JAC to seek the comments of one or two judges – depending on the vacancy – on the shortlisted candidates. For vacancies below the High Court, the JAC will see comments from one judge, whilst comments from two judges are sought for vacancies in the High Court.

Recommendation

The JAC's Commissioners will decide who to recommend for appointment, guided by the selection panel's assessment of the shortlisted candidates and taking into account the comments procured through statutory consultation. The Commissioners must recommend only persons of good character, and must therefore consider the results of character checks (which can include financial, criminal and professional checks). In making their recommendation, the Commissioners must select only on merit, but having regard to the need to encourage diversity in the range of persons available for selection. Where there are two or more candidates who are assessed as being of equal merit, the Commissioners can recommend a candidate for the purpose of increasing diversity using the 'equal merit' provision introduced by the Crime and Courts Act 2013. In 2015–2016, 14 recommendations were made following the application of the equal merit provision.

The JAC makes its recommendation to the Lord Chief Justice (for judicial positions below the High Court), the Senior President of Tribunals (for most tribunal positions) or the Lord Chancellor (for the High Court and above), depending on the vacancy. In each case the appointing authority can accept or reject the recommendation or ask the JAC to reconsider.

Senior appointments

Statute specifies the membership of panels for selection for judicial office in England and Wales above the High Court. These panels operate as 'committees' of the JAC.

The selection panel for appointments to the Court of Appeal comprises: (i) the Lord Chief Justice (or a nominee who must be a Head of Division or a member of the Court of Appeal), who chairs the panel; (ii) a Head of Division (usually the Master of the Rolls) or a member of the Court of Appeal designated by the Lord Chief Justice; (iii) the JAC's Chair (or a person designated by the Chair); (iv) a lay commissioner of the JAC; and (v) a person nominated by the Lord Chief Justice, in consultation with the JAC Chair. The panel determines the selection process to follow, and makes its recommendation to the Lord Chancellor, who can accept or reject it, or ask the panel to reconsider.

For the appointment of Heads of Division, the panel comprises: (i) the Lord Chief Justice (or nominee); (ii) the most senior England and Wales Supreme Court Justice (or that person's nominee); (iii) the JAC Chair (or nominee); (iv) a lay commissioner on the JAC; and (v) a person nominated by the Lord Chief Justice, in consultation with the Chair of the JAC. The panel determines the selection process to follow, and makes its recommendation to the Lord Chancellor, who can accept or reject it, or ask the panel to reconsider.

For the appointment of the Lord Chief Justice, the panel comprises: (i) the Chair of the JAC, who also chairs this panel; (ii) the most senior England and Wales Supreme Court Justice; (iii) two Commissioners designated by the JAC Chair, one of whom must be a lay commissioner; and (iv) a judicial panelist designated by the current Lord Chief Justice. The panel is free to determine its selection process, subject to the statutory requirement to consult with the Lord Chancellor and the First Minister for Wales. The panel makes its recommendation to the Lord Chancellor, who can accept or reject it, or ask the panel to reconsider.

Appendix IV

About the cover image

Despite the old adage about not judging a book by its cover, when it comes to choosing an image for a book about judges it can be hard to break new ground. Images of judges – typically white and male – or judicial buildings and/or the architecture of the court abound. From the outset we wanted an image that would capture the individual judge and the institution of the judiciary, at the same time as pointing to the distinctive outlook of the collection: namely, the need to do more to secure a more diverse and representative judiciary. A trawl of various image databases confirmed that this was a tricky task.

Isobel Williams is an artist who 'draws people, sometimes in places where cameras are not allowed'. She has spent many days sitting in the public seats of the Supreme Court drawing the Justices, lawyers and architecture of that court. Her blog – *Drawing from an Uncomfortable Position* – documents many of the key cases heard by the Court. She is not, to use Les Moran's words 'so much a courtroom artist, commissioned to produce court pictures for an image hungry media, but an artist interpreting her courtroom experiences in words and pictures'.[1] Erika had met Isobel at a workshop organized by Les Moran and Linda Mulcahy as part of the AHRC *Judicial Images* network and remembered an image which Isobel had sketched while at that workshop. That image had captured two judicial robes either side of Christopher Allan, Ede & Ravenscroft's Court and Ceremonial Manager.[2] So we wrote to Isobel to see if she'd be interested in drawing something inspired by that image for the cover of our book. Other than this our brief was vague: 'What we're looking for is an eye-catching image of "judges", "judging", "diversity", "judicial appointments" that is different to the usual images of men in wigs/images of Justice'.

Happily this was enough. Isobel produced an experimental sequence of pictures in which the robes moved from being static on a tailor's dummy to being

1 L. J. Moran 'Judging Images', *Counsel*, February 2014.

2 You can see that image here: 'Judicial Images: Costume Drama', *Drawing from an Uncomfortable Position*, 8 November 2014. Online, available http://isobelwilliams.blogspot.co.uk/2014/11/judicial-images-costume-drama.html (accessed 23 February 2017).

inhabited and finally became the evocative and powerful 'ink splodges' that we chose for the cover.[3]

There are a number of reasons why the ink splodge image appealed so strongly to us both. We liked that while various echelons of the judicial hierarchy – the robes represent circuit bench, the High Court and the Court of Appeal – were represented, none was elevated over the other. They appeared here as a group, mirroring the community of judges that make up the judiciary. We also liked the element of ambiguity of the 'team colours'. While the circuit bench and High Court are immediately recognizable, the Court of Appeal strip bears a remarkable similarity to that of the Supreme Court. We especially liked the fact that the image was blurry: that although the image was of the ceremonial aspect of judging, it wasn't an image of judicial perfection, but rather a truer image reflecting the difficulties not only of day-to-day judging but of making judicial appointments. Above all, we liked that the robes were uninhabited – that they were, if you like, waiting for someone to put them on, something especially appropriate for a book on judicial appointments. The uninhabited robes force us to imagine who will inhabit them in their future.

Isobel and the editors would like to thank Christopher Allan, Court and Ceremonial Manager at Ede & Ravenscroft, who kindly showed Isobel the various judicial robes on which she based her drawings.

You can see more of Isobel's wonderful work on her blog at http://isobelwilliams.blogspot.co.uk/.

3 Isobel has written about the evolution of the cover, complete with pictures, here: 'Cover, Book, Judge', *Drawing from an Uncomfortable Position*, 18 October 2016. Online, available http://isobelwilliams.blogspot.co.uk/2016/10/cover-book-judge.html (accessed 23 February 2017).

Index

www.ingramcontent.com/pod-product-compliance
Ingram Content Group UK Ltd.
Pitfield, Milton Keynes, MK11 3LW, UK
UKHW022115190926
475702UK00013B/1461
* 9 7 8 0 3 6 7 3 3 6 8 2 0 *